concepts

thinking|media

series editors
bernd herzogenrath
patricia pisters

concepts

a travelogue

edited by
bernd herzogenrath

BLOOMSBURY ACADEMIC
NEW YORK • LONDON • OXFORD • NEW DELHI • SYDNEY

BLOOMSBURY ACADEMIC
Bloomsbury Publishing Inc
1385 Broadway, New York, NY 10018, USA
50 Bedford Square, London, WC1B 3DP, UK
29 Earlsfort Terrace, Dublin 2, Ireland

BLOOMSBURY, BLOOMSBURY ACADEMIC and the Diana logo
are trademarks of Bloomsbury Publishing Plc

First published in the United States of America 2023
Paperback edition published 2024

Volume Editor's Part of the Work © Bernd Herzogenrath
Each chapter © of Contributors

For legal purposes the Acknowledgments on p. xi constitute
an extension of this copyright page.

Cover design: Daniel Benneworth-Gray
Cover image © Paolo Sanfilippo

All rights reserved. No part of this publication may be reproduced or transmitted in any form or by any means, electronic or mechanical, including photocopying, recording, or any information storage or retrieval system, without prior permission in writing from the publishers.

Bloomsbury Publishing Inc does not have any control over, or responsibility for, any third-party websites referred to or in this book. All internet addresses given in this book were correct at the time of going to press. The author and publisher regret any inconvenience caused if addresses have changed or sites have ceased to exist, but can accept no responsibility for any such changes.

Library of Congress Cataloging-in-Publication Data
Names: Herzogenrath, Bernd, 1964- editor.
Title: Concepts : a travelogue / edited by Bernd Herzogenrath.
Description: New York : Bloomsbury Academic, 2022. | Series: Thinking media | Includes bibliographical references and index. | Summary: "This book makes concepts from other languages and cultures available and fruitful for (media) philosophical issues by presenting concepts drawn from the cultures of 4 continents and 26 different languages"– Provided by publisher.
Identifiers: LCCN 2022019231 (print) | LCCN 2022019232 (ebook) | ISBN 9781501375330 (hardback) | ISBN 9781501375309 (paperback) | ISBN 9781501375323 (epub) | ISBN 9781501375316 (pdf) | ISBN 9781501375293
Subjects: LCSH: Mass media. | Critical theory.
Classification: LCC P90 .C63725 2022 (print) | LCC P90 (ebook) | DDC 302.2301–dc23/eng/20220804
LC record available at https://lccn.loc.gov/2022019231
LC ebook record available at https://lccn.loc.gov/2022019232

ISBN: HB: 978-1-5013-7533-0
       PB: 978-1-5013-7530-9
       ePDF: 978-1-5013-7531-6
       eBook: 978-1-5013-7532-3

Series: Thinking Media

Typeset by Integra Software Services Pvt. Ltd.

To find out more about our authors and books visit www.bloomsbury.com
and sign up for our newsletters.

... wherever the rain falls...

this book is dedicated to
jukka-pekka puro
who fixed the roof as if it was the last thing he would ever do ...

Contents

List of Figures		x
Acknowledgments		xi
Introduction: Concepts Bernd Herzogenrath		1
1	*Anaesthesis, Sensoma, Veoma*: Cyborg Life Modes of Immersion After Deleuze Liana Psarologaki	35
2	*Antropofagia*: Devouring Experimentations of a Manifesto Toward a Kinosophy to Come Sebastian Wiedemann	45
3	*Autofotografija*, Or; A Nonhuman Selfie Ana Peraica	55
4	*Bazaar*: The Persistence of the Informal Bhaskar Sarkar	63
5	上善若水/ Be (Like) Water: Media Dynamics and Multiple Realities Helena Wu	75
6	*ćmiatło* and *świecień*: Jacek Dukaj's Concepts in the Perspective of Philosophy of Visual Media and Telecommunication Agnieszka Dytman-Stasieńko and Jan Stasieńko	87
7	*Darshan*: Vision as Touch and the Stakes of Immediacy Kajri Jain	99
8	*Dhvāni*: Resonance Budhaditya Chattopadhyay	113
9	*Gestell*: Heidegger's Cyborg and the Vicissitudes of the Machine | Body Bernd Herzogenrath	121

10 Góng (空) | Saek (色): The Ineffable Persistence of Becoming   133
    Woosung Kang

11 Hiljaa: Silent and Slow Media Use   143
    Jukka-Pekka Puro and Veli-Matti Karhulahti

12 kō kō kà, the Sound of Colonial Shoes: Forgotten Words of a
    Yoruba Song of Success   153
    Babson Ajibade

13 L'Implèxe: What's in a Situation?   165
    Holger Schulze

14 Ljom—A Meditation   175
    Erik Steinskog

15 Māya: A Measured Response in and to Cinematic Virtual Reality   183
    Soudhamini

16 Mediataju: A Sense of Media   195
    Jukka Sihvonen

17 Myslet médii. Thinking in, With, or Through Media: Images,
    Interfaces, Apparatuses   205
    Vít Pokorný

18 Naqqāli: Iranian Storytelling in Two Films by Ali Hātami   217
    Behrooz Mahmoodi-Bakhtiari

19 肉声: The Fleshly Voice   231
    Gretchen Jude

20 OTKA3 (OTKAZ): From Expressive Movement to a
    Figure of Thought   243
    Julia Vassilieva

21 رند, or Rend   253
    Mohammad Hadi

22 Sankofa—A Synthesis   261
    Didi Cheeka

23	*Saudade*: (De)mythologizing a Portuguese Concept Susana Viegas	269
24	*Schalten und Walten*: Toward Operative Ontologies in the Digital Iconosphere Lorenz Engell	279
25	*Seken*: Webs and Networks of In-Betweenness Sebastian Kawanami-Breu and Shintaro Miyazaki	291
26	*Tathāgatagarbha*: Translating the Untranslatable Victor Fan	299
27	*Todetita*: Facebook's Ontological Malady Bogdan Deznan and Andrei Ionescu	313
28	*Togliere di scena* Lucia D'Errico	321
29	*Ubuntu*: Be-ing Becoming (Capable of Being Affected) Chantelle Gray	331
30	*Uri (우리 [uri])*: Sound and the Porous Self Suk-Jun Kim	339
31	*"Utbrytningsdröm"*: Swedish Audio-Visual Expressions of a Desire for Leaving Far Andreas Jacobsson	349
32	*Wellevenskunst* Rick Dolphijn	357
33	Line and Bump Cora Bender	365

Contributors	376
Index of Subjects	387
Index of Names	391

Figures

1.1 A macropod image of the Hawaiian bobtail squid and the glowing bacteria *V. fischeri* showing in its bi-lobed light organ and ink sac in the center of the squid's mantle cavity. Image credit: Mark Smith and Annette Evans. 2015. Macroscopic Solutions, LLC. www.macroscopicsolutions.com   36

12.1 An illustration of how the kō kō kà sound is produced   155

18.1 A typical *parde* used for a one-man show   219

18.2 A *Parde-dār* and his screen   220

18.3 *shar-e farang*, and the images of the story of Hassan the Bald   222

18.4 The beginning of the story of Hassan the Bald   224

18.5 The story of Hassan the Bald continued   225

18.6 Prologue for the story of *Bābā Shamal*   226

18.7 The story of *Bābā Shamal* continued   227

18.8 The story of *Bābā Shamal* continued   229

25.1 Etymological illustrations of the characters *se* (shi) and *ken* (jiān) in Chinese handwriting. Images reproduced from *Zìyuán cháxún* (Etymological Sources for Chinese Characters) http://qiyuan.chaziwang.com   292

Acknowledgments

I would like to express my gratitude to Bloomsbury for giving us and me the opportunity to publish this book and try out "new things."

Thank you! also to all those wonderful people that contributed to this volume—it has been a pleasure!

Special thanks go out to Yusuf Buhurcu, for all the work you've put into this!

Introduction: Concepts

Bernd Herzogenrath

> *Yes, that's what a theory is, exactly like a tool box. [...] A theory has to be used, it has to work. And not just for itself. If there is no one to use it, starting with the theorist himself who, as soon as he uses it ceases to be a theorist, then a theory is worthless, or its time has not yet arrived. You don't go back to a theory, you make new ones, you have others to make. It is strange that Proust, who passes for a pure intellectual, should articulate it so clearly: use my book, he says, like a pair of glasses to view the outside, and if it isn't to your liking, find another pair, or invent your own, and your device will necessarily be a device you can fight with.*
> (Deleuze 2004: 208)

The idea of "theory as a tool box," here related to French philosopher Gilles Deleuze,[1] has gained notoriety since the early 1980s, gained impact at the turn of the century, and is still in academic currency.

In this collection, we would like to challenge this idea of the "theory toolbox" in order to come up with an update of this idea. The problem with the toolbox idea is that Deleuze's improvisation with the term led to an approach that, in our perspective, runs counter to the practice it has seemingly inaugurated. If we link Deleuze's observation to his idea (or: concept) of the philosophical concept, we see that what he has in mind is not the idea of a menu of theories to draw from that can be mechanically applied to find solutions for a particular problem: in the case of the Theory Toolbox, these are the "problems" of authority, subjectivity, ideology, culture/nature, etc. This is not to say that these are not important and prevailing issues, what we want to point out is the disrelation of the concept and the problem/solution nexus.

The problem with "problems" is, that they are seen as "fixed objects" that only require a specific "problem solving" theory (a "special tool" from the theory-toolbox) to make it "disappear." Such a "knowledge designates only the generality of concepts or the calm possession of a rule enabling solutions" (Deleuze 1994: 164). Problems in this perspective thus appear to be close to questions of the *Who wants to be a Millionaire?*-type, questions to which there is (hopefully) only one possible answer—choose the right tool! But this approach completely ignores at least two things: a) a problem is an event that is connected to multiplicity of other events—it is not an isolated object, and b) a problem is an event also in a temporal sense—it is not isolated as a "point in time." For Deleuze, problems are ways of creating possible futures: Deleuze gives the examples of the incredible complexity of the eye, the "photosynthesis-machine" of plants, and different "schools" of painting as creative ways to pose (and deal with) the "problem" of light. Problems thus do not disappear—problems change, and can never be solved once and for all. For Deleuze the solution to a problem is off the point altogether. Instead, the point of philosophy is the thinking itself of problems and their solutions as ongoing repetitions, and to try to ensure that solutions are not in any case final ... hence the need for the creation of ever new concepts.

Now, what happens if we shift perspectives from problem/solution to concept, and from theory to philosophy? A first look at the etymology of the word "concept" gives us various perspectives to look from: originating from the Latin verb "*concipere*" (to conceive), the word "concept" relates to the following (semantic) fields:

- to create (an embryo) by fertilizing an egg
- (of a woman) to become pregnant
- to form or devise (a plan or idea) in the mind
- to form a mental representation of; imagine
- to become affected by (a feeling)

in addition, there is also the meaning of "concept" as "an experimental model to test the viability of innovative design features," for example, of a car or other vehicle. All these issues can be found in Deleuze's concept of the concept in philosophy: philosophy is "the art of forming, inventing, and fabricating concepts" (Deleuze 1994: 57).

Philosophy is (and concepts are) thus inventive, giving rise to new thoughts. And "thoughts" here does not refer to knowledge or recognition, but to new ways of experiencing the world: "Do not count upon thought to ensure the relative necessity of what it thinks. Rather, count upon the contingency of an encounter with that which forces thought to rise up and educate the absolute necessity of an act of thought or a passion to think" (Deleuze 1994: 139).

Deleuze here distinguishes between two strategies of knowing, of thinking, of making sense. The one is what we might call [re]cognition, which simply relies on matching our experience with our culturally acquired knowledge, ideology, habits, and beliefs. It only confirms our expectations, what we already know, and this lack of friction does not allow for real thinking. This other strategy is what Deleuze calls an encounter. An encounter challenges our habitual ways of experiencing and perceiving the world. It creates a fundamental break with our strategies how to conceive the world. Making or perceiving art is an encounter that opens up possible worlds, and it is "the object in question" that determines the strategies with which you "make sense." Such a concept/strategy is by necessity heuristic, not methodic, improvised, not composed, fluent, not static: creative. And this creativity is what both distinguishes *and* combines the different approaches of philosophy, the sciences, and the arts. Deleuze's concept is basically a force field composed of three tensors that generate each other: the label "concept" actually denotes the terms' own conceptuality, while the new ways of seeing and perceiving that it opens up are called the percept, and the force with which it hits us is the affect. These three moments/movements cannot be thought separate from each other: the perception of a sensation remains dull without the conceptual sharpness of the concept, and without the energy of affect, the thinking that is conceptualized does not get moved and moving by what it perceives.

If the task of philosophy is the "creation of concepts" (Deleuze and Guattari 1994: 5), then this entails a definition of philosophy that goes beyond its traditional territorialization, one that is extensional, forming assemblages rather than propositions, what—again—Deleuze has called "the new image of thought."

Following this approach, the terms "philosophy" and "thinking" do not necessarily refer to rational propositions and|or a purely neural activity, though. Thinking is not just a representation of the world as "it is"—as Deleuze puts it, "*something in this world* enforces thought. This something is the base of a fundamental encounter, and not of a recognition" (Deleuze 1994: 182). While the idea of "thinking as (re-)cognition" is based on the verification of ideologies, of pre-collected knowledge, customs and articles of faith, the notion of "thinking as an encounter" shatters our epistemological and experiential habits, it produces a break in our "normal," habitual perspective of the world and enables the possibility to approach alternative points of view and means of thought and to question our common practices. According to Deleuze these are especially new perspectives on concepts of images, time, space, and movement (concepts which are grounded in the peculiarity of the medium as a stream of "moving images").

In an interview with Raymond Bellour and François Ewald, Deleuze stated, "I've never been worried about going beyond metaphysics or any death of philosophy. The function of philosophy, still thoroughly relevant, is to create concepts" (Deleuze 1995: 136). This affirmative function of philosophy is also a call to transdisciplinarity, so that even when Deleuze was working on "painting and cinema: images, on the face of it ... [he] was writing philosophy books" (137). In defense of Deleuze against Sokal|Bricmont's attempt to control and regulate the limits of the disciplinary fields, Paul Harris points out that Deleuze's work in contrast shows "how productive it is to work with and think through material from others and other fields ..., working with ideas cooked up in geology and geography, zoology and ornithology, archeology and paleontology, and even mathematics and physics" (Harris 2010: 24–5). The philosophical practice of "creating concepts," as a creation of "newness" as well, necessitates, according to Deleuze, that philosophy enters into manifold relations with arts and sciences, since philosophy "creates and expounds its concepts only in relation to what it can grasp of scientific functions and artistic constructions. ... Philosophy cannot be undertaken independently of science or art" (Deleuze 1994: xvi). It is these resonances and exchanges between philosophy, science, and art that make philosophy "creative," not reflective. These relations—from the perspective of philosophy—are vital for reasons internal to philosophy itself, that is, vital for the creation of "concepts," and—from the perspective of Film Philosophy—in resonance with the percepts and affective logics and modalities of art in general, and film in particular.

If we take this a step further, relating this approach to the whole range of media (production), but also take a step back, and see what this approach basically means, we begin to see the seeds of a "media philosophy"—not talking *about* media by way of "philosophy proper," but by realizing the "philosophical qualities and impacts" of the medium: it all starts from the assumption that our memory, perception, and thinking are not just a given, as a body- and weightless, immaterial logics, reason or internal process that takes place behind the walls of our skull and is purely mental—there is always a "material basis": as Nietzsche had already claimed, *our* writing equipment takes part in the forming of *our* thoughts. From here, we can derive the media-philosophical insight that media (help us) think (differently). Media thus reveal themselves as the body (or, better: different bodies) of thought. It is important to note that these "bodies" are not "retroactive" to those thoughts that they "materialize," just like the telescope is not retroactive to the discovery of planets—media are coextensive to the thoughts they "allow." Media Philosophy is an event, even a praxis—but *of* the media *themselves*. It takes place *through* and *in* the media in question. To do philosophy in this way thus is "to fabricate concepts in resonance and interference with the arts," to facilitate an encounter "in which both art and thought come alive and discover their resonances with one another" (Rajchman 2000: 115).

In a 1972 conversation between Gilles Deleuze and Michel Foucault, both philosophers discuss a new relationship between theory and praxis. This relationship is "fragmentary and partial" (Deleuze 2004: 206), rather than one being the application of the other. To Deleuze in particular, theory is invariably local, related to a limited field, and subsequently applied in another sphere.

Deleuze uses the concept of the "relay" to explain how he understands theory and practice to be interrelated: "Praxis is a network of relays from one theoretical point to another, and theory relays one praxis to another. A theory cannot be developed without encountering a wall, and a praxis is needed to break through" (206). This new relationship between theory and practice is thereby ultimately one where "[t]here is no more representation. There is only action — the action of theory, the action of praxis, in the relations of relays and form networks" (207).

Concepts then could be seen as a "shorthand" for these relays. And concepts never work isolated—the have to refer to other concepts, echo them, enter other relationships. Ultimately, concepts create a kind of logic—not the "rational logic" which sometimes is regarded as the only logic, but a new kind of logic (like, e.g., Deleuze's own *Logic of Sense*, *Logic of Sensation*). This logic of concepts and relays is not subjected to the notion of ratio, or the notion of truth—"[r]ather, it is categories like Interesting, Remarkable, or Important that determine success or failure" (Deleuze and Guattari 1994: 82).

Concepts thus seem to work best when created in that interspace between theory and praxis, between philosophy, art, and science. Deleuze himself has generated many concepts in this encounter between philosophy and nonphilosophy (art, literature, film, botany, etc.): his ideas of affects and percepts, of becoming, the stutter, movement-image and time-image, the rhizome, to name but a few.

Most of these concepts were taken from other disciplines, and/or the arts, that is, from "the other" of philosophy, from a decidedly nonphilosophical terrain. For Deleuze (and Guattari), "[p]hilosophy needs a nonphilosophy that comprehends it; it needs a nonphilosophical comprehension just as art needs nonart and science needs nonscience" (Deleuze and Guattari 1994: 218), in order to focus on the ways in which art, philosophy, and science ask the same kinds of questions and relate to each other's "findings," as it were. In that respect, whereas science involves the creation of functions, of a propositional mapping of the world, art involves the creation of blocs of sensation (or affects and percepts), and philosophy involves the invention of concepts. Yet, since "sciences, arts, and philosophies are all equally creative" (Deleuze and Guattari 1994: 5), it might be fruitful, as Deleuze proposes, "to pose the question of echoes and resonances between them" (Deleuze 1995: 123).

Such a question of echoes, affinities, and resonance can be best posed as an heuristic, not as a clear-cut method—it is a question of probing and inventing, not defining and cataloguing. A heuristic does not denote a clear-cut method—the term *method* in fact denotes a μετά όδός, meta-hodos, a *way afterwards*, a retroactive abstraction, a recipe: the one problem/one solution habit), but is more related to a (nonfinite) inventiveness, an improvisation. It can only work because of this interdisciplinary cross-fertilization.

In our case, the "other" is the "other" to English language/culture (and its philosophy): what happens, if instead of "other disciplines," we take other cultures, other languages, other philosophies? Does not the focus on English as a hegemonic language of academic discourse deny us a plethora of possibilities, of possible *Denkfiguren*, of possible concepts? The English language dominates much of media theory and media philosophy. This fact does not only make it tougher for non-English native speakers to have a voice, it also makes media theory and media philosophy all the poorer because of that, because of all the "untranslatables" or "only-quite" translatables that would open up a new perspective on issues in theory and philosophy in general, and in media theory and media philosophy in particular, in this case.

This collection is a kind of travelogue. The journey does not follow a particular trajectory—some countries are not on the map; some are visited twice. So, there is no claim to completeness involved here—it is rather an invitation to answer to the call … there is much to explore! Traveling always includes the hope to be changed when returning home—changed by contact, we return to a home we then see with new eyes, sometimes maybe as if for the first time. And as such the hope is to also contribute to what Dipesh Chakrabarty has called the "provincializing of Europe," to counter the hegemony and coloniality of Western Philosophy (or, in this case: Anglo-American Media Philosophy): Europe/The West/the English *lingua franca* is not the Center of the World! Thus, in the best of all worlds, the concepts collected in this book will become media of new world-experiences—media of new worldings.

*

Liana Psarologaki
Anaesthesis, Sensoma, Veoma: Cyborg Life Modes of Immersion After Deleuze

This essay acknowledges that sensed conditioning (aestheton) is most challenged in contemporary experience of human life within the built environment. It aims to interrogate matter and mind of subject and architecture in mutualism of lived experience in three observations. These axiomatics use an assemblage of linguistic references from ancient and modern Greek terms synthesized with English and Latin. The somatization of architecture (the built surroundings responding back behaviorally) and the human pathology of aesthesis in the time of information dynasty (the now) are two creases in the same fold: that of the fabric of the world in reference to Gilles Deleuze after Leibniz and Antonio Damasio after Spinoza. In fact, we are talking about the post-human aesthetics (an-aesthetics), which Psarologaki defines as *anaesthesis* to differentiate from classical aesthetics (form, judgment) and new aesthetics (atmospheres, affect). Such is shaped by the repercussions of advanced capitalism which according to Rosi Braidotti is manifested in two polarized modes of life: "zöe" (ζωή) as the autopoietic lived condition and "veos" (bios, βίος) segregated to habitual consumption of goods, data, and services. The first is the default mode of life that sustains ecosystems (human and nonhuman) and the second concerns the current habit of people to use technological as bodily extensions and define the human-society as network according to Deligny.

The self-consumption of the post-human lived entity (what Psarologaki will call enfleshed) is a kind of aesthetic coma that becomes definitive of our experience of life (bios in an advanced capitalism condition): post-human subject becomes cyborg—an *anaesthesis* (first observation). Architecture may acquire capacities (affordance) to invert the aesthetic coma of a subject who becomes one with system and network they engage with virtually but remain situated by flesh. Psarologaki defines this as *sensoma*; the architectural cyborg (second observation)—a system of built form, human flesh, and consciousness. The third observation acts as umbrella for the previous two. It sees the lived experience as a haecceity and highlights the role of affect toward a new definition of a posthuman lived condition defined as *veoma* (third observation). These three neologisms—anaesthesis, sensoma, and veoma—are presented here as triplet for the first time. They seek to become the basis for the elaboration of an experimental post-human lexicon that may act as the long-anticipated metalanguage of contemporary environmental (post)humanities and technoculture.

Sebastian Wiedemann
Antropofagia: Devouring Experimentations of a Manifesto Toward a Kinosophy to Come

Following Deleuze and Guattari's call to experiment rather than to interpret or explain, Wiedemann does not aspire to give an account of the concept of Anthropophagy, but rather to put it in motion and differentiation. (So, what we have here is really a Brazilian concept faked by a Colombian. As Orson Welles and Deleuze remind us, faking opens up new dimensions of thought through the power of fabulation.) It means to make of the writing a gesture of thinking in presence of the cannibal forces that emerge from the ideas of Brazilian poet, writer, and philosopher Oswald de Andrade in his 1928 Manifesto Antropófago (Cannibalist Manifesto). The procedure used in this philosophical experimentation is the one Brazilian poet and translator Haroldo de Campos calls transcreation (a devouring translation). To be precise, a cinematic transcreation that could help to establish what Wiedemann will call kinosophy, a wild and tropical Media Philosophy.

Ana Peraica
Autofotografija: Nonhuman Self-Portrait or a Human Selfie?

In the urge of producing new words to be distinctive from Serbian language (following the political and economic separation from Serbian and other ex-Yugoslavian republic speaking the same or similar language with the war for independence of Croatia, 1991–5), the Croatian Institute of Language compiles newly formed words but also coins some new words. The way of forming new words is in their logic of literary translations, sometimes overly vulgar and descriptive, similar to the language formation of Croatian Second World War regime, collaborating with Nazi regime, and engaging into similar language separation and linguistic purification. Independent State of Croatia (1941–5) has brought *The Law on Human Language, Its Purity and Grammar,* and founded the state office for language. The politics of this office was often seen as very aggressive in eliminating Serbian and other imported words from clean language. One of the words invented in this period was *svjetlopis* (Croatian, lightwriting, or photography), never used.

In contemporary Croatia, Croatian Institute for Language proposes Croatian alternative to the concept of selfie. Milica Mihaljević from this institution thus proposed alternatives; sebić (selfich) and samoslika (self-image). A serial of other proposals included autofotografija, autoslika, egoslik, fotoautoportret, jaslik, ja-slika, licić, osobna fotografija, osobna slika, osobnica, osobnjača, osobnjak, samnica, samnić, samo klik, samo slika, samoljubić, samoportret, samosličak, samoslik, samoslika, samoslikanje, samoslikavanje, samoslikić, samotret, seba, sebeljubić, sebeslik, sebič, sebičlika, sebičnost, sebičnjača, sebičnjak, sebić, sebićnica, sebifotkić, seboslik, segled, selbić, selfasnjača, selfić, solić, soloslika, svojfotkić, svojica, vlastoslik, zrcalka, zrcalnica, svojka, svojofot, samokid(ač) …

Each of these concepts puts focus on a separate element of the image reflection. There is a substantial difference among the word autofotografija and selfie, the first one reverberating an automatic process (as also autoslika), or the ones organized around mirror (zrcalka, zrcalnica…), each defining the technology of the image differently. Whereas selfie means recording oneself as a human, autofotografija reverberates the automatism of photography recording itself, or at least a machine recording itself. Although the fact that self-reflection in the mirror-based medium seems as referring to the reflexive technology of mechanical SLR (self-reflexive camera) or a digital DSLR, is a narrowing one, there are also some other changes of meaning which are connoted.

This difference among most of the concepts is maybe the most visible among the images of any selfie produced by a human and a so-called selfie produced by a nonhuman agent (such as the accidental photographic shot made by a machine on the Moon surface). This article will analyze differences between the human selfie and unhuman autofotografija, basing its reading on definitions of unhuman photography, as well as on previous aspects of selfie photography in the domain of post-humanity, but also trying to analyze different other constructs which are set in use (as sebić, Croatian, to-oneself-ie).

Bhaskar Sarkar
Bazaar: The Persistence of the Informal

In spite of its non-Anglophone origins, the word bazaar/bazar has found its place in the Oxford English Dictionary. Defined as a specific kind of market, marketplace, or fancy fair, it is typically qualified by "Oriental" or "eastern," and invariably conjures a certain informality, energy, and exotic appeal. Indeed, etymology confirms the word's Persian origins, and subsequent adoptions into Hindustani and Turkish; from the latter, it came into English via Italian. But more than its linguistic roots, it is the sense of exuberant, if chaotic, excess associated with the bazaar in Euro-American imaginations that makes the qualifier necessary. In othering such markets in terms of geographical-cultural designation, the OED seeks to capture something untranslatable inhering in the lexicographic signifier.

The gap between the market and the bazaar is born of cultural differences, consolidated via the colonial encounter, and targeted for elimination to improve market efficiency under capitalist modernity. Commercial laws seek to formalize modern economic transactions, minimizing their social, political, and cultural complexities. And yet, the bazaar remains a site of romanticism, of simultaneous enchantment and disorientation. But for large segments of the global South, the bazaar is the space of commerce that works on local terms—tacit contracts, homegrown protocols, and informal institutions—to promote local interests.

Drawing on the informal economies of the global South, Sarkar elaborates on the contemporary cultural and material dimensions of media piracy in which the untranslatable elements of the bazaar persist: not as vestiges of a past that should have disappeared with modernity, but as a constitutive element of southern capitalist modernities.

Helena Wu
上善若水/ Be (Like) Water: Media Dynamics and Multiple Realities

The expression "be (like) water" was most notably used by classical philosopher Laozi in *Dao De Jing* [Tao Te Ching] during the Warring States (fourth to second centuries BCE) of ancient China, international film star and founder of *Jeet Kune Do* Bruce Lee in the 1960s and Hong Kong pro-democracy protesters in the post-handover era. Water as a substance, medium and discursive entity is explored in this essay as to how various actors are connected and disconnected in the construction of varied realities of a particular space-time. The Hong Kong anti-extradition law protests that started in June 2019 provide a point of entry: Not only that the expression "be water" gained oral currency and is practically adopted as a resistance strategy; languaging also occurs—from Laozi's philosophical undertaking in classical Chinese to Bruce Lee's and Hong Kong protesters' engagement with the term in English ("be [like] water" [sic])—leaving room for thought along the line of its transmissibility and translatability. In this regard, the phenomenal popularization of the term during the territory-wide pro-democracy movement in Hong Kong can be regarded as an accumulative outcome of the city's entangled social, cultural, and political landscapes, for being a British colony once (1842–1997) and thereafter a Special Administrative Region (SAR) that practices the controversial "one country, two systems" policy with the People's Republic of China (PRC).

With an eye to the contextualization of liquid embodiment via the discourses of globalization (Saldana 2008) and modernity (Bauman 2000, 2005), Savat's (2013) extrapolation of Guattari and Deleuze's (1987) usage of viscosity offers a vantage point to weave media with politics. The potentiality of *fluid* as entity and characteristic is, for instance, spelt out under the framework of "fluid politics" in the domain of digital technology, where Savat named examples of "electronic civil disobedience" such as virtual sit-ins and hacker-activist activities as perceptible political actions. At this juncture, Wu's approach to media philosophy undertaken in this essay is inspired by Savat's exploration of the political dimension of digital media, but steers away from his proposition to have a clear-cut boundary between solid and fluid politics where the former signifies the "sedentary" space of the State (*polis*) and the latter marks the realm of the nomads (*nomos*). Rather, this essay focuses on how realities in the postmillennial age are not just multiplied by cultural production, utterances and media, but are also felt through their interaction and mediation. Hong Kong in 2019 precisely exemplifies the multifarious realities in contact and clash with one another on different discursive, physical, and virtual dimensions, as the protest activities in the city are varyingly manifested and perceived according to one's value systems, positioning of a Hong Kong identity and treatment of narratives of different wavelengths and ideological orientations. The essay concludes by highlighting the inevitability of being partially bounded by existing discourses (cf. the political discourses available in pre- and post-handover Hong Kong) and the possibility to strike newer relations and bestow differing meanings to changing contexts by way of media dynamics.

Agnieszka Dytman-Stasieńko and Jan Stasieńko
ćmiatło and *świecień*: Jacek Dukaj's Concepts in the Perspective of Philosophy of Visual Media and Telecommunication

One of the most important and recognizable novels of the Polish science-fiction writer Jacek Dukaj, written in 2007 entitled **Ice**, was set by the author in the early twentieth century. The plot of the novel takes place mainly in the ice-covered tsarist Russia, although all of Europe at the time is depicted in it as a place of the spread of the mysterious ice creatures "lute" that appeared on Earth after the impact of the Tunguska Event. Although the novel is described by the author and also by its readers as a very original version of the philosophy of history, it may also be interesting in the context of media philosophy. For the purpose of the book Dukaj creates various types of transformations and alterations of existing physical properties that occur as a result of ice. After the explosion of the meteoroid, new chemical elements (*tungetyt* "tungetite") and materials (*zimnazo* "cold iron") extracted in Siberia appear. From the perspective of media theory, the most interesting element of the new dark ice physics is the *ćmiatło* ("shlight")—a phenomenon that is the opposite of light, resulting from the burning of *zimnazo*. However, this is not a shadow, but a specific type of dark emanation, having its source and casting glow on objects that do not leave a shadow as if by light, but so-called *świecień* ("shine shadow"). All these terms are very difficult to translate into English, but at the same time, they can refer to new interesting contexts related to the philosophy of light in visual media. If for instance the theory of film starts from the light projection toward the screen the Dukaj's novel would suggest possibility of alter-cinema based on darkness and shadows. In the paper, we consider the potential of using the concept of *ćmiatło* and *świecień* in the interpretation of various aspects and conditions of both projection media and photography as well as selected properties and varieties of telecommunication in the perspective of the original concepts coined by Dukaj.

Kajri Jain
Darshan: The Gaze as Vision, Touch, and Spatial Presence

Darshan is usually described as a specifically South Asian concept to describe a type of engagement with divine or otherwise auspicious and powerful personages, including icons and gurus. It has been deployed in studies of South Asian cinema, media, and art, particularly—but not exclusively—in relation to religious and mythological forms. What makes it untranslatable is its simultaneous connotation of seeing and being in the presence of an image or person. Here the visual and the tactile or spatial are inseparable, for being present to the other via vision, which entails occupying the same space, becomes a form of touching via the gaze conceived as a fluid, involving a material exchange of substance. Darshanic engagement has been the basis for visual anthropologist Christopher Pinney's influential notion of "corpothetics" as a "sensory, corporeal aesthetics" opposed to a putatively "anaesthetizing" Kantian aesthetics centered on a distanced, disembodied, disinterested beholder (see Pinney 2004: 8, 23, 193). Jain would argue, however, that this subalternist valorization of South Asian corporeality against an anemic Western opticality, perhaps better labeled Cartesian, doesn't take into account the hegemonic–indeed oppressive– nature of touch, as is the case in South Asia where the social hierarchy of caste is still operational. Caste is organized around touch, purity, and pollution, exchanges of material substances, and spatial exclusion. Here the Brahmin priests who mediate and transact with the divine are at the top, while at the bottom, or rather entirely abjected from the social, have been the so-called outcastes or Untouchables, now self-identifying as Dalit or oppressed. Arguably, then, in the sensorium of caste all the other senses can be seen as interconvertible with touch as ritually fraught contact. This also has a gendered dimension, as it extends to menstruating or reproductive women as well. A discussion of the concept of darshan therefore pushes back both against the commonsense of the hegemony of vision in Western media and visual studies, and the generalized celebration of the haptic in the critique of ocularcentrism. Further, Jain suggests that when brought into conversation with work on spatial exclusion and regimes of violent touch, particularly in relation to race, the implications of this concept are perhaps more generalizable than has been considered so far.

Budhaditya Chattopadhyay
Dhvāni: Resonance

Dhvāni is a Sanskrit concept, which denotes resonance. This essay aims to unpack the conceptual premises of Dhvāni that emerge from an Indian epistemology-informed approach to sound and listening, emphasizing the role of the listener, the inter-subjective and affective contexts as the theoretical framework toward construing sonic, performative and artistic experiences. Contributing to current research in sound studies and existing knowledge in South Asian aesthetics and philosophy, Chattopadhyay will also unpack interconnected concepts, for example, *Sphōta* (sound grasped by the intellect) and *Rasa* (emotive context). By discussing these concepts, he examines the role of the "self" and inter-subjectivity, against an overarching emphasis on sonic object permeating in the Western artistic and scholarly traditions. Departing from the sonic object, the essay hints at the formation of fertile and evolving "auditory situations" where the selfhood and subjectivity of the listener can be considered in a reciprocal manner. In doing so, the essay develops an understanding of the role of chance and contingency in sound experience as a mode of creating temporal disjuncture for the "divine intervention" as Indian musician Gita Sarabhai informed John Cage in 1946 helping to shape Cage's subsequent work with chance composition. Such culturally inclusive approach to sound, resonance, and listening expands the contemporary sound studies discourses.

Bernd Herzogenrath
Gestell: Heidegger's Cyborg and the Vicissitudes of the Machine | Body

In his essay, Herzogenrath relates three artistic instances of what he considers to be marvelous marriages between the human and the machinic, to Heidegger's notion of the *Gestell*, and to a set of other theoretical approaches that deal with this relation and|or employ a machinic metaphor when it comes to the question of the human subject. Thus, following the lead that the meaning of *techne* as both art and technics/technology provides, the bits, pieces and engineers of this machine|text in search of an "originary machinism" are: Martin Heidegger, Jacques Lacan, Deleuze & Guattari, Stelarc, Mark Pauline, and *Tetsuo*, the 1989 movie by Shinia Tsukamoto. As a result, Herzogenrath argues that both the cultural/speaking body *and* the "real body" are machinic.

Woosung Kang
Gong (공空) | *Saek* (색色): The Ineffable Persistence of Becoming

Originally a Buddhist idea that teaches *sunya* (emptiness) of what exists, the notion of *góng* is always coupled with its conceptual opposite, *saek*, which connotes multiple shapes of being in the world. Philosophically, the wisdom of *Prajnaparamita* depends on the assumption that these antagonizing concepts are but two paths of becoming infinite. In China, Taoism tends to identify *góng* with *wu* (nothing) and puts it over *saek*, contrasting the ontological emptiness of the world with the shadow of substantial Being. Heavily influenced by Confucianism imported from China, Korean culture equates *góng* with the secular ethics of *musoyu* (non-possession), thereby downplaying the notion of *góng* into a nihilistic ideology and reducing *saek* to the object of desire. Wonhyo is an exception in that he warns of the danger of petrifying *góng* as substance: *góng* is also empty (*gonggong*). For Wonhyo, *góng* and *saek* are only different in form that they assume in reality, two contrasting but interdependent ways leading to the enlightenment, which requires the constant struggle with human desire. Kang argues that the secularization of two concepts in Korea derives from the overvaluation of the role human desire takes in everyday experience. Traveling through historical mutations of both notions, Kang demonstrates the way this unlikely pair becomes secularized and sexualized in Korea in terms of human desire.

Jukka-Pekka Puro & Veli-Matti Karhulahti
Hiljaa: Silent and Slow Media Use

In this essay we introduce a Finnish adverb *hiljaa* (n. *hiljaisuus*, adj. *hiljainen*) as a basis for conceptualizing media use that is silent, slow, and calm in a specific way, that is, controlled or easy in contrast to excessive and stressful. The nature of *hiljaa* in historico-cultural and phenomenological contexts of Finland points toward a rich semiotic meaning in which stillness in space (slowness) and lack of noise (silence) are merged into a single term, as positively perceived "calmness" or "tranquility" more generally. Using media *hiljaa* is a subjectively satisfying technological practice that allows one to interact with mediated content without undermining enactive agency.

Babson Ajibade
kõn kõn kà: The Sound of Colonial Shoes—Forgotten Words of a Yoruba Song of Success

By the time the industrial revolution made it prudent to abolish slave trade in 1807, varying degrees of devastation had swept through sub-Saharan Africa. Within the territories themselves, while Christian missionaries and the colonial enterprise were using the bible and the gun to negotiate new identities, it seems that self-cultural loathing was subtly encouraged among indigenous populations. Within the colonial missionary school system, children learnt the inferiority of Africa's denigrated culture and imbibed the longing for the colonial Western cultures. Also, dressing in western attires was hardly negotiable for natives working for the institution at all levels, making it clear that life's joys and successes were synonymous with western values, represented in western ways of dressing.

Among the Yoruba of southwest Nigeria, this situation did not go unrecorded in public memory. Knowing that success in colonial life was tied to living like *awon oyinbo* (white people), parents either sent their wards to missionary schools or embedded them to live with and serve missionaries. Through this embedded servitude to missionaries, many young people got scholarships to study abroad, to triumphantly return at a much later date. In the end, socioeconomic becoming gained a western coloration that was visible in one's western dressing. In the Yoruba societies of the time, the western-style heel shoe was the icon of this becoming, and all parents would remind their wards to aspire to it. But, in popular imagination, it was not the shoe itself that was the icon of this modernity and success; it was the sounds—*kōn kōn kà*—made by the shoes' heels, as the white man walked by. It was made into a song that parents sang and children learnt:

Bàtà rē á dún kōn kōn kà	Your shoe will sound *kōn kōn kà*
Bàtà rẹ á dún kōn kōn kà, bí ō b á kàwé rẹ	Your shoe will sound *kōn kōn kà*, if you study
Bí òò bà kàwé rẹ, bàtà rẹ á dún ṣẹrẹrẹ ní lẹ̄	If you don't study, your shoe will sound *ṣẹrẹrẹ* on the floor

In this song, the coveted modernity of *kōn kōn kà* was contrasted with the backwardness of the sound *ṣẹrẹrẹ* (akin to one made by a flip-flop) that indigenous shoes made on the same floor. Up until the early 1980s, when the Nigerian economy collapsed, this song was very popular. In his essay article, Ajibade uses a review of literature and field work to interrogate the social history and economic extensions of the cultural notions about *kōn kōn kà*. In particular, he seeks to analyze the link between economic collapse in the 1980s Nigeria and the dearth of *kōn kōn kà* in Yoruba popular culture.

Holger Schulze
L'Implèxe: What's in a Situation?

The concept of the implex was first used by poet and thinker Paul Valéry in his famous "Cahiers" in the late nineteenth century (Valéry 1965, 2007). In the early twenty-first century, though, essayist and science fiction-novelist

Dietmar Dath took up this long forgotten, seemingly quirky concept in order to rethink dialectical processes in historical transformations and social progress (Dath and Kirchner 2012). The implied trajectories, tendencies, inclinations, the implied complex goals of one person or a larger group of people can be conceptualized then as a vector exerting and unfolding its impact along the way.

This rediscovered concept of the implex is now useful to reinterpret and understand the concept of sonic fiction, proposed and employed by Kodwo Eshun (Eshun 1998). An implex, according to Valéry and Dath, must be regarded as the generative nucleus of a sonic fiction: the implex of a situation is then defined as an intrinsic inclination toward a certain direction of further development or action, implying—if not demanding—a collective or individual action. This situation can be characterized as a sonic, sensory, political, or economical one: in all of these cases, the implex describes an implied trajectory that can, but must not be manifested.

As soon as one outlines the implex of a sonic or social situation, one starts unfolding the latent sonic or social fiction implied in this situation. This unfolding is the utopian, the maieutic and the heuristic impact of the implex (Schulze 2020).

Erik Steinskog
Ljom: Norwegian Noise/Echo/Reverberation

The Norwegian word ljom comes from Old Norse hljómr, which is also one of the etymologies for the English word "loud." The Norwegian word is both a noun ("ljom") and a verb ("å ljome"), and as such describes both a sonic phenomenon, but also the making of said phenomenon.

It would, however, be a mistranslation to simply say that "ljom" is equivalent to "loud." Rather, translating "ljom" one needs access to a number of concepts of sound: echo, reverberation, arguably noise, as well as "sounding" or "to sound." It is this movement from one word—in both its versions as noun and verb—to a multiplicity of words for sonic phenomena, that this article takes a point of departure and line of flight. What happens, one may ask, when trying to think a cluster of words and terminology, with a foreign vocabulary, a vocabulary where the relations between the different terms are reshuffled or imagined differently?

The Norwegianness of the term ljom also opens for a renegotiation between so-called "natural" sounds and "cultural" sounds, that is, ljom can also be used to describe echoes and reverberations as they are heard between mountains or across fjords, and while this use could be seen as (hopelessly) nationalist and/or romantic, in this piece this will rather be used as a way to question how one might think about "natural" sounds (or sounds in nature) as cohabiting how sounds found in "culture"—from cityscapes to music—are interpreted.

Soudhamini
Māya: A Measured Response to and in Cinematic Virtual Reality

Both Pierre Levy's and Gilles Deleuze's interpretations of the term virtual are strikingly similar to the Vedic *Kavi's* (poet-seer's) intuition of *māya* as a generative and creative force. Yet by the time *Advaita Vedanta* becomes established as a philosophical schema, *māya* comes to imply that this world is just an illusion, but so compelling an illusion that it is mistaken for real. The VR apparatus (technology + ideology) attempts to achieve precisely this—to provide so complete an immersion that it supersedes reality rather than simply intervening in it. VR in other words aspires to a condition of *māya*. But where *Vedanta* seeks to dispel the illusion by invoking the notion of the *atman-* consciousness, VR seeks to sustain it. This essay brings to bear the structural configuration of *māya:atman* as an organizing principle in Cinematic Virtual Reality (CVR) as an aesthetic, ethical, and ecological alternative to the sensorial immersion the market offers.

Jukka Sihvonen
Mediataju: A Sense of Media

The Finnish word—*mediataju* ("a sense of media")—is a composite of two concepts, "media" and "taju" [pronounced as *ta-you*]. In the online dictionaries *taju* would translate into English as "consciousness," "sense," "flair," "grasp," "appreciation," "savvy"—all of which could be used also in this connection. Though *mediataju* is a somewhat weird word in Finnish there is another and as such a much more common word that also has *taju* in it: *rytmitaju*—roughly meaning "a sense of rhythm." When a word such as *taju* is used, there may be an assumption that it can (or cannot) be innate; and/or, that it is possible to learn it as a skill. This term is offered as a concept in the discussions on media education, to promote *mediataju* instead of "media literacy." Media education requires not just "reading skills" but also "sensing skills." The article discusses the notion of *sense* from the viewpoint in which Gilles Deleuze explores it in his book *Logique du sens* (1969). Furthermore, Paul Auster's film *The Inner Life of Martin Frost* (2007) is discussed as an example in which the problematic of sense becomes explored in a tangible way.

Vít Pokorný
Myslet médii. Thinking In, With, or Through Media: Images, Interfaces and Apparatuses

Vít Pokorný's essay aims to think about thinking, to think about what thinking is and how it is. Pokorný starts from the assumption that thinking is always somehow connected with the medium and that it is inseparable from the practices and techniques of its expression. M. Petříček bases his analysis of what it means to *think through images* on the fact that an image is not a representation of reality and that it does not relate to it from outside, but from inside. B. Herzogenrath in his project of *practical aesthetics* claims that practical aesthetics does not want to think about art, but with art, with images, sounds, and so on. Thinking here means thinking through/in/with something, that is, not only through speech and text and not only through images, but generally through any means of expression in which thinking can manifest. This study also interprets media as *interfaces*, as generally defined by B. Hookway, that is as a relational system emergent to its constitutive parts.

Thinking *with* always operates through something, it is always mediated, as well as mediating, but it also always takes place somewhere, that is, as an embodied and situated activity of the organism in the environment. In this context, I want to interpret the concept of thinking also in light of Deleuze's text *Proust and the signs* according to which we seek the truth not because we want to, but because we are forced to do so by the violence of signs.

However, thinking *through*, *with* or *in* something also means that we, as the authors, are not fully autonomous. Thinking does not originate from within the free, disembodied will and depends on the interface of its action by whose possibilities it is limited. In her essay "On the practice of theory," K. Krtilová therefore asks, on the one hand, how to accept the technological or media determination of thinking and, on the other hand, how to "think 'thinking'" as a free activity that is able to exceed each of its technological determinations.

Behrooz Mahmoodi-Bakhtiari
Naqqāli: The Case of Ali Hātami's Movies

Naqqāli is a typical method of storytelling in Iran, in which the storyteller (Naqqāl) stands by a painted screen, points at different parts of the painting with a specific stick, and tells a folklore or epic story by using his body language, singing, and acting. Ali Hātami, the famous Iranian film director, was greatly interested in traditional Iranian performances, and has shown some of them (including Naqqāli) in his movies. An important feature in his films is that he starts two of his movies with Naqqāli. These films are Hasan Kachal (Hassan the Bald, 1970), and Bābā Shamal (1972), which will be studied in this article.

Gretchen Jude
Nikusei: The Fleshly Voice

This essay will discuss the Japanese term "*nikusei*" (肉声), whose denotative meaning refers to voice in its electronically unamplified and unmediated state. In this sense, the term fills a lacuna in the English lexicon, which does not provide a concise way to express this fundamental phenomenon. While writing her dissertation on the history of Japanese vocal processing and performance, Jude found the term not only practically useful, but also metaphorically appealing, as the Sino-Japanese characters literally indicate "meat-voice"—which she chose to gloss in English as "the fleshly voice." This anchoring of the sonic phenomenon of vocal vibration in a particular and inescapably embodied source seems conceptually crucial for avoiding abstracted and metaphorical uses of the term "voice."

Cases in which the word *nikusei* expands beyond its denotative meaning also push against the limitations of English, as Jude illustrates with discussion of two Japanese vocal recordings, one of singing and one of speaking. Folk singer Tomokawa Kazuki's 1976 *Nikusei*, glossed in English as *A Natural Voice*, indicates an emotional rawness that resonates with the artist's regional, working-class roots, rather than indicating an "unplugged" or all-acoustic album. Descriptions of a historical recording of an early-twentieth-century speech given by General Nogi Maresuke draw on the term *nikusei* to indicate the sense of startling directness across distance (in this case, temporal distance). Both uses of the Japanese term indicate the need for a term in English to elaborate the complex connection between voice and its body of origin (not to mention the bodies of its listeners).

Finally, Jude examines the use of *nikusei* by Japanese media and critical theorists in translations of the French term *parole*. Not only does this sense of the Japanese word underline the connotations of directness and embodiment that the Japanese term carries (unlike a pedestrian English translation of the denotation "unamplified voice"), it also highlights the contextual and relational nature of any act of translation (in this case, between English, Japanese and French)—as well as any act of voice. Jude's triangulations of the various uses of *nikusei*, a translation-resistant term, will be of interest to sound, media, and voice studies scholars who aim to expand theorization in their fields beyond the limitations of the Western canon.

Julia Vassilieva
ОТКАЗ *(OTKAZ)*: From Expressive Movement to a Figure of Thought

ОТКАЗ/OTKAZ is a Russian term which reigns supreme in celebrated Revolutionary director Sergei Eisenstein's theory and practice. Often translated as *recoil*, a term borrowed from theater studies to denote a particular trajectory of stage movement—a zigzag line, a spiral or a semi-spiral, each of them recording the movement toward the aim in a roundabout way—for Eisenstein the word acquired an extended meaning, which cannot be adequately captured through translation. In ОТКАЗ/OTKAZ, "that movement which, when you wish to make a movement in one direction, you initially make in the opposite direction (in part or completely)," Eisenstein saw, first of all, the essence of the expressivity arguing "This is one of the fundamental laws inevitably met at all levels and in all varieties of expressive movement" (quoted in Law and Gordon 1996: 192). ОТКАЗ/OTKAZ serves as the paradigm of expressive movement because its trajectory presents a physical outline of conflict, staging the dynamic of two opposing forces or motives—away and toward the aim of movement, and the notion of conflict is central for Eisenstein.

In Eisenstein's theoretical writings detailed discussion of ОТКАЗ/OTKAZ can be found in his numerous analyses focusing on *mise en scène* and trajectories of movement on stage. He praises Chinese director Mei Lanfang and Japanese kabuki theater for their skillful mobilization of OTKA3/OTKAZ; he refers to Lessing's notes on hand movements; and he highlights the exaggerated use of OTKA3/OTKAZ movement in the ritual dancing of North American indigenous people. And in his cinematic work Eisenstein insists on the necessity of breaking down the movement into two phases—the initial one, away from its aim, and the amplified second phase, toward the aim—to achieve maximum expressive effect. He uses OTKA3/OTKAZ in all his films—from *Strike* (1924) and *Battleship Potemkin* (1925) to *Ivan the Terrible* (1942-6); it can be observed at the level of individual actors and in the collective movement of Eisenstein's famous invention, the "mass protagonist." Yet, as Luka Arsenjuk demonstrated recently, for Eisenstein, OTKA3/OTKAZ is not only an epitome of expressive movement in its ability to dramatize conflict, it is also, and more importantly—a figure of thought, that takes physical movement as a point of departure for a new, purely cinematic dialectics, dialectics arising from the fact the cinema is an art of the moving image. OTKA3/OTKAZ enacts the synthesizing possibility of cinematic thought by dramatizing splitting of (apparent) unity and the overcoming of this splitting through the dialectical logic of "negation of negation" (Arsenjuk 2018: 6). As such it is only cinema that can realize the full potential of OTKA3/OTKAZ as an instrument of thinking and in its full measure OTKA3/OTKAZ for Eisenstein is no less than an embodiment of a unique potential of cinema, its capacity to engage with division and alienation, and a possibility to overcome this division.

Mohammad Hadi
رند, or Rend

Mohammad Hadi's essay, without dealing with the historical facets inherent in semantic and pragmatic evolutions of the Persian figure *Rend* رند, deals with the deep-rooted reluctance or even disinclination in رند in having her translated. It argues that رند is a *perfect* expression of (un)translatability. Rend has undergone various connotations from mercenary gangster to the one who drinks wine and practices the generous life with others, to lout and debauchee. All this hints at an unceasing attempt in رند to break away from the imposed religious or secular norms and establishments in a way that is against Zahed زاهد, or the ascetic who is content with his preordained sanctimonious, self-righteous, and hypocritical deeds.

As the antithesis to زاهد who, by dissembling his true emotions and passions, constantly professes a search for ascension, رند is in harmony and equilibrium with herself, without pretense or hypocrisy. Ironically speaking, such lack of pretension in رند, makes its translation harder, simply because she combats authoritarian inauthenticities rooted in culture, thought, and language and eludes the securities of ell-embracing rules and regulations by sneaking through the back doors of morality.

If زاهد recoils from human condition and takes the edge off life by having to resort to his dogmas and principles, رند remains faithful to the intensities she experiences and does not pretend NOT to have been affected. This brings yet another key point to forth: رند notices *Stimmung*. She allows for all possibilities which might befall her life, all ways of affecting and being affected.

Didi Cheeka
Sankofa: It Is not Taboo to Return

"Lingering spirit of the dead, rise up."

Among the Twi language-speaking people of Ghana is a word, Sankofa, which literally means "Go back and get it." The term, which is usually depicted by a bird flying forward while reaching with its beak an egg delicately balanced on its back, is, among an artistic intellectual layer of African Americans, synonymous with the black experience—in the sense that, disconnected from the American reality, their sense of rootlessness could be overcome by reaching out to the motherland, Africa. A major disagreement with this attitude is with its return to the source tendency—an inability, or reluctance, to theorize, Sankofa in philosophic psychologic terms beyond a mere [metaphysical] return to one's spiritual roots. The beginning quote is from the movie, *Sankofa*, by Haile Gerima—it is the chant of the Divine Drummer, named Sankofa, that opens the movie and signifies his communion with the enslaved ancestral spirit of the black diaspora. The lingering spirit, invoked from the dead, takes possession of the protagonist and transports her, in the body of a slave, into the past "to live the life of her enslaved ancestors" in an American plantation. In seeking to deploy the concept of Sankofa, Didi Cheeka cites this film not to engage with black slavery nor extend the debate on superiority of cultures but, rather, as the film itself does, to highlight the healing power of history and memory: the characters who suffer less are the slaves with memory of their homeland—their memory of their history acts to heal the wounds imposed by slavery. Cheeka approaches Sankofa as the filmmaker himself: "to move forward, you must reclaim the past. In the past, you find the future and understand the present." Contained in this statement is a philosophic psychologic possibility inherent to the Sankofa concept.

Susana Viegas
Saudade: (De)Mythologizing a Portuguese Concept

For centuries, Portuguese philosophers have considered the concept of *saudade*, an untranslatable word from Galician-Portuguese origin, which can be understood as a state of mind of being nostalgic, to long for or to miss someone/something. The sentiment itself is created by a feeling of distance from someone/something that is loved and that is loosed. This poetic feeling was object of the Portuguese Saudade School as something that could existentially define a whole nation. But more than a Portuguese feeling, *saudade* is a universal experience of time, a time that seems not to pass. Considered within this conceptual framework, the experience of time is thought as an eternal present moment, taken as an everlasting moment: it remains between a past that is remembered and a future that is desired. Because it is never complete, this desire, or expectation, is destined to fail, or at least to be postponed indefinitely. Even if the analysis of a metaphysics of time seems to be logically guided by hopeless and vain longings, we find it to be a very effective concept, since its power lies not in its logical mode of thought but in what we can do with it. What are the existential and cultural problems that lie at its origins? And how are we to deal with illusory expectations? One possible answer turns out to be a reactionary and retrogressive effect, against difference and innovation. If, for example, following Walter Benjamin's ontology of images, we think of images as being dialectical, doubles by nature—past and present, mobile and immobile, part and whole—we realize that *saudade* persists by restraining its true progress into something faultless and improved. It has a messianic nature, but not in a dialectical (historical) way. As will become evident in the following analysis, taken in this sense *saudade* creates more obstacles than developments. *Saudade* has unconsciously shaped an idea of historical power and the development of greatness that has real effects both in political and economic decisions and in cultural and social movements. Media philosophy explores how these movements are represented and perceived. Recent conservative political and social movements may also be clarified through this concept, since critical thought of this nature is relevant, for example, to postcolonial visual studies, such as critical thought on how the colonies are represented, either in cinema, the news, advertising, social networking, or mass media in general.

Lorenz Engell
Schalten und Walten: An Access to Operative Ontology

In German, *Schalten und Walten* is a rather common and quite widespread idiom that can be found in everyday life. Whoever, the idiom stipulates, is able to execute *Schalten und Walten* has the power to act, has freedom of decision and power of disposition. *Switching and Ruling* might be accepted as English versions, but quite an unbridgeable difference remains.

Although both terms are mentioned together and belong together in the German expression *Schalten und Walten*, they are nevertheless complements to each other. They both refer to the exercise and existence of domination, disposal, or power, but they designate nonetheless two quite different modes of being. *Schalten* is not so much sheer command over something, but government or management. It is linked to control, intervention, and change, in short: it is operative and goes along with distinctive measures and cause-and-effect relations. The English equivalent *switching* reflects this more or less adequately.

Walten, on the other hand, is not articulated. It is not divisible, is not based on distinctions or decisions, and does not come in the form of interventions or distinct operations. *Walten* is not a technique of domination, but rather dominance or dominion as a given state of being, a form of existence without outside, without any question, or alternative to it. *Walten* has neither origins nor causes. Where the German language separates *Walten* from *Schalten* precisely by drawing them together, the English *ruling* includes both sides, both that which is simply there and therefore rules, and the technique of domination, such as the setting of rules.

Schalten on its turn brings with it *Walten* like its own shadow, and, of course, media theory is interested in this remaining ontological shadow of digitization and of mediatization in general. But there is even more than the necessary pertinence of *Walten* even under digital conditions. *Walten* is not only the unavoidable substrate of *Schalten*, it can also emerge from it. Earlier investigation focused on the material conditions and the interactions between philosophical and organic operations, hence between switchings and rulings. Media philosophy now adds to this the consideration of the technical and medial bodies.

Sebastian Kawanami-Breu and Shintaro Miyazaki
Seken: Webs and Networks of In-Betweenness

This essay will look into the etymology and cosmology of the Indian concept *loka*, translated roughly as a world filled with activity, and compare this to the Japanese version pronounced *seken* (世間 in Chinese characters), where the meaning has shifted to an amalgam implying a meaning close to inter-meshed in-betweenness. While the cosmos in Indian, Hinduist, and ancient Buddhist thinking has a concentric, onion-like architecture, this view transformed slowly into the metaphor of a web of human affairs. Unlike European thinking based on alphanumerics and geometry, East Asian thinking also embeds stroke-based graphics. This cosmotechnical difference shows itself in various facets of the term *seken*, whose semantic and historical contrasts to the European concept "society" we will examine in further detail in the second part. The essay closes by pondering about the implications of this concept for theories of media or of sociotechnological spaces.

Victor Fan
Tathāgatagarbha: Translating the Untranslatable

In comparative literature and philosophy, translating concepts that are deemed *untranslatable* is often necessary for the purpose of enabling scholars from different linguistic and cultural perspectives to access and partake in a discourse. Nonetheless, as Lydia Liu argues, in an act of translation, signs that have different values in their respective languages are often "thrown together" into a "super-sign." The result is a new system of differences that does not help readers of the target language to interpret directly the sign originated in the source language. Rather, this super-sign constitutes a new discursive space that often takes an established discourse originated in the target linguistic sphere to a new direction.

In his essay, Fan uses the historical conversation between Buddhism, Taoism (Daoism), and European philosophy on the meaning of Tathāgatagarbha as a case study to scrutinize what it means by translating the untranslatable. The Sanskrit term Tathāgatagarbha literally means the *garbha* (womb) from which Tathāgata (a being/non-being that is neither coming nor going, neither not coming nor not going) is generated. This "womb" is considered by many Buddhist scholars as the meontological ground of all interbecomings and interdependent relationalities. The concept itself is regarded as inarticulable in and untranslatable into language. This case study, Fan argues, demonstrates that by enabling two different, but mutually relatable, philosophical systems to talk to one another, scholars can foster a *potentiality of translatability* from the untranslatable. Such an act can also inspire scholars from different linguistic and cultural ecologies to rewrite their own epistemes, based on a new *topos* reconfigured by the act of translation itself.

Andrei Ionescu and Bogdan Deznan
Todetita: Facebook's Ontological Malady

In his *Six Maladies of the Contemporary Spirit* the twentieth-century Romanian philosopher Constantin Noica articulates, through a close engagement with both the arts and the sciences, a typology of six ontological pathologies. The concepts he creates to account for this taxonomy are derived from Ancient Greek terms and introduced in the Romanian language as idiosyncratic neologisms. In this article, we will investigate the usefulness of one of these concepts—*todetita*—in an exploration of the structure and functions of social media, with a specific focus on Facebook. *Todetita* is characterized by a deficiency of individuality and a blockage within generality, thus by an inability to deal with the specificity of concrete phenomena. Although Noica discusses this concept mostly in connection to literature, science, and religion, we will argue that his analyses can be expanded to also shed novel light on crucial aspects of new media. The introduction of this concept in the vocabulary of contemporary media philosophy will have the advantage of clarifying and systematizing previously neglected aspects of social media, such as the deficiencies that their functionality and ontological status engender.

Lucia D'Errico
Togliere di scena

Literally translating as "taking out of the stage" with the implication of "unstaging," the Italian locution *togliere di scena* was employed by Italian theater director and actor Carmelo Bene to describe his own counter-theatrical practice. If traditional theater deals with staging ("mise en scéne," or *mettere in scena* in Italian) plays that are conveyed primarily through a textual dimension by means of adding elements to the text (stage, costumes, action, diction, music, etc.), Bene pursues the opposite aim: to subtract, amputate, mutilate the text, to take it away from the stage, in order to block the re-presentation of the already said, the already happened, the work as *Abfall* or cadaverous remainder of practices irremediably sedimented.

In his short essay *One Less Manifesto*, Gilles Deleuze comments on several subtractive strategies employed by Bene to give life to what Deleuze calls a "minoritarian" practice. He enumerates the elements that Bene amputates in the original plays: structure, constants, diction, action. In her essay, D'Errico focuses on the central role that sound plays in Bene's operation. Physical sound, with its infinite microvariations, is called by Bene *phoné*. If the immediate reference for this term seems Jacques Derrida, the use that Bene makes of this term has implications that widely diverge from those drawn by the French philosopher: phonic substance is far from representing the logocentric voice which, in dialogue with itself, would reinstate the primacy of phonocentrism and the metaphysics of presence. Quite the contrary: sound becomes a subtractive force, that which springing from the text but always in friction and excess with it manages to jeopardize the textual. Instead of a metaphysics of presence, Bene pursues absence— again, the *togliere*, not the *mettere*. By obliterating the text through its own excess, Bene's stagings point to what is outside the scene and can never be represented because it is unrepresentable. Bene calls this locus *l'osceno* ("the obscene"), which through a productive paraetymology becomes the *obskené*, the outside-the-scene, but also a reference to that which cannot be said, shown, put on a stage.

This essay will also discuss two apparent paradoxes that make Bene's use of sound unique and still relevant in today's reflections on the ontology of sound and its relation to writing. The first regards Bene's need to remain anchored to texts from the great theatrical tradition (such as Shakespeare, Laforgue, or Wilde) instead of losing his own theater from the fetters of any tradition, and consequently his sound from the necessity of a text (a quest that might resemble more Antonin Artaud's project). The second concerns the pursuit of absence through what is perceived as an almost baroque excess: not only through the abundance theatrical props and costumes, but also importantly through the saturation of the sonic environment, both in terms of pace, by means of a superposition of voices that can be compared to the use of fast-paced montage in cinema (including Bene's own cinema) and in terms of range, through the extreme exploitation of what Bene calls *fascia* ("sonic band").

Chantelle Gray
Ubuntu: Be-ing Becoming (Capable of Being Affected)

In *Uncontrollable Societies of Disaffected Individuals* (2013), Bernard Stiegler laments the ubiquity of disaffected individuals in our contemporary societies of hyper-control, which is to say persons no longer capable of being affected. He attributes this to the reduction of the *totality* of life to consumption so that even individuation and transindividuation processes—the processes by which we become—are short-circuited by what has become automated processes. For Stiegler, it is not automation *per se* that is a problem—all societies, individuals, and even cells deal with sets of automatisms which, in fact, are the basis of life. The problem, rather, lies with the way in which *digital* automations short-circuit the purposeful functions of the mind, thereby instantiating disindividuating processes which, for Stiegler, unlike Simondon, is not a neutral operation that forms part of all individuation processes but implies, on one level, the short-circuiting of individuation (ontogenetic) and transindividuation (sociogenetic) processes and, on another level, the proletarianization of knowledge or, to put it differently, the short-circuiting of epistogenetic individuation processes. This loss of knowledge provokes a veritable becoming-unreasonable of the world because as noetic life is automated and reticulated, a loss of reason, and reasons for living, is induced. The shift to digital automation is thus not merely technical for Stiegler, meaning a transition from analogue to digital, but *organological*, a question of life; that is, of the cosmos and the living subject.

It is here that we find a curious link to *ubuntu*, a Nguni term translating as "personhood" or "humanness," but which denotes African ontology, epistemology, and ethics. Generally, *ubuntu* is associated with the individuation of persons and the social being from which emerges a knowledge of how to live an ethical life. Thus, it is often described as a humanistic ethic though, properly speaking, *ubuntu* surpasses a concern with human dignity and even the human as such because it is, more substantially, occupied with cosmic harmony and well-being. Although *ubuntu* is associated with the organic and inorganic, it is neither commonly nor theoretically aligned with technology. There is, however, some use in alloying the two concepts, which is to say, placing the two heterogeneous series into continuous variation with the aim of provoking an encounter. In doing so, it is Gray's hope that it prompts the beginnings of a response to what Peter Frase calls the two specters of the present-day in his book, *Four Futures: Life After Capitalism* (2016), namely the ecological crisis and automation.

Suk-Jun Kim
Uri (우리 [uri]): Sound and the Porous Self

Talking about and sharing with others our aural experiences is a notoriously difficult task. Even when we hear the same sound, the same aural phenomenon, at the same time and in the same place, as soon as we try to share our experiences from it, we realize that there is so much we do not agree, so much in the sound about which we do not think we understand each other. What's clear is that we can at least acknowledge that we are not listening to the same things in it despite our temporal and spatial togetherness. The difficulty in talking about our aural experiences of a sound event, let alone highly structured aural phenomena like a piece of composition, is common and widespread like an innocuous ailment. In this article, Kim aims to examine this difficulty in the collective aural by exploring the problematics of the (concept of) the audience and the division of hearing-listening and those of language in our attempts to share aural experiences. Finally, Kim proposes to consider *uri (우리)*, a Korean word meaning "we," and its tacit inclusiveness or a being-togetherness in a shared experience, in the hope that it will offer us a porous self with *parallax hearing* (based on the *parallax view* by Žižek) that may open up a gap or space for the collective aural.

Andreas Jacobsson
Utbrytningsdrömmar: Swedish Audio-Visual Expressions of a Desire for Leaving Far

In his book *La grande aventure du cinéma suédois* (1960), French film historian Jean Béranger describes Ingmar Bergman's film *A ship bound for India* (1947) as an "*Utbrytningsdröm*," a concept he finds impossible to translate into French with precision. The concept according to Béranger captures being imprisoned emotionally and structurally in the bourgeois Swedish society, and dreaming of breaking free from these specific contextual restraints. In *A Ship Bound for India* the dream is manifested as an actual desire to travel. But "Utbrytningsdröm" is also relevant to understand as an abstraction of the feeling of being restrained and suffocated in a welfare state (Folkhemmet)—without obvious (material) reasons for feeling this way. A Utbrytningsdröm is not restricted to describing thematic concerns, the term also captures an aesthetic dimension of many of Bergman's films and fits the description of a number of other Swedish films from this era. In his essay,

Jacobsson expands on the concept and develop a discussion of contemporary audio-visual expressions of "Utbrytningsdrömmar," in relation to a changed socio-political landscape.

Rick Dolphijn
Wellevenskunst

Wellevenskunst is a concept coined by the Dutch philosopher Dirck Volckertsz Coornhert, who had an enormous influence on art and philosophy in the Netherlands in sixteenth century. The Netherlands, at that time, was still a nation to come, struggling with wars, with Calvinism gaining popularity, but also with the freedoms of the Renaissance touching ground, and allowing artists and philosophers to think creatively, to question the powers of the church. Coornhert, hardly known within philosophy today, played a crucial role in this emancipation process. He finished his book "zedekunst is wellevenskunst" in 1584, making it the first ethics ever written in a native language in Europe. Coornhert was known to be very outspoken about the importance of freedom of religion and the move away from the dogma's key to the moralities, key to Christianity.

Coornhert, though his many publications search for ways to educate the masses, writing an ethics that would not just serve one part of the population but that would benefit all. Very much written in the Stoic tradition of Seneca and Cicero and always emphasizing how human passions need to be overcome, Coornhert, preceding his artistic and philosophical peers from the Golden Age (the seventeenth century in which the Netherlands became the European center of art and philosophy) succeeded in laying the foundation of the time to come, so crucial to the history of Europe. The term Wellevenskunst played a crucial role in his work and therefore needs a special place in the philosophical lexicon.

Cora Bender
Line and Bump

What benefit can a transcultural media theory gain from reflecting, integrating, and experimenting with non-Western media concepts? What can be pitfalls and problems of this process? An especially interesting example of transcultural theorizing is the confluence of South American indigenous thinking and the philosophical work of Gilles Deleuze and Felix Guattari in the concept of *perspectivism and the Other*, coined by the noted Brazilian anthropologist and public intellectual Eduardo Viveiros de Castro. In the present article, I would like to use another aspect of Deleuze's and Guattari's "concept of concepts": that of *signature, regeneration*, and *geography*. As an exemplary case, I introduce the transcontextual encounter of indigenous thought and Western media theory in the essay of anthropologist and linguist Dorothy Lee to a journal edited in Toronto by Edmund Carpenter and Marshall McLuhan with the title *Explorations* (1953–7). In doing so, I seek to highlight, first, the role of anthropological mediators of indigenous concepts, and second, the question of what an indigenous concept's signature might be, and to whom it belongs. What I aim to come up with, in the end, is an argument to first and foremost treat indigenous concepts as *indigenous media* with a specific and complex signature of both translation *and* sovereignty.

Note

1 See also Brian Massumi in his "Translator's Foreword" to *A Thousand Plateaus*:
> Deleuze's own image for a concept is not a brick, but a "toolbox." He calls his kind of philosophy "pragmatics" because its goal is the invention of concepts that do not add up to a system of belief… [Which]… pack a potential in the way a crowbar in a willing hand envelops in energy of prying … The question is not: is it true? But: does it work? What new thought does it make possible to think? What new emotions does it make it possible to feel? What's new sensations and perceptions does it open in the body? (Deleuze and Guattari 1987: xv).

Works Cited

Arsenjuk, L. (2018), *Movement, Action, Image, Montage: Sergei Eisenstein and the Cinema in Crisis*, Minneapolis: University of Minnesota Press.
Bauman, Z. (2000), *Liquid Modernity*, Cambridge, UK: Polity Press.
Bauman, Z. (2005), *Liquid Life*, Cambridge, UK: Polity Press.
Dath, D., and B. Kirchner (2012), *Der Implex: Sozialer Fortschritt: Geschichte und Idee*, Berlin: Suhrkamp Verlag.
Deleuze, G. (1994), *Difference and Repetition*, trans. P. Patton, New York: Columbia University Press.
Deleuze, G. (1995), *Negotiations 1972–1990*, trans. M. Joughin, New York: Columbia University Press.

Deleuze, G. (2004), *Desert Islands and Other Texts 1953–1974*, NY and LA: semiotext(e).
Deleuze, G., and F. Guattari (1987), *A Thousand Plateaus*, trans. B. Massumi, Minneapolis: University of Minnesota Press.
Deleuze, G., and F. Guattari (1994), *What Is Philosophy?*, trans. H. Tomlinson and G. Burchill, New York: Columbia University Press.
Eshun, K. (1998), *More Brilliant Than the Sun: Adventures in Sonic Fiction*, London: Quartet Books.
Harris, P. A. (2010), "Deleuze's Cinematic Universe of Light: A Cosmic Plane of Luminance," *SubStance* 39 (1): 115–24.
Law, Alma H., and Gordon, Mel (1996), *Meyerhold, Eisenstein, and Biomechanics: Actor Training in Revolutionary Russia*, Jefferson, NC: McFarland.
Nealon, J., and Giroux, S. S. (2012), *The Theory Toolbox: Critical Concepts for the Humanities, Arts, and Social Sciences*, Lanham, ML: Rowman & Littlefield.
Pinney, C. (2004), *"Photos of the Gods:" The Printed Image and Political Struggle in India*, London/New Delhi: Reaktion/Oxford University Press.
Rajchman, J. (2000), *The Deleuze Connections*, Cambridge: MIT Press.
Saldana, A. (2008), "The Political Geography of Many Bodies," in Kevin R Cox, Murray Low and Jennifer Robinson (eds), *The SAGE Handbook of Political Geography*, London: SAGE, 32334.
Savat, D. (2013), *The Uncoding the Digital: Technology, Subjectivity and Action in the Control Society*, Hamsphire: Palgrave Macmillan.
Schulze, H. (2020), *Sonic Fiction*, New York: Bloomsbury Academic.
Valéry, P. (1965), The Collected Works of Paul Valery – Part V: Idee fixe: A Duologue by the Sea, translation by D. Paul, Preface by J. Mathews, Introduction by P. Wheelwright, Princeton, NJ: Princeton University Press.
Valéry, P. (2007), *Cahiers/Notebooks 3*, transl. N. Rinsler, P. Ryan, B. Stimpson, based on the French Cahiers edited by Judith Robinson-Valéry, Frankfurt am Main: Peter Lang.

1

Anaesthesis, Sensoma, Veoma: Cyborg Life Modes of Immersion After Deleuze

(Origin Greek)

Liana Psarologaki

Introduction

In her seminal book *The Posthuman* (2013), Rosi Braidotti makes an important statement about the problematics of the binary distinction between life as previously (or so far) *bios* assigned to Man and *zöe* assigned to nonhuman living, toward a living subject that is part of nature-culture continuum. In the context of the necropolitics of advanced capitalism, she sees a life-death continuum of *zöe* that seizes to be the distinctive quality of nonhuman life. In fact, it is one that may (or should perhaps) ontologically and ethically define the posthuman subject: "the crisis of Anthropos—she says—relinquishes the demonic forces of the naturalized others. Animals, insects, plants and the environment, in fact the planet and the cosmos as a whole, are called into play" (2013: 66). The common standard for man as center of cosmic axis mundi is displaced, warped. Rather, the human organism, closest as ever to both machine and animal is de-wired but reconnected to a plethora of sources, forces, flows and transformative drives—sometimes connected sometimes disconnected, but always an interconnected hybrid. To understand this alliance of life, let us look at the interdependent affordance between organism and environment as flesh[1]-machine, what Braidotti defines as "an embodied affective and intelligent entity" (2013: 139). She says "being environmentally bound and territorially based, an embodied entity feeds upon, incorporates and transforms its environment constantly. Being embodied ... in ecological manner entails full immersion in fields of constant flows" (2013: 139–40), immersion being the operative term here.

This is very close to what neurobiologist Rob DeSalle describes as quorum sensing in his book *Our Senses: An Immersive Experience* (2018). Par example, in the case of the Hawaiian bobtail squid (Euprymna scolopes) and the bioluminescent bacterium Aliivibrio fischeri that lives in its light-producing organ, squid and bacteria have a dynamic mutualistic relationship. Its organ only works with this single species of bacteria that live Not Within Its Cells but within the squid and make up the organ. A (molecular) mechanism is in place because the bacteria need to know when to light up otherwise "it would be a terrible waste of energy to stay lit up all the time" (DeSalle 2018: 9). It's not just that this sustainably evaluates and responsively decides when to light up, but a molecular lock-and-key mechanism is in place to assess the population size and therefore determine its zöe and bios networks within the (lived) environment. In fact, organ, organism, and environment (as entour^2/entourage) become ontologically constitutive to one another. They become together an immersive, embodied (enfleshed perhaps), and intelligent reterritorialization—a Simondonean modulation to quote Anne Sauvagnargues "a common system, an associated milieu ... an operation of individuation, through a continuous exchange of information" (2013: 69). In essence, the bacteria and organ (ink sack) act as bioclimatic synthesis machine-in-flesh and become a bios/zöe based environmentally responsive shutter system, a haecceity of an immersion (Figure 1.1).

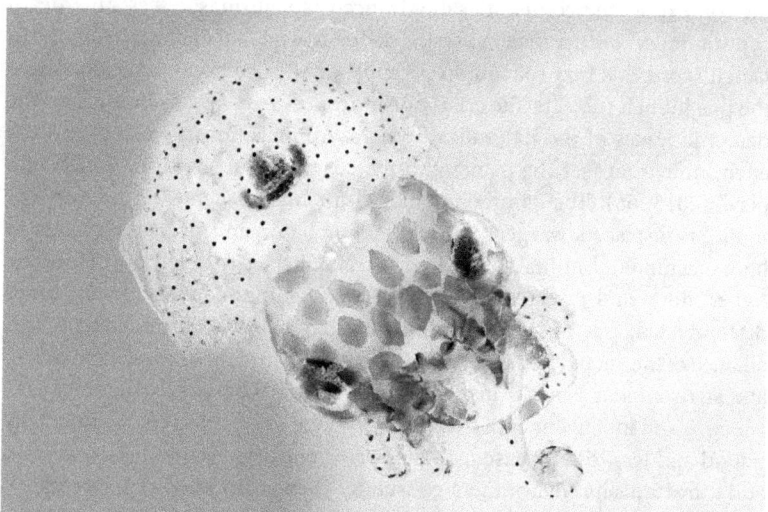

Figure 1.1 A macropod image of the Hawaiian bobtail squid and the glowing bacteria *V. fischeri* showing in its bi-lobed light organ and ink sac in the center of the squid's mantle cavity. Image credit: Mark Smith and Annette Evans. 2015. Macroscopic Solutions, LLC. www.macroscopicsolutions.com.

Immersion: Affective Contemplation

In humans, immersion comes or used to come in states of affective contemplation; a temporal phase of regression from the will to desire, which is not to be found in any other living entity as we know it. In such contemplative state (the veomatic state as I define it, later), we reconnect with the fabulative: the imaginary, our mythic selves. We become as Donna Haraway says in *The Companion Species Manifesto* "alert to the emergent historical hybridities actually populating the world at all its contingent scales" (2003: 11). As Byung-Chul Han notes in his book *Scent of Time* (2017), the post-anthropos-machine-animal lives in temporal crisis—with acceleration of sequences of life "intensified to the point of hysteria" not permitting "any contemplative lingering" (2017: 18) and therefore no immersion. Han stresses the importance of acceleration as constitutive term of modernity which in post/supermodernity (now) becomes a flickering of superfluous interchange of aesthesis (our gateway to life according to) to say that "the increasing plurality of temporal sequences irritates the individual human being and asks too much of it" (2017: 32). The mythical and the contemplative that possess narrative tensions are lost. We are losing what Anne Sauvagnargues calls Fernand Deligny's "dans l'écrit" in her book *Artmachines* (2016)—a transcript: "a bold contraction that turns the line into the participle of the gesture, the unfolding of an act—is derived from the network (réseau) eating into the trace (tracé) ... To "trace is to act" (2016: 162–3) to slow time toward a contemplative state and immerse "not in an inconsistent or continuous flux but rather a distinct process of operation: a [virtual] creating" (2006: 27) after Peter Hallward's reading of Gilles Deleuze and the philosophy of creation in the book *Out of this World*.

Anaesthesis: A Super-Modern Tedium

This inconsistent flux that hinders creating (and contemplative thought) is typical of our era, characterized by pathologies of the flesh that are immunological and neurological, and which have their roots in modernity and whatever followed, with today's experiences and life characterized by "poor transitions" (Han 2017: 37). This is not an issue of acceleration, the default characteristic assigned to modernity, says Han, but between the accelerated points that define life as sequence "necessarily yawns and emptiness, an empty interval in which no sensation takes place" (Han 2017: 17). From lingering (wandering) we ended up zapping (Han 2017: 41) and scrolling, living an affect-poor life. Our excitement and desire are trapped and our capacity to contemplate and become content is minimal.

Paul Beatrice Preciado in their novel-essay-diary *An Apartment on Uranus* assigns this to the problematics of contemporary subjectivity that is fractured and wounded by binary oppositions. "The entire universe is cut on half ... we are human or animal" (2019: 35). Just as our social and professional selves are found in a condition of immaterial affective labor (Hardt 1999).

Under currency and goods that are digitally mediated and deterritorialized, our gratification comes from a screen that has an orgasm and demands a strange type of discipline. We have come far from modernity to now, from acceleration to deferral. Preciado characteristically mentions for instance Candy Crash Saga as "an immaterial prison proposing a constant deferral of desire and action ... by making the screen into a surrogate masturbation surface" (2019: 62–3). The hand that once was used for self-gratification and labor, is now working immaterially to masturbate the screen of cognitive capitalism. This condition of passive affective surrogate anorgasmia I define as *anaesthesis*—a posthuman tedium. Anaesthesis is the incapacity of the super-modern subject to become immersed in contemplation and put their trust, will and desire over a cognition-rich event of relaxed concentration over the nowness. Its pedigree and genome lie primarily with modern boredom and aboulia.

Anson Rabinbach presents almost a clinical philosophy on aboulia in the chapter of *The Human Motor* called "Mental Fatigue, Neurasthenia and Civilisation" (1990: 146–78), identifying it as a malady of modernity linked to intellectually tasked individuals as "a diminution of the will" (1990: 159) and where "a desire to act exists but is impotent" (1990: 167). Where in zöe this becomes a principle of efficiency through the law of the least effort (1990: 172), in modern bios it overrules desire through impotence of will. This is however different to states of regressive experience that are affective (immersions). We are, as such, close to becoming animal[3] because we suffer a loss of attention that is contemplative and affective. Instead, we are, as Byung-Chul Han asserts this time in *The Burnout Society* "hypertension ... a rash change of focus between different tasks, sources of information, and processes" (2015: 13). It is very interesting to note the title of the chapter: "Profound Boredom."

After Svendsen who notes that boredom "is the 'privilege' of modern man" (2005: 21) Michael Gardiner[4] titles boredom "the default mood of our age" defining it as "as a state of emotional flatness and resigned indifference, something that grips us, more or less involuntarily, without necessarily having an identifiable cause, shape, or object" (2020: 57). In Heidegger's terms and the triad of boredoms[5] this definition is close to the third and most profound type where "one feels timeless, one feels removed from the flow of time" (1995: 141). Allan Kaprow in conversation in *DOMUS* (1980: 4–5)[6] makes a significant turn noting intellectual boredom as a state that does not afford "getting lost in the myriad of thoughts, desires, and judgements that continuously make claims upon awareness" comparing this to the Buddhist principle of Zen as "being in the present,"[7] which is surprisingly close to contemplative immersion (an aboulia of ecstasy). In absence of such, the modern super ego becomes super-modern ideal ego and the human subject (psycho-) becomes posthuman project (schizo-) that cannot distinguish between experience [Erfarhrung] and experiencing [Erlebnis].

Sensoma: The Affective Cyborg

To understand what (aesthetic) "experience" means we will have to re-examine our relationship to the cosmos. Antonio Damasio in his book *Descartes' Error* (1994) questions the famous quote by the thinker who shaped aesthetics—cogito ergo sum that is—prioritizing feeling: I feel therefore I live (as of experience life) therefore; I think. Stephen Shaviro on the other hand in his book *Discognition* (2016) explores unanswered questions of life: what is it like to be a dog, a robot, or a tree—or even a human being? ... What does it mean to be conscious, to think, to feel, or to know? Such questions he says seem to have obvious answers until we try to answer them. He tries in seven chapters named Thinking Like. Thinking Like: A Philosopher, a Computer, an Avatar, a Human Being, a Killer, an Alien, and Slime Mold. To approach how we experience we will turn to Chapter 1: Thinking Like a Philosopher and Mary's story; the most prominent physio-philosophical debate of all times: Mary, a neuroscientist that knows all about color has never empirically sensed any color specificity; she lives in a grey-scale condition. What happens when she steps out and experiences a red rose? This implies that the relation to surrounding matter and flesh is mediated and fluid. Soma and cosmos are resonating parts of a mutant twofold, a hybrid double (Psarologaki 2018: 65).

We need to understand the divergence implied from processes of conscious thought in favor of pre-perceptible processes that humans share with other living beings (as opposed to sapience). This is not a difference by kind but by degree (of), notes Shaviro. Affect becomes as such (if we agree that beings—living entities- do experience) the infrastructure for experience to be produced and is related to both life what we feel/sense. It is also no coincidence that affect is also related to the strongest of sensations: that of fear and suffering.[8] As Schopenhauer notes, "[t]he basis of all willing is need, lack, and thus pain, which is its primordial destiny by virtue of its essence. If, on the other hand, it lacks objects to will, its former objects having been quickly dispelled as too easily achieved, it is seized with a terrible emptiness and boredom: i.e., its essence and its being itself become an intolerable burden to it" (2010: 338). We can interpret this as a condition of temporal emptiness between bodily (enfleshed) entities and cosmic matter—one that is productive and affirms life, a tedium of intellectual potency. I call this an intensified sensoma: A body of flesh situated in the cosmos and hinged by its sensory capacities and imagination; able to linger, immerse, and contemplate ... again.

Veoma: The Lived Event

The post-human entity[9] is preoccupied more and more with what each experience accounts for and progressively less with what each experience *is,* and this becomes a constitutive term of contemporary (and future) bios. It is manifested in the tedium of the everyday and the mundane objecthoods that frame our aestheton and surrounding matter. Architect and philosopher Aristide Antonas in his essay-novela *The Pulp of Things* presents the modern handbag as the proof of human misery, our pathetic attachment to things. "Humanity and reality are the same malady" he says (2020: 55). Our crisis is not as much neurological and immunological per se. As neurasthenia, our malady (reality after Antonas) is symptomatically rooted in our capacity to be in a reciprocal relationship with the immediate world, which includes our sensorium (and therefore us, as enfleshed entities). We have become by lifestyle inherently short of things that can evoke contemplative immersions and sensoma-tic (and potently dynamic) tedium. We have become bloated by exaggerated meaning and this is perhaps the essence of our nausea of reality, but we are still short of grains of meaningful sensory matter, says Antonas (2020: 78–9), what Shaviro describes these grains as qualia (2016: 27).

These missing things go beyond the phenomenological account because they regard entities that are not simply embodied subjects but closest as ever to machine and animal. They are haecceities, "sensible encounter[s]" (Sauvagnargues 2016: 68), "the emergence of singularities on whatever scale: a human idea, a molecular encounter, a distinct atmosphere, five o'clock in the afternoon" (Sauvagnargues 2016: 65). I define these haecceities as *veomata.* They are lived, contemplative, and therefore memorable experiences, deterritorialized events, slices of history interrupted by granular nowness.[10] A veoma is a becoming in flesh of sensoria and worlds, an immersive event. It would be short-sighted to imply that veomata will become the panacea for the maladies we called reality and life as neurological and immunological suffering. They can be however possibilities[11] for regressive lingering, contemplation, creating of imaginative narratives, and slowing down from an accelerative sensory saturation that is not only superfluous but symptomatically meaningless and therefore adverse.

Immersive Reflections

Through repositioning life (zöe and bios) framing it with current biopolitical and ecosophic reference, we have been able to approach closely some key ideas. These relate to the posthuman capacity to sense, experience, and therefore consciously live through particular conditions as potentially emancipated and still enfleshed entity. Approaching the posthuman entity as cyborg, we have been able to focus on interactions of flesh that are much more gradient and less binary when compared to the compartmentalized manner of looking at the mind as what the brain does or the experience as a phenomenon of embodiment. Instead, the politics of the experience led us to a basis of a nascent lexicon that concisely picks up the ontology of our post-human experiences. It is characteristic of our times to (re)invent terms and linguistic expressions that manifest as abbreviations, xeno-infusions, and slang. It is however surprisingly uncommon to observe widely adopted neologisms that delve into meaning and successfully reposition our etymological comprehensions. In response, we introduced three key terms of philological science fiction: anaesthesia, sensoma, and veoma.

The conceptual definition of anaesthesia, sensoma, and veoma has allowed a reflection that is in itself contemplative. It leads moreover to a conceptual breakthrough. So far, the philosophical treatise of immersion defines the latter primarily as heightened sense of concentration and mental involvement. This definition has penetrated the etymological and encyclopedic dictionaries. Immersion—as we have negotiated—can be seen as a state of regression, a condition of contemplative reverie, a phased down ecstasy. As such, it can be perceived as symptomatically mimetic to aboulia. This brings forward a possibility of hope and through new terms, we can expect a future where our reflexive impotence (Fisher 2009: 21) can be addressed and overcome before we reach a threshold of sensory syncope.

Notes

1. I intentionally distinguish here between notion of embodiment as phenomenological entity and therefore use "flesh" as a post/meta-phenomenological term instead of "body." For more, read commentary on the late and unfinished work of Maurice Merleau-Ponty (which attempted to transcend it phenomenological starting point) by Diana Cole (2010). This remains debatable as still strongly based on notions of traditional (human) subjectivity and humanism.
2. This is a reference to Fernand Deligny's notion of "entour" and "entourage" as (lost) quality of surrounding network, which he identifies as mode of life more diverse than society because the network allows for multiplicity of species, in *The Arachnean and Other Texts*.
3. Byung-Chul Han mentions "… the animal is forced to divide its attention between various activities … incapable of contemplative immersion … The animal cannot immerse itself contemplatively in what it is facing [Gegenüber]" (2010: 12–13).
4. Gardiner also turns to Bifo and the architectonics of the soul noting that "Bifo means all the embodied, affective, and aesthetic capacities of the human being as these are manifested intersubjectively, and which have now become diffused throughout society as a whole" (2020: 70).
5. "becoming bored by something," "being bored with something," and "it is boring for one" (Heidegger 1995: 141). This is also tied to traditional subjectivity of an "I" and a world.
6. For a reflective analysis of the Kaprow interview and boredom, see Christian Parreno's "Boredom in Domus" (2021: 137–8).
7. This is interestingly associated with line of flight and artistic creating.
8. See also, Caballero's "Perfect Boredom: From Disillusion to Creativity" (2020: 238).
9. I refrain here from referring to this entity as subject, to diverge from traditional subjectivity and phenomenological embodiment.
10. See also Psarologaki, L. (2019), "Artistic spatiotemporal experiences after Gilles Deleuze, Alain Badiou, and Brian Massumi; a theory of becoming." https://doi.org/10.2307/j.ctvmd83nt
11. Virtualities, following from Massumi. See also, Psarologaki (2019).

Works Cited

Antonas, A. (2020), *Ο Πολτός των Πραγμάτων (The Pulp of Things)*, Athens: Antipodes.

Braidotti, R. (2013), *The Posthuman*, Cambridge: Polity.

Caballero, S. G. (2020), "Perfect Boredom: From Disillusion to Creativity," in J. R. Velasco (ed), *The Culture of Boredom*, Boston: BRILL, 236–56.

Coole, D. (2010), "The Inertia of Matter and the Generativity of Flesh," in D. Coole and S. Frost (eds), *New Materialisms: Ontology, Agency and Politics*, Durham and London: Duke University Press, 92–115.

Damasio, A. (1994), *Descartes' Error: Emotion, Reason and the Human Brain*. New York: Avon Books.

Deligny, F. (2015), *The Arachnean and Other Texts*, Minneapolis: Univocal Publishing.

DeSalle, R. (2018), *Our Senses: An Immersive Experience: Gateways to Consciousness*, New Haven and London: Yale University Press.

Fisher, M. (2009), *Capitalist Realism*, Aylesford: Zero Books, John Hunt Publishing.

Gardiner, M. (2020), "The Multitude Strikes Back? Boredom in an Age of Semiocapitalism," in J. R. Velasco (ed), *The Culture of Boredom*, Boston: BRILL, 55–75.

Hallward, P. (2006), *Out of This World: Deleuze and the Philosophy of Creation*, London: Verso.

Han, B. C. (2015), *The Burnout Society*, Stanford, CA: Stanford University Press.

Han, B. C. (2017), *Scent of Time: A Philosophical Essay on the Art of Lingering*, Cambridge: Polity.

Haraway, D. (2003), *The Companion Species Manifesto, Dogs, People and Significant Otherness*, Chicago, IL: Prickly Paradigm Press.

Hardt, M. (1999), "Affective Labour," *Boundary 2*, 26 (2): 89–100.

Heidegger, M. (1995), *The Fundamental Concepts of Metaphysics: World, Finitude, Solitude*, Bloomington: Indiana University Press.

Kaprow, A. (1980), "Forum: Interview with Allan Kaprow, on the Various Possibilities to Interpret and Utilize Boredom in Art and Life," *DOMUS*, 605: 4–5.

Parreno, C. (2021), *Boredom, Architecture, and Spatial Experience*, London and New York: Bloomsbury.

Preciado, P.B. (2019), *An Apartment on Uranus*, London: Fitzcarraldo Editions.

Psarologaki, L. (2019), "Artistic Spatiotemporal Experiences after Gilles Deleuze, Alain Badiou, and Brian Massumi; a theory of becoming," in Paulo de Assis and Paolo Giudici (eds), *Aberrant Nuptials: Deleuze and Artistic Research*, Orpheus Institute Series, Leuven: Leuven University Press, 317–24. https://doi.org/10.2307/j.ctvmd83nt

Psarologaki, L. (2018), "The Fourth Dog Perspective," in D. Damian-Martin (ed), *On Time: A SPILL Reader*, Ipswich: Pacitti Company, 64–75.

Rabinbach, A. (1990), *The Human Motor: Energy, Fatigue, and the Origins of Modernity*, Berkeley and Los Angeles: University of California Press.

Sauvagnargues, A. (2016), *Artmachines: Deleuze, Guattari, Simondon*, Edinburgh: Edinburgh University Press.

Schopenhauer, A. (2010), *The World as Will and Representation*, Vol. 1, Cambridge: Cambridge University Press.

Shaviro (2016), *Discognition*, London: Repeater.

Svendsen, L. (2005), *A Philosophy of Boredom*, London: Reaktion Books.

2

Antropofagia: Devouring Experimentations of a Manifesto Toward a Kinosophy to Come

(Origin Brazilian)

Sebastian Wiedemann

Perhaps one of the greatest teachings of the Anthropophagy proposed by the wild thought of the Brazilian poet, writer, and philosopher Oswald de Andrade in his 1928 *Manifesto Antropófago* (Cannibalist Manifesto), is to remind us that without body there is no thought. And as a filmmaker and philosopher who feels that his body occupies a singular point of view when entangled with equally singular means and practices, it is up to me to devour this proposition—without body there is no thought—experimenting that there is only thought as a gesture of making body with the world from cinematic means and practices. Means and practices as modes of experience that, far from being restricted to a single mode of expression, proliferate through the most diverse surfaces (of thought). That is, thinking is always thinking by other means. Thinking is always a media practice that from the point of view of an experimental filmmaker can only give rise to a Media philosophy that in the encounter with Guattari's (2012) concept of Ecosophy, I risk calling Kinosophy.

Kinosophy, as this adventure of constructing imminently cinematic problems from cosmopolitical concerns (Stengers 2005), as cinema in reverse, as metamorphic cinema that can certainly be independent of film or as it is happening right now, can become cinema by other means as can be writing and its practice of conceptualization. Kinosophy as a program in delirium, always open and unfinished, as a proposition in the act and in movement. Always toward …, experimenting how to pass …

In this sense and accepting Deleuze and Guattari's (1996) call to experiment rather than to interpret or explain, we do not aspire here to give an account of the concept of Anthropophagy, but rather to put it in motion and differentiation, to make it work in a devouring way by making an aberrant and kinosophical translation, that is, in a cinematic and delirious tone, of its own Cannibalist Manifesto. To make of Anthropophagy a practice that self-phagocytes in the act in the encounter with cinematic potencies of thought and therefore of a tropical and wild Media philosophy that in its unreason we could well call Kinosophical Anthropophagy. A thought in the act of voracious appetite, that tastes, chews, and swallows, that devours making translation a betrayal or even in the words of the Brazilian poet and translator Haroldo de Campos a transcreation (Campos 2019) (Tapia and Nobrega 2013).

A practice of rewriting (Ferraz 2008) (Wiedemann 2020), of (re)montage of a speculative found footage cinema in reverse, which transforms everything into ruin and remains as generative and composting material for new dispositions of thought that operate close to the logics proposed by the Armenian filmmaker Artavazd Peleshian in his theory of Montage-at-a-Distance (2015). A cinema by other means, an anthropophagic becoming of a writing cinematic thought that is also affected and infected by the transcreative force of delirium and appetite present in the manifestos of the Brazilian filmmaker Glauber Rocha, *Estética da fome* (An Aesthetics of Hunger) and *Estética do sonho* (An Aesthetics of Dreams) (Rocha 2018).

Our banquet is based on gestures such as those of the contemporary Brazilian indigenous artist Denilson Baniwa (2021) with his text and painting *ReAnthropophagy*.[1] In the same way, the main ingredient of the banquet that we will devour is Leslie Bary's translation of the *Manifesto Antropófago* (de Andrade 1991) and Beatriz Azevedo's critical study entitled *Antropofagia—Palimpsesto selvagem* (2018).

Seeking to be on the side of the emerging, of the new, and of what is in the process of being made, this travelogue to the inside folds of the concept of Anthropophagy proposed by Oswald de Andrade and devoured from a Deleuzian perspective,[2] as speculative rewriting and experimentation, ultimately transcreates an obliquitous in-between-space (Nodari 2019) of thought for a kinosophy to come, as a Media philosophy engaged with a permanent decolonization of thought (Viveiros de Castro 2017), which in the following lines aims to gain a certain degree of consistency, even if fragile and unstable.

*

Kino-Manifesto Antropófago (Cannibalist Kino-Manifesto)

Each aphorism transcreated is followed by its original pair in Leslie Bary's translation (de Andrade 1991).[3]

Antropofagia: *Devouring Experimentations*

1. Image alone unites us. It crosses us corporally. Spiritually. Existentially.
   (Cannibalism alone unites us. Socially. Economically. Philosophically.)

2. The world's single law. Kino-Affect, the moving not of an image of thought, but of the without-image that is undisguised expression of all worlds that do not surrender to being one.
   (The world's single law. Disguised expression of all individualism, of all collectivisms. Of all religions. Of all peace treaties.)

3. Kino, or not kino that is the question. That is our becoming.
   (Tupi or not tupi, that is the question.)

4. Down with every representation. And down with the mother of dogmatisms.
   (Down with every catechism. And down with the Gracchi's mother.)

5. I am only concerned with what is not mine. Law of becoming. Law of the image without image.
   (I am only concerned with what is not mine. Law of Man. Law of the cannibal.)

6. We're tired of all the Cinemas. Hollywood and Cannes put an end to the mystery and proliferation of cinematic modes of experience.
   (We're tired of all the suspicious Catholic husbands who've been given starring roles. Freud put an end to the mystery of Woman and to other horrors of printed psychology.)

7. What clashed with the truth of the relative was representation, the raincoat placed between the universe and the pluriverses. The reaction against the enclosure of sense. The performativity of experimental cinema will inform us.
   (What clashed with the truth was clothing, that raincoat placed between the inner and outer worlds. The reaction against the dressed man. American movies will inform us.)

8. Children of the shadows and silence, mother of the images that we are and become. Discovered and loved ferociously, with all the blindness of light, by the enlightened ones, the literates, and those who carry reason. In the land of the people of light and whispers, whose light cannot be seen, but can be heard.
   (Children of the sun, mother of the living. Discovered and loved ferociously with all the hypocrisy of "saudade," by the immigrants, by slaves and by the "touristes." In the land of the Great Snake.)

9. It was because we never had grammars, nor vision machines. And we never knew what genres, a priori forms, and Grand Narrative were. Lazy, glued to the experience and body of the world. A participatory consciousness, a rhythmics of minor existences.
   (It was because we never had grammars, nor collections of old plants. And we never knew what urban, suburban, frontier and continental were. Lazy in the mapamundi of Brazil. A participatory consciousness, a religious rhythmics.)

10. Down with all forms that want to fix the imagetic flows. The palpable existence of life. And the aberrant meaningless logic for television to study.
    (Down with all the importers of canned consciousness. The palpable existence of life. And the pre-logical mentality for Mr. Lévy-Bruhl to study.)

11. We want the Spectral Revolution. Greater than the French Revolution. The unification of all productive revolts toward the more than human. Without us, the visible wouldn't even have its poor museums. The Golden Age of the cathedrals. The Golden Age. And all the *xapiripë* spirits.
    (We want the Carib Revolution. Greater than the French Revolution. The unification of all productive revolts for the progress of humanity. Without us, Europe wouldn't even have its meager declaration of the rights of man. The Golden Age heralded by America. The Golden Age. And all the "girls.")

12. Heritage. Cinema before Cinema. Godard, Brakhage, Weerasethakul. From black cube to white cube. The Walpiri Dreamtime. Karrabing Film Collective. We push onward.
    (Heritage. Contact with the Carib side of Brazil. Où Villegaignon print terre. Montaigne. Natural man. Rousseau. From the French Revolution to Romanticism, to the Bolshevik Revolution, to the Surrealist Revolution and Keyserling's technicized barbarian. We push onward.)

13. We were never filmmakers. We live by and through somnambulistic cinematic modes of experience. We made the image without image to be born in the luminous darkness of the forest. Or in the abyssal bottom of the sea.
    (We were never catechized. We live by a somnambulistic law. We made Christ to be born in Bahia. Or in Belém do Pará.)

14. But we never permitted the birth of the hero's journey among us.
    (But we never permitted the birth of logic among us.)

15. Down with Griffith. Author of our first loan, to make a commission. Capital asking for hero and narration. A cinema-nation was born. Griffith, potency of creation. Forgetting almost everything, brought us montage.
    (*Down with Father Vieira. Author of our first loan, to make a commission. The illiterate king had told him: put that on paper, but without a lot of lip. The loan was made. Brazilian sugar was signed away. Vieira left the money in Portugal and brought us the lip.*)

16. The spirit refuses to conceive a spirit without the body. Cinema of the body. Experience of the world as cinema of the body. Kinosophical vaccine. To maintain our instability, against the clear iconicity of the image. And against inquisitions that don't want the image without image.
    (*The spirit refuses to conceive a spirit without a body. Anthropomorphism. Need for the cannibalistic vaccine. To maintain our equilibrium, against meridian religions. And against outside inquisitions.*)

17. We can attend only to the orecular world of the invisible images.
    (*We can attend only to the orecular world.*)

18. We already had the visible, the codification of the invisible. The audible, the codification of the inaudible. Kinosophy. The permanent transformation of the invisible and inaudible into movement of thought.
    (*We already had justice, the codification of vengeance. Science, the codification of Magic. Cannibalism. The permanent transformation of the Tabu into a totem.*)

19. Down with the reversible world, and against motionless movement of dichotomies. The stop of thought that is dynamic. The image as victim of measurement. Source of perceptive injustices. And the forgetting of the conquests of being because one is flight, one is clandestine and always to come.
    (*Down with the reversible world, and against objectified ideas. Cadaverized. The stop of thought that is dynamic. The individual as victim of the system. Source of classical injustices. Of romantic injustices. And the forgetting of inner conquests.*)

20. Flight. Flight. Flight. Flight. Flight. Flight. Flight.
    (*Routes. Routes. Routes. Routes. Routes. Routes. Routes.*)

21. The instinct of the people of light and whispers.
    (*The Carib instinct.*)

22. Death and life. Metamorphosis. Cosmomorphic and impersonal cinema. Existential practice. Kinosophy.
    (Death and life of all hypotheses. From the equation "Self, part of the Cosmos" to the axiom "Cosmos, part of the Self." Subsistence. Experience. Cannibalism.)

23. In communication with the generative matter of worlds.
    (Down with the vegetable elites. In communication with the soil.)

24. We were never filmmakers. Without essence the image crosses us. Cosmic inter-body that we carry and carries us.
    (We were never catechized. What we really made was Carnaval. The Indian dressed as senator of the Empire. Making believe he's Pitt. Or performing in Alencar's operas, full of worthy Portuguese sentiments.)

25. We already had the senses. We already had the look. The Golden Age. Sensation, pure affect. Blind, listening. Deaf, seeing. Existential tones. Minor tones.
    (We already had Communism. We already had Surrealist language. The Golden Age.)

26. Magic and life. The image had us. Multi-sensoriality without judgment. And we knew how to transpose mystery and death with the help of some cinematic modes of experience. Cinema before Cinema.
    (Magic and life. We had the description and allocation of tangible goods, moral goods, and royal goods. And we knew how to transpose mystery and death with the help of a few grammatical forms.)

27. I asked the people of light and whispers what Law was. They answered me that it was the possibility to exist. They ate me. There is only becoming, an always fugitive image. We, the image always to come.
    (I asked a man what the Law was. He answered that it was the guarantee of the exercise of possibility. That man was named Galli Mathias. I ate him.)

28. Down with the histories. Cinema already in the dream of the world. Stories without histories, of sensation, of body, without name. Kino-deformation. Without an author. Experiences alone.
    (Down with the histories of Man that begin at Cape Finisterre. The undated world. Unrubrified. Without Napoleon. Without Caesar.)

29. Without progress, cinema of involution. A world that is not fixed to the screen. World-screen in transmutation.
    (The determination of progress by catalogues and television sets. Only machinery. And blood transfusers.)

30. Down with the transcendences. Always creeping images. Imaginal fertilizer.
    (Down with the antagonistic sublimations. Brought here in caravels.)

31. Down with the dogmatic image, the sagacity of a kinosophy of drifting images.
    (Down with the truth of missionary peoples, defined by the sagacity of a cannibal, the Viscount of Cairu:—It's a lie told again and again.)

32. They were fugitives from the reason that fixes everything. We are eating, the images say. We in their stomachs.
    (But those who came here weren't crusaders. They were fugitives from a civilization we are eating, because we are strong and vindictive like the Jabuti.)

33. God, pure creativity, the Uncreated Image of all images without image.
    (If God is the consciousness of the Uncreated Universe, Guaraci is the mother of the living. Jaci is the mother of plants.)

34. We had divination. Orecular image, which is always oracular. We had Politics as perceptive distribution.
    (We never had speculation. But we had divination. We had Politics, which is the science of distribution. And a social system in harmony with the planet.)

35. The migrations. Always. Migrant images, wandering lives in between. No tedium, pure speculation.
    (The migrations. The flight from tedious states. Against urban scleroses. Against the Conservatories and speculative tedium.)

36. From William James and Deleuze. The transfiguration of the being of the image into imaginal becoming. Kinosophy.
    (From William James and Voronoff. The transfiguration of the Taboo into a totem. Cannibalism.)

37. Without a moral of the image: kino-madology + errant value theory of the intervals.
    (The paterfamilias and the creation of the Morality of the Stork: Real ignorance of things + lack of imagination + sense of authority in the face of curious offspring.)

38. To arrive at the idea of God, because the flight of the image is everywhere. One must depart from the non-image, but the people of the light and the whispers have the darkness and the silence.
    (One must depart from a profound atheism in order to arrive at the idea of God. But the Carib didn't need to. Because he had Guaraci.)

39. What do we have to do with that? With Cinema, nothing. With cinema before cinema; next, the cinematic modes of experience. The object.
    (The created object reacts like the Fallen Angels. Next, Moses day dreams. What do we have to do with that?)

40. Before Cinema was created, cinema was the surface of the whole world.
    (Before the Portuguese discovered Brazil, Brazil had discovered happiness.)

41. Down with the representation. The image as supplantation and falsification of itself.
    (Down with the torch-bearing Indian. The Indian son of Mary, the stepson of Catherine of Medici and the godson of Dom Antonio de Mariz.)

42. The breath of cinema is the imaginal surface of the world in motion.
    (Joy is the proof of nines.)

43. In the matriarchy the image is a celebrated flight.
    (In the matriarchy of Pindorama.)

44. Memory of no one and all worlds. The image as creative oblivion made cinematic mode of experience.
    (Down with Memory as a source of custom. The renewal of personal experience.)

45. We are concretists. Let's get rid of the immaterial excess of abstractions. The image, abstract materiality, and concreteness of the invisible and inaudible. Speculation that creates the sensible.
    (We are concretists. Ideas take charge, react, and burn people in public squares. Let's get rid of ideas and other paralyses. By means of routes. Believe in signs; believe in sextants and in stars.)

46. Exhausting the "down with," until affirming without having to perceive the affirmation that wants to legislate the inconstant soul of the image.
    (Down with Goethe, the Gracchi's mother, and the court of Dom João VI.)

47. The breath of cinema is the imaginal surface of the world in motion.
    (Joy is the proof of nines.)

48. The Uncreated Image of all images without image. Absorption of the sacred enemy. Devoration of God. Creative immanence. Kinosophy. Image. Affect. Spinoza. No contradiction, pure composition.
    (The struggle between what we might call the Uncreated and the Creation—illustrated by the permanent contradiction between Man and

his Taboo. Everyday love and the capitalist way of life. Cannibalism. Absorption of the sacred enemy. To transform him into a totem. The human adventure. The earthly goal. Even so, only the pure elites managed to realize carnal cannibalism, which carries within itself the highest meaning of life and avoids all the ills identified by Freud—catechist ills. What result is not a sublimation of the sexual instinct. It is the thermometrical scale of the cannibal instinct. Carnal at first, this instinct becomes elective, and creates friendship. When it is affective, it creates love. When it is speculative, it creates science. It takes detours and moves around. At times it is degraded. Low cannibalism, agglomerated with the sins of catechism—envy, usury, calumny, murder. We are acting against this plague of a supposedly cultured and Christianized peoples. Cannibals.)

49. Exhausting the "down with," until affirming without having to perceive the affirmation that wants to legislate the inconstant soul of the image. *(Down with Anchieta singing of the eleven thousand virgins of Heaven, in the land of Iracema—the patriarch João Ramalho, founder of São Paulo.)*

50. Our co-dependence, always proclaimed. We are images between images. We must expel at the will of clarity. We are fog. It eats us, swallows us.
(Our independence has not yet been proclaimed. An expression typical of Dom João VI: "My son, put this crown on your head, before some adventurer puts it on his!" We expelled the dynasty. We must still expel the Bragantine spirit, the decrees and the snuff-box of Maria da Fonte.)

51. Down with the given reality,—the unrealized and hungry reality of images. Kinosophy, interval, flight of thought as image without image. *(Down with the dressed and oppressive social reality registered by Freud—reality without complexes, without madness, without prostitutes and without penitentiaries, in the matriarchy of Pindorama.)*

Notes

1 See and read here: <https://brooklynrail.org/2021/02/criticspage/ReAnthropophagy>
2 As Orson Welles and Deleuze remind us, by faking there are opened new dimensions of thought through the power of fabulation. (Deleuze 1986).
3 For a deep understanding of the context and references made by Oswald de Andrade in the manifesto, see the generous notes that follow the translation of Leslie Bary (Cf. de Andrade 1991).

Works Cited

Azevedo, B. (2018), *Antropofagia—Palimpsesto selvagem*, São Paulo: SESI-SP Editora.

Baniwa, D. (2021, February 2), "ReAnthropophagy," *The Brooklyn Rail*. https://brooklynrail.org/2021/02/criticspage/ReAnthropophagy.

Campos, H. de. (2019), *Metalinguagem e outras metas* (4ª edição). São Paulo: Perspectiva.

de Andrade, O. (1991), "Cannibalist Manifesto," trans. L. Bary, *Latin American Literary Review*, 19 (38): 38–47.

Deleuze, G., and Guattari, F. (1996), *What Is Philosophy?*, New York: Columbia University Press.

Ferraz, S. (2008), "A fórmula da reescritura," *Seminário Música Ciência e Tecnologia*, 1: 41–52.

Guattari, F. (2012), *Chaosmosis: An Ethico-Aesthetic Paradigm*, trans. P. Bains and J. Pefanis, Sydney: Power Publications.

Nodari, A. (2019), "Alterocupar-se: Obliquação e transicionalidade na experiência literária," *Estudos de Literatura Brasileira Contemporânea*, 57: 1–17. https://doi.org/10.1590/2316-4018573

Pelechian, A. (2015, December), "Montage-at-a-Distance, or: A Theory of Distance," trans. J. Vassilieva, in *LOLA*. http://www.lolajournal.com/6/distance.html.

Rocha, G. (2018), *On Cinema*, ed. I. Xavier, trans. S. Dennison and C. Smith, 1st edition, New York: I.B. Tauris.

Stengers, I. (2005), "The Cosmopolitical Proposal," in B. Latour and P. Weibel (eds), *Making Things Public*, Cambridge: MIT Press, 994–1003.

Tapia, M. and Nobrega, T. M. (2013), *Haroldo de campos—Transcriação* (1ª edição). São Paulo: Perspectiva.

Viveiros de Castro, E. (2017), *Cannibal Metaphysics*, trans. P. Skafish, 1st edition, Minneapolis: University of Minnesota Press.

Wiedemann, S. (2020), "Azul profundo como escritura y re-escritura metamórfica de politritmicidades: Una performance filosófica como contrapedagogía radical ante la forma-academia," *Saberes y prácticas. Revista de Filosofía y Educación*, 5 (1): 1–11.

3

Autofotografija, Or; A Nonhuman Selfie

(Origin Croatian)

Ana Peraica

At the time a seminal book on self-portraiture in the arts, Gen Doy's *Picturing Self* (2004), was published—we did not have a distinctive term for selfies. Nonetheless, by 2013, Oxford Dictionary had dubbed the word *selfie* the world's word of the year. Since then, the concept of the selfie has been adopted by a plethora of other languages. However, in countries where language is actively engineered, where new words are created not only to satisfy translation requirements, but also to distinguish the language from other, similar languages, the situation is quite different.[1] In many cases these new, artificially engineered words are ridiculous. Yet, as this chapter will demonstrate, some of the proposed neologisms can be quite useful in defining various (sub)types of selfies.

Selfies are a type of photographic self-portrait, and as such, they appeal to our intrinsic motivations for self-appreciation. In contrast to conventional photographic self-portraits, they are taken with the frontal or rear camera of a mobile phone and are thus either within the reach of an extended arm or as a mirrored reflection. They are carefully chosen, refurbished, and reworked network images, typically from a larger set of recorded images. Today, in 2021, numerous terms have been coined to differentiate between different types of selfies, with helfie, belfie, and drelfie being the most popular pictures of self-representation of one's hair, buttocks, and workout. Nonetheless, in this chapter, I'd like to discuss a type of selfie that goes unnoticed—the failed or unsuccessful selfie.

As already mentioned in definition of the genre, for every successful selfie, there are numerous failed ones that do not meet the definition of a selfie as a networked image. This chapter will attempt to distinguish between these, successful and unsuccessful selfies. To delve deeper into the concept of failure, it will also consider mobile photographic self-portraits that are not the result of Narcissism, such as those created by machines. Thus, it would deal with two types of automatic images: those created in a serial of images from which to choose the successful selfie and those created specifically for the purpose of machine operation. To address these distinctions, I will borrow two of the numerous concepts proposed by the Croatian Institute for Language as a translation of selfie.

Among other solutions, for the translation of the concept of selfie, the Croatian Institute for Language proposed two intriguing concepts: *samoslika* (self-picture) and *autofotografija* (self-photography). Both *self-picture* and *autofotografija* are tautological terms that refer to a visual form of self-reference Luhmann named the one of autopoiesis in the cultural domain (Luhmann 1990). Although both definitions refer to the act of photographing oneself, there are numerous distinctions between them. The first one, self-picture, refers to selfie through general field of visuality, while the second, of *autofotografija*, by specifying its technology, the medium of photography.

The first concept, of self-picture, is present in the idea of picturing self and as such does exist in English language. Interestingly, the neologism self-picturing, as used in English and for example appearing in the subtitle of Doy's book, is not a noun but a verb, referring directly to the act of picture taking, or photographing, which fits the process of yearning for the best self-image. Another term, auto-fotografija, conjures up images of an automated, mechanical process. Whereas a selfie is a recording of oneself as a human being, autofotografija echoes the automatism of photography recording itself, or at the very least a machine recording itself.

Contextualizing the scope of two distinct concepts, the first definition is derived from visual studies and image theory (in the self-picture that results from the self-depiction process), while the second definition is derived from media theory (in the self-reference made by the medium itself). To be more precise, the first concept, pointing to self-reference in pictures, has by now been discussed in some detail in self-portraiture theory, including very frequent psychoanalytical interpretation of a genre, while the second, which would define the logic of the medium's processualism, has not been discussed yet.

For that reason, in this chapter, I intend to focus on the second. My intention is, yet, to use both concepts to clarify the process of self-referential image making in cases where the image is not a satisfactory self-image or is made without any self-image present. Thus in definition and distinction between two definitions, this chapter will propose the use of the term self-picture to refer to images created in order to match one's self-image through the creation of an unsatisfactory picture (or self-picture), and autofotografija to refer to images created automatically, and without pre-existing self-image.

Failed Selfies

Photographs have become pervasive. Unlike in the days of glass plate negatives or twelve-shot negative film shot or developed by professionals, photographic cameras are now integrated into a variety of other pieces of equipment, ranging from mobile phones to monitoring devices. As photography becomes a more integral part of various technologies, the number of photographic images continues to grow at an uncontrollable rate. However, not all of these captured images would fulfill the original purpose of photography—to preserve the moment for future viewers. Some of them will never be seen.

A common example of a human-created image that is not retained is an unsuccessful image. Given that the majority of today's mobile phone users are neither skilled nor educated photographers, the new method of recording is an attempt-mistake one rather than one based on parameter selection (based on their combinatorics of angle, recourse, framing, exposure, shutter speed). Yet, not only as a result of numerous technically failed images, the number of unsuccessful images continues to grow. Certain images, such as selfies, are the result of more profound and complex dissatisfactions.

Selfies are a delicate form of photography. They are primarily self-portraits captured with a mobile front camera or a back camera equipped with a mirror. Apart from being photographed by mobile phones, a selfie is also a network image or one that is uploaded to platforms, where it is combined with various types of text, such as geolocations, tags, or a simple type of message. What is not apparent in these networked images is how frequently they are reworked, retouched, and filtered. Different poses, angles, and frames are practiced with slight variations in order to select the perfect image. Additionally, various expressions are practiced. Thus, the selfie, which can be considered the genre's fourth characteristic, is a satisfactory self-portrait chosen from a large series of images. This is the image we chose from the plethora of other images captured.

The majority of these images that are not chosen to be uploaded to the web are immediately deleted. Nonetheless, some remain unnoticed on the mobile device and are stored alongside successful ones on external hard drives or in the cloud. Whether sad or beautiful, scared or insane, even failed images have an effect on reality, as selfie is a delicate self-approaching form. Each time we record ourselves, we gain access to and interact with our self-image, healing, nurturing, and destroying it. The consequences of these processes are not trivial.

Numerous attempts to create the perfect selfie may result in an obsession with selfies, dubbed *selfitis*, which has already become a meme. Jessica

Helfand reported in her book *Face: A Visual Odyssey* (Helfand 2019) that a British teenager took approximately 200 selfies per day in 2014, spending, in his own words, ten hours per day attempting to create the perfect selfie.[2] He even attempted suicide by overdosing on drugs after failing in his endeavors. Apart from this sad story, we rarely learn about the number of failed selfies, despite the fact that the majority of us choose selfies from a long list of failed attempts.

However, unsuccessful selfies (and unsuccessful photographs in general) are not the only ones that go unnoticed. We know from postphotographic theory that some images captured by machines also exist outside the visible range, although they are not useless, in contrast to failed images. This category of images captured for no reason is those that will never be seen, as they are created "by machines for other machines" (Paglen 2010: 6, 5–13). Their sole purpose is to operate machines. Among these machine-made images, there are some that are defined as a device's self-portrait as well. So, it might be useful to analyze differences between hidden and often destroyed (self) images created by humans and those invisible ones created by machines.

Machines Self-Recording

When Lisa Gotto published "Strike a Pose: Robot Selfies" in 2018, there were only a few images in which machines, primarily robots, took what we name selfies, albeit inadvertently (Gotto 2018). Among these early pictures machines made of themselves, the most well-known examples are Google's Gigapan and NASA's Curiosity Mars rover's self-image (Jean Luc Nancy also writes in his *Portrait*).[3] Soon after these, already by 2019, scientists from Columbia University had installed a camera in a robot to help it visualize itself and consequentially develop something that might be defined as self-awareness. It was assumed that seeing oneself would aid the machine in being more accurate and efficient, particularly in spatial coordination. "We conjecture that this separation of self and task may have also been the evolutionary origin of self-awareness in humans" the project's authors noted (Kwiatkowski and Lipson 2019). Self-picturing has made significant advancements in the spatial coordination of robots and has become a popular method of programming in the modern era. Cameras in robots are expected to become more prevalent in the future, to the point where machines will exhibit something resembling true self-awareness; at least, that is what some renowned technology institutes predict.[4] Self-consciousness is a natural progression in the development of artificial intelligence, which is already capable of self-development and learning, as well as concluding autonomously and without human guidance. But does machine, if having a picture of self, necessarily have a self-image, that would be the first line defining selfie as self-portrait?

Self-Image

In psychology, the term "self-image" refers to one's perception of oneself and, while it does include the concept of an image, it has little to do with visuality. Rather, it refers to the conscious awareness of one's own inner psychological state, defining a certain look toward the inside. This view is all but simple. Although self-image is formed primarily by the way we see ourselves, it is also conditioned by the way society sees us, the way we see our community seeing us, and the way we see ourselves seeing ourselves. Thus, as a synthesis of multiple agents' perspectives, this image, an amalgam of hopes, projections, interpretations, and various insight attempts, bears little resemblance to self-knowledge. Moreover, as a complex web of circumstances, self-image is hardly fixed and objective. Thus, rather than being defined by a single, fixed image, self-image may be defined by the large number of photographs taken, those with which we are or are not satisfied. To further elucidate these distinctions, it may be necessary to revise the fundamental distinction in visual studies between images and pictures.

Image vs. Picture

WJT Mitchell's distinction between image and picture was one of the most profound in visual studies, defining the field and allowing for substantial differentiations between visual imagination and concrete artifacts. In the introductory pages to his book *What do Pictures Want?* Mitchell distinguishes between images and pictures by the presence of the medium; "By 'image', I mean any likeness, figure, motif, or form that appears in some medium or other. [...] By 'medium', I mean the set of material practices that brings an image together with an object to produce a picture" (Mitchell 2012: XIII). According to Mitchell, the image represents an abstract concept, a preconception, whereas the picture represents a tangible material object. To put it simply, an image is an idea, a prejudice, whereas a picture is something that can be hung on the wall. While the image is ideal, a picture is a material, making it transient and biodegradable. There can be numerous pictures; only a few can be related to ideal images, while others appear to be unable to.

Even in photography there are images, on the level of preconception. Incorrectly exposed photographs, strange shots, defocused and decentered photographs are all examples of failure of picture to meet the image, what someone imagined and what it turned out to be. Thus, clearly, there is a difference between self-image and self-picture. The picture would be an objectified version of our self-image or interpretation of self.

However, images captured by machines cannot be said to have a self-image or a preconception of self. These images are just operative, and we need another concept to capture these types of selfies. Thus, I would propose to use the term *autofotografija* to refer to locations where the self-image is captured but there is no reference to the self-image. Machines record mechanically and, while they do gain self-knowledge, they rarely experience the self-image problems associated with projections. They are unconcerned with what society thinks of them and make no attempt to understand how they see themselves.

Conclusion

Our self-images are formed by our self-conceptions, the perceptions others have of us, the perceptions we have of the perceptions others have of us, and the perceptions we have of the perceptions others have of us. Thus, self-picture does refer to self-image, but with varying degrees of success. This instability and insecurity result in a number of self-portraiture failures.

Whether destroyed or not, even failed images contribute to our sense of self-worth. Or, the relationship between self-picture and self-image is not purely passive; self-image also changes with each attempt at recording it. Specifically, more failures will have a detrimental effect on our self-image, resulting in an insecure version of ourselves. Every attempt to make a self-picture out of own self-image changes it.

Machines also can generate a large number of self-portraits that are invisible to humans. Despite this, the quality of these images is completely different. Unlike humans, machines are unaffected by hormones, emotions, changing physical conditions, or subconsciousness. And this is where the vast number of pictures recorded by humans and those recorded by machines, even when they are made for its operation, are profoundly different.

In contrast to machines, which have a controlled relationship with their image, our relationship with our own face is also uncontrolled and unconscious. Whereas humans can despise their faces, engines cannot be dissatisfied with their appearances, or perform to improve their self-image. Thus, it would be beneficial to distinguish between self-portraiture as a selfie and mechanical autographic portraiture, between tense and dynamic relationship among self-image and self-picture, contrary to formal one of *autofotografija*.

Notes

1 The Croatian Institute of Language compiles newly formed but also coins some new words, often making them on the base of the language politics of Independent State of Croatia (1941–5), a collaborationist creation during the Second World War which issued The Law on Human Language, its Purity and Grammar, and founded the state office for language. The politics of this office was often seen as very aggressive in eliminating Serbian and other imported words from the "clean" Croatian language. One of the words invented in this period was svjetlopis (Croatian, lightwriting, or photography), rarely used. The institute was created with a regained independency of Croatia in 1991. Language engineering during that time was also influenced by strong will to introduce from Croatian to other languages that are grammatically and vocabulary similar, if not even being the same, such as Serbian language. Contemporary post-war Croatian language context also reverberates the linguistic separation between countries once sharing the country of Yugoslavia, but also a great deal of language similarities.
2 Aldridge, Gemma, and Kerry Harden: Selfie addict took two hundred a day—and tried to kill himself when he couldn't take the perfect photo. *Mirror*. Mar. 23, 2014. https://www.mirror.co.uk/news/real-life-stories/selfie-addict-took-two-hundred-3273819.
3 Nancy's reference is brief, he notes that existence represents or imitates nothing (Nancy 2018: 100).
4 See for example: Karlsruhe Institute of Technology Press Release 046/2019. On the Way towards Self-aware AI? New Technology Foresight Project Addresses the Vision of "Conscious" Machines. https://www.kit.edu/kit/english/pi_2019_046_on-the-way-towards-self-aware-ai.php informs on the project "Clarification of Suspicion of Consciousness in Artificial Intelligence (AI Consciousness)" lead by Prof. Karsten Wendland.

Works Cited

Andrews, B. (2019), "Scientists Gave This Robot Arm a 'Self Image' and Watched It Learn," *Discover*, Jan. 30, 2019. doi: 10.1126/scirobotics.aau9354.

Doy, G. (2004), *Picturing the Self: Changing Views of the Subject in Visual Culture*, London: I.B. Tauris.

Gotto, L. (2018), "Strike a Pose: Robot Selfies," in Julia Eckel, Jens Ruchatz and Sabine Wirth (eds), *Exploring the Selfie*, New York: Springer, 285–301.

Helfand, J. (2019), *Face: A Visual Odyssey*, Cambridge: MIT Press.

Jones, A. (2006), *Self/Image: Technology, Representation and the Contemporary Subject*, London: Routledge.

Kennedy, A. (2019), *From Self to Selfie: A Critique of Contemporary Forms of Alienation*, London: Palgrave Macmillan.

Kwiatkowski, R. and Lipson, H. (2019), "Task-agnostic Self-modeling Machines," *Science Robotics*, 4 (26): Jan. 30, 2019.

Luhmann, N. (1990), *Essays on Self-Reference*, New York: Columbia University Press.

Mitchell, W. J. T. (2012), *What Do Pictures Want? The Lives & Loves of Images*, Chicago: Chicago University Press.

Nancy, J. L. (2018), *Portrait*, New York: Fordham University Press.

Paglen, T. (2010), "Invisible Images: Your Pictures Are Looking at You," *Architectural Design*, 89 (0): 22–7.

Peraica, A. (2017), *Culture of the Selfie*, Amsterdam: Institute of Networked Cultures.

4

Bazaar: The Persistence of the Informal

(Origin Persian)

Bhaskar Sarkar

The Bazaar as Exotica

In a celebrated scene from *Monty Python's Life of Brian* (Terry Jones 1979), the film's eponymous hero finds himself in a crowded market square full of petty peddlers, customers, and curious onlookers, and a bunch of would-be prophets seeking their publics. A fugitive closely pursued by Pontius Pilate's legionaries; Brian comes upon a stall selling fake beards. Elated at this prospect of a quick and easy disguise, he is ready to pay up the twenty shekels that the merchant asks for. Aghast at his customer's hurried compliance, the merchant insists that Brian will not get the beard unless he bargains to bring the price down. During the exchange that follows, alternating in tone between banter, complaint, and imploration, Brian gets a crash course in the time-honored art of haggling—an informal, intense, and often hyperbolic form of bargaining over price-quantity combinations. But the shopkeeper's concern about Brian's naivete, his offhand willingness to give his unfamiliar customer a crash course in shopping etiquette, indexes a social field where the buyer-seller relationship involves a bit more than just economic transaction. As conjured in this British comedy hovering between satire and farce, the custom of haggling is an essential aspect of all marketplace transactions, whether in Roman-occupied Judea or, by implication, in the seventies' Middle-East. The film puts its hapless hero, and along with him its audiences, squarely in the realm of the *bazaar* or the "Oriental" market, imagined as a transhistorical public space of bizarre encounters, exotic commodities, and mystifying protocols.

The *Oxford English Dictionary* traces the word *bazaar* back to the Persian *bāzār*, market, adopted into Hindustani and Turkish, the word comes to English via Italian *bazarra* (Genoese for market-place, c1340). The OED goes onto furnish three main definitions of the bazaar, all specifying the geographic and/or fanciful association of this market-concept: 1a) "a Middle Eastern marketplace or permanent market"; 1b) "a market in a [colonial] Middle Eastern camp"; and 2) a "fancy fair in imitation of a Middle Eastern bazaar", often in support of a charity or a religious group, or "a shop, or arcade of shops, displaying an assortment of fancy goods." The *Hobson-Jobson Glossary of Anglo-Indian Terms* also points to the Malay adoption of the term as *pāsār*, which then comes back to parts of India as a term denoting merchandise. The word's sphere of circulation, from North Africa and Turkey to Southeast Asia, roughly corresponds to colonial notions of "the Orient."

As invoked in English and other European languages, the term *bazaar* is never simply the *market*. Folded into layers of Orientalist fantasies, the term, like the Arabic souq or souk, widely conjures a public gathering of merchants and buyers, touts and brokers, even healers and tricksters. Embedded in kinship and clientelist networks, affective structures of trust and reputation, religious observations and seasonal variations, as well as archaic customs like haggling, economic transactions in the bazaar seem to be so much more—and, by the same token, so much less—than what they are in modern markets. Informality and chaos, uncertainty and speculation, enchantment and excess appear to be quintessential aspects of the bazaar. To reiterate the organizing logic of this volume: something in the bazaar does not quite translate into the modern idea of the market.

When people in Asia, Africa, and Latin America speak of the bazaar, souk, and mercato, the referent is either the bustling urban markets that have a permanent location and are open most days of the week, or the temporary farmer-artisan markets that meet once or twice a week. Writing about Bengal at the cusp of the medieval and the modern, historian Sudipta Sen records the "various *kinds* of markets, permanent and temporary: markets specific to products, markets of rice, markets of vegetables, temporary markets afloat on boats on the rivers of eastern Bengal during the height of the monsoon, markets secured to temples, mosques, and hospices" (Sen 1998: 5). Sen also points to the marketplaces that came up alongside seasonal *mela*s or fairs, the convergence points of "resident and itinerant communities" (5). Sen's larger point is that "medieval Indian society" had a much more capacious sense of "wealth and power" that it "shared with other parts of the pre-modern world: rights, family honor, possession, ritual well-being, and the power to withdraw and redistribute objects of value" (4). Many of these considerations and forms continued into "the age of British expansion into India," complicating the "social life as well as the moral economy of the market" (4). Collapsing these ambiguities into a stereotype, invocations of the bazaar in the transnational Anglophone sphere invariably summon a heterotopia, a site of raucous and frenetic transactions exuding allure as well as risk.

Moreover, in the global-popular imagination, the bazaar as conceptual space frequently gets conflated with legendary marketplaces and built structures—the magnificent gateways and labyrinths of the Khan el-Khalili in Cairo, the Grand Bazaar of Isfahan, and the Al-Hamidiyah Souq in Damascus, or even Bombay's colonial Crawford Market dating back to the 1870s, with its fabulous clocktower and frieze. This perfunctory association, which grounds the romance of the bazaar in materiality sedimented over time, points to the category's liminal status.

The bazaar *is*, in fact, a heterotopic space in a more profound sense. As scholars of South Asian commerce and industry have noted, in accommodating a vast range of aspirations, energies, and activities, the bazaar brings together capital and community, business and charity, the sacred and the profane (Ray 1995; Birla 2009; Jain 2012). In its extensive material-symbolic mediations between modernity's polarized realms (public/private, rational/superstitious, economic/social, etc.), the modern-day bazaar presents an actually existing, operative structure for economic exchange, without having to either dissociate the economic from the rest of the social or to institute exchange value as the primary measure of everything. In fact, the bazaar would seem far more feasible than the abstract, idealized "market" of (neo)classical economic theory. More feasible, as well as more habitable; for the market, in pursuing efficiency narrowly construed in terms of *optimal* outcomes, and in seeking the fungibility of all things, actively works to eliminate various non- and extra-economic factors as distortion, corruption, or noise, even when such factors are crucial to the relations comprising human lifeworlds.

The Bazaar in Modernity

Because of the historical primacy of Western modernity and its attendant social forms—key among which are the sovereign people, the public sphere and, most pertinent to the focus of this chapter, the market economy—any perspective willing to accept the bazaar as a modern, viable space for economic transactions remains occluded. Charles Taylor has pointed out that the advent of these new forms, which were constitutive of a modern social imaginary, announced "a new conception of the moral order of society" around the figure of the individual (Taylor 2004: 2). In the increasingly disenchanted Europe of the eighteenth century, with both religious and martial values on the wane, social order needed a fresh domain, and a fulcrum around which it could reassemble itself. Already the Treaty of Westphalia (1648), which privileged mercantile interests over military ones, had recognized commerce as that domain. In posing the whole question of rationality in terms of self-interested agents, this new compact also heralded the emergence of the individual subject as the bulwark of modern social orders.[1] The rational individual had the right to be ambitious and industrious, as well as a sense of obligation toward the collective; they entered a contract in which civility, not force, was to be the primary enforcer of order. Even with the sense of community denuded by market imperatives, a contractual civility was expected to temper unbridled self-interest, keeping aggression and duplicity in check.

It is via such disaggregations as well as enfoldings that the market, a thoroughly self-interested, competitive domain, came to be invested with new kinds of moral authority. The assumption that the more abstract the economic contracts, and the more effective their stipulations in nullifying sociocultural opacities (social hierarchies, habits and customs, gaps in information, personal histories, etc.), the smoother the functioning of the market, became a governing principle. Emerging technologies, institutions, and instruments (statistics and projection models, laws and insurance companies, options and shares) abetted and accelerated the processes of disembedding and abstraction, grounding the market's moral authority in disinterested technicity. Adam Smith's "invisible hand" is, perhaps, best understood as a figure for this technicity.

In short, the ascendancy of the modern market required a set of conceptual and institutional shifts, and the repression of anterior domains of economic transaction whose modes now stood devalued as antiquated, informal, and risky. By the time industrial capitalism came around, the European colonization of the Americas and Asia was in full swing: the "Oriental" bazaar proved to be an expedient category to encapsulate the modalities that slowed down the wondrous becoming of the modern homo economicus. What was striking was the extent to which this narrative of historical change was turned into a morality tale, with two models of the space of exchange recast in (misrecognized) civilizational terms. As Rajat Ray observes, the market/bazaar dichotomy became a key element of the colonial enterprise: "the economic confrontation between East and West was perceived as a confrontation between Gemeinschaft and Gesellschaft" (Ray 1995: 449).

Translated into English as "community" and "society" respectively, *Gemeinschaft* refers to social bonds, values, and behavioral patterns that congeal out of informal, personal, and proximate exchanges, while *Gesellschaft* has to do with supposedly more evolved social relations, orientations, and actions that are based on formalized, impersonal, often remote interactions. Socialites associated with Gemeinschaft have been characterized as traditional and custom-bound, affectual, and capricious; the rules of association are usually tacit, ad hoc, and not uniformly enforceable; individual sovereignty is often compromised by strong and extended kinship structures and groupthink. Gesellschaft, on the other hand, is understood to consist of more sophisticated social relations sanctioned by the Law, designed to eliminate the tyranny of customs and habits, and oriented toward the promotion of rational choice in all spheres of life; interactions are categorical, governed by formalized protocols, and geared toward promoting information flow; and at least in principle, individual sovereignty is upheld as inviolable. The dichotomy sets up an explicit teleology: the gradual overcoming of Gemeinschaft, an antecedent and circumscribed community form, to establish Gesellschaft, a modern and dynamic society.

In the colonial imagination, the market was a singular expression of Gesellschaft, while the bazaar was aligned with Gemeinschaft. That the dual categories of social organization were introduced by sociologist Ferdinand Tönnies in the late 1880s, soon after the Berlin conference known as the "Scramble for Africa," is not just a matter of coincidence. The dichotomy between the idealized market and the vestigial bazaar was elaborated and played out in a series of binary oppositions—formal/informal, organized/chaotic, networked/isolated, dynamic/traditional, industrial/artisanal, standardized/ragtag, sophisticated/basic, professional/dilettante, objective/emotional, consistent/erratic, scientific/speculative, and on and on. The gathering resonance across these reiterations of affirmation/negation produced a sense of compulsion: since the realm of the economic had eclipsed all other sectors as the epicenter of (capitalist) modernization, vastly augmenting volumes and complexities of commercial transactions, the bedlam of the antiquated bazar had to give way to the systemic coherence, organization, and efficiency of the modern market.

While admittedly the Monty Python oeuvre lampoons everything under the sun, the film's zany depiction of the middle-eastern bazaar points to the continuing purchase of such colonial perceptions. From "universal" modernist perspectives, the bazaar ought to wither away, or gradually transform into the market; when it persists in some regions as the preeminent space of exchange, this is attributed to the unfinished modernization of those societies and the limited nature of their market institutions. In short, the bazaar is always discounted as an antecedent, partial, failed, incomplete version of the market; it is simultaneously the market's malapropism, and its eternal *not yet*.

Rationalizing the Bazaar

Until the mid-twentieth century, academic contributions from western historians and anthropologists mostly characterized the "bazaar economy" as a system of the East, a fragmented and degraded space that has been absorbed within, and relegated to the fringes of, the capitalized world economy centered in the West. Starting in the 1960s, anthropologist Clifford Geertz began to study seriously "the bazaar economies," first in Indonesia and then in Morocco. In his understanding, bazaar economies were characterized by a very large number of small peddlers, lack of coordination and networking, inconsistent pricing, patchy accounting, and a failure to exploit untapped marketing possibilities. While proceeding from this common understanding, Geertz challenged attendant perceptions of chaos and illogic, looking instead for the singular forms of rationality that organized bazaar operations.

Drawing on ethnography conducted in Sefrou, a Moroccan town, Geertz zeroes in on information flows as a significant determinant of bazaar modalities. He argues that "in the bazaar information is poor, scarce, maldistributed, inefficiently communicated, and intensely valued"; and that most bazaar practices seek to overcome the lack of reliable information about "market possibilities," "product quality and going prices," as well as to exploit others' ignorance opportunistically (Geertz 1978: 29). Geertz isolates two "procedures" of "information search," *clientelization* and *bargaining*. The first involves the establishment of continuing relationships between buyers and sellers through repeated transactions, allowing agents to narrow down "a diffuse mob into a stable collection" of "familiar antagonists" (since clientship involves neither dependency nor patronage, but antagonistic competition for information). The adversarial nature of bazaar transactions is perhaps more evident in bargaining, which Geertz characterizes as multidimensional (entailing manipulations of quality or quantity for a certain price, or surreptitious adjustments in credit arrangements) and intensive ("the exploration in depth," via bargaining, "of an offer already received," instead of seeking out further offers) (31). Geertz's point is that seemingly shambolic bazaar operations generate certain cogent outcomes, including recognizably logical practices and institutions: bazaar economies evince their own rationality.

In his emphasis on informational constraints, Geertz was following a new generation of innovative economists who had begun to move away from the idealistic model of perfectly competitive markets to address real-life transactions in situations of less-than-ideal information and communication. Just a few years ago, economic theory seemed to have reached its apogee with the influential Theory of General Economic Equilibrium. Economists Kenneth

Arrow and Gerard Debreu had deployed complex mathematical modeling to "prove" that under certain simplifying assumptions, it was possible to figure out a set of prices such that the market for every commodity in the economy would clear, that is, the aggregate demand for each commodity would equal its aggregate supply. While such theoretical models are impressive in their rigor and sophistication, the esoteric assumptions that shore them up (e.g., perfect competition, "convex" preferences) are hardly realistic. (Arrow and Debreu 1954) Moreover, when uncertainties about future states come into play, gaps in information and communication cause some markets to remain *incomplete*; for instance, certain goods and services in demand are not available for transaction, with potential suppliers choosing to stay out of those markets because of underlying risks. Here again, mid-century economists proceeded from a debatable assumption: that advanced capitalist societies were capable of developing market instruments and designing contracts that would provide insurance coverage for every possible future contingency, allowing economic agents to engage in complex transactions across space and time. All markets were rendered "complete" *in theory* in terms of their capacity for the contractual mitigation of future risks.

For some economists who came into professional prominence in the tumultuous decades of the 1960s and 1970s, this disciplinary strategy of assuming away key questions about the market proved dissatisfying. Their experiential horizon compelled them to treat contingency, incompleteness, and disequilibrium as serious research problems. A particularly salient subset of the incomplete market problematic features transactional imperfections/costs arising from asymmetric access to information. Situations in which one party (the agent) withholds information key to the transaction from the other party (the principal) lead to some form of "moral hazard." The challenge is to come up with contracts that provide incentives for agents to divulge more information about themselves (i.e., self-screen). A familiar instance, whose dynamics Geertz found to be akin to bazaar modalities, is provided by the interactions between the used car salesman and the buyer, the former (the agent) potentially hiding aspects of the car from the prospective buyer (the principal). The moral hazard amounts to the possible sale of a "lemon" at a price higher than what is warranted. As economist George Akerlof argues convincingly, market mechanisms may actually lead to a decline in the quality of cars available for sale over time (Akerlof 1970).

Geertz was clearly drawn to the emerging work on incomplete markets which sought to address and incorporate sociocultural factors in models of economic transactions. However, in making the gaps in information/communication the defining if not the sole problematic of bazaar economies, Geertz effectively reduced them to an archaic version of incomplete markets;

all other imperatives that animated the bazaar as a space of transactions were evacuated. The rationality of the bazaar, as presented by Geertz, was no more than a feeble and compensatory trace of market rationality.

Bazaar Genealogies

Historical evidence, argues Rajat Ray, does not support such widely prevalent notions of the bazaar as either the humble antecedent or the bastardized copy of the modern capitalist market. (Ray 1995) While Asian commercial networks had clearly not reached the levels and dynamisms of the British, the Dutch, or the French capitalist enterprises before the Europeans arrived on the scene, they did not just amount to the limited and isolated trade of local farmers, artisans, and hawkers (Geertz's starting premise). Noting the polysemic circulation of the term in Asia, Ray observes that in British India, what the Controller of Currency referred to as the bazaar was "an expanding intermediate sphere" of indigenous "commercial credit operations," situating itself between the business enterprises of European corporations and the "vast areas of subsistence agriculture and peddling trade" (455). This indigenous money market used "promissory notes, bills of exchange, and other negotiable instruments" to finance "the wholesale and forward trade over the longer distances" (452). And in addition to the bank rate of interest, the Controller of Currency regularly published a *bazaar rate*, with the latter dictating the financing of "the bulk of the inland wholesale trade of British India" (452-3). Even before European capitalism entered Asia, Chinese commercial operations had developed all over Southeast Asia, and corresponding Indian circuits across the Arabian Sea were honing crucial skills of marine travel, "account-keeping, and the handling of money" (454). Now, these well-placed Asian merchants and financiers were able to take advantage of the new political and commercial assemblages and consolidate their operations in the overseas communities of the Dutch East Indies and British East Africa. Hence, the encounter that took place, Ray claims, was a "confrontation ... between two gesellschaften" (449).

Clearly, market and bazaar histories come thoroughly entangled, and it is difficult to make an unequivocal case for the conceptual and/or operational superiority of the market paradigm unless one is reciting from the capitalist playbook for global transformation. For the past several centuries, capitalism has been unrelenting in its efforts to universalize the market paradigm as the benchmark and endgame for all regimes of economic transaction. The historicity of those efforts tells a complex story: of the bazaar's marginalization in the modern economic imagination *and* its persistence in contemporary economic life. Staying with the South Asian context, we find one such account in historian Ritu Birla's study of the Indian indigenous capitalists' negotiations in the late nineteenth and early twentieth centuries of the new British colonial legislations intended to govern market practices (Birla 2009). Birla notes that both colonial administrators and the nationalist intelligentsia expressed concerns about local capitalists' vernacular modes of conducting business, their dependence on extended kinship structures and familial networks, their lack of ambition, and their inability to recognize emerging trends and to take advantage of fresh opportunities. For the indigenous capitalists, the arguments against bazaar practices did not always stand up to the sheer evidence of their experience. As Birla demonstrates for the period between 1870 and 1930, "even as they folded their bazaar idioms into new languages of capitalist development," (6) local capitalists challenged many of the new economic diktats in their spheres of operation as well as in court: for instance, the equation of vernacular speculative practices with gambling, thus framing such practices as immoral; or the dismissal of local accumulation strategies as mere hoarding (usually of jewelry), and therefore unproductive. In fact, local businessmen's efforts to transform themselves into the "New Economic Man" were effectively undercut by colonial liberalism's intrinsic contradictions, a spectacular expression of which was the bifurcation in British India's legal system. One set of laws applied to the public realm, which included the economy/market, and another set— "personal law," a category born from colonial liberalism's acknowledgement of traditional structures and customs– applied to the private realm, which included culture. Crucial aspects of commercial life were affected by personal law stipulations, for instance with respect to joint property ownership and inheritance; incommensurabilities between these traditional *cultural* norms and the abstract rules of market economy would delay legal settlements inordinately. This dual dynamic, "the utilitarian call to economic progress" and the simultaneous "paternalistic imperative of cultural preservation," placed indigenous capitalists as simultaneously internal and external to the emerging economic system, burdening them with a perpetual need to perform their legitimacy as economic agents (3–4). The broad impact of the "legal infrastructure for colonialism's developmental regime," Birla argues, was the institutionalization of the market "as a *public* venture." The new laws orchestrated and "enforced an abstract, or […] 'disembedded' vision of society as a public of exchanging, contracting actors" (4). Neoliberalism's monetization of all aspects of life, its reduction of everything into fungible assets, had already begun under colonial liberalism. But the intransigent bazaar, marked as necessary roadkill in this script of order-via-capture, has consistently muddied that teleology by refusing to wither away.

Bazaar Affirmations

In stark contrast to the views of the market proponents, particularly their dismissal of the bazaar as a vestigial structure and their predictions of its impending demise, the following three examples offer evidence-based affirmations of the bazaar form and ethos, of their continuing vitality in contemporary economic and community life in most of the world.

The first affirmative instance comes from Kyrgyzstan. As political scientist Regina Spector notes, the country scores low on "global indicators related to rule of law and security of property rights" because of its "weak state capacity, frequent political instability, and high levels of corruption" (Spector 2017: 2). Spector's research reveals a surprising trend: while post-Soviet polities in Central Asia may lack rule of law, local merchants in many places have organized themselves and developed bottom-up institutions in the bazaar to bring back order and security. Spector argues that aggregative economic statistics and governance indexes, computed according to global standards, fail to recognize and account for these "local islands of order" that emerge in the bazaars where "people on the ground … create meaningful work environments" (179–80). They do so precisely by forging norms and organizations "based on prior ideas and experiences" that, in post-Soviet societies, are very likely be at odds with capitalist market institutions (180).

The second instance has to do with the role of bazaar modes in popular culture. Art scholar Kajri Jain argues that in South Asia, the bazaar has served as a key "infrastructure" for a number of vernacular popular forms, from what is known as "calendar art"[2] or "bazaar art" to popular cinema. (Jain 2021) From the late nineteenth century, print technologies enabled the mass reproduction of sketches, paintings, photographs, posters, and illustrated pamphlets, sold at affordable prices by vendors in the marketplace, outside temples, at the fair, and at street corners. Modern South Asian commercial-popular art emerged from these informal congeries at the intersections of commerce and religion, high and low taste cultures (Jain 2012). Despite its tremendous popularity, twentieth-century art critics and historians generally dismissed bazaar art as aesthetically impoverished and ideologically compromised (banal, derivative, crass, conservative) in comparison to the more abstract, critical-reflexive "modern art" of elite galleries and museums. Note that the commercial-popular Hindi cinema of Bombay, now known as Bollywood, has been subject to similar charges of mediocre quality, bastardized aesthetics, low levels of professionalism, and criminal connections. With the transformations wrought by globalization, the industry has faced challenges of organization, formalization, and standardization (Punathambekar 2013).

And yet, after more than two decades of far-reaching corporatizing efforts, well-established family-based production houses (Dharma Productions, Yash Raj productions) are faring much better than the relatively new entrants in the Indian media sector with impeccable market reputation (e.g., Disney India recently ended its film production operations). Elements of the bazaar live on, indeed reign, in one of the biggest global culture industries.

A third set of phenomena that affirm the bazaar as a generative space is to be found in the realm of the piratical, consisting of practices that emerge in the gap between what the state institutes as legal and what the people consider to be legitimate (Sarkar 2016). Two of the most salient piratical activities have to do with the unauthorized reproduction of media products (from books to mp4 files) that boost circulation while gnawing at corporate profits; and the recycling, rewiring, and repurposing of media technologies, which foil the planned obsolescence that companies now build into their products, often expanding what consumers can do with their appliances well beyond sanctioned uses. The pirates' sense of legitimacy is fueled by outrage over the exorbitant prices set by transnational corporations, frustration about the shrinking lifetimes of "durable" goods, and the sheer pleasure of going DIY with intricate technologies usually developed and patented in more advanced societies. The nodes[3] for such piratical activities which dot the global South—neighborhood repair shops, street corner convenience stores, and battery-charging stations, as well as the more itinerant VCD and pen drive peddlers and unlicensed pavement vendors—are a significant component of the massive *informal* economy, that largely unaccounted for material reality that forces an expansion of the conceptual space of the bazaar. Like South Asian bazaar art, "southern" piratical practices affirm the bazaar as a structure for generative transactions; and in turn, the two realms are made possible by the bazaar as infrastructure, through the bazaar's affirmative interactions.

Notes

1 How the self-interests of individuals map onto the self-interests of entire societies—or how individuals constituting a "people" develop into the rational, right-bearing citizen-subjects of modern polities, has remained an enduring problematic of political theory.
2 Named after the illustrated calendars that businesses give their clients as gift to mark the new year.
3 Sometimes the nodes appear as *chorbazaars*—flea markets or, literally, thieves' markets.

Works Cited

Akerlof, G. (1970), "The Market for 'Lemons': Quality Uncertainty and the Market Mechanism," *The Quarterly Journal of Economics*, 84 (3) (August 1970): 488–500. https://doi.org/10.2307/1879431.

Arrow, K. J. and Debreu, G. (1954), "Existence of an Equilibrium for a Competitive Economy," *Econometrica*, 22 (3) (July): 265–90. https://doi.org/10.2307/1907353.

Birla, R. (2009), *Stages of Capital: Law, Culture, and Market Governance in Late Colonial India*, Durham, NC: Duke University Press.

Geertz, C. (1978), "The Bazaar Economy: Information and Search in Peasant Marketing," *The American Economic Review*, 68 (2) (May 1978): 28–32. https://www.jstor.org/stable/1816656.

Jain, K. (2012), "Mass Reproduction and the Art of the Bazaar," in Vasudha Dalmia and Rashmi Sadana (eds), *The Cambridge Companion to Modern Indian Culture*, Cambridge, UK: Cambridge University Press, 184–205.

Jain, K. (2021), "Bazaar," *BioScope: South Asian Screen Studies*, 12 (1–2) (June & December, 2021): 35–8.

Punathambekar, A. (2013), *From Bombay to Bollywood: The Making of a Global Media Industry*, New York: NYU Press.

Ray, R. K. (1995), "Asian Capital in the Age of European Domination: The Rise of the Bazaar, 1800–1914," *Modern Asian Studies*, 29 (3) (July): 449–554. https://doi.org/10.1017/S0026749X00013986.

Sarkar, B. (2016), "The Pedagogy of the Piratical," in Katarzyna Marciniak and Bruce Bennett (eds), *Teaching Transnational Cinema: Politics and Pedagogy*, New York: Routledge, 191–201.

Spector, R. (2017), *Order at the Bazaar: Power and Trade in Central Asia*, Ithaca, NY: Cornell University Press.

Sen, S. (1998), *Empire of Free Trade: The East India Company and the Making of the Colonial Marketplace*, Philadelphia: University of Pennsylvania Press.

Taylor, C. (2004), *Modern Social Imaginaries*, Durham, NC: Duke University Press.

5

上善若水 / Be (Like) Water: Media Dynamics and Multiple Realities

(Origin Chinese/English/Cantonese)

Helena Wu

"*Shangshan ruoshui / seung sin yeuk seui*" 上善若水 ("excel like water") is the four-character expression that opens the eighth chapter of *Dao De Jing* [*Tao Te Ching*], a classical text that was believed to be written by Taoist philosopher Laozi during the Warring States period of ancient China. Explaining why water is valorized as a virtue, the text describes water as something that is beneficial to all things without competing with them and that resides in places preferred by no one, or close to the way (i.e., "*dao*").[1] Centuries went by, the human-matter relationship embedded in this mode of thinking suggests not just a de-anthropocentric tendency but also an individualized and collective experience that is simultaneous. Shifting from resemblance to becoming, the idea of "be water" [*sic*] was philosophized by the US-born Hong Kong-raised international film star Bruce Lee in the early 1970s to convey agility, adaptability, and resilience. Arriving at the twenty-first century, the watery state was evoked *en masse* in Hong Kong, a former British colony from 1841 to 1997 and thereafter a Special Administrative Region (SAR) practicing the "One Country Two Systems" policy with the People's Republic of China. During the Anti-Extradition Law Amendment Bill (Anti-ELAB) Movement in 2019, the city's pro-democracy population recontextualized the "be water" [*sic*] concept into a myriad of resistance strategies.[2] Just when the pandemic broke out and the protests were forced to subside in 2020, the Cantonese term "yam seui" 飲水 ("drink water") was integrated into some colloquial greetings, widely circulated as a piece of health advice to stay hydrated as well as an unspoken reference to other watery imageries, among the traumatized population.[3]

In this regard, expressing different modes of water embodiment by way of classical Chinese, English and Cantonese not only unveils the countless encounters with entangled cultures and contested identities in the history of Hong Kong; but the condition of being (like) water—as advocated by Laozi in ancient time; by Bruce Lee in a transnational context; and by all walks of life in a critical moment—also turns out to be a sedimentation of different temporal, spatial, and lived experiences. This chapter will offer a critical examination of liquid embodiment by way of viscosity, liquidity, fluidity, and water and extend the lines of inquiry to discourses of globalization, modernity, digital media, and the body. Thinking with intersectionality will enable us to connect with different localized yet diverse experiences within and beyond Hong Kong. Building on these local and translocal trajectories, I contend that liquid embodiment and the motto "be water" should be understood on not just a metaphorical level nor as figurative speech, but as an active enactment and lived experience grounded in situated reality through the lens of Hong Kong.

Being Viscous

In physics, viscosity is the resistance of a fluid to flow.

In light of the body politic, geographer Arun Saldanha recontextualized viscosity as a political-geographical dimension of human bodies next to sensuousness, variation, and locatedness, with a view to addressing a "global interconnectedness" that is grounded on corporeality (Saldanha 2008: 331). As a spatial process where flows and networks intersect, viscosity encompasses the condition of motion and stasis of different groups and formations. In Saldanha's words, viscosity is a "dynamic emergence" of "collectivities of people based on attributes like sex, skin colour, nationality, economic power or fear" and is manifested in "governments, social movements and corporations," among other structures and events on different scales (Saldanha 2008: 325). What is noteworthy about the embodied perspective of "many bodies com[ing] together as bodies" is the co-presence of their differences, on the one hand, and the condition of "togetherness, of coordinated flowing and relative stability," on the other (Saldanha 2008: 330). With reference to Saldanha's interpretation of Spinoza's materialist approach and Deleuze's political ontology, it has been suggested that pluralism and the engagement with variation that is made visible through the lens of materiality and viscosity are the keys to achieving what Saldanha contemplated as a "democratic body politic" (Saldanha 2008: 332).

Being Liquid

Liquid retains a higher viscosity than gas.

While Saldanha sought to "counter the general tendency towards solidification" (Saldanha 2008: 331) in the domain of political geography, sociologist Zygmunt Bauman (2000) differentiated liquid from solid in his conceptualization of liquid modernity. Liquid, which is characterized as light, quick, diffused, and network-like (Bauman 2000: 25), was explored serially by Bauman along the lines of love (2003), life (2005), fear (2006), and time (2007). Bauman discussed five aspects—emancipation, individuality, time/space, work, and community—of the "liquid modern" state of the globalized world, which were not only reflected in the individuation, fragmentation, and fluidity of human relations, social forms, and experiences but also in a series of paradoxes, conflicting discourses, and contradictory positionings. Bauman also observed that individualization has become "a fate, not a choice" (Bauman 2000: 34) in the contemporary world, posing a critique of free will by questioning its authenticity and practicability beyond the oft-mentioned context of the market and consumers' choice. In a similar vein, the fluidity gained by different entities can empower individuals, but it also intensifies the "panoptical technique of power" per se. What Bauman deemed problematic is the gap between the public and the private, seemingly unfillable due to the absence of any effective agency as it has become increasingly difficult to "translat[e] private problems into public issues" (Bauman 2000: 51). Bauman also pointed out the impact of the disparity between individuals and society on emancipation: autonomy "cannot fulfil itself anywhere except in the autonomous society" (Bauman 2000: 52).

Being Fluid

A fluid can be a liquid or a gas—to be fluid is equivalent to not being (a) solid.

The discussion of liquid embodiment will disclose one's unavoidable connection to politics (body, life, etc.) in one way or another. Likewise, in the digital sphere, media scholar David Savat's (2013) conceptualization of "fluid politics" offered yet another viewpoint that wove media with politics. In particular, extrapolating from Guattari and Deleuze's notion of flow and nomad, Savat invited readers to think of "politics and political action as not being the action of solids" (Savat 2013: 179). In this light, the "language of solid politics" uses "fluid" to describe situations that are "hard to predict and analyze" by "solid actors" (Savat 2013: 179–80). Contrarily, fluid politics emphasizes flows and the rate of flow that are enacted by networked and scattered actors during their exchanges, communication, and connections. In screen reality enhanced by digital media, a political action is "anything that affects the constitution of flow, whether that be in the ability to participate in a flow, the ability to constitute a flow in the first instance, or any change in an already constituted flow" (Savat 2013: 183). Virtual sit-ins and hacker-activist activities—examples of "electronic civil disobedience" (Meikle 2014: 143)—are perceptible political actions in the networked space, aiming to influence the physical world and hence transgressing different levels of tangibility and intangibility, accordingly.

While Savat pinned down a rather clear-cut understanding of spatiality between solid and fluid, or the "sedentary" space of the State (*polis*) in solid politics and the realm of the nomads (*nomos*) in fluid politics, Luce Irigaray's essay "The 'Mechanics' of Fluids" warned of potential blind spots, as fluid "allows itself to be easily traversed by virtue of its conductivity"; in other words, intermixing is not without problems, especially when dilution and homogenization result in unbalanced power relations (Irigaray 1985: 111). In a similar fashion, Saldanha located politics in the "mutual reinforcement/ challenge" of human encounters (Saldanha 2008: 11), just as Bauman reminded us of the "inner paradox of communitarianism" under the circumstances of being, or wanting to be, a part and simultaneously not a part of a community (Bauman 2000: 169). Considering the array of disciplines involved, these lines of investigation cross over geography, sociology, feminist studies, cultural theory, and digital media while all pointing to different degrees of materiality pertaining to our engagement with fluid/liquid—from empirical observation (physical state, properties, etc.) and discourse (metaphor, representation, etc.) to embodiment (experience, affect, etc.).

The Strength of Water

"Excel like water."—Laozi
"Be water, my friend."—Bruce Lee

Revisiting *Dao De Jing*, the second mention of water is toward the end of the book: in Chapter 78, the liquid state of water is reflected upon as an analogy of strength and power:

> In the world there is nothing more submissive and weak than water. Yet for attacking that which is hard and strong nothing can surpass it. This is

because there is nothing that can take its place. That the weak overcomes the strong. And the submissive overcomes the hard, everyone in the world knows yet no one can put this knowledge into practice. (Lau 1989 [1963]: 113)[4]

Centuries later, Bauman was also inspired by the agility of liquid and employed a similar reading of having the powerful overturned by the nature of liquid: "The game of domination in the era of liquid modernity is not played between the 'bigger' and the 'smaller', but between the quicker and the slower" (Bauman 2000: 188). While *Dao De Jing* suggested that the strength of water was known but hardly applied, Bauman associated liquid with the speed of the human condition, while exposure to the liquid-modern state was accumulative and was not up to a person to decide. Bruce Lee proposed a set of practices so as to be empowered by the strength of water. The actor and founder of Jeet Kune Do said in a television interview conducted in English in 1971:

> Empty your mind, be formless, shapeless, like water. Now you put water into a cup, it becomes the cup. You put water into a bottle, it becomes the bottle. You put it in a teapot, it becomes the teapot. Now water can flow, or it can crash. Be water, my friend.[5]

Lee was re-enacting what he felt most represented his core belief in an accessible language. Lee's student Stirling Silliphant, who was a screenwriter by profession, wrote these lines to express Lee's philosophy about the body and martial arts when designing a cameo role for Lee in the US crime drama *Longstreet* (1971). Lee appeared in four episodes and played a character called Li Tsung, who was a Jeet Kune Do practitioner and a martial arts instructor for the title character. According to Lee, the character was not just speaking about his philosophy but *was* himself, hence unveiling the overlapping layers between the acting body, the martial art body, and the actor's corporeal body across the text, the screen, and the different time-space where Lee and his audience were located.

Lee's emphasis on the body and the self manifested a liquid embodiment in actuality. Whereas Lee's posthumous legacy has become almost inseparable from the sweeping term "Chinese kung fu," especially in the popular cultural sphere, in his own words Lee reiterated the importance of delimiting the understanding of race, nationality, and martial arts at large: rather than simply being a set of combative and defensive skills, martial arts is "self-knowledge" and "the art of expressing the human body." Moving from a discursive to an actual but no less abstract level, Lee—who had been making appearances on the silver screen since he was a few months old and who came of age in the media's spotlight as Hong Kong's champion in boxing and cha-cha—articulated the difficulty of expressing oneself "honestly" in the name of "un-acting acting" and "acting un-acting." In this regard, Lee showed his awareness of the performativity embedded in and constantly relayed through one's body through the amalgamation of his screen personae accumulated from the roles he played, his star image as an international action film actor, and his spectacular movements and well-trained physique when practicing martial arts, both onscreen and offscreen. Between training and intuition, the will to genuinely express oneself by way of the body and/or language and the wish to achieve the know-how bring not just the natural-artificial paradigm into question but also body politics and the politics of representation into dialogue, against the discussion of different disciplines that have been explored in earlier parts of this chapter. Lee's speech act was inevitably complicated by his bodily engagement, his interpretation of his own body, and his audience's perception of him and his screen image. His body could not escape from being an agent of action and interaction with other bodies, as well as a site of mediation and representation, both physically and visually, resulting in a paradoxical relation lingering between being and performing. As Lee mentioned in the interview, he was (still) "being Bruce Lee" in the characters he portrayed as a Jeet Kune Do practitioner and attributed it to the success of those roles (like "Li Tsung"), which allowed him to express himself and his body.

Since his death in 1973, Bruce Lee's philosophy has been repeatedly, if not overly, interpreted and appropriated. In addition to the circulation in real life as well as popular culture, Lee's charismatic reminder to "be water, my friend" was adopted as the title of a book published by his daughter, Shannon Lee, in 2020, in which the "teachings of Bruce Lee" were equated as the "'be water' philosophy." In the same year, it was also used in the title of a documentary about Bruce Lee directed by Bao Nguyen. It is noteworthy that Bruce Lee's "philosophy" could not escape from being represented and mediated by himself or others. Although Lee did not live to see Bauman's observed liquid modernity, nor the digital age in which Savat contextualized the notion of "fluid politics," Lee's martial arts practice and teaching demonstrated a high degree of viscosity, to borrow Saldanha's use of the term. In this case, corporeality was emphasized by bringing together different bodies not only to spar and train together but also to experiment and experience the hybridity Lee located in the mixed application of different forms and schools of martial arts. The resulting cultural influences were exerted by Lee's iconicity and the networked communities of his family, followers, fans, and viewers through the generations. While Lee advocated an "honest" expression of the self as formless and shapeless, foregoing the indoctrination of any style, did his conceptualization introduce yet another form that he himself had strived to deconstruct? Jeet Kune Do, which literally means the "way of intercepting fist," was still formatted, to a certain extent, according to what Lee conceived, practiced, and propagated as a martial artist during his lifetime on both discursive and physical levels.

Last, but not the least toward the end of the said interview, Lee was asked to address his identity as a "Chinese" or a "North American." Refusing to be labeled by race, ethnicity, or nation-state at that instance, the star said that he considered himself a "human being" and added that "it just so happened that people are different." In fact, Lee's star image was very much built on his transnational appeals, racialized masculinity, and transpacific crossing: He first gained popularity in Hong Kong with his roles in Hollywood (such as Kato, a fictional character of Asian origin, in *The Green Hornet* series produced between 1966 and 1967), and rose to international stardom at the age of thirty-one with the release of *The Big Boss* (Lo Wei and Wu Chia Hsiang 1971), the star's first project with Golden Harvest, a studio founded in 1970 in Hong Kong that would become a major agent in popularizing the city's action cinema around the world.[6] Whereas Lee's witty response to the host's question might be a diplomatic answer for a celebrity who had made appeals to different local, diasporic, and transnational communities studded with varying cultural upbringings, linguistic identities, and political orientations, it revealed one possible application of liquid embodiment, not just in bodily terms but also in dialectic thinking. In any case, Lee's rhetoric was consistent in his emphasis on difference, rather than sameness. Though Lee's own project was left incomplete upon his death, what Bauman identified as the obstacle to being autonomous amidst the widening gap between individuals and society is worth re-examining in the context of 2019 Hong Kong.

Be(ing) Water

In retrospect, 2019 was only the starting point of consecutive eventful years to come in Hong Kong, which not only unpacked the geopolitics of neighboring places but also impacted international relations, policy making, and security issues around the world. In its early stage, the Anti-ELAB Movement was the population's response to the Hong Kong SAR Government's plan to implement extradition to China. In the first half of the year, public opinion remained ambivalent, with a relatively low turnout in a related demonstration in May 2019. However, the June 9 and June 16 protests, in which reportedly one million and two million citizens participated respectively, broke records for the most attended protests in the history of Hong Kong. These two rallies, together with the police-civilian clash on June 12, set the momentum for a myriad of protest activities, resistance strategies and everyday tactics to emerge, encompassing both nonviolent and valiant approaches in a wide spectrum. The insistence on a leaderless mode and decentralized methods of mobilization was a lesson learnt from the 2014 Umbrella Movement, with an aim to rule out any chance of being misrepresented and misappropriated.[7] Under these circumstances, Bruce Lee's advice to "be water" became a motto that circulated through digital communication (e.g., Internet forums, social media platforms, and instant texting applications) and was practiced in real-life scenarios (e.g., dispersal techniques, planning, and the selection of protest sites) over the course of the Anti-ELAB Movement.

The diverse resistance strategies—ranging from rallies, civil disobedience acts, petitions, song singing, crowd-funding campaigns, and advertisements in newspapers to the use of consumer power—revealed the diversity of not just the Anti-ELAB Movement from a macroscopic view but also the pro-democracy faction's preferred methods and accepted approaches of protest.[8] The pursuit of solidarity in how conflicts were managed was attributed to the driving force of the protests (Lee 2020), and the protesters' simultaneous emphasis on collectivity and individuality played a key role in maintaining a high degree of intra-movement liberty. While collectivity was sustained by the motto "no splitting," individuality was constantly reflected on by the shared imagery of "brothers climbing the mountain," another oft-used catchphrase which pointed to the determination to achieve the same goal, albeit through different means (Holbig 2020; Ting 2020).

In the digital age of the twenty-first century, social movements have multiplied through competing narratives, utterances, and cultural production as media/mediated/mediatized phenomena, which reverberate online and offline through the interactions and intermediations of emotions, behavior, and representations. In Hong Kong, the Anti-ELAB Movement exemplified such multifarious realities in contact and clash with one another in different discursive contexts and across physical and virtual dimensions concurrently. In hindsight, the undertaking of events—including the territory-wide social movement and different stakeholders' actions and reactions—was inseparable from individuals' and the community's perception of the protest in a broader sense and of its different components (e.g., formats, tactics, and narratives). The reception process continuously shaped the resistance campaigns and reflected the recipient's value system, identity, and ideology in the situated present, complicating political leanings that were often traditionally perceived in dualism.

From classical Chinese and English to Cantonese, the discourse on water has revealed languaging as an accumulative outcome of the city's entangled social, cultural, and political landscapes—from a postcolonial perspective, cultural studies scholar Rey Chow referred to languaging as a "condition of being caught between languages" (Chow 2014: 39).[9] From philosophy and critical theory to everyday practice, water embodiment, its transmissibility, and its translatability engender a site for different times, spaces, cultures, and disciplines to cross over one another. From "excel like water" to "be [like] water," another lesson to learn from water is about striking a relation between the self and the other, transgressing boundaries, and maintaining a critical awareness of these affinities and activities. With regards to the differing perception of Bruce Lee, cultural scholars have been critical of the nationalistic sentiments and the ideological implications derived from his image and body (Li 2001; Lo 1996, 2005; Berry 2006). In the early 2000s, Li Siu Leung, for instance, read the ambiguous signification resulted as an example of the "hollowness of Hong Kong identity to be 'filled out' by other bodies" (2001: 528). On the other hand, with the rise of local consciousness in the postmillennial era, cultural objects, icons, and memories were continuously re-invented, complicating while renewing existing discourses and relations (Wu 2020). In the lead up to the Anti-ELAB Movement and over its course, water embodiment—amidst various lineages and trajectories (including Bruce Lee's)—not only strengthened identification, but also fueled intermediation through localization (e.g., Bruce Lee's/resistance motto, "Baltic Way"/"Hong Kong Way" human chain, #MeToo/#ProtestToo hashtag), echoing the democratic body politic explored in the beginning of this chapter.

Extrapolating from viscosity, liquidity, and fluidity, the water embodiment in Hong Kong's pro-democracy movements—amidst the entangled processes of cultural referencing, appropriation, and mediation from countless local and translocal nodal points—epitomized the possibility of attaining multiple positionings and demonstrated the simultaneous understanding of the self as a member of a crowd as well as an active individual. Enabled by technological means and changing media dynamics, "be water" as a travelling concept has demonstrated the possibility of striking newer relations and driving innovations based on the fluid flow of differences and discords. Although the pursuit of the democratic body politic has been distressed by tightened control, forced monologism, and unbalanced power relations, the concept of "be water" has travelled again to places outside of Hong Kong and has found resonances among members of the diasporic communities who continued to voice grievances and concerns over Hong Kong matters,[10] as well as resistance movements in Belarus, Thailand, and Myanmar among other places in the post-2019 era.[11]

Notes

1. The original text is: 水利萬物而不爭, 處眾人之所惡, 故幾於道
2. In a column series titled "Anti-ELAB Movement Keywords" published on the supplementary of Hong Kong newspaper *Ming Pao*, cultural studies scholar Yiu-wai Chu (2019) mentioned that "be water" is a resistance tactic as well as a "management strategy."

3   The image of water is at times deployed to implicate an affective connection with Hong Kong. For instance, a group of diasporic Hongkongers, including some self-exiled activists, named a magazine they established in 2021 as "Flow HK" 如水. The Chinese title literally means "be water."

4   The original text is: 天下莫柔弱於水, 而攻堅強者莫之能勝, 其無以易之。弱之勝強, 柔之勝剛, 天下莫不知, 莫能行

5   In December 1971, Bruce Lee spoke on *The Pierre Berton Show* hosted by the namesake Canadian television personality and journalist. The episode was later renamed "The Lost Interview" as it was re-discovered in 1994, almost two decades after the interview had taken place.

6   Bruce Lee (1940–1973) was no stranger to showbiz, even before his venture into Hollywood during his twenties and his later breakthrough upon returning to Hong Kong. His father, Lee Hoi-chuen, was a famous Cantonese opera actor and film actor in Hong Kong, and Bruce Lee played in movies since he was, literally, a baby.

7   The Umbrella Movement was a civil disobedience campaign that lasted for seventy-nine days between September and December 2014 in Hong Kong. The Umbrella Movement and the Anti-ELAB Movement shared similar pro-democracy demands, such as universal suffrage entitled by the Basic Law.

8   Scholars have observed the trend of tactical radicalization in Hong Kong since the late 2000s. In particular, the Anti-ELAB Movement showed an augmentation of the public's acceptance of radical action (Lee et al. 2021).

9   From the data collected in 2018, the Census and Statistics Department of the Hong Kong SAR Government reported that 88.8 percent of the population in Hong Kong identified Cantonese mother tongue (2019); however, in reporting the same set of data in an individual report titled "Use of Language in Hong Kong in 2018" published 2020, there was no mentioning of mother tongue.

10 For instance, "be water" is the name given to a global rally that took place in at least fifty cities around the world to commemorate the second anniversary of the Anti-ELAB movement in 2021 (Griffiths 2021).

11 The "be water" tactic was discussed by political scientists as to how Belarusian pro-democracy protesters learned from their Hong Kong counterparts to "void capture by the authorities" in the mass protests that broke out in August 2020 (Way 2020: 24). In October 2020, Thai pro-democracy protesters' adoption of the "be water" tactic was widely reported by international news outlets such as Reuters and Agence France-Presse (Kittisilpa et al. 2020; *France 24* 2020). In analyzing the protests against the military rule in Myanmar that began in February 2021, a report by the United States Institute of Peace (2021) also cited Hong Kong and Thailand as the inspiration for the "leaderless and fluid" "be water" methods of the "generation z."

Works Cited

"'A Moving Current': Thai Protesters Adopt Hong Kong Tactics" (2020), *France 24*, October 20, 2020, https://www.france24.com/en/live-news/20201020-a-moving-current-thai-protesters-adopt-hong-kong-tactics

Bauman, Z. (2000), *Liquid Modernity*, Cambridge: Polity.

Bauman, Z. (2003), *Liquid Love*, Cambridge: Polity.

Bauman, Z. (2005), *Liquid Life*, Cambridge: Polity.

Bauman, Z. (2006), *Liquid Fear*, Cambridge: Polity.

Bauman, Z. (2007), *Liquid Times*, Cambridge: Polity.

Berry, C. (2006), "Stellar Transit Bruce Lee's Body or Chinese Masculinity in a Transnational Frame," in F. Martin and A. Heinrich (eds), *Embodied Modernities: Corporeality, Representation, and Chinese Cultures*, Honolulu: University of Hawaii Press, 218–34.

Chow, R. (2014), *Not Like a Native Speaker*, New York: Columbia University Press.

Chu, Y. W. (2019), "Be Water," *Ming Pao* (August 7, 2019).

Griffiths, N. (2021), "Vancouver Protesters Join Global Demonstration in Support of Hong Kong," *Vancouver Sun*, June 12. https://vancouversun.com/news/local-news/vancouver-protesters-join-global-demonstration-in-support-of-hong-kong

Holbig, H. (2020), "Be Water, My Friend: Hong Kong's 2019 Anti-Extradition Protests," *International Journal of Sociology*, 50 (4): 325–37.

Irigaray, L. (1985), *This Sex Which Is Not One*, trans. C. Porter and C. Burke, New York: Cornell University Press.

Kittisilpa, J., Tanakasempipat, P. and Setboonsarng, C. (2020), "'We are all leaders today': Arrests Don't Stop Thai Protests," *Reuters* (October 18): 2020.

Laozi, "*Dao De Jing*," https://ctext.org/dao-de-jing

Lau, D. C. (1989) [1963], *Tao Te Ching*, Hong Kong: The Chinese University Press.

Lee, F. L. F. (2020), "Solidarity in the Anti-Extradition Bill Movement in Hong Kong," *Critical Asian Studies*, 52 (1): 18–32.

Lee, F. L. F., Cheng, E. W., Liang, H., Tang, G. K. Y., and Yuen, S. (2021), "Dynamics of Tactical Radicalisation and Public Receptiveness in Hong Kong's Anti-Extradition Bill Movement," in *Journal of Contemporary Asia*, (April 2021). doi: https://doi.org/10.1080/00472336.2021.1910330

Li, S.L. (2001), "Kung Fu: Negotiating Nationalism and Modernity," *Cultural Studies*, 15 (3): 515–42.

Lo, K.C. (1996), "Muscles and Subjectivity: A Short History of the Masculine Body in Hong Kong Popular Culture," *Camera Obscura*, 39: 105–25.

Meikle, G. (2014), *Future Active: Media Activism and the Internet*, New York and London: Routledge.

Oo, Z., Ford, B., and Pinckney, J. (2021), "Myanmar in the Streets: A Nonviolent Movement Shows Staying Power," United States Institute of Peace. https://

www.usip.org/publications/2021/03/myanmar-streets-nonviolent-movement-shows-staying-power

Saldanha, A. (2008), "The Political Geography of Many Bodies," in K. R. Cox, M. Low, and J. Robinson (eds), *The SAGE Handbook of Political Geography*, London: SAGE, 323–34.

Savat, D. (2013), *Uncoding the Digital: Technology, Subjectivity and Action in the Control Society*, Hampshire: Palgrave Macmillan.

"Thematic Household Survey Report - Report No. 66," (2019), Hong Kong: Census and Statistics Department, HKSAR Government, https://www.censtatd.gov.hk/en/data/stat_report/product/C0000086/att/B11302662019XXXXB0100.pdf

Ting, T. Y. (2020), "From 'Be Water' to 'Be Fire': Nascent Smart Mob and Networked Protests in Hong Kong," *Social Movement Studies*, 19 (3): 362–8.

Way, L. A. (2020), "Belarus Uprising: How a Dictator Became Vulnerable," *Journal of Democracy*, 31 (4): 17–27.

Wu, H. (2020), *The Hangover after the Handover: Places, Things and Cultural Icons in Hong Kong*, Liverpool: Liverpool University Press.

6

ćmiatło and *świecień*: Jacek Dukaj's Concepts in the Perspective of Philosophy of Visual Media and Telecommunication

(Origin Polish)

Agnieszka Dytman-Stasieńko and Jan Stasieńko

> "... Then, beyond the entryway to the corridor, in the other wall, the eastern wall, we saw this young man trapped in the ice. There are no photographs, you must trust my memory."
>
> I was rubbing my eyes, twice blinded—from darkness and lightness—sure that under my eyelids my pupils are still pulsating like the giddy flames of ćmiatło.
>
> Jacek Dukaj "The Ice"

One of the most important novels by a Polish sci-fi writer Jacek Dukaj, "The Ice"[1] from 2007, is set by the author in the early years of the twentieth century. The story takes place mainly in ice-covered Tsarist Russia, however, the entire Europe of that time is presented as a place of spreading of mysterious ice formations—*frostens*,[2] which in the book are often ascribed the features of autonomous beings, and which appeared on Earth after the impact of the Tunguska meteor.

Although the novel constitutes primarily a highly original metaphor for the philosophy of history, it can also prove appealing in the context of the philosophy of the media. For the purpose of the book, Dukaj has created various types of transformations and opposites of the existing physical properties that occur due to the action of the ice. After a meteor blast, the new elements (*tungetite*) and materials (*zimnazo*[3]) mined in Siberia appear.

From the perspective of media theory, the most striking element of the new dark physics of the ice is *ćmiatło*—a phenomenon that is the opposite of light, resulting from, among others, burning *zimnazo* and *tungetite*, but also present in many other forms and places, for example, as dark auroras (*Chernoye Sijaniye*). Nonetheless, it is not a shadow, rather a specific type of dark emanation, which has its source and casts a glow on objects that do not leave a shadow as in light, but the so-called *świecień*.

The terms discussed are relatively difficult to translate. In the novel, Dukaj, trying to reflect the specificity of his characters' speech, has applied terms from several languages, primarily Russian and French. He has also occasionally referred to English, hence we know that he wants *ćmiatło* to be translated as *shlight* (a combination of shadow and light).[4] Nonetheless, this translation seems to reflect not entirely all the semantic contexts and "shading" of this concept.

It has become known that the idea of a frozen world presented in Dukaj's novel, grounded in innovative phraseology, may refer to new gripping contexts related to media theory. Therefore, our goal is to indicate in which passages and in what form the unique concept of *ćmiatło*, and also the broader "dark" philosophy of the ice created in the novel, can contribute to better understanding of both visual media and forms of remote communication.

Sean Cubitt began his classic work "Practice of Light" (2014) with an in-depth analysis of blackness as an indispensable element of both traditional and digital media. These analyses relate, among others, to observation that blackness as the absence of color has potential to evoke anything and hence is terrifying, it "is an absence that nonetheless weighs like a presence" (Cubitt 2014: 21). On the other hand, according to Cubitt, blackness is "only ever virtual" as we are never able to reach its perfect degree. Due to this inability, blackness is not only frightening but also alluring (Cubitt 2014: 21).

This theory of blackness would seem to be a convenient field for interpreting media contexts of *ćmiatło*, were it not for the fact that "blackness" for Cubitt is shown from the perspective of the role of light in the structure of visual media, and thus placed in opposition to it. A similar expressive opposition is also applied by Burik (2019), who searched for philosophical references to the metaphors of light and darkness—and his conclusions are quite the contrary. Analyzing the philosophy of Heideger, Derrida and the religious assumptions of Daoism, he attempted to indicate that there are many significant reasons to appreciate darkness in combination with light in philosophical terms. Nonetheless, *ćmiatło* eludes such definitions built in opposition to light. *Ćmiatło* in Dukaj's concept is not blackness.

The nature of this phenomenon is not entirely explained in the novel. Benedykt Gierosławski, the main character of the book, describes its properties in this way:

> Ćmiatło was not, howbeit, a simple reverse of light; it did not pass around obstacles in straight lines, and the very boundaries of gloom

and świecień did not remain unchanged. The cabinet did not move, ćmieczka did not change its position, and yet a rectangle of a glow on the wallpaper behind the side wall of a piece of furniture was shrinking, and then puffing up, the line of light and darkness was bending ellipsoidally outside, and then inside, from the upper corner of świecień, every now and then a funnel-shaped extension of the glow was growing, extending up to the ceiling, just to curl up into itself and plunge with the crooked tooth of darkness into the depth of świecień ... The frantic flapping of light and ćmiatło did not slow down even for a second.

(Dukaj 2016a: 67)

The nature of *ćmiatło* seems to place this phenomenon in the novel not in opposition to light but to constitute a phenomenon that deconstructs the light, or rather deconstructs the basic opposition between light and darkness. Hence, *ćmiatło* would set alongside all the major notions characteristic of Derridean deconstruction, such as pharmakon, arche—writing and *différance*. They were coined to deal with Derrida's essential binary oppositions, namely signifier—signified, audible—written, speech—writing, presence—absence, etc. Derrida mentioned the light–darkness opposition by naming it "the founding metaphor of Western philosophy as metaphysics" (Derrida 2010 [1978]: 31); however, he did not formulate a category that would deconstruct this opposition. Dukaj seems to aid this need of a French philosopher with his *ćmiatło*.

Ćmiatło as a word refers in Polish not only to "dim," but also to "smoulder" and "eclipse." Therefore, in this matter, it comprises a mystery, indescribability that cannot be combined with light. Conversely, light appears as a specific condition of truth and certainty, as in a Polish expression "to come to light," which means disclosure of hidden facts.

Alternative media theory, taking into consideration the above properties of *ćmiatło*, but also the wider awry physics related to the domination of the ice, could comprise three forms of the media: cinema, photography, and telegraph, which the author implicitly deconstructs through his complex vision of the "frozen" reality.

Ghosts in the Absence of Cinema

If to seek any clear references to both visual media and telecommunications technologies in the novel, it becomes apparent that the ice-covered reality is devoid of many media performances and services; however, in fact, it is the result of a more common tendency to inhibit the development of technologies known before the "Age of the Ice."

One of the protagonists defines this problem as follows:

> ... And why are inventions that have caught on there not being accepted here? Why is electrification of our cities progressing so reluctantly? And automobiles? The closer to Winter, the fewer vehicles on the streets. And this invention of the cinematograph—did you, Miss, ever see a film, moving pictures? In Warsaw, maybe. And books, what we read? And the melodies that are played at balls and in parlours? Why won't radio receivers sell in Russia? And there are few who are willing to send their voice and music to homes with wireless telegraph. Am I talking wrong? Mister Benedykt? (Dukaj 2016a: 300)

The closer to the epicenter of the ice at the site of the meteorite impact, the worse all the media of wired and wireless communication work; however, the problem is wider as it involves various forms of social communication and cultural activity. It is difficult to find, for example, references to the theater in the plot. Although we know that it exists, it is more often shown as an architectural object exposed to *frostens*. The real visual "attraction" is sometimes displays of sparkles, once in the form of light fireworks, once *shlight frierenworks (ćmietlne frirtwerki)*.[5]

The cinema, as it occurs, is also absent in the book. We know that it exists and films are shown in picture theaters; however, there is also no detailed knowledge of how this new (the novel takes place in the first half of the twentieth century) form of visual media develops (or does not develop) "under the ice." This nonexistence of the cinema in the mainstream of narrative strongly prompts us to search for an alternative and deconstructed vision of a moving image. In the novel, we encounter a peculiar ritual in which one can seek an awry antithesis and a critical version of a film screening. It is a séance witnessed by the main character, Benedykt Gierosławski. Although the time of the action is a historical moment in which séances were still quite popular all over the world, as the characters of the novel indicate, such gatherings become especially frequent in ice-covered Russia.

In a séance, as in the whole idea of *ćmiatło*, nothing is certain; the assembled are shown strange light phenomena related to *świecienie* and outlines of mysterious figures. The protagonist of the novel—Benedykt, accidentally becomes the main actor of the performance, a kind of apparition illuminated by a revolver made of *zimnazo* hidden in a vest. In the fumes of the so-called *śmieczki* he looks to the gathered people like Christ in religious pictures, from whose breast a ray of light beams.

The traditional cinema apparatus (its projection machinery) as understood by Baudry (1986) constructs a reception relationship from clearly delimited elements, such as a viewer, a projector, a cinema room, which he likens to a Platonic cave, a film screening evoking the impression of a dream. The apparatus of a séance with the use of *ćmiatło* is not, however, as in the cinema, a passive reception of a previously recorded image, which is provided through a device that generates light, but becomes the apparatus that actively and "live" absorbs the human agent, whose biology interacts with *zimnazo* to create a light spectacle. They become (both the spectacle and the agent) the disturbance of darkness generated by *ćmiatło*, a by-product of a shadow. In this instance, the projector is thus inseparable from the participant of the show, it becomes a biomedium, in the sense given to it as one of the first by Eugene Thacker (2003) as informatization of the body and embodied materiality of information.

This séance also brings to mind the reflections of Paul Scons (2000)— a spiritualistic show becomes the most expressive reflection of his idea of "haunted media," on the one hand, aimed at communicating with the world of non-material beings, and on the other hand, being the effect of specific technologies of such contact.

Unfortunate Fate of Photography

As we have indicated above, the presence of *frostens* significantly modifies the physics of the earthly world, therefore the inventions and technologies to date do not have the possibility of such dynamic development as before. Thus, the cinema falls victim to the new icy reality because its dynamics and documentary potential do not match this reality. The medium that would seem to better correspond with the specifics of the world of the ice is photography, and undeniably in the novel we can find many descriptions of photographs, which for the main character become a source of information needed to solve the mystery of the missing father. Nonetheless, photography as a medium often falls victim to *ćmiatło*. This is because *ćmiatło* is hard to capture with a photographic camera. A clear example of these problems is attempts to capture people who previously underwent rituals of the so-called *odćmieczanie* initiated by Nikola Tesla, who Dukaj made one of the protagonists of the novel. Tesla is an inventor of a pump that allows for sucking out *ćmiatło* from living organisms. People undergoing this procedure feel more clear-headed and it is easier for them to think. A side effect is the visual after-images that accompany the *odćmieczony* ones—their silhouettes appear blurry, fuzzy. In the photographs, in turn, they become shadowy apparitions without clear lines and details, they become visible gaps in the picture, spaces after themselves.

As one of the protagonists describes such a photograph:

There is such a photograph in the hall of the Holey Palace, take a walk one day and see, in nineteen-thirteen when they put up the manufactories of zimnazo, everyone took souvenir photographs there, a panorama of the new city, roofs, chimneys, fires and frostens in the back, and here in front, the whole brigade, and so in this photograph they came out, every other like a wraith chased away from the grave, the face is black like a Negro's, eyes, mouth, hair, everything awry, and some of them even illuminated and only a stain is like a man, instead of a man. And you are asking me! I can see well. (Dukaj 2016a: 296)

We can find a similar description in other passage:

It was difficult to say with certainty, and to say anything, about the details of his appearance: the men were standing against the white ice slopes and snowy taiga, but in the place of Balloon Mute there emanated a black hole in this old photograph, there was a blur of dense oćmiata, and instead of facial features of Mute, instead of eyes, hair—only a few strokes of świecień glistered in the darkness reflected on the film, like star constellations in the night sky. (Dukaj 2016b: 356)

Interestingly, the ritual of *odćmieczenie* is described by Dukaj with categories related to photography. Suction of *ćmiatło* appears in this description as an *expressis verbis* deconstruction of photography. Here is how Tesla himself *odćmiecza*:

… The left arm, this motionless one, was the first to blur. As if someone was obliterating the image in an old photograph—as if the photographic film had been exposed for too long. (…) Tesla was falling into the shadow, behind the vertical veil of grey twilight, like a fluttering airy after-image, but fluttering not from heat but from cold, and not in a stunning glare, but in darkness, that is in ćmiatło—you could see its black sparks, like negatives of electrical discharges, but blurry, slow, growing out along gentle arcs and in tight bundles, in woolly flocks and flames of black fire (…). With the window in front of him, lightness was flashing behind his back—a bright świecień of a tall silhouette, far clearer than any shadow normally cast in daylight. Nikola Tesla was disintegrating into his own negative and a negative of a negative, laid down with a white stain on the carpet, the door, the compartment wall. (Dukaj 2016a: 196)

Vilem Flusser (2000 [1983]) wrote about photography as a medium that is often uncritically treated as a window into reality. The observer of photography is unaware or forgets that photography is a result of the ideologically and historically shaped apparatus (Flusser 2000: 15). Nonetheless, photography "displayed" to exposure to *ćmiatło* becomes its own critical alter ego, which is unable to attempt to represent reality, and thus reminds us of being a form of illusion and an ideological construct.

When photography ceases to fulfil its basic functions—it stops accurately reflecting shapes and silhouettes—it is necessary to look again for phenomena and forms that would take over the role of a medium that preserves reality in this oneiric world. The ice itself appears to have such properties. Dukaj has often employed the term "froze" in the novel to denote events that have become permanent or have happened in an irreversible way or opinions and decisions that have been decidedly taken and are difficult to change.

This freezing and capturing of reality, which we so often attribute to photography in our world, finds another unusual outlet in the book. *Frostens* themselves and their nests (*soplicowa*) in a way become new visual forms—they seize all the elements of the human world and create macabre collages from them.[6] To a certain degree, their aesthetics resembles dioramas, known from scale modeling, made with the use of resin, in which the displayed objects and figures are embedded, often presented as frozen in motion. This is why *frostens* are subject to censorship similar to that which affects traditional media. Censorship of these mysterious ice forms clearly shows that their "communicative" potential is perceived and considered a threat to the political system.

The Mammoth Roads—Macro Time Telegraph

The third subversive form of communication in the book, which proves to be something between telematic and visual media, is the so-called mammoth roads or paths. In Dukaj's concept, the ice spreads around the world after the Tunguska event, moving both above the ground and primarily under the ground in a manner slightly similar to the flow of electrical impulses in a telegraph cable. The paths of the underground ice movement are also compared to underground black rivers ("the Ice tide geomatic horoscopes"— the Ice is capitalized in the entire book to emphasize its importance). These mysterious underground channels, however, prove to be not only a place where the ice moves, but also, according to the beliefs of the tribes of Tungus, Buryats and Yakuts inhabiting the epicenter of the ice, a way to cover distances by not only frozen selves and bodies of shamans and other chosen ones.[7] The main character, Benedykt Gierosławski, who wants to find his missing father in ice-covered Siberia, faces this problem. In many rumors he is referred to as the so-called Father Frost, who, as a being that can withstand the closeness of the ice, is also able to travel on the Mammoth Roads.

Dukaj's idea of the Mammoth Roads seems to fall directly within Sconce's haunted media concept, where he wrote that the beliefs and concerns associated with the fact that the means of communication, such as the telegraph, are the habitat of ghosts, result from the typical combination of the three agents of "flow": electricity that drives technology, information that inhabits the medium and the consciousness of viewers/listeners (Sconce 2000: 8). It seems that the category of flow, hugely present in media theory (Berelson, Gaudet, and Lazarsfeld 1944; Csikszentmihalyi 1990; Williams 1992 [1974])[8] could greatly benefit from Dukaj's critical vision.

The strangeness of the mammoth roads system is emphasized by the fact that no regularities can be detected in them. Therefore, they become in a way the rhizome of Deleuze and Guattari (1987), which eludes plans and maps created by people. This is confirmed by the fact that the universal Holy Grail of the world of the ice is the mythical Grochowski's Card—a complete map of cold deposits that everyone wants to get, and which is only a legend. Thus, the mammoth roads fall within the definition of decentralized networks, and there is no logical justification for their structure and location. Their character resembles a parody of the global Internet network.

Why is it worthwhile to consider the Mammoth Roads as a deconstructed version of the telegraph? First, unquestionably, both in religious-mystical and scientific approaches to the ways of spreading the ice, they are treated as sources of information and channels of its flow. Nonetheless, this information is entropic in nature, it cannot be specified in any way, the mystery related to physics, including the geology of the ice, means that the inhabitants of Dukaj's world are constantly occupied clarifying this information, interpreting it and developing theories around it.

Second, immateriality of messages carried along the Mammoth Roads is deconstructed. The ice is entirely material and carries material artifacts, remains, and debris instead of encoded information. Moving along the Mammoth Roads, the ice eludes the definition of an inanimate substance. This relocation takes place through the so-called blood of *frostens*, that is liquid helium. This element behaves truly peculiarly under the physics of the ice. As Benedykt describes the experiment on "blood of *frostens*":

> It looked almost as if one of the simplest elements in its most primitive form was suddenly acquiring properties of a living organism under

the Ice. The more frozen—the more lively. This was the black-physical physiology of frostens. (Dukaj 2016b: 271)

Third, the ice is the antithesis of the speed of information transmission through wires. Despite dynamics of the spread of *frostens*, which can dominate urban spaces overnight, the ice is slow compared to any "human" technology of information transfer. This slowness makes the Mammoth Roads a kind of telegraph of "deep media time" as perceived by Zieliński or, in other words, telegraph of macro time.

Frostens develop faster and more densely in cities—the mammoth paths become a form of unsolicited, incomprehensible, and ineffective information transmission, the one that is impossible to control and supervise. The carcasses of mammoths "spat out" to the surface are here an ironic antithesis of telegrams and telepresence, understood by telegraph historians as the first expression of the sense of immaterial presence and dematerialization of the body (Gitelman 2006: 4). They become geo-transmission, in which the encoded messages are replaced by portions of frozen prehistoric life.

*

Friedrich Kittler, by specifying his approach to the media, built the famous triad—gramophone, film, and typewriter (Kittler 1999). He treats these media as technologies for a deconstruction of the existing, primary model of the medium, which is writing. In his model, people from active writing agents become inscription surfaces for new technologies (Kittler 1999: 210). Submitted by Dukaj to the critical reflection and experimental exposure to the novel's *ćmiatło*, another triad of the media brings different deconstructive possibilities. The film, the black parody of which is a séance, the photography that captures shadows instead of objects, and the sluggish and incomprehensible telegraph of the ice world, the Mammoth Roads, deconstructed in the novel, realize the possibility of building broader "ironic" media theory, which would be based on an antithesis, on pointing to the domination of noise and incomprehension, on showing communication delays that could dominate the speed of providing information. This deconstructive approach would mean picking cracks and illogicality in the dominant discourse of media theory, it would be related to the glitch poetics.

On the other hand, deconstructive media theory, inspired by Dukaj's not entirely translatable word-formation creations, could draw from this misapprehension. Can the media, by definition, communicate faults and falsehood and understatement?⁹ Can you imagine technologies which communicate nonobviousness and intentionally cause delays? It seems that many concepts related to the research of deception and surveillance technology, as well as the interpretation of contemporary fake news or deepfakes, could draw from this approach. Concepts of Zielinski's media anarchaeology (Zielinski 2006), pointing to the value of blackness in Cubitt's visual media theory of light (Cubitt 2014), also seem to correspond with this approach.

The geological approach to the media in Dukaj's book, in turn, appears to be extremely consistent with the concept of the geology of the media by Jussi Parikka (Parikka 2015). In his view, on the one hand, material residues of the media and related toxic waste may become subject to archaeological analyses. On the other hand, Parikka focused on materiality of minerals and elements sourced from Earth and required for production of media devices. He also indicated that the environment can be understood as a medium, for example, when it captures and registers the geological and chemical transformations of our planet. In the passage devoted to glaciers, this is how they are treated: as recording devices (Parikka 2015: 84). Dukaj's ice world seems to generate the metaphorical exemplification of the phenomena discussed by Parikka, and the ice ecosystem and the role of *ćmiatło* in this system become a critical tool for looking at the media around us.

Finally, it remains to ask what, in the context of *ćmietlana* media theory, is associated with Father—the most important figure of the novel. It seems that this metaphor may occur to be more understandable in light of the geology of the media. In one of the most important scenes of the work, in which Benedykt Gierosłowski finds his father in the Siberian wilderness, he proves to be a Frankensteinian creature, artificially held by the ice that after the thaw breaks down into fragments of the body of a previously alive man. Thus, Father only seems to be the "so-called human" ("so-called Man," "der sogenannte Mensch"), as Kittler defined the essence of humanity, pointing to our disappearance as cognitive and self-determined agents (Kittler 1999). Father, as a hybrid of the ice, frozen flesh, and memories, communicates with his son in a greatly limited way before final disintegration. He ironically becomes a message generated, or rather "spat out," by the ice on the Mammoth Roads; the Figure of Father Frost thus embodies one of the most important philosophical issues that Benedykt has repeatedly discussed. It is related to the statement that "history is a form of communication between man and God." This issue is an attempt at a coherent approach to three orders—metaphysical, biological, and technological. Father, as a hybrid creature with unclear ontology, is at the same time divine in his supernatural possibilities and images of the people of Siberia, historical as history is personified in the book by the ice, and also human due to potential to accumulate memories of his human life on the Roads of the Dead (the ice "geotechnology" of memory) and integration with the ice of the biological remains of his body.

Notes

1 In quotations we use Polish edition from 2016 divided into three volumes (Dukaj 2016a) (Dukaj 2016b) (Dukaj 2016c).
2 Dukaj has referred here to the archaic meaning of the Polish word *luty*—February as *zimny*—cold, *mroźny*—frosty.
3 The combination of the Polish words *zimny*—cold and *żelazo*—iron.
4 In Dukaj's work, *ćmiatło* is not the only word in the family of words composed of a combination of root words derived from the root words of *ćmić*—dim and *światło*—light. In the novel, there is also a noun *ćmieczka* (like *świeczka*—a candle), an adjective *ćmietlny* (like *świetlny*—luminous) or a verb *odćmieczyć* (to suck out *ćmiatło*)—this one should derive from the verb *odświeczyć*; however, such a form does not exist in Polish; the current form is *odświetlić* (illuminate). If we were to follow the word-formation rules, then a verb *odćmietlić/odćmietlać*, like illuminate: lighten, ablaze, reflect, should appear in the text.
5 German *frieren*—to freeze.
6 See the quotation from the book: "In relation to the nest, *soplicowo* is what the nest is in relation to a single *frosten*. But in the case of *soplicowo*, we know exactly that it is something more than a simple assemblage of *frostens*. The photographs captured trapped in the ice fragments of agricultural equipment, household items, half the table, a pot, an icon, a part of an anvil, and less durable items like a cereal crumpet, a bunch of onions, a ring of sausage, and parts of human and animal bodies, and their internal organs, and objects that are completely impossible to recognize in this black and white picture. The ice formations seem to correspond with their shape to the props enclosed in them. A sloping icicle rising from the ground, in which a quarter of an obese woman hangs over the plain, is crowned with a strange caricature of a human foot" (Dukaj 2016a: 54–5).
7 Sconce described historical instances of a religious approach to the telegraph related to the spiritualist movement. Spiritualists believed that the living can contact with the dead through séances, and that contact with the medium took place through the "spiritual telegraph," see the chapter "Mediums and Media" in (Sconce 2000).
8 Although Csíkszentmihályi's flow theory arose on the psychological grounds, we place it within media theory as it has a huge impact on its various areas, for example, game studies.
9 Compare to the book "Deceitful Media" (Natale 2021), in which the author considers Artificial Intelligence as such a deceitful medium.

Works Cited

Baudry, J. L. (1986), "The Apparatus: Metapsychological Approaches to the Impression of Reality in Cinema," in Philip Rosen (ed), *Narrative, Apparatus, Ideology: A Film Theory Reader*, New York, NY: Columbia University Press, 299–318.

Berelson, B., Gaudet, H., and Lazarsfeld, P. F. (1944), *The People's Choice. How the Voter Makes up His Mind in a Presidential Campaign*, New York: Duell, Sloan & Pearce.

Burik, S. (2019), "Darkness and Light: Absence and Presence in Heidegger, Derrida, and Daoism," *Dao*, 18 (3): 347–70.

Csikszentmihalyi, M. (1990), *Flow: The Psychology of Optimal Experience*, 1st edition, New York: Harper & Row.

Cubitt, S. (2014), *The Practice of Light: A Genealogy of Visual Technologies from Prints to Pixels*, Leonardo Book Series, Cambridge, MA: The MIT Press.

Deleuze, G., and Guattari, F. (1987), *A Thousand Plateaus: Capitalism and Schizophrenia*, Minneapolis: University of Minnesota Press.

Derrida, J. (2010 [1978]), *Writing and Difference*, ed. Alan Bass, Transferred to digital print 2006, Repr. Routledge Classics. London: Routledge.

Dukaj, J. (2016a), *Lód. 1 1*, Kraków: Wydawnictwo Literackie.

Dukaj, J. (2016b), *Lód. 2 2*, Kraków: Wydawnictwo Literackie.

Dukaj, J. (2016c), *Lód. 3 3*, Kraków: Wydawnictwo Literackie.

Flusser, V. (2000 [1983]), *Towards a Philosophy of Photography*, London: Reaktion Books.

Gitelman, L. (2006), *Always Already New: Media, History and the Data of Culture*, Cambridge, MA: MIT Press.

Kittler, F. A. (1999), *Gramophone, Film, Typewriter*, Writing Science, Stanford, CA: Stanford University Press.

Natale, S. (2021), *Deceitful Media: Artificial Intelligence and Social Life after the Turing Test*, 1st edition, New York, NY: Oxford University Press.

Parikka, J. (2015), *A Geology of Media*, Electronic Mediations, vol. 46, Minneapolis and London: University of Minnesota Press.

Sconce, J. (2000), *Haunted Media: Electronic Presence from Telegraphy to Television*, Console-Ing Passions, Durham, NC: Duke University Press.

Thacker, E. (2003), "What Is Biomedia?," *Configurations*, 11 (1): 47–79.

Williams, R. (1992 [1974]), *Television: Technology and Cultural Form*, ed. Ederyn Williams, London: Routledge.

Zielinski, S. (2006), *Deep Time of the Media: Toward an Archaeology of Hearing and Seeing by Technical Means*, Electronic Culture: History, Theory, Practice, Cambridge, MA: MIT Press.

7

Darshan: Vision as Touch and the Stakes of Immediacy

(Origin Hindi)

Kajri Jain

Scenes of translation

In "The Ochre Robe", *Agehananda Bharati writes,* "*There is absolutely no parallel to the conception of darshan in any religious act in the West* ...".
(Eck 1998: 6; Bharati 1970: 161)[1]

This line is from an influential book first published in 1981 by Diana L. Eck (currently Professor of Comparative Literature and Indian Studies at Harvard Divinity School), which instituted *darshan* as a famously untranslatable, South Asia-specific conception of the gaze. That this untranslatability is itself necessarily mediated via multiple sites of translation is made doubly evident by the fact that the Hindu Dasanami monk whom Eck cites here, Agehananda Bharati, was also an Indologist and a professor of Anthropology at Syracuse University, born in Austria as Leopold Fischer (he was conscripted as an interpreter for the German army's Free India Legion during the Second World War).

This essay will briefly sketch the intellectual journey of this much-discussed concept in its "untranslatability," through its various deployments in the Anglophone academy after emerging from European philological scholarship on classical Sanskrit texts.[2] It does so to point to another possible direction in this journey. Here it moves from the politically fraught presentation of *darshan* as a specifically—if not essentially—"Indian" modality of vision to a different type of attention in recent scholarship to contemporary deployments of classical Indian philosophical concepts in lived social experience, particularly in relation to untouchability, touch, and the sensorium of caste. It seeks, in the process, to disassociate untranslatability from indexing "cultural" difference. Instead, it brings mutuality and deconstructive play back into the problematic, and relatively recent, formulation of "cultures" *as* essentially different (Trouillot 2003)—a formulation that elides the relational circumstances, not least colonialism, that made comparisons possible in the first place. I use the Anglophone career of *darshan* to demonstrate how a media philosophical approach to the complexity of everyday knowledge and experience in postcolonial spaces must contend with the Eurocentrism *both* of the legacies of Orientalist knowledge *and* of immanent critiques of hegemonic Western frames. Further, since all spaces are postcolonial spaces in that they exist in the wake of colonialisms past and present, in such an understanding this and other putatively untranslatable concepts may have greater resonance across contexts than considered so far.

The Visual Turn

Darshan entered circulation in the Anglophone academy from religious studies as a concept describing South Asian devotional engagements with divine or otherwise auspicious and powerful bodies, including icons and gurus, but also extending to holy sites (shrines, landscapes). Its Sanskrit root *drish* means "glance" or "look," but what makes it untranslatable is its simultaneous connotation of seeing and being in the presence of an image, person, or place. *Darshan* has a transactional quality; as Eck points out, people commonly speak of "taking" *darshan*, while a revered personage "gives" *darshan*. Against a Cartesian model of the gaze that institutes a distinction between subjects/agents and objects, *darshan* is framed as a reciprocal, two-way exchange: "it is not only the worshiper who sees the deity, but the deity sees the worshiper as well. The contact between devotee and deity is exchanged through the eyes" (Eck 1998: 6–7). Crucially, Eck outlines the conception of vision in practices of *darshan* as a form of contact or touch. Here she draws on the Dutch Indologist Jan Gonda's study of vision in Vedic texts (he never actually visited Asia), and the Viennese art historian Stella Kramrisch, who synthesized extensive on-site observation with canonical Sanskrit textual prescriptions in a two-volume study, *The Hindu Temple*. Eck cites Kramrisch:

> Seeing, according to Indian notions, is a going forth of sight towards the object. Sight touches it and acquires its form. Touch is the ultimate connection by which the visible yields to being grasped. While the eye touches the object, the vitality that pulsates in it is communicated ...
>
> (Kramrisch 1976: 136; Eck 1998: 9)

Kramrisch's conflation of "Indian" with "Hindu" and "Hindu" with ancient Sanskrit texts and classical temples was standard operating procedure for Indologists of that era, and indeed beyond. This played into both implicitly and explicitly Hindu-hegemonic civilizational discourses whose baleful hierarchical and exclusionary effects continue to shape Indian social and political life (I return to these below).

Darshan was quickly mobilized beyond religious studies by various disciplines dealing with South Asian images, including anthropology, cinema and media studies, and art history/visual culture. Here it was placed on a continuum with broader South Asian invocations of a tactile, efficacious gaze such as the Persian term *nazar* (Ruffle 2020), extending to non-ritual scenarios such as the evil eye or the gaze between lovers (Taylor 2003; Dean 2011).[3] However, despite the identification of *darshan*'s key feature as the inextricability of sight and touch, and an insistence on devotion as a multisensory experience, all these expansions remained firmly within the primary organizing frame of visuality. If this stemmed from the obvious centrality of images in much Hindu worship, it also rested on an unquestioned assumption that the most salient modality of engagement with images is a visual one. In this regard, attention to *darshan* arose from a specific context of translation: the "visual turn" in the Anglophone humanities and social sciences following the uptake of critical theory and the emergence of film, media, and cultural studies in the 1960s and 1970s.

This is abundantly clear from Eck's treatment. Consider the sequence of subheads in her book's first chapter, itself titled "Seeing the Sacred Image" (nothing about touch here): A. Darshan; B. The Visible India; C. Film Images. Even as she writes that, "In the Indian context, seeing is a kind of touching," on the next page we hear that "India is a visual and visionary culture, one in which the eyes have a prominent role in the apprehension of the sacred" (Eck 1998: 9, 10).[4] Touch, in this account, merely ends up modulating vision as a form of knowledge, although here vision is "not only an activity of the eye" but also a matter of inner, "visionary" perception (regrettably, if unavoidably, consistent with Orientalist stereotypes of the mystical East; Eck 1998: 9). We gain no sense of how touch in this "visionary culture" organizes relations among bodies: of deities, people, and images.

Embracing the Haptic

A similar primacy of the visual frame, but now opening onto bodies, appears in a key article following Eck's book that same year by the anthropologist of religion Lawrence Babb. As suggested by its title, "Glancing: Visual Interaction in Hinduism," Babb's main concern is again with visuality and the gaze; he combines an ethnographic analysis of ritual practices in two Hindu sects with a section on a mythological film. However, in his emphasis on "interaction" and reciprocity in the religious gaze, *darshan* re-emerges as a flow of material substance. Babb's ethnography echoes the conception of vision as a form of fluid touch in the textually based citation from Kramrisch above (although his account ultimately takes this in a psychologistic direction):

> In the Hindu world "seeing" is clearly not conceived as a passive product of sensory data originating in the outer world, but rather seems to be imaged as an extrusive and acquisitive "seeing flow" that emanates from the inner person, outward through the eyes, to engage directly with objects seen, and to bring something of those objects back to the seer. One comes into contact with, and in a sense becomes, what one sees.
>
> (Babb 1981: 396–7)

Further, Babb is keenly aware that in "trying to make a point about vision" his essay "greatly simplifies what is actually a very complex conception," particularly when it comes to the role of sound (Babb 1981: 401, n4).

Babb's footnotes and acknowledgments indicate that he was influenced by the anthropologist McKim Marriott's formulation of Hindu bodies as "dividual." By contrast with the "individual" subjects of Western modernity's self-understanding, "dividuals" are porously co-constituted (as we now say) through fluid, processual transactions of variously purity- or pollution-laden substances across ritually charged social situations including worship, but not confined to that (Marriott 1976). Marriott's path-breaking (albeit essentializing) work pre-empted elements of the later "new materialist" turns to embodiment, the senses, performativity, materiality, affect, and distributed agency. Babb's uptake of Marriot's formulation in relation to *darshan* provided the segue to a focus on corporeality in the scholarship on South Asian popular images and devotion in general. This dovetailed with the consolidation in the 1990s of feminist, art historical, postcolonial, phenomenological, and other critiques of post-Enlightenment ocularcentrism and the Cartesian mind-body split.[5]

A paradigmatic instance of the emphasis on embodiment in the *darshanic* scene at this moment, inspired by Babb, Walter Benjamin, and Maurice Merleau-Ponty, is the anthropologist Christopher Pinney's neologism "corpothetics" (Babb 1981: 261; Pinney 2004: 8–9). This invokes a multisensory, corporeal, tactile aesthetics that responds to the icon's own embodiment of the deity as a receptacle for divine presence: an embodiment that Pinney extends beyond statues in temples to reproduced photographs and prints.[6] Corpothetics is opposed to colonial "anaesthetics" or "dominant class 'Western' practices, which privilege a disembodied, unidirectional and disinterested vision" (Pinney 2004: 18–19, 193). For Pinney, this aesthetic is not confined to South Asia: he signals the "continuities and resonances" of "*darshan*-related practices" with "popular visual practices elsewhere" (Pinney 2004: 193).

This treatment of *darshan* takes a Subaltern Studies inspired approach, ranging dominance and resistance along binary axes: colonizer *vs.* colonized; elite *vs.* popular; Kantian aesthetics *vs.* embodied corpothetics. Consequently, the critique of ocularcentrism turns *darshan* into a site of subalternity. Here, as is often the case, scholarly attention to the body slides into uncritically valorizing corporeality and the haptic as somehow inherently resistant. What this binary model leaves out, however, are the multiple forms of hegemony and oppression *within* the colonized or the "popular," in this case those of gender and caste. So here again, as with the visual turn, the very embrace of the corporeal plunges *darshan* into another scene of translation with its own elisions in relation to *darshanic* touch. Presupposing the hegemony of Aristotelian, Cartesian, and/or Kantian orderings of the senses (or of theories of spectatorship or spectacle that uphold the primacy of certain understandings of vision) reinforces a kind of meta-hegemony, for it consolidates and re-centers putatively hegemonic Western regimes of the senses at the expense of other hierarchical regimes that might actually be more germane to much subaltern experience in South Asia.[7]

Spatiality and the Senses

Given these unquestioned assumptions in discussions of *darshan* about the nature and force of vision, it is unsurprising that a major breakthrough should come from a material culture oriented scholar of smell and aromatics in South Asian religions, James McHugh. Drawing on classical texts, reconstructions of the aromatic materials these texts describe, and accounts and observation of rituals, McHugh argues for an "intersensorial" (note: not "multisensory") understanding of *darshan* that draws on the varying but in some ways overlapping philosophies of the senses in pre-Islamic South Asian Hindu, Buddhist, and Jain traditions (McHugh 2007, 2011, 2013). Of particular interest here is an ordering principle of the senses that is shared across early Buddhist phenomenological analyses, a foundational text of Ayurvedic medicine, and ritual manuals for the spatial organization of Hindu temples, in which a key distinction between the senses is the rapidity and proximity—that is, the immediacy or otherwise—of their activation or address (Colas 2005: 26–7; McHugh 2011).

In this spatiotemporal logic, sight works at the greatest distance, followed by hearing, smell, taste, and touch. This phenomenologically tracks the devotee's approach to the temple icon in its sanctum, from *darshan* (as vision), to the smell of incense and flowers, the taste of sanctified *prasad* (ritual food offerings) and holy water, and some form of *sparshan* (touch): heat from a lamp, ashes, vermilion, or flowers, even the feet of the icon—for those who are permitted that kind of access. This permission did not traditionally extend to those abjected by the caste order, the "Untouchables" as they were known during the colonial period, now self-identifying as Dalit or oppressed. Nor did it include women in the ritually polluted state of menstruation. Both forms of exclusion are now unconstitutional but subject to legal loopholes, informal adherence, and politicized controversy. McHugh does not address the temporal aspects of access to the divine, but Samuel Parker notes how, in South India, temporally delimited cyclical festivals bringing designated icons out of temples for public procession provided *darshan* to those excluded from the sanctum. Parker also relates the elaborate carvings on temple towers (*gopuram*s), visible yet unreachable, to a similar function (Parker 2008: 149).

What does this tightly controlled spectrum of mediation and access to the divine do to the conflation of vision with touch at the heart of *darshan*? In a 2012 overview, religion scholar John E. Cort cites McHugh to support his argument that the monolithic account of *darshan* needs nuancing through attention to Jain understandings where *darshanic* seeing, unlike in many Hindu philosophies, does not involve physical contact or a reciprocated gaze (Cort 2012: 9, citing McHugh: 170, n45).[8] Cort also takes up McHugh's intersensorial approach to focus on singing hymns as activating an affective "muscle memory" in the worshipper's throat. But again, this enthusiasm for affect ignores the broader context for McHugh's assertions, where vision's advantage as a "hands-off" form of contact is geared toward avoiding the inauspicious effects of ritual pollution (McHugh 2011: 170–1). There is a hierarchical "distribution of the sensible" at work here: the sensory infrastructure of the social/political regime of caste (Rancière 2005; Jain 2021).

In *darshan* of an auspicious body or site, visual contact is usually considered less efficacious than the more spatially proximate contact of the skin. By the same logic, pollution via physical touch—including the touch of an "Untouchable"—has traditionally been more perilous for caste Hindus than an inauspicious sight or smell. However, even the latter can precipitate purificatory rituals since, as canonical accounts of *darshan* suggest in relation to sight, all the senses are ultimately considered varieties of touch. Why else would a Brahmin cross the street to avoid even the shadow of a Dalit? Cort does not attend to these deeper, caste-related implications of McHugh's cautiously insightful framing of the spatiotemporal logic of the senses: "The structures of worship spaces might therefore be productively analyzed as exploiting the phenomenology of materials in order to regiment perceptions, not just positively but also negatively, hierarchically, and quite possibly politically" (McHugh 2011: 169).

Experience in and against Translation

For the political implications of McHugh's insights on the sensory regimes of pre-modern South Asian ritual spaces to gain traction in the Anglophone academy, they needed to move from scenes of translation by Indological religious, anthropological, or art historical study to one of sensing and making sense of social experience in and of South Asia in the present: a present where gender- and caste-based discrimination, vilification, and violence are inescapable social facts. This experience is the focus of a burgeoning discussion of the senses in relation to caste and untouchability (Guru and Sarukkai 2012 and 2019; Rao ed. 2013; Guru 2016; Lee 2017; Jaaware 2019). For instance, in *Caste, Experience, and the Everyday Social* (2019), Gopal Guru and Sundar Sarukkai argue for an intersensory understanding of the social that challenges the primacy of vision as a basis for knowledge, and the attendant distinction between subjects and objects of social theory. But rather than simply celebrating touch or the other senses, their account describes how *all* the senses inform *both* egalitarian or resistant *and* hierarchical practices of the social. Sound and smell receive the most thorough treatment here, including via McHugh, since these are well suited to their idea of the social as invisible yet pervasively sensible. The social for them is a kind of atmosphere, like the "wind" that carries smell (Guru and Sarukkai 2019: 57); sound is a *vyapti* or pervasion that enables strangers to "socialesce," to coalesce into sociality (62–3). Smell is closely related to taste and touch, again as a form of contact.

Neither McHugh nor Guru and Sarukkai explicitly frame a discussion of *darshan* within contemporary political stakes.[9] Doing so, however, reveals a capacious assemblage of sense regimes whose "untranslatable" translation of sight to touch is shared between *darshan* and untouchability. *Darshan* and untouchability emerge as different aspects of the same set of charged fluid transactions: *darshan* shares in intersensorial flows of auspicious presence where viewing, hearing, tasting, and smelling are all desirable forms of touching as proximity; untouchability is the avoidance by distancing of pollution via senses that are ultimately interconvertible with touch within a logic of shared material substance.[10] This sensorium is informed by multiple traditions of thought and practice with varied conceptions of the nature and workings of sense-perception and consciousness, as well as the objects and media of perception—and indeed, the very distinction between subjects and objects. These conceptions remain at odds with those of secular post-Enlightenment European traditions, *as well as their critiques,* even as these European traditions are also efficacious in South Asia.

What these South Asian traditions appear to share, to the extent that they inform social experience in the present across religious boundaries, is an idea of proximity to truth, power, and/or the divine achieved through a form of material contact that includes but also exceeds *sparshan*, the touch of skin. In this sensorium, caste and gender untouchability includes but also exceeds physical touch. All the senses are mediated via matter, such that touch is on the one hand generalized and spatialized, interconvertibly with the other senses, and on the other it is a singular sense (*sparshan*). The singular term "touch" does not distinguish between the two. In this sensible regime, where flows of sense data are organized in terms of spatiotemporal access to an ultimate truth, questions of perception, knowledge, experience, and ethics unfold as issues of immediacy: of shared or exclusionary spaces and times. This regime undergirds hierarchies encompassing caste, gender, and species both mortal and supernatural, a distribution of the sensible that surely perpetuates the obdurate force of untouchability, its material infrastructure reinforced every day in millions of acts of *darshan*, grand and humble. This has come into further assemblage with other forces, not least those of governmentality and the global flows of bodies and matter attendant on capitalism. Here the discourses and practices of hygiene, toxicity, and ritual pollution coalesce: we know how to keep matter in its proper place; we have always known "social distancing."[11]

Framing *darshan* via untouchability offers a powerful corrective to the approach of the Anglophone academy so far, with its local, "provincial" presuppositions and enthusiasms: its post-textual visual turn, its love affair with corporeality, and indeed its new materialist excitement about the agency of things (for instance Ruffle 2020; in a sensorium where subjects are not quite intact agentive bourgeois individuals but constituted by flows of matter, surely the question of agency is vexed both for people and for things). But how context-specific, how "untranslatable" is this sensorium? For Guru and Sarukkai, as for Agehananda Bharati in the opening quote, the sensible regime described here is specific to "the everyday socials of societies like the Indian and many similar non-Western societies" (Guru and Sarukkai 2019: 17). However, if we think of the "West" as co-constituted with and by "non-Western" societies through the massive project of European colonialism, we can refuse the obfuscation of colonialism's epistemic legacies by recognizing the translations at the heart of untranslatability, and returning our analyses to everyday sociality everywhere. In the case of *darshan*, this means challenging the hegemonic commonsense of the hegemony of vision and the generalized celebration of the haptic in the concomitant critique of ocularcentrism, so as to reformulate touch-as-immediacy not as something to valorize, but as a mediatic infrastructure of oppression. This opens the way to bringing untouchability into conversation with other regimes of spatiotemporal exclusion and violent touch—including those of structural racism and gender oppression in the heart of Western modernity, with its legacies of slavery, indenture, settler colonialism, and heteropatriarchalism. That would be to inhabit other, differently efficacious, scenes of translation.

Notes

1 While Eck and others use diacritics, given the non-specialist readership of this volume I have substituted the more intuitive Romanized spellings of South Asian terms. Many thanks to Anusha Sudhindra Rao for her research assistance and to participants in the University of Toronto, Mississauga's Centre for South Asian Civilizations Works-in-Progress Workshop, particularly Srilata Raman and Francis Cody, for their enormously helpful and generous feedback on a draft of this essay.
2 For a detailed overview of *darshan* as a "super-category," see Cort (2012). As will become clear, however, Cort's aims are different from mine: his are historicizing and spatializing, while mine are more "contemporanising" in the temporally nonlinear sense outlined by Banerjee et al. (2016) in their comparativist approach to theory.
3 Indeed, in another act of translation, Karen Ruffle's account of Shia Muslim "visuality" explicitly supplements the Hinduism-centric term *darshanic* with the Islamicate *nazranic* (Ruffle 2020).
4 Subsection C ("Film Images") goes on to discuss cinematic and photographic images of Indian rituals as ways of understanding religious practices, citing Rudolf Arnheim and Susan Sontag. The book was intended as a companion to an annotated list of audio-visual materials for college teaching (Cort 2012: 6).
5 For instance Butler (1990), Crary (1990), Mitchell (1991), Jay (1993), and Grosz (1994). The scholarship on South Asian images in this vein includes Babb and Wadley (1995); Brosius and Butcher (1999); Ramaswamy (2003); Pinney (2004); Jain (2007).
6 Richard Davis makes a distinction between the "aesthetics of presence" characterizing Hindu temple icons as embodiments of the divine and a

"semiotic aesthetics ... conveying a message separate from the image itself" (Davis 1999: 32). This embodiment of presence is similar to what Hans Belting (1994) describes for Christian icons.

7   An instance from cinema studies of a valorization of the corporeal and the haptic that unwittingly serves to reinforce the hegemony of the hegemony of the visual, explicitly within a scene of "intercultural" translation, is Marks 2000. At another scale, this is homologous to the way postcolonialism was reappropriated through the 1990s to focus attention on easily recognizable and assimilable objects of study pertaining to the colonial encounter, at the expense of actually engaging the complex histories and life-experiences of the colonized. This meant, for instance, Western universities "diversifying" English departments while closing down programs in South Asian languages.

8   In this footnote the admirably careful McHugh adds the caveat that "we always need to be extremely cautious of assuming that philosophical and ritual theories always operate seamlessly as one coherent system." While this supports Cort's emphasis on the specificity of North Indian Digambar Jain practices, it also suggests that there is some overlap between different theories and systems, not to mention inconsistencies between theory and practice. I can attest to this from personal experience, given the range of Hindu ritual practices that my own North Indian Digambar Jain extended family adopts in varying contexts.

9   McHugh discusses *darshan* but not in the present; Guru and Sarukkai discuss the present but not *darshan*. An obvious issue here is the ahistorical use of ancient texts to think about contemporary experience—hence McHugh's hesitancy, but Guru and Sarukkai's analysis deploys concepts from Nyaya philosophy (see commentaries in Rao 2013). Banerjee et al. (2016) challenge the Eurocentric asymmetries in distinguishing "theoretical" as opposed to "historical" concepts, pointing out that issues of anachronism are seldom raised when recent thinkers invoke Greek philosophy. Further, scholars of caste, religion, art, medicine, and other arenas of praxis demonstrate how canonical texts and performative prescriptions based on earlier philosophical traditions undeniably inform everyday practices in South Asia (Davis 1999; Holdrege 2015). But this happens in messy ways: practices do not neatly correspondence to theories; current practices do not always follow "original" texts (to the extent that these are available or even specifiable), instead mobilizing translations and reformulations; practices are not consistent within "subjects" of experience or categories of identity. These overlapping fields of efficacy of South Asia's multiple philosophical, aesthetic, and practical traditions—including those of "Western" modernity and modernism—extend to the ongoing, historically layered, palimpsestic presence not only of accruing texts but also of built and crafted forms, and the practices that they call forth.

10 Similarly, though not in the context of untouchability *per se*, Melanie Dean sees the *aratti* or priestly circling of the icon with a camphor flame as removing any traces of the inauspicious "evil eye" of worshippers (Dean 2011). In her study of the evil eye in South India, Dean argues that auspicious *darshan* and the inauspicious evil eye partake of the same logic of material flows, whose attendant rituals have ramifications for the performance of social status.
11 Ashish Rajadhyaksha (2020) relates the social proximities that initiate re-distancing back to processes of globalization and the migration of laboring bodies.

Works Cited

Babb, L. A. (1981), "Glancing: Visual Interaction in Hinduism," *Journal of Anthropological Research*, 37 (4) (1981): 387–401.

Babb, L. A., and Wadley, S. S. (eds) (1995), *Media and the Transformation of Religion in South Asia*, Philadelphia: University of Pennsylvania Press.

Banerjee, Prathama, Nigam, A., and Pandey, R. (2016), "The Work of Theory: Thinking across Traditions," *Economic and Political Weekly*, LI (37) (Sept. 10, 2016): 42–50.

Belting, H. (1994), *Likeness and Presence: A History of the Image before the Era of Art*, Chicago and London: University of Chicago Press.

Bharati, A. (1970), *The Ochre Robe*, New York: Doubleday.

Brosius, C. and Butcher, M. (eds) (1999), *Image Journeys: Audio-Visual Media and Cultural Change in India*, New Delhi: Sage Publications.

Butler, J. (1990), *Gender Trouble: Feminism and the Subversion of Identity*, New York and London: Routledge.

Colas, G. (2005), "Rites among Vaikhanāsas and Related Matters: Some Methodological Issues," in Jörg Gengnagel, Ute Hüsken, and Srilata Raman (eds), *Words and Deeds: Hindu and Buddhist Rituals in South Asia*, Wiesbaden: Harrassowitz, 23–44.

Cort, J. E. (2012), "Situating Darsan: Seeing the Digambar Jina Icon in Eighteenth- and Nineteenth-Century North India," *International Journal of Hindu Studies*, 16 (1): 1–56.

Crary, J. (1990), *Techniques of the Observer: On Vision and Modernity in the Nineteenth Century*, Cambridge, MA: MIT Press.

Davis, R. (1991), *Ritual in an Oscillating Universe: Worshipping Shiva in Medieval India*, Princeton, NJ: Princeton University Press.

Davis, R. (1999), *Lives of Indian Images*, Princeton, NJ: Princeton University Press.

Dean, M. (2011), "From Darśan to Tirusti: 'Evil Eye' and the Politics of Visibility in Contemporary South India," unpublished doctoral dissertation, University of Pennsylvania. *Dissertations available from ProQuest.* AAI3485603. https://repository.upenn.edu/dissertations/AAI3485603

Eck, D. L. (1998; first published 1981), *Darśan: Seeing the Divine Image in India*, New York: Columbia University Press.

Grosz, E. (1994), *Volatile Bodies: Toward a Corporeal Feminism*, St. Leonards: Allen and Unwin.

Guru, G. (2016), "Aesthetic of Touch and the Skin: An Essay in Contemporary Indian Political Phenomenology," in Arindam Chakrabarti (ed.), *The Bloomsbury Research Handbook of Indian Aesthetics and the Philosophy of Art*, London and New York: Bloomsbury, 297–315.

Guru, G. and Sarukkai, S. (2012), *The Cracked Mirror: An Indian Debate on Experience and Theory*, Delhi: Oxford University Press.

Guru, G. and Sarukkai, S. (2019), *Experience, Caste and the Everyday Social*, New Delhi: Oxford University Press, 2019.

Holdrege, B. A. (2015), *Bhakti and Embodiment: Fashioning Divine Bodies and Devotional Bodies in Krsna Bhakti*, Abingdon: Routledge.

Jaaware, A. (2019), *Practicing Caste: On Touching and Not Touching*, Hyderabad: Orient Black Swan.

Jain, K. (2007), *Gods in the Bazaar: The Economies of Indian "Calendar Art"*, Durham, NC: Duke University Press.

Jain, K. (2021), *Gods in the Time of Democracy*, Durham, NC: Duke University Press.

Jay, M. (1993), *Downcast Eyes: The Denigration of Vision in Twentieth-Century French Thought*, Berkeley: University of California Press.

Kramrisch, S. (1976; first published 1946), *The Hindu Temple*, vol. 2, Delhi: Motilal Banarsidass.

Lee, J. (2017), "Odor and Order: How Caste Is Inscribed in Space and Sensoria," *Comparative Studies of South Asia, Africa and the Middle East*, 37 (3): 470–90.

Marks, L. U. (2000), *The Skin of the Film: Intercultural Cinema, Embodiment, and the Senses*, Durham, NC: Duke University Press.

Marriott, M. (1976), "Hindu Transactions: Diversity without Dualism," in Bruce Kapferer (ed.), *Transaction and Meaning: Directions in the Anthropology of Exchange and Symbolic Behavior*, Philadelphia: Institute for the Study of Human Issues, 109–42.

McHugh, J. (2007), "The Classification of Smells and the Order of the Senses in Indian Religious Traditions," *Numen*, 54 (4): 374–419.

McHugh, J. (2011), "Seeing Scents: Methodological Reflections on the Intersensory Perception of Aromatics in South Asian Religions," *History of Religions*, 51 (2): 156–77.

McHugh, J. (2013), *Sandalwood and Carrion: Smell in Premodern Indian Religion and Culture*, Oxford: Oxford University Press.

Mitchell, T. (1991), *Colonising Egypt*, Berkeley: University of California Press.

Parker, S. K. (2008), "Sanctum and Gopuram at Madurai: Aesthetics of Akam and Puram in Tamil Temple Architecture," in Martha Ann Selby and Indira V. Peterson (eds), *Tamil Geographies: Cultural Constructions of Space and Place in South India*, Albany: State University of New York Press, 143–72.

Pinney, C. (2004), *"Photos of the Gods": The Printed Image and Political Struggle in India*, London: Reaktion Books.

Rajadhyaksha, A. (2020), "I Hope You've Washed Your Hands": The Rebirth of the Untouchable," *Inter-Asia Cultural Studies*, 21 (4): 566–74.

Ramaswamy, S. (ed.) (2003), *Beyond Appearances? Visual Practices and Ideologies in Modern India*, New Delhi: Sage.

Rancière, J. (2005), *The Politics of Aesthetics*, London and New York: Continuum.

Rao, A. (ed.) (2013), "Kitabkhana," *Comparative Studies of South Asia, Africa and the Middle East*, 33 (3): 378–416.

Ruffle, K. (2020), "Gazing in the Eyes of the Martyrs: Four Theories of South Asian Shi'i Visuality," *Journal of Material Cultures in the Muslim World*, 1: 268–90.

Taylor, W. (2003), "Penetrating Gazes: The Poetics of Sight and Visual Display in Popular Indian Cinema," in Sumathi Ramaswamy (ed.), *Beyond Appearances? Visual Practices and Ideologies in Modern India*, New Delhi: Sage, 297–322.

Trouillot, M. (2003), *Global Transformations: Anthropology and the Modern World*, New York: Palgrave Macmillan.

8

Dhvāni: Resonance

(Origin Sanskrit)

Budhaditya Chattopadhyay

In a keynote given at the Media Art History conference 2015 in Montreal, where I was present, Christine van Assche, the chief curator of Centre Pompidou Paris, proclaimed that sound as an artistic medium and scholarly field will come to the foreground in the next ten years and occupy a central position in the contemporary arts and media scholarship. Indeed, within Arts and Humanities, sound studies have established itself as a vibrant and productive academic field since the last decade resulting in a profusion of scholarly and artistic works, including numerous publications, conferences, and major research projects: three consecutive compendia such as *The Routledge Sound Studies Reader* (2012), *The Oxford Handbook of Sound Studies* (2013), and *The Routledge Companion to Sound Studies* (2018) have been complemented with *Journal of Sonic Studies*, *The New Soundtrack* and a number of other peer-reviewed journals that are entirely dedicated to the studies of sound. These publications in the last decade established sound studies as an interdisciplinary field of immense significance receiving wider academic attention within fields of media art history, cultural studies, musicology, digital culture, film and media studies, et al. As we all know here, sound arts too have gained currency in contemporary arts since a number of major exhibitions were held in the last decade, such as *Soundings* (2013) at MoMA, and *The Listening Biennial*.[1]

In this canonical body of work, however, an astounding absence of Global South sound thinkers and artists is observed. The predominant attention clearly has been invested in studying sound within a Euro-American media cultural context. Sounds in South Asia, Africa, and the Middle East—broadly termed the *Global South*, have largely remained underexplored, although they contribute significantly to global outputs in audiovisual media, South Asia being the largest producer. Yet sound studies and sonic arts largely ignore voices of sound thinkers and practitioners from the Global South. Does that mean non-Europeans cannot think critically in the realm of sound and listening? If we make an effort in assessing some of the literature and aesthetic experiences in sound and listening in South Asia alone, we find a different narrative. There are important treatises existing in South Asia, for example, *Dhvāni Theory*, having the potential not only to enrich the field but also radically reconfigure and address some unresolved areas in sound studies, for example, temporality, subjectivity, and chance. This is the reason why early figures in sonic arts, such as John Cage and La Monte Young changed the course of their artistic trajectories to redefine sound practice in the West upon engaging with sonic thoughts from South Asia, for example, *Dhvāni*.

Cage and Dhvāni

John Cage underwent a composer's block in the 1940s and was going through a lack of enthusiasm for public performance. His compositions were not appreciated well by the public, and he became quite disillusioned with the idea of art as communication. In the middle of this phase, in 1946, Cage met Gita Sarabhai, an Indian musician who came to the United States concerned about Western influence on the music of South Asia. Sarabhai wanted to spend several months in America, studying Western music. She took lessons in counterpoint and contemporary music with Cage, while she taught him about Indian music in return. Through Sarabhai Cage became acquainted with Indian music, and its sonic aesthetics and philosophy. The purpose of music, according to Sarabhai's teacher in India, was "to sober and quiet the mind, thus rendering it susceptible to divine influences" (Robinson 2011: 180; Chattopadhyay 2022). This definition of chance composition became one of the central philosophies of Cage's view on music, sound, listening, and art impacting his subsequent works.

Around the same time, Cage also began studying Indian art historian Ananda K. Coomaraswamy's works. Among the ideas that influenced Cage was the South Asian aesthetics of rasa and the subjective states of *permanent emotions* (Thampi 1965: 76). According to *Rasa Theory*, these emotions are divided into two groups: four white (humor, wonder, erotic, and heroic) and four black (anger, fear, disgust, and sorrow). They are the first eight of the navarasas or "nine emotions," and they have a common tendency toward the ninth of the navarasas, which is *Santam* or tranquility, a state that was highly endorsed by Gita Sarabhai who believed that the purpose of music and art in general was to quieten the mind, freeing it from the ego, and thus rendering it open to mystical experiences. These ideas resonated very much with Cage, and helped him come out of the composer's block. Drawing ideas from the East and South Asian sound worlds and their aesthetic knowledge systems, such as Dhvāni Theory and resonance (Malik 1999), Cage eventually developed a new style of performative music based on the ideas of indeterminacy whereby certain compositional elements, such as duration, tempo, and other musical dynamics were kept open-ended for chance events. This approach already existed for many of years in South Asian music and sonic performances, for example, Dhrupad and Khayal and in its everyday listening. But this was a novel intervention in Western sound worlds dominated by written scores. This intervention, arguably, was at the heart of the genesis of sound arts—the way it was developed from Cage's work with new sense of temporalities, and inter-subjectivities.

Besides John Cage, other canonical figures in the field of sound arts and music were deeply influenced by South Asian sound practices and thoughts, particularly the Buddhist philosophical thoughts and ways of listening; to name a few, Pauline Oliveros, Eliane Radigue, Terry Riley, Marion Zazeela, and La Monte Young. Young studied under Hindustani practitioner Pandit Pran Nath for thirty years, which fundamentally reshaped his sonic world especially in the formation of American minimalist school of music with a signature fascination for Drone sounds of Tanpura and sustained chords found in South Asian sound performances. I have been researching these intercultural sonic encounters and confluences in my postdoctoral project *Sonic Perspectives from the Global South: Connecting Resonances* (2023).

South Asian Sound Practices and Thoughts

What was new knowledge for Cage and Young while engaging with South Asian sound practices and thoughts? I contend that the new knowledge were the ideas of resonance, temporality, attention, chance, and inter-subjectivity, through which one can comprehend the role of the (sensitive) listener in a shared sonic experience, such as a music performance or improvisation. For these Western-trained artists, sound practices and thoughts in South Asia opened up a whole new world in which the subject—object dichotomy in sound perception held in Western listening traditions, was broken down into a multiplicity of sensing and meaning-making, as suggested by the idea of *Dhvāni*. This multiplicity resonated with the critical thoughts of South Asian aesthetics scholar Ānandavardhana, who proposed the Dhvāni Theory and stated that good performing arts and good poetry should offer many possible interpretations upon its reception. Ānandavardhana (c. 820–90 CE) the author of *Dhvanyāloka* (In the Light of Sound, Bhattacharya 1972) articulated the philosophy of "aesthetic suggestion" (in any sonic expression or Dhvāni). The philosopher Abhinavagupta (c. 950—1016 CE) wrote an important commentary on it, the Locana (The Eye, Gupta 2017). Ānandavardhana is credited with creating the Dhvāni Theory along with later commentaries. He wrote that *Dhvāni* (meaning sound, or resonance) is the "soul" or "essence" (ātman) of human (sonic) expressions, such as a song or poetry. "When the poet writes," said Ānandavardhana, "he creates a resonant field of emotions" (Bhattacharya 1972). To understand the poetry, the reader or hearer must be on the same wavelength with the performer or speaker as an evolving inter-subjectivity. The method requires sensitivity on the parts of both the performer and the listener. Ānandavardhana conceived and expanded the idea of *Dhvāni* from its literal meaning of sound and resonance through a reinterpretation of the concept of *Rasa* (Barlingay 2007) that was central to the seminal text of Indian aesthetics on dramatic and performing arts, *Natyashastra* (fifth century BCE to the seventh–eighth century CE). With Abhinavagupta's significant scholarly contribution to the concept of *Dhvāni* in the eleventh century, these ideas were further expanded into the Dhvāni Theory to comprehend the essence of the aesthetic experience of performing arts and oratory. Ānandavardhana also drew upon the idea of *Sphōta*, another very useful concept for sound studies, meaning sensing and comprehension of a sensory (sonic) experience in a flash or cognitive explosion or bursting out of meanings, after suggestion (*Dhvāni*).

In Indian aesthetic theory, the topic of (inter-)subjectivity and selfhood embedded in sonic phenomena has been discussed in-depth. From S. S. Barlingay's writings (2007), we know a concise explanation about this concept of *Sphōta*, which indicates, "A sound changes into (subjective thinking) and language, and acquires meaning only after a certain explosion of sounds" (Barlingay 2007: 27), as part of an inter-subjective affective association in the listening process. Such a perspective is useful and contributes greatly to current discourses in sound studies in relation to subjectivity and objectivity, for example. The key aspect of the aesthetic conceptualization of sonic and sensory experiences as performed and received in terms of concepts like *Dhvāni* and *Sphōta*, is the way it bridges the dichotomies of subject and object, word and meaning, experience and sensing, sound and listening. Aesthetician and philosopher V. K. Chari notes:

> Dhvani is primarily a theory about levels of meaning. It understands suggestion simply as a special function of language, and it inquires into the conditions in which a word or sentence may give rise to a meaning other than the literal.
>
> (Chari 1977: 392)

Dhvāni is understood then as the principle of suggestion and the essential element to communicate medial and performing arts to the *Sahrdayas* (sensitive listener) in which sounds (e.g., voice, spoken words, and musical or instrumental performance, as well as other oral presentations) transcends the mere vibrational aspects of sound and its source or object (literal meaning) to touch upon an affective resonance with the full consideration for the subjectivity of the listener and his/her/their context or mood. In this theory, the usage of metaphors would not be enough if a performer or poet requires to follow the dictates of logic in the use of language. The true poet, orator, performer, musician or artist, according to *Dhvāni* Theory, uses language creatively. The usage must be necessarily unique in order to create the kind of resonance that connects the listener affectively. Such usage of sound lends itself to creating *Dhvāni* or suggestiveness. Without this element of suggestion there can be no art or poetry.

The aesthetic approach of suggestion in any sonic or oral performance, termed *Dhvāni*, allows negotiation between the realms of reality and appearance. A number of Indian philosophers and aesthetic theorists divided the sonic subject in terms of *Dhvāni* (sound heard by the ear) and *Sphōta* (sound grasped by the intellect), recognizing sound's multiple possible interpretations upon listening (Barlingay 2007). Indian rhetoricians have made meticulous studies of both the meaning and emotive context of sound. According to them, sounds have at least two meanings, one suggestive meaning, which is described as *Dhvāni*, and the other echoing the literal meaning of sound but going beyond it to accommodate the emotive context of the listener as *Sphōta* or "bursting out" of the multitude of sonic associations is released upon its occurrence in the immediate reality, and further in the listener's mind grasping it in inter-subjective contemplation. This perspective on the multiplicity of sonic interpretations helps understanding the issues related to the perception of sound.

Classical South Asian aesthetics emerge from the interpretation of performing arts, for example, songs, elocution, and dance in ritual settings. In addition to analysis of the metaphoric and literal dimensions of language, this aesthetic model relies on an understanding of listener's context and moods that are identified as *Rasa*. South Asian philosophers advanced this inter-subjective conceptualization of sound by propounding the doctrines of *Dhvāni*, and *Sphōta*, by which the highest aesthetic bliss is experienced through suggestion and the performativity of voice and other sounds.

Chance, Connectivity and Inter-Subjectivity— the Dhvāni Project

Addressing this question of affect in sound perception and cognition beyond causality, in my work, I often draw ideas from Dhvāni Theory dealing with the mood (*Rasa*) of the listening subject, inter-subjectivity, and inwardness associated with listening. The consideration for manifold and multilayered sonic experience beyond its object-hood led me to divide sound phenomenon into *Dhvāni* (sound heard by the ear) and *Sphōta* (sound grasped by the intellect), recognizing sound's multiple possible interpretations upon listening. This multiplicity of sonic interpretation helps explain the streams of thoughtful, contemplative states sounds may generate inside the itinerant mind of the listener. Sounds' two meanings, one suggested meaning, described as *Dhvāni*, and the other perceived meaning, as *Sphōta*, helps to resolve issues in sound studies and sonic arts related to selfhood, chance and emergence.

Emphasizing the sonic subject's essentially withdrawn, inward-looking, and contemplative realm of thoughts and its capacity to connect outwardly through an inter-subjective listening, I have made experiments in my own artistic works, especially, in Dhvāni project (2020–3).[2] My argument for advocating an intercultural and inter-sonic confluence as resistance to colonial and neo-colonial imbalances in power manifests in my media artworks, such as Dhvāni, which is a series of self-regulating, responsive, and autonomous installations driven by AI and Machine Learning. It incorporates ritual and traditional practices from South Asia, for example, temple bells, Buddhist Gongs, wind chimes, and Ghungroo, among others. The project emerges from a research creation in re-listening to and re-telling of South Asia's auditory cultural history in the contemporary moment of crisis, informing the AI-driven surveillance and controlled societies of today about the values of inter-connectivity, community and reciprocal ways of life, often found in the ritual practices of the Global South. The work aims to envision a geological equity to hear the Global South, rendering the linear curves of Western-modernity-dominated sense of temporality a recursive one by focusing on memory, and engaging with South Asian performing arts, and the indigenous listening practices. This temporal mélange may help in finding answers to the crises of today, such as climate breakdown, and global inequality. Dhvāni in its exhibitions (2020,[3] 2021[4]) creates fertile, evolving, and autonomous auditory situations that are relational, performative, and participatory, whereby the inter-subjectivity of the listening is considered in an affective context.

This mode of co-creating and co-listening encourages a reciprocal approach in realizing a shared and communal artistic experience through a bio-mimic network of traditional objects, such as temple bells or indigenous wind chimes. Taking an Indian epistemology-informed approach to sound and transcendental listening, the work underscores the role of the listener, inter-subjectivity, and situational context of the audience as the primary triggers toward construing an artistic experience, and examines the role of the "self" against an overarching emphasis on artistic object embraced in the Western art traditions. This shift in perspective and approach toward contingency and new temporalities helps develop an understanding of the value of chance and indeterminacy in sonic and performative experiences, creating temporal disjuncture for a "divine influence" as Indian musician Gita Sarabhai informed John Cage in 1946 (Cage 1973; Robinson 2011: 180). The aim of the project is to reflect on the idea of chance, inter-connectivity, Network, and co-dependence in contemporary societies marred by global pandemic, climate catastrophes, and racial conflicts.

Epilogue

Sound travels from one body to another, and on its path it makes connections. An utterance connects a voice to its listener, and in this way, knowledge is shared in the societies and cultures of the Global South. To me this social capacity of sound is significant. When it comes to Global South concepts like *Dhvāni*, in the West such non-European concepts are either ignored, or appropriated or understood through a colonial-minded "Orientalist ear," but one must acknowledge the profound injustices and inequalities that are concealed under these exotic ontological perspectives. From sound-based curatorial practices to sonic research, non-White artists and scholars have often been denied dignified entry to these fields. The dominant discourses are often Eurocentric, and such Eurocentrism is often celebrated rather than questioned. One must acknowledge that there is a question of affordability— lack of support and funding curtails many of the aspirations in worlds outside Europe, for example, the Global South, and after entering Europe such voices face a new kind of structural inequality. Therefore, before we romanticize on exotic concepts like *Dhvāni* through colonial ears, we need to understand the context in which such terms developed and engage with that historical contextual framework from an interest of critical engagement rather than seeing them as exotic. Contemporary renditions of these concepts and knowledge systems are necessary to unpack in an equitable field of sound (studies and arts).

Notes

1 Further information is available on the website: https://listeningbiennial.net/
2 See the project website with further readings and listening: See: https://budhaditya.org/projects/connecting-resonances/dhvani/

3 The premiere exhibition of the pilot version of Dhvāni project took place at the Experimenta – la Biennale Arts Sciences in Grenoble, 2020. More information to be found on the biennale website: https://www.experimenta.fr/dhvani/
4 A fuller version of the Dhvāni project was premiered at the Rewire Festival 2021, in Den Haag. See: https://www.rewirefestival.nl/artist/budhaditya-chattopadhyay

Works Cited

Barlingay, S. S. (2007), *A Modern Introduction to Indian Aesthetic Theory: The Development from Bharata to Jagannåatha*, New Delhi: D. K. Print World.
Bhattacharya, B. (ed.) (1972), *Dhvanyaloka of Anandavardhana [Uddyota II]*, Edited with an elaborate English exposition, Calcutta: K. L. Mukhopadhyay.
Bull, M. (2018), *The Routledge Companion to Sound Studies*, London: Routledge.
Cage, J. (1973), *M: Writings '67–'72*, Middletown, CT: Wesleyan University Press.
Chandra, A. (2013), "Revisiting Dhvani in the Context of the Aesthetics of Experience in Film," *CINEMA*, 4: 44–61.
Chari, V. K. (1977), "The Indian Theory of Suggestion (dhvani)," in *Philosophy East and West* 27 (4), Honolulu: University of Hawai'i Press, 391–9.
Chattopadhyay, B. (2023), *Sonic Perspectives from the Global South: Connecting Resonances*, New York: Bloomsbury Academic (forthcoming).
Chattopadhyay, B. (2022), *Sound Practices in the Global South: Co-listening to Resounding Plurilogues*, London: Palgrave Macmillan (in press).
Chattopadhyay, B. (2021), "Uncolonising Early Sound Recordings," *The Journal of Media Art Study and Theory*, 2 (2) (Special Issue: Sound, Colonialism, and Power) November 2021, 81–8.
Gupta, Neerja A. (2017), *Abhinavagupta's Comments on Aesthetics in Abhinavabharati and Locana*, Newcastle upon Tyne: Cambridge Scholars Publishing.
Malalasekera, G. P. (1967), "Some Aspects of Reality as Taught by Theravāda Buddhism," in C. A. Moore (ed.), *The Indian Mind: Essentials of Indian Philosophy and Culture*, Honolulu: University of Hawaii Press.
Malik, S. C. (1999), *Dhvani: Nature and Culture of Sound*, New Delhi: Indira Gandhi National Centre for the Arts.
Pinch, T. and Bijsterveld, K. (2013), *The Oxford Handbook of Sound Studies*, New York: Oxford University Press.
Robinson, J. (2011), *John Cage*, Cambridge, MA: The MIT Press.
Sterne, J. (ed.) (2012), *The Routledge Sound Studies Reader*, London: Routledge.
Thampi, G. B. M. (1965), "Rasa as Aesthetic Experience," *The Journal of Aesthetics and Art Criticism*, 24 (1): 75–80.

9

Gestell: Heidegger's Cyborg and the Vicissitudes of the Machine | Body

(Origin German)

Bernd Herzogenrath

Wait a minute, Doc. Are you telling me you built a time machine ... out of a DeLorean?

Marty McFly in *Back To the Future*

While writing this essay, I felt like I was fast-forwarded Back not to the Future, but the late 1980s. Most of the theoretical and cultural references point to this, have that 1980s/1990s vibe ... So, climb into the *Gestell* and enjoy the ride (I hope): If my calculations are correct, when this baby hits eighty-eight miles per hour, you're gonna see some serious s***.

*

The relation of the human to technology has more often than not been reduced to a strategy opposing man and technics. In philosophy, Martin Heidegger occupies a prominent position, having scrupulously questioned this simplistic opposition underlying the Question Concerning Technology, and showing the difficulty of thinking man and technology *together*. For Heidegger, the "world" of the subject is a way of "understanding being," making possible the encounter of people and things. However, there are no things-as-such, waiting for the subject to simply "realize" them as objects in the act of "understanding." Things can "be" in a twofold way: as an object "ready-to-hand" [*Zuhanden*], and as an object "present-at-hand"

A very early draft of this essay appeared in 2000 in the long-defunct online student-journal *Enculturation* as "The Question Concerning Humanity: Obsolete Bodies and (Post)Digital Flesh." *Enculturation* 3.1 (Fall 2000)

[*Vorhanden*]. The object "ready-to-hand" can be roughly equated with both tools and symbolic actions, machines, and speech-acts.

One important method of "making sense of the world" is the "technological understanding of being," which implies an understanding of technology itself. At first, he saw technology basically as a threat because of man's will to control, mastering technology in the service of his own needs. Man-as-subject sees himself as the bottom/reason/foundation of all being, the *Grund allen Seins*. In his later work, however, Heidegger realized that the essence of technology was not a way of subjects using and controlling objects: "that man becomes the subject and the world the object, is a consequence of technology's nature establishing itself, and not the other way around" (Heidegger 1971: 112). Language and technology thus partake in the same subject/object grammar, "enframing" the subject in the dangerous and misleading realm of instrumental reason. This notion of the instrumentality of technology was a concept he sought to dethrone in his essay "The Question Concerning Technology." First, Heidegger states that "the essence of technology is by no means anything technological" (Heidegger 1997a: 287). It is exactly this notion that blocks our understanding of what technology *really* is. In the following, Heidegger deconstructs the *instrumental* interpretation of technology's essence by referring to Aristotle's analysis of the *causa*, ultimately showing that what we see as *causa efficiens*, as the "standard for all causality" (Heidegger 1997a: 291), has a completely different meaning in Aristotle. In Greek thought, the *causa* is nothing instrumental, but a "bringing-forth [that] brings out of concealment into unconcealment" (Heidegger 1997a: 293), and thus has a close relation to the revealing of truth Truth. In contrast to the "revealing" of *physis* (bringing-forth in itself) and *poiesis* (bringing-forth in another), modern technology, though still a mode of revealing [*Entbergen*] and bringing-forth, is "something completely different and therefore new" (Heidegger 1997a: 288). "Technology" comes to signify the efficient ordering of resources: "Everywhere everything is ordered to stand by, to be immediately at hand, indeed to stand there just so that it may be on call for a further ordering. Whatever is ordered about in this way has its own standing. We call it standing-reserve [*Bestand*]" (Heidegger 1997a: 298). Technology erases the object *as* object ("Gegen-stand" in German literally means "standing against," that is "having a standing of and for its own"). Man, according to Heidegger, is "challenged to exploit the energies of nature" (Heidegger 1997a: 299). This being said, the question arises that "[i]f man is challenged, ordered, to do this, then does not man himself belong even more originally than nature within the standing-reserve" (Heidegger 1997a: 299).

Since Heidegger explicitly links the words *techne* and *episteme*, both of which are "terms for knowing in the widest sense" (Heidegger 1997a: 294), it is no big step to the insight that today it is information that ultimately makes objects cease as *Gegen-Stand*. Thus, Heidegger almost uses cybernetic vocabulary to comment on the essence of technology: "[u]nlocking, transforming, storing, distributing, and switching" (Heidegger 1997a: 298) are technology's strategies of challenging-forth, a challenging-forth; however, that "never simply comes to an end" (Heidegger 1997a: 298). For this obscene circularity of technology which is no longer grounded in any external reference, Heidegger uses the word *Gestell*. Despite his insistence that technology itself is nothing technological, Heidegger himself acknowledges that *Gestell* in its "ordinary [but also: technical] usage means some kind of apparatus" (Heidegger 1997a: 301), for example, "frame," "mount," "support," or "shelf." Also, it has the German verb *stellen* in it, which means placing. A *Ge-stell* places man and things, is a kind of exoskeleton, an en-framing that supportingly places. Technology somehow works and functions in and for itself, simultaneously *producing* man *as* subject (because of man's "more originally belonging within the standing-reserve") and *erasing* the subject as an autonomous entity in control. It is exactly this "paradigm word" I want to use in a more apparatus-oriented reading as a guiding image/metaphor throughout this article.

Jacques Lacan's notion of the symbolic is clearly indebted to Heidegger in this respect—like Heidegger's *Gestell*, language oscillates between being both a constituting and constituted factor with regard to the subject. The symbolic, the machine of culture and language, "places" the human speaking subject in a universe regulated by logic and reason—it thus could be argued that the *Gestell* and the symbolic are but different names and|or manifestations of that (machinic) logic that situates, places, *and* produces the human being *as* subject. Yet, Lacan's notion of the machine is a quite particular one—the subject is a "symbolic machine," and any reference to a machinic notion of the *corporeal* is somewhat bypassed, is inferred negatively as something impossible which nevertheless has effects within the representational registers—the real.

Whereas Lacan's "symbolic machines" might generate a particular kind of pleasure, a *machinic jouissance* of a more material kind is certainly at stake in the work and theatrical performances of Mark Pauline and the *Survival Research Laboratories* (SRL),[1] founded in 1978. Putting engineering skills in the service of *bricolage*, SRL's objective was to present mechanical spectacles, "operating as an organization of creative technicians dedicated to re-directing the techniques, tools, and tenets of industry, science, and the military away from their typical manifestations in practicality, product or warfare ... developing themes of socio-political satire."[2]

SRL's spectacles, always engaging in ever increasing machinic violence—some staging employ flame-throwers and shock-wave cannons—are not so much a critique of technology, but show a delight in extremes: "We build machines of a fairly large size—they are very extreme ...—some of the machines are very large and weigh up to a couple of tons. ... Running the V-1 in a closed building—that's pretty intense, like being in the middle of a storm or war zone" (see Hertz 1995: n.p.). However, machine parts are not the only material involved in Pauline's spectacles. In 1981 and 1982, Pauline joined the machines with dead animals (or animal parts), biological bodies in the purest sense. *Rabot*, for example, mechanically animated the body of a dead rabbit, harnessing and chucking the animal into a frame/mount/*Gestell*, causing it to walk. Other animal-machine hybrids were staged in *A Cruel and Relentless Plot to Pervert the Flesh of Beasts to Unholy Uses*, featuring "a machine incorporating the remains of a dog, mounted on an armature and anchored to a radio-controlled cart. Actuated, the dog-machine lunges forward, its head spinning in goulish imitation of cartoon violence" (Dery 1996: 118). These spectacles, in which the body is controlled and animated by a machine, neatly parallel Pauline's own relation to the machine. They exemplify what Pauline sees to be

> the mark of a true machine consciousness—when a mechanical system gets to a point where there's a disjunction between you and what's going on because what's going on is just too complicated or too intense. Systems are getting so complicated that they're out of control in a rational sense.
>
> (Dery 1993: n.p.)

Note that in this quote, the term "machine consciousness" is quite open in respect to whom it applies: machine, machine-controller, or a fusion of both.

In this respect, Pauline's *Rabot* and his other "organic robots" are a perfect illustration of both Heidegger's enframing of man and the Lacanian subject, staging the real body *within* and *as animated by* a machine/the symbolic, which Lacan, in his reading of Freud's *fort/da* game, saw ultimately based on an originary binarism, 1/0, thus relating it to cybernetics. Although the real (body), strictly speaking, is excluded from the representational registers, it both *has* effects and *is itself a belated effect* of the symbolic: in a paradoxical logic, "[t]he first [speaking] body produces the second [biological] one, by incorporating itself in it" (Lacan 1970: 61), producing it by en-framing it, "housing" it. For Lacan, the subject "inhabits the signifier" and possesses a "real" "body whose essence it is said is to dwell in language" (Lacan 1990: 23).[3] In language, in its en-framing *Gestell*, man-as-subject is supported.

Thus for the subject, for whom culture is in fact its most "natural habitat," the machinic proves to be a constituting factor (see e.g. Stiegler 1998). However, if on the other hand the symbolic/machinic is seen solely in terms of a tool being at the subject's disposal, the house becomes a "prison-house," finally alienating the subject from its "true" self. The question, then, accordingly, is if and how we can gain a free relation to the machinic.

As already noted, *beyond* the representational realms of the Symbolic and the Imaginary, the subject participates in what Lacan calls "the impossible real:" the body of the drives that cannot be reduced/tamed/represented in those two registers that constitute reality. Lacan describes the drive as a kind of feedback circuit: since "the drive may be satisfied without attaining what, from the point of view of a biological totalization of function, would be the satisfaction of its end of reproduction, ... its aim is simply this return into circuit" (Lacan 1991: 179). This circuit is described in terms of an input/output loop that Lacan captures in the paradoxical formula "*se faire* ..." (Lacan 1991: 195), "to make oneself ..." eat, shit ... even walk: see in this respect Pauline's and Stelarc's various *Walking Machines*.[4] Underneath the regulated drift of desire that ties the human subject to the phallic machine, there is thus the rhythmic pulsation of the drives, another machine, removed from the "typical manifestations in practicality, product or warfare."

Terry Harpold, in his reading of *Tetsuo*, has connected a refusal of the "fetish model of prosthesis" (Harpold, unpublished, n.p.) based on the Oedipal scenario of castration and lack of the sexuated subject, with Lacan's myth of the lamella, where Lacan highlights the "immortal ... irrepressible life" (Lacan 1991: 198) of the drive energy. The lamella is the human being as pre-sexual, pre-subject substance, that something in the *human* subject that is *not* reducible to the pure digitality of the symbolic. Lacan even calls it the organ of the libido, the paradoxical organ of a "life that has no need of no organ" (Lacan 1991: 198).

Tetsuo: The Iron Man is more a montage of nonstop surrealistic images than your average movie. It is a montage sped up by its extensive use of stop-motion photography, which emphasizes the overall feverish atmosphere. *Tetsuo* begins in an abandoned factory with a man slashing his thigh open and trying to insert a metal rod into his leg. This man, credited as "the metal fetishist," is then hit by a car driven by an anonymous businessman, accompanied by his girlfriend. Rather than report it, the businessman dumps the injured but not dead victim in the woods and escapes. Waking up the next morning, the businessman finds a metal hair growing out of his cheek. Soon, his body seems to burst open, revealing metal and machinic parts inside. To make things even worse, the businessman starts having sexual fantasies even more bizarre than his reality, and they start coming true: when his penis turns into a rotating drill, he impales his girlfriend. It all turns out to be the metal fetishist's work—due to their "contact" made through the accident, a telepathic bond seems to have been developed between them. In a final battle, both fetishist and businessman merge into a gigantic engine, ready to go for the world.

Commenting on Slavoj Zizek's interpretation of the lamella in the work of David Lynch, Harpold rightly sees Zizek's restriction to figures of "the flayed, skinned body, the palpitation of raw, skinless red flesh" (Zizek 1995: 208) as too limiting, because "too biological" (Harpold, unpublished, n.p.). Harpold observes that later in his seminar, Lacan shortly returns to his notion of the lamella, giving as some of the most ancient examples of the incarnation of the lamella in the body the practices of "tattooing, scarification" (Lacan 1991: 206). Presuming that Lacan would include other forms of bodily modifications in this list as well, Harpold then goes on "to extend this lamella-function to other artificial interventions on the body" (Harpold, unpublished, n.p.), interventions that play a predominant role in *Tetsuo*. The materializations of the lamella that Lacan has described have "the function ... of situating the subject ..., marking his place in the field of the group's relations .... And, at the same time, it obviously has an erotic function" (Lacan 1991: 206). Whereas the "situating function" doubles the logic of the *Gestell*, the "erotic function" "inscribe[s] the substantiality of the body on its substance" (Harpold, unpublished, n.p.), and it is exactly that which combines these practices with the libido-organ, the lamella.

How does *Tetsuo* fit in with all this? Following Terry Harpold, *Tetsuo* can be read as displaying—in its obsessiveness with bodily modification, in its conjunction of flesh, machinery, and pornography—a maybe more up-to-date version of the lamella:

> what is revealed in the movie when surfaces are peeled back, or when they burst open from within, is: a tangle of cables and conduits, steaming solder and blossoming rust. The stuff of the real body in *Tetsuo* is metal ...; what might be otherwise understood as electromechanical extensions of human flesh are revealed to be its essence.
>
> (Harpold, unpublished, n.p.)

In *Tetsuo*, the logic of the drive is visualized and manifested in wires, scrap, and power-drills. Thus, the machinic body has to be situated *at:as* the interface between the body of the drives and the body of desire, it is the "polymorphously perverse" body|machine that finally aims at "spreading" the truth, a truth that the mysterious, manically laughing TV in the movie knew all the time: that the machine *is* the essence of the body. In the final scene of *Tetsuo*, the ambivalence of Tsukamoto's epilogue to this paper becomes apparent in its full force: the final sentence of the movie, "We can mutate the whole world!" can be either read as a menace, realizing the worst nightmares of the technophobic, or as a liberating, utopian promise to create a libido-machinic society, the process of which has been shown to be a very painful one for the individual ....

In *Tetsuo*, the ultimate aim of the drive is not satisfaction, but insatiability, not function, but *jouissance*, which can be seen exactly as that which does not serve anything. Function, in contrast, is closely related to the law, since it is the essence of the law to regulate enjoyment, to set constraints upon its open-endedness.

Even if Lacan is more concerned with the subject—whereas for Deleuze and Guattari this is quite an obsolete idea, they are more concerned with lines of force and, ultimately, politics—I think that on a structural level a cautious and tentative analogy can be drawn between the Lacanian differentiation between pre-oedipal drive and post-oedipal desire and the "pure/molecular machine" (desire machine) and the "operational/molar machine" (social machine). Desire machines, according to Deleuze/Guattari, "are of a molecular order ...: formative machines, whose very misfirings are functional" (Deleuze and Guattari 1992: 286). Like the Lacanian drive, desire machines are "engaged in their own assembly (*montage*), ... machines in the strict sense, because they proceed by breaks and flows, associated waves and particles, associative flows and partial objects" (Deleuze and Guattari 1992: 286–7). Again, what is at stake is not a matter of oppositions pure and simple. Since the subject's reality *is* its psychic reality, fantasy and reality share the same structure, are one and the same thing judged from different perspectives. The difference is thus not between fantasy and reality, desire and utility, but a difference of register, a difference of conditions: the molar "society machines" are molecular machines under "determinate conditions" (Deleuze and Guattari 1992: 287), ultimately two states of one and the same machine. *Beyond* function, beyond culture, the polymorphous drive reacts against repressive, phallic desire, a "Rage against the machine" not from the (however illusory) position of a non-machinic other (see also Herzogenrath 2000), but a "Rage of the (pure) machine against the (oedipal) machine," a "*rage against the Symbolic*" (Kristeva 1982: 178). The common-sense opposition between machine and human being thus has to be re-written as the opposition between the signifier-machine and the signified-machine. Since there is no escaping the machine, there is only the *machine-that-acknowledges-being-a-machine* and the *machine-that-claims-to-be-natural*. This perspective does not claim nature and the machinic as oppositions: once within the symbolic (culture), the machinic is our most natural condition. With regard to Heidegger, this comes close to saying that once within the

Gestell, the subject can only think of an illusory realm *before* the *Gestell* as a belated effect of *always already* having been *within* the *Gestell*. The body can thus not be seen as determined by biological parameters alone anymore. In Félix Guattari's re-definition of the Lacanian object *a* as a "*object machine petit 'a'*" (Guattari 1984: 115), the subject is constituted in "a pure signifying space where the machine would represent the subject for another machine" (Guattari 1984: 117–18). Whereas the Lacanian object *a* is still a fragment of the real (body), here the body as a whole is—not replaced—but affected by the machinic: the whole body is an "objet-machine petit 'a.'" For Deleuze and Guattari, "[d]esire does not lack anything; it does not lack its object. It is, rather, the *subject* that is missing in desire, or desire that lacks a fixed subject; there is no fixed subject unless there is repression" (Deleuze and Guattari 1992: 26). If, according to Lacan, the object *a* is the "'stuff'" (*Écrits* 315) of the subject, then, in that "pure signifying space," where the subject *as* subject is missing, it is in fact the *objet-machine petit "a"* that is the stuff of the "subject:" body and machine become one, the body is part of what Deleuze and Guattari call the *machinic phylum*. This *machinic phylum* is first of all a "flow of matter" (Deleuze and Guattari 1993: 9): it is "materiality, natural or artificial, and both simultaneously; it is matter in movement, in flux, in variation, matter as a conveyor of singularities and traits of expression" (Deleuze and Guattari 1993: 409). In *Tetsuo*, this *machinic phylum*, which, strictly speaking, "is not a life-force, since the phylum is older than life" (DeLanda 1991: 9), is *metallic*: it traverses the ancestry of both the organic and the nonorganic, the human and the robot, etc. It is thus only fitting that for Deleuze and Guattari, the *machinic phylum* is "essentially metallic or metallurgical" (Deleuze and Guattari 1993: 410), since metal "is neither a thing nor an organism, but a *body* without organs" (Deleuze and Guattari 1993: 411, emphasis in the original). With regard to this notion of the *body without organs*, the schizzo-body escaping the organ-ization of the symbolic machine, one can see how *Tetsuo* markedly differs from, let's say, *Terminator 2*: the raw "*bricolage* spirit" of the montage of *Tetsuo*, I argue, relates more to the notion of the *machinic phylum* than the elegant morphing in *Terminator*. Whereas *Terminator 2* relentlessly shows off the skills and power of the "digital machine," *Tetsuo* revels in a "machino-authentic" Old Skool Lo-Fi ... the "real stuff" ...

Because of the *machinic phylum*, both human and robot bodies would "ultimately be related to a common phylogenetic line" (DeLanda 1991: 7). Following Spinoza, Deleuze reads the body in machinic, computational terms:

> In the first place, a body ... is composed of an infinite number of particles; it is the relations of motion and rest, of speeds and slownesses between

particles, that define a body, the individuality of a body. Secondly, a body affects other bodies, or is affected by other bodies; it is this capacity for affecting and being affected that also defines a body in its individuality.
(Deleuze 1988: 122)

A body is thus not simply a form, a container, but a "complex relation between differential velocities, between deceleration and an acceleration of particles" (Deleuze 1988: 123), affecting and being affected by other such complex relations: desiring-machines connected to and coupled with other desiring-machines. Since this definition of bodies does without any "substance," it can be applied to any "body," and it can be known and assessed only with respect to changes happening to, in, or between bodies. Bodies thus only ever are in states of "becoming," entering relations with their milieu which in turn is a part of a larger body of particles, et ad infinitum. The body thus becomes-what-it-is by forming assemblages with other such bodies (human or nonhuman). Following Manuel De Landa, Deleuze and Guattari's example of the wasp and the orchid (an example of "unnatural coupling") can thus be extended, seeing "the role of humans ... as little more than that of industrious insects pollinating an independent species of machine-flower" (DeLanda 1991: 3). However, as Deleuze's reading of Spinoza suggests, since the *machinic phylum* crosses any transversal becoming, the relation described in De Landa's example should not be read one-way: machines affect humans and *vice versa*, they are not separate entities but connected in a mutual phase of "becoming."

This, I argue, is at stake in the art and strategy of the Australian performance artist Stelarc. Whereas Mark Pauline is working with machine parts and body parts of dead animals, Stelarc has turned to his own body as his "experiment ground." Employing robotic and medical devices, Stelarc's work probes and extends the capabilities of the human body. In performances that make extensive use of cyborg and post-human metaphors, Stelarc questions the issue of "biological evolution" and comments on the human body's (mal) adaptation to an environment that has become increasingly technological: "A BODY IS DESIGNED TO INTERFACE WITH ITS ENVIRONMENT— its sensors are open-to-the-world (compared to its inadequate internal surveillance system)" (Stelarc no year). Because of this poor adaption of the human to its environment, Stelarc's objective is to "redesign[.] the body" (Stelarc 1997: 243) and by this redesigning to "redefin[e] what is human" (Stelarc 1997: 243).

Having started with a series of suspension-performances, probing the limitations of the human body, his later work concentrates on enhancing this very body. Later performances include a "Third Hand," a five-finger robotic hand activated by his abdominal and leg muscles; a "Stomach Sculpture" to be inserted into the artist's "internal space," etc. More recently, Stelarc has been creating amplified and "virtual" body performances, using prosthetic technologies that "affect" his body with remote and direct muscle stimulation (his muscles in fact affect the system and *vice versa*): These "machinic dances" stage a choreography of machinic movements and involuntary gestures and body motions ultimately uncontrollable by the artist.

According to Stelarc, "[t]he information explosion is indicative of an evolutionary dead end. ... In our decadent biological phase, we *indulge in information* as if this compensates for our genetic inadequacies" (Stelarc 1997: 241). Comparable to Heidegger's *Gestell*, "INFORMATION IS THE PROSTHESIS THAT PROPS UP THE BODY" (Stelarc 1997: 241), supporting and placing it. Because of the human body's "*outmoded Pleistocene programme*" (Stelarc 1997: 241, emphasis in the original), we have to get rid of the body.

However, I think Stelarc's comments on his own work have to be read as a *manifesto* more that to be taken at face value. His stressing of the human being's *post-evolutionary* status makes sense only as long as we read "evolution" only referring to a "natural law" being applied to nature only. As soon as we take the notion of a *machinic phylum* into account, an evolution encompassing both man *and* machine, the phrase "post-evolutionary" becomes redundant. Also, a statement like "THE BODY IS OBSOLETE" (Stelarc 1997: 242) is maybe too catchy and simplistic in the long run, since what is obsolete is the body as a container of the soul, the body taken as autonomous subject, the body "as we know it." But what comes to the fore, what resurfaces, even resurrects, is exactly the body *as* machinic, the body as a site of affection. Thus, what I see Stelarc aiming at is not so much a fashionable transformation into a cyborg—he is not a willing victim of the human being's domestication through technology (see Virilio 1995)—but a project to stage the endless project of *becoming*, of *body-becoming-machine*, and, ultimately, *machine-becoming-body*.

Thus, the *machinic phylum* enjoys a curious relation to both the body of the drives and Heidegger's *Gestell* (here, Stelarc's *proper name* bears a relationship to that "paradigm word" of science, the *Stel* of *stele* is present in both). The body of the drive, itself *machinic*, is placed within the "determinate conditions" of the *Gestell*. The *Gestell* somehow uncovers [*entbergen*] what is ultimately already inherent in the *machinic phylum*/body of the drives, but places it in the service of control and mastery, a mastery that itself has to be mastered (or condemned) by its own creation. Stelarc stages this conflict in his work, and in drastically showing the subject's endless oscillation between the biological and the machinic.

Given his credo that THE BODY IS OBSOLETE: why does Stelarc's body still look like "a body"? In this respect, design—after all, Stelarc's proclaimed objective is the "re-designing of the body"—is more than just memory, nostalgia: it shows that in the end, meat matters in the process to fill the gap created by the hegemony of the human body's post-biological status by a non-symbolic flesh.

Notes

1 See *SRL*'s website http://www.srl.org
2 See http://www.srl.org/bio.html
3 This notion ultimately refers to Heidegger. He essentially elaborates this idea in his essay "Building, Dwelling, Thinking." Heidegger puts forward the idea of the close relationship between being, dwelling, and language, as well as man's disturbed relationship with language, acting "as though *he* were the shaper and master of language, while in fact *language* remains the master of man" (Heidegger 1977b: 348). See also Heidegger's "Letter on Humanism," where he states that "[l]anguage is the house of Being. In its home man dwells," in its en-framing *Gestell*, man-as-subject is supported. In: Barrett, W. and H.D. Aiken (eds), *Philosophy in the Twentieth Century: An Anthology*, New York: Random House, 1962, 270–302, 271.
4 See, for example, Stelarc's performance "Exoskeleton: Event for Extended Body and Walking Machine."

Works Cited

De Landa, M. (1991), *War in the Age of Intelligent Machines*, New York: Swerve.
Deleuze, G. (1988), *Spinoza. Practical Philosophy*, trans. R. Hurley, San Francisco: City Lights Books.
Deleuze, G. and Guattari, F. (1992), *Anti-Oedipus. Capitalism and Schizophrenia*, trans. R. Hurley, M. Seem, and H. R. Lane, Minneapolis: University of Minnesota Press.
Deleuze, G., and Guattari, F. (1993), *A Thousand Plateaus. Capitalism and Schizophrenia*, trans. B. Massumi, Minneapolis and London: University of Minnesota Press.
Dery, M. (1993), "Out of Control," *Wired*, 1 (4), http://www.srl.org/interviews/out.of.control.html.
Dery, M. (1996), *Escape Velocity. Cyberculture at the End of the Century*, London: Hodder & Stoughton.
Guattari, F. (1984), *Molecular Revolution*, trans. R. Sheed, Harmondsworth: Penguin Books.

Harpold, T. "Negative Prosthesis. Tsukamoto's *Tetsuo: The Iron Man*," I am indebted to Terry Harpold for kindly emailing me a copy of his unpublished paper.

Heidegger, M. (1962), "Letter on Humanism," in W. Barrett and H. D. Aiken (eds), *Philosophy in the Twentieth Century. An Anthology*, New York: Random House, 270–302.

Heidegger, M. (1971), "What Are Poets For?," in *Poetry, Language, Thought*, New York: Harper & Row, 89–14.

Heidegger, M. (1977a), "The Question Concerning Technology," in David Farell Krell (ed.), *Martin Heidegger: Basic Writings*, New York and San Francisco: Harper and Row, 284–317.

Heidegger, M. (1977b), "Building, Dwelling, Thinking," in David Farell Krell (ed.), *Basic Writings*, New York: Harper and Row, 347–63.

Hertz, G. (1995), "Beyond the Realm of Humans. A Discussion with Mark Pauline of Survival Research Laboratories," http://www.conceptlab.com/interviews/pauline.html

Herzogenrath, B. (2000), "Stop Making Sense: Fuck 'em and Their Law (… it's only 1 and 0 but I like it …)," *Postmodern Culture*, 10: 2.

Kristeva, J. (1982), *Powers of Horror: An Essay on Abjection*, New York: Columbia University Press.

Lacan, J. (1970), "Radiophonie," *Scilicet*, 2/3: 55–99.

Lacan, J. (1990), *Télévision: A Challenge to the Psychoanalytic Establishment*, trans. Denis Mollies, Rosalind Kraus, and Annette Michelson, ed. Joan Copjec, New York: Norton.

Lacan, J. (1991), *The Four Fundamental Concepts of Psycho-Analysis*, trans. A. Sheridan, Harmondsworth: Penguin.

Stelarc (no year), Excerpt from "Absent Bodies," http://stelarc.org/?catID=20317

Stelarc (1997), "From Psycho to Cyber Strategies: Prosthetics, Robotics and Remote Existence," *Cultural Values*, 2: 241–9.

Stiegler, B. (1998), *Technics and Time 1. The Fault of Epimetheus*, Stanford: Stanford University Press.

Virilio, P. (1995), *The Art of the Motor*, Minneapolis: University of Minnesota Press.

Zizek, S. (1995), "The Lamella of David Lynch," in R. Feldstein, B. Fink and M. Jaanus (eds), *Reading Seminar XI: Lacan's Four Fundamental Concepts of Psycho-Analysis*, Albany, NY: State University of New York Press, 202–22.

10

Góng (空) | *Saek* (色): The Ineffable Persistence of Becoming

(Origin Korean)

Woosung Kang

Góng and Its Discontents

Originally a Buddhist idea that teaches the ephemerality of what exists, *śūnya*, the notion of "góng" (空 being in the state of empty) in Korea has witnessed various conceptual mutations ever since it was first introduced into native soil with the arrival of Buddhism in ancient time (Yun 2007: 272). With the long domination of Confucian culture and the proliferation of Christianity as a reaction to it, the Buddhist notion of *góng* now loses its religious meaning having mostly been transformed to designate a state of utter nothingness or an unwavering state of mind. In ancient India, *śūnya* or *śūnyata* takes the central place of Buddhist teaching, a substantial principle of the universe (Gironi 2012: 3). It originates from the direct teaching of Buddha himself and proliferates later, throughout East Asia, by Chinese philosophers who imported the notion of *śūnya* with the help of Taoist concept of "wu" (無 nothing) and "dao" (道 path of truth), two fundamental philosophical ideas in ancient China (Murti 1998: 337). The notion of *śūnya* constitutes the basic tenet of Buddhism in all its Asian variants, the gist of which is epitomized in *Prajnaparamita* (般若經), a book which explicates the way to the perfect transcendence beyond the present world.

As is well known, it was Nagarjuna (龍樹 150–250) who developed and popularized the thought of *śūnya* as a primordial principle of the universe, making it a sort of Buddhist cosmology as well as a spiritual goal to arrive through individual enlightenment (Lee 2014: 152). When Nagarjuna's *śūnya* was introduced to the mainland China, its complex implications were not transmitted as they stand; it was adopted into Chinese thinking as a philosophical concept in close connection with the popular Taoist concept of "*wu*" for their similarity in meaning (Yun 2007: 275). Taoist appropriation of a Buddhist idea in China heavily depends upon the so-called "analogical method" (格義) of interpretation, a method characteristic of the Confucian thinking in China (Chan and Shiu 2011: 170). Confucianism has a tendency to digest a heterogeneous system of thinking within itself by finding a conceptual analogy. Indeed, Confucianism as a systemic philosophy rests on the analogical method with which it establishes the tight connection between the invisible substance and visible phenomena, like the one between yin (陰) and yang (陽) elaborated in *I Ching* (周易). The Confucian analogy of the universe makes it possible to link the notion of Buddhist *śūnya* with *wu* in Taoism and with the idea of interdependent arising (緣起) in Buddhism (Yun 2007: 278). As a result, Buddhist *śūnya* was renamed as Taoist *góng* in China and directly assimilated to the concept of *wu*, having been naturalized to mean "substantial nothing" from which derives everything phenomenal (Mou 2014: 208).

Native Taoism and Confucianism in China collaborate in naturalizing the unfamiliar notion of *śūnya* in order to dehydrate, as it were, its religious implication. *Śūnya* was thus generally misconstrued as the minor concept propagating the Taoist philosophy of nihilism, in contradistinction with the moral philosophy of Confucianism and the transcendental wisdom of Taoism (Chan and Shiu 2011: 170). In ancient China, *śūnyatā* (空性 truth of emptiness) becomes indistinguishable from the nihilistic principle of *wu*, a law of pure negation that denies the ontological status of existing entities (有 *yǒu*). The original meaning of *śūnya* or Buddhist *góng*, however, has no implication of negation. It is much closer to the Taoist and Confucian notion of universal "zong-dao" (中道 middle path), which refers to the void emptiness beyond being and nothing, from which every phenomenal being and even noumenal nothingness originate (Chan and Shiu 2011: 175). Analogically linking the notion of *śūnya* with the nihilistic idea of *wu* in Taoism, Confucianism is able to maintain its status of dominant ideology.

The peculiar way of appropriating *śūnya* into the system of Chinese philosophy clearly demonstrates the strong persistence of Confucianism and its power to co-opt the subversive potentiality of heterogeneous ideas within its own turf. The dominant Confucianism is prone to allow only a minor significance to *śūnya* by letting it identified with the nihilistic idea of *wu* in Taoism (Mou 2014: 136). As a result, Confucian ideology effectively eliminates the cosmological connotation of *śūnya*, thereby neutralizing the uncanniness of *śūnya* as a subspecies legitimizing the system of Confucian thinking (Mou 2014: 141). It was only with the translation of *Prajnaparamita* and Nagarjuna's writings into Chinese that the original teaching of *śūnya* could be understood.

With the method of analogy and its theory of the unity of non-difference (不二 not-two), however, the notion of *góng* as the force of pure negativity, according to which "being and nothing are not to be distinguished" (非有非無), can be attached to the Confucian thinking: the transcendental principle that unifies the noumenal and the phenomenal, substance (體) and its function (用) (Mou 2014: 141). The essential philosophical principle of non-difference between *wu* and *yŏu* in Confucianism looks similar to the Kantian idea of transcendentalism in that it explains the possibility of phenomenal world according to the presupposed world of noumena behind it. But it differs from Kant since it does not presuppose the thing in itself (*das Ding*) as a primordial entity or God as the first cause: there is nothing substantial behind or beyond the phenomenal world in Confucianism (Mou 2014: 121).

What is singular in the Chinese notion of *góng*, therefore, is not the transcendental unification of the analogical universe but the negation of itself as the ultimate substance. *Góng* does not refer to the metaphysical truth of supersensible substance but displays the way all things become interdependent in the middle path. Or rather, it is *the* path-on-the-move to the constant becoming and enlightenment. But in Confucianism, the enlightenment of *góng* as the middle path to the interdependent becoming cannot be possible without the function (用) of language. In Buddhism, Nagarjuna himself also does neither disregard language as a phenomenal *yŏu* nor thinks little of it as the temporary representation of *śūnya*. Language is the excellent means of becoming which makes it possible for ordinary people to be on the path of enlightenment (Yun 2007: 280). In short, the world of *góng* cannot be intuited or manifested without the function of language. No wonder then that proponents of *góng* constantly emphasize the crucial role of learning through dialogue as well as of correct usage of language reflecting the cosmic analogy. This also explains why the word *góng*, not those of *śūnya* or *wu*, has to be the Chinese name for the middle path toward universal becoming. The whole cosmos revolves around the principle of fundamental *góng*, it being neither to be equated with substance nor to pure negativity.

In contrast to this valorization of *góng* as the principle of cosmic becoming beyond *wu* and *yŏu*, however, there still persists a strong tendency in Chinese Confucianism that takes the notion of *góng* as a representative of Taoist escapism from reality. Confucian scholars of this orientation often think of the Taoist *wu* as a false belief or a bad faith which easily deludes ordinary people into believing the simple denigration of the world of being. They suggest that the Taoist concept of *wu* or inaction (無爲) is contaminated in essence since it proclaims the total worthlessness of the present in contrast with the blissful hereafter of *wu* (Park 2008: 32; Mou 2014: 126) But the notion of inaction in Taoism does not refer to the total retreat from the here and the now; it means the active way of distancing from the worldly interest.

In Confucianism, the secular world of *yŏu* represents the empty form of *wu* and the world of *wu* in turn implies the ultimate emptiness of *yŏu*, which means that nothing is self-generative or has self-identity in the cosmic universe (Mou 2014: 83–4). From this dialectic of cosmic becoming between *wu* and *yŏu* comes the peculiar notion of *saek* (色), which designates the sensible shape or color of everything extant including the world of *wu* and human body. "The sensible shape of all things (*saek*) appears separate as *sui generis*, as it were, totally independent of the world of nothing (*wu*). But the middle path (*dao*) of *góng* means that the so-called natural shape of things is developed or evolved from nothing self-generative" (Yun 2007: 288).

In Korean version of Confucianism, however, a different conceptualization of *saek* predominates popular imagination. While the emptied-out mind (*góng*) can possibly achieve the state of enlightenment with the help of Taoist *wu*, the allure of *saek*, that is, the obsession with phenomenal shape of things, cannot easily be emptied out or superseded since it has to do with our innate human desire. With this notion of *saek* as the obsession of sensible or even sensual form of desire, *góng* finds itself on the verge of being identified with the concept of inaction (無爲), which illustrates the active distanciation from fatal desire itself.

The Speculation of *Gonggong*

In Chinese Buddhism, however, the notion of *saek* has not particularly to do with desire. As previously indicated, the nature of every being lies in non-self-identity (非自性), the utter interdependence without self-genesis (Lim and Lee 2020: 177). Here *saek* is only equated with the object of Kantian intuition. Visible or not, *saek* refers to something perceptible in our daily experience but that which could not be limited to sensible phenomena or our body. It is rather the *form* that everything perceptible takes in the present, including nothing (*wu*). Its objective reality cannot be confirmed even if it appears to the subject as what actually exists (Lim and Lee 2020: 180). Every being as *saek* does not have its own separate entity, only to be temporarily available as the sensible form of interdependent arising between yin and yang. Thus the essence of *saek* is paradoxically not distinguishable from the rhythm of *góng*, whose movement through the world of *saek* is critical in the Confucian dialectic of nothing and being. Indeed, as in various Buddhist classics, "*góng* is *saek*; *saek* is *góng*" (Wonhyo 2012: 241). With this interchangeability, *saek* denotes only the temporary form of every being on its way to ultimate *góng*, presenting itself as phenomenal to the subject.

But in Korean Buddhism, the fundamental principle of *góng* and its identity with *saek* undergo a drastic change. As is well known, Korean Buddhism originates from the Chinese Buddhism of analogical method, but it develops its own distinct system with the speculative redefinition of the Chinese notion of *góng*. It was the famous monk Wonhyo who meditated on the possibility of *góng*'s ossification into substance. For him, the basic idea of *śūnya* in *Prajnaparamita* and the Chinese *góng* became, under the strong influence of Confucianism in China, a sort of empty transcendental substance: pure negativity on the basis of which every phenomenal being ultimately generates.

For Wonhyo, to insist on the originarity of *góng* and its interconnection with *saek* is not enough. Wonhyo argues that *góng* amounts to the metaphysical explication of essential emptiness concerning being and nothing and showcases the highly metaphysical characteristics of Chinese Buddhism; it fails to grasp the reason why *góng* presides over all the speculations on being and nothing. For Wonhyo, the notion of *góng*, or what he renamed as *gonggong* (空空), having lost any connection with *saek*, dismissed too easily the possibility of its being fixed as Supreme Being or the Kantian notion of noumena (Lim an Lee 2020: 175). Wonhyo's *gonggong* expresses the idea that even *góng* itself is not above its own rhythm of perpetual emptiness.

Gonggong indicates the potential emptiness of *góng* itself: it has no necessary connection with primal mover or pure causality as the synthesis of beings and nothingness. Wonhyo later likens the notion of *gonggong* to "suchness"(眞如) of cosmic becoming and to the "univocity of mind" (一心) (Wonhyo 2007: 105–6). From the perspective of cosmic "suchness," the supposition of noumenal substance and the conceptualization of *saek* as its phenomenal representation are none other than the dismissal of the potential shadowiness or formal illusoriness (相) of *góng* and/as *saek*. Without the ineffable, even mysterious, way of how cosmic becoming persists through *saek*, it is highly plausible for individual subjects to immediately substantiate *góng* and *saek* respectively into an original principle of *ex nihilo* and the object of desire.

The ephemeral rhythm of cosmic becoming (*gonggong*), its "suchness," in Wonhyo's thinking finds its best expression in the enigmatic phrase: "*Gonggong* means that *góng* is also empty" (空相易空) (Wonhyo 2007: 107). What is manifest here is that *góng* is neither the final empty causality nor pure nothingness: *gonggong* is far from the emptiness of *zero* out of which positivity and negativity are able to take shape. In Wonhyo's notion of *gonggong*, everything constantly revolves around everything else according to the cosmic way (*doh*) of infinite becoming: "suchness" or "univocity of mind" does not amount to any ontological principle of universe (Wonhyo 2007: 108). In this respect, *gonggong* looks very much similar to the Hegelian idea of dialectics in that the double emptiness of *góng* and *saek* comes close to the synthetic sublation (*Aufhebung*) of double negation. Wonhyo's *gonggong* differs, however, from Hegelian dialectics since it does not allow the mediation of negativity and any prospect of final synthesis. Indeed, *gonggong* has nothing to do with dialectics; it involves with the infinite becoming ("suchness") of cosmic universe. *Gonggong* is rather closer to the rhythm of double affirmation (Wonhyo 2007: 234–5).[1]

But what is the status of *saek* in this notion of *gonggong* as infinite becoming? What about its unity with *góng* as the basic principle of suchness? If *saek* is just the form of shadowiness of everything ephemeral including beings and nothing, how is it possible for it to get conceived of as another name of *góng*? Wonhyo here further explicates the notion of *gonggong* in terms of human desire toward the world of *saek*. For him, the form of *saek* constitutes the reservoir of all human desires which are not only shadowy but contaminated as well (Wonhyo 2007: 276–7).

Everything in the universe perpetually revolves around everything else in the middle of infinite becoming, that is, in the pivotal "suchness" of cosmic path (*doh*), while it makes itself manifest through various stages of contamination in the world of *saek*. In this relentless circuit of cosmic becoming, it is not enough to simply negate the illusory world of shadows once and for all (Mark 2015). For Wonhyo, everything in the universe is not just something ephemeral that could be stripped away with meditation; the world of *saek* stands fundamentally contaminated by human desire (Wonhyo 2007: 286). But the contamination of the ephemeral world of *saek* should not be mistaken to indicate that phenomenal world itself is without significance or empty of meaning.

The contamination of *saek* denotes the present state of intense reification (物化) that effectuates the illusory substitution of the law of the interdependent arising with that of physical entities, or what Georg Lukács calls "phantom objectivity" (Lukács 1968: 83–6). In terms of everyday experience of ordinary subjects, *gonggong* has to pass through the ambiguous process of reversal that the delusive fixation of *saek* imposes upon human desire.

The Secularization of Gong and Saek

In order to explain why the world of *saek* appears reified or contaminated, Wonhyo concretizes the five aspects of *gonggong*, which roughly correspond to the five ways of *saek*'s rhythm of contamination and decontamination

(Wonhyo 2012: 59). In the detailed explication of *gonggong*, Wonhyo first posits the idea that three worlds of human desire, actual things, and invisible elements are without self-identities, altogether empty in themselves and always interdependent (Muller and Nguyen 2012: 138–9). And he further complicates the notion of *gonggong* by insisting that the law of causality in secular affairs be empty and temporary because what causes human suffering in the present cannot be attributed to the sins of the past. He rather requires the full acknowledgment of human desire itself (Muller and Nguyen 2012: 102).

Wonhyo argues that the object of desire is no more empty and shadowy than the desiring subject. Seen from the infinite movement of suchness, there is neither an absolute origin of negative contamination nor a hidden source of decontamination; the world of *saek* is the very form or path of infinite becoming that human desire takes toward enlightenment (Wonhyo 2007: 44). What is thus critically at stake is neither the negation nor the transcendence of desire itself. Whether the objective world appears reified to human being, that is, whether human desire blocks the intuition of cosmic becoming, does not matter for Wonhyo since these doubts themselves are empty, futile, and illusory.

The only question worth asking would rather be about the potentiality of our following a sort of dialectical rhythm of *gonggong* and *saekgong* (色卽空 空卽色), our enlightenment *as* desiring subject in the unfolding of suchness of infinite becoming (Wonhyo 2007: 146–7). No wonder the primary aim in Wonhyo's teaching about five stage of *gonggong* in accordance with five contaminations in *saek* rests on our constant interdependence with cosmic rhythm. Of course, this path of enlightenment requires an endless practice of emptying out desire itself, not the repression or negation of particular desires. We are responsible for confronting our world of reified desire (*saek*) itself as a necessary stage toward enlightenment. He calls this excellent state of emptying out desire itself by the term "authentic *gonggong*" (眞空), metaphorizing it to the blossoming of lotus flower out of muddy soil.[2]

After Confucianism has been established as the dominant cultural ideology since Chosun Dynasty on, Wonhyo's version of Korean Buddhism was stigmatized as mysticism and completely marginalized. The central teachings of Buddhism were often undervalued as the religious code of conduct or even reduced to the premodern forms of esotericism. Confucian philosophers often denigrate the notion of *gonggong* or *saekgong* as an escapist precept promoting the meaninglessness of the present reality (Lim and Lee 2020: 181). Buddhist and Taoist temples were tightly monitored having been driven away to mountain area. *Saekgong* was identified with the nihilistic negation of existing order, which denies the significance of reality and human will to control nature. Despite this suppressive control, however, the notion of *gonggong* ironically became widespread among populace who felt frustrated by the growing corruption of Confucian ideology.

Instead of conforming to the existing order, ordinary people more and more absorb the teachings of *gonggong* as the principle of individual ethics, imbibing them as the noble attitude of secular mind. In this way, *gonggong* comes to put more emphasis on the value of life in the hereafter. The unity of *gonggong* and *saek* was eventually broken apart. While *gonggong* refers, with rapid modernization, to an individual attitude of forgoing worldly possessions, *saek* designates all the seductions of secular interest. Especially, in a society where sexuality has been long repressed by the strict moral code of male-oriented Confucianism, *saek* is overwhelmingly equated with the danger of women's sexuality. The cosmological principle of suchness in *gonggong* or *saekgong* was completely forgotten, thereby reduced to either a strict rule of religious sect or a secular ethics of asceticism against the snare of feminine sexuality. Likewise, the Confucian lesson of *doh* gets shrunk to signify the strait path between the nihilistic denial of secularity and the hedonistic enjoyment of desire. *Gonggong* becomes spiritual transcendence while *saek* denotes the dirty secret of sexual desire. In their stead, the notion of *musoyu* (無所有 the denial of earthly possession) proliferates as an ethical attitude toward minimalism (Park 2015: 183–4).

The secularization of *gonggong* and *saekgong* remains dominant throughout Korean history in which any subjugation to sexual desire amounts to the failure of one's integrity. Furthermore, *saek* often instigates misogyny, victimizing women as the object of sexual desire, a far cry from the original meaning of the sensible form of emptiness. But *gonggong* still retains its positive implication when it comes to the matter of achieving creative power by emptying out the form of selfhood. Unfettered from the sexualized world of *saek* and shorn of social implication, *gonggong* becomes the path of individual enlightenment which, within the contaminated world of *saek*, secures our sublimation toward spiritual decontamination. Though individualized, Wonhyo's idea of cosmic suchness survives as the ethics of secular life whose power lies in the achievement of non-possession beyond the world of desire.

Notes

1 Instead of adopting emptiness and suchness for *góng* and authentic *góng*, the translator of Wonhyo's Collected Works rather takes new idioms, "voidness" and "thusness" for each meaning.
2 Interestingly, "authentic *gonggong*" also connotes the absolute vacancy of any particle in physics.

Works Cited

Chan, W., and Shiu, C. H. H. (2011), "Introduction: Mou Zongsan and Chinese Buddhism," *Journal of Chinese Philosophy*, 38 (2): 169–73.

Gironi, F. (2012), "Sunyata and the Zeroing of Being," *Journal of Indian Philosophy and Religion*, 15: 1–42.

Lee, J. (2014), "Tradition of Western Metaphysics and Ethics: Nagarjuna and Hua-yen Literature," *Journal of Criticism and Theory*, 19 (2): 149–78.

Lim, S. and Lee, S. (2020), "The Analysis of Ontology of Wonhyo's Sunyata," *Journal of East-West Philosophy*, 96: 169–87.

Lukács, G. (1968), *History and Class Consciousness*, trans. Rodney Livingstone, Cambridge, MA: The MIT Press.

Mark, E. (2015), "Wonhyo," *World History of Encyclopedia*, Aug. 30, 2015. Web.

Mou, Z. (2014), *Works of Mou Zongsan*, ed. John Makeham, trans. Jason Clower, Boston: Brill.

Muller, A. C., and Cuong T. Nguyen (2012), *Wonhyo's Philosophy of Mind*, Honolulu: University of Hawai'i Press.

Murti, T. R. V. (1998), *The Central Philosophy of Buddhism*, New Delhi: Munshiram Manoharlal.

Park, J. Y. (2008), *Buddhism and Postmodernity: Zen, Huayan, and the Possibility of Buddhist Postmodern Ethics*, Plymouth: Lexington.

Park, K. R. (2015), "The Seon Philosophy in Ven. Beobjeong's Non-Possession," *The Journal of the Korean Buddhist Research Institution*, 70 (1): 283–309.

Wonhyo. (2007), *Cultivating Original Enlightenment: Collected Works of Wonhyo*, Vol. 1, trans. Robert E. Buswell Jr., Honolulu: University of Hawai'i Press.

Wonhyo. (2012), *Wonhyo: Selected Works*, trans. A. Charles Muller, Jin Y. Park, and Sem Vermeersch, Seoul: Jogye Order of Korean Buddhism.

Yun, J. (2007), "A South Korean Change and Development of the Emptiness of Nagarjuna and Wonhyo's Exposition of Vajrasamadhi Sutra," *The Journal of Korean Philosophical History*, 21: 271–303.

11

Hiljaa: Silent and Slow Media Use

(Origin Finnish)

Jukka-Pekka Puro and Veli-Matti Karhulahti

A Cultural History of *Hiljaisuus*

The cultural history of the term *hiljaisuus* is twofold. On the one hand, the term was utilized to describe Finns, written by European explorers, such as Giuseppe Acerbi (1773–1845). Acerbi's travel book through Scandinavia (1798–9) was published in 1802, and his description about mysterious Finns and "Laplanders" with their cultural habits became seminal in the European understanding of people in the dark North.[1] According to Acerbi, Finns were polite but poor and introverted, and the Finnish language reflected cold and hard living conditions. The use of local language was an intrinsic part of Finnish life. Compared to the neighbor Sweden in particular, the difference was vast (see Englund 2005). Sweden was in constant cultural exchange with central Europe and vivid European communal life, whereas the isolated Finns lived desolate lives in small and dark cabins. In these conditions, people concentrated on survival and shelter, and *hiljaisuus*—as a special type of "silence"—was a means to adapt to the environment.[2]

Over the years, *hiljaisuus* evolved into a part of the cultural self-image of the Finns themselves, too. As silent but hard-working and determined, the Finns perceived themselves differently from the Swedes and the Russians. This served as a pivotal element to national awakening and, finally, independence in 1917. Acerbi's stereotypes stood the test of time. During the first years of independence, Finnish literature and movies created characters that walked hand in hand with their *hiljainen* image: stubborn but unselfish people forming strong social and cultural cohesion—and respecting listening skills. The Finnish idioms from the nineteenth century, repeated by Finnish novelists, politicians, and educators, underpinned how "speaking is silver, listening is gold." *Hiljaisuus* was something to be compared, for example, to *kuulua* (v., "to be perceptible through hearing"), which at the same time signifies intersubjectivity as a very basic, existential concept (Peltola 2018).

During the first decades of Finland's independence, *hiljaisuus* (as "silence") signaled respect toward other people and was a natural condition of daily life. Culturally unique artifacts, such as the Finnish sauna, were unquestionably silent places (Puro 2009). In Finnish heritage, the sauna is a place of birth and dying. During winter times, saunas were usually the only warm place as well as clean enough to wash newborn babies and deceased family members. In one sense, the sauna served as a church, as another Finnish idiom puts it. In both places people are supposed to be silent, respecting new or lost lives, and the spiritual dimensions of human existence.

In Acerbi's Europe, religion was fundamentally anchored to the "Word" to be hermeneutically found in the Bible itself (Larkin 2003). European spiritual life was full of sermons, religious speeches, and outspoken priests, and the Word, as it was conceptualized in Christianity, spread around in churches and marketplaces as a part of versatile cultural life. In Finland, the Word was rather perceived to be hidden in the silent nature of the people, however. Nature was harsh and everyday life was full of adversity; according to Acerbi, the Finns appeared to cope with these conditions by their strong faith and by listening to silent ambience. *Hiljaisuus*, when conceptualized in terms of "silence," was something exquisite and emblematic. It projected not only the long physical distances between people, but also cognitive distances: silence voiced the independence of the mind, namely, human existence.

During the 1800s, German priest Johann Tobias Beck (1804–78), the founder of Finnish "biblicism," wrote his seminal works on "genuine Christian life." Beck was a well-known theologian in central Europe, but "beckism" was one of the most fundamental cornerstones of Finnish Christianity in the 1800s (Luukkanen 2015). Beck changed radically the understanding of religion and religious life. For Beck, God emerged in the Bible, not in sermons or the spoken word. God revealed himself silently in the pages of the Bible to anyone pursuing sacred life. Instead of gospelling, as in most European countries, beckist bishops and priests declared in Finland that the Word needs no gospelling. Instead, the most genuine understanding of God's will is found personally, directly from the Bible, without anyone's interpretations or explanations. The Word reveals itself to the humble and the silent, in silence.

Juha: the Silent Protagonist

Since its original roots, constructed by travelers like Acerbi and reformers like Beck, silence grew up to be a cultural mirror of Finnish life. The birth of Finnish nationalism in the 1800s and early 1900s exploited the idea about humble and composed people, oppressed first by the Swedes and then Russians, ultimately finding their identity as a silent but strong nation. The "silent strong Finn" was a heroic stereotype first in local literature and later in films, which echoed the same stereotype. Along with the literary adaptations to film, the stereotypes spawned numerous popular caricatures, such as the one depicted in the versions of *Juha*. Originally a novel written by Juhani Aho (1861–1921)—the first full-time Finnish novelist and one of the most influential local authors—*Juha* has been filmed several times, as in 1937 by Nyrki Tapiovaara, in 1956 by Toivo Särkkä, and by Aki Kaurismäki in 1999.

The protagonist Juha is a Finnish, middle-aged, hard-working man, who loses his wife to talkative Shemeika. It is not an accident that Shemeika is a handsome, young Russian, who enters Juha's property, representing something nationally and culturally alien. Juha perhaps knows what he should say and do, but Shemeika is better and faster at talking to Juha's wife, Marja. To the reader and movie audiences, Juha was something to identify with; it explained, in prosaic form, many of the verbally awkward social tensions and misunderstandings. Both the novel and the movies by Tapiovaara and Särkkä underline the tragedy that was hidden in silence: being a strong national feature, but also involving the unwillingness or inability to be open and receptive.

Unlike the above, Aki Kaurismäki's version of *Juha* (1999) is a silent movie. Kaurismäki uses Juha as an allegory of the society: Finland, as a silent nation, is both tragic and ridiculous in its imagined glory of silence (Kääpä 2010). As it has been pointed out by many critics, however, the movie also challenges its self-image; Finns are not, in fact, more silent than others, but it is rather a myth that was built up in historical and religious contexts, and it should be abandoned. The tragedy is not silence, but the stereotypes and representations that are based on puritan interpretation of Lutheran history, with fictional protagonists, such as Juha.

Hiljaisuus Today

After twenty years from Kaurismäki's film, the *hiljainen* stereotype has been reformed and the understanding of Finland's sociocultural roots as well as economic status has changed. With many other countries, Finland suffered a major economic depression period in the early 1990s, followed by an economic boom at the end of the decade and culminating into the Dot-com bubble crash by 2002. A motor for the latter events was the local company Nokia, which quickly became the world-leading mobile phone developer in the world. In the early 2000s, the number of mobile phones per head of population in Finland was the highest in the world (Puro 2002). Considering the previously summarized history of Finland as the "silent country," how come a machine for ubiquitous talking break through there in particular? One could entertain the Finns' suppressed need to converse to have discharged as a line of Nokia phone production; however, we suggest that modern media technologies, including the Nokia phone, complicate the meaning of (English) "silence" by empowering non-aural, non-visual, and non-spatial means for communication, which at the same time reflect and conflict with Finland's historic trademark, *hiljaisuus*.

While "Juha" remains a product of agricultural Finland, the Finnish millennials "were born with cell phones in their hands," as it was often phrased by the local media echoing the rise of Nokia during the late 1990s. The mobile phone (before the smartphone), despite its technological roots in the "telephone," was designed with several features that had little to do with "talking" as such. One key feature in the late 1990s Nokia phone was the text message, which enabled remote communication without vocal expression. In addition to being free of sound, the text message was also spaceless and timeless: it could be sent and received without eye contact, and unlike the phone call, a message would be waiting to be read until needed, thus removing time-criticality and potentially slowing down the pace of communication. Apart from its (customizable and mutable) notification sound, the text message was a "silent" means for communication, which also supported the user's potentially "slow" pace of life and facilitated social interaction also for those who felt uncomfortable in face-to-face situations.

The example of the text message as a "silent medium" or means for "silent communication" represents a concept that goes beyond "silence" in the English language. Whereas the English term "silence" (n.) is somewhat limited to "an absence of all sound or noise" (OED 2021), the Finnish counterpart, *hiljaisuus*, is multisensory: next to "silence," other accurate translations for the word are "slowness" and "stillness." Unlike most cultures that perceive silence in negative terms (Berry 2011), *hiljaisuus* is also associated with positive valence, as in "calmness." In other words, the Finnish language has the same word indicating the absence of sound, speed, and haste—and, instead, a pleasurable presence of tranquility.

In the use of modern communication media in particular, *hiljaisuus* thus intersects with techno-cultural development and its multisensorial phenomenology. Having a "chat" may now be entirely soundless and take place in written language, but at the same time, the exchanges can occur at a fast pace and involve hectic dialogue. Moreover, while the dialogue may involve pauses with lengthy intervals, these "silent" gaps may involve other sorts of sensory stimulation, either in the same medium, device, or via multitasking with other media and devices. In this context, *hiljaa* (adv.) becomes a "method" of sorts, no longer connected to the "silence" in a stereotype, but an approach to configuring devices that mediate human interaction in space and time. Using media *hiljaa* is an attribute, which reflects a controlled experience of use.[3]

Using Media *Hiljaa*

After the Dot-com crash of 2002, media use has changed radically. Text messages still exist, but in many diverse forms; from ephemeral Snapchat and public Twitter messages to Kakao, WhatsApp, and other platforms that are primarily designed for written personal dialogue. This interaction is multisensory and multimedial by default, for "messaging" now also involves audio, emojis, images, and videos. Outside private communication (and sometimes inside it too), the message may also serve "liking" systems, which have made it possible to instrumentalize social interaction into a game of positive feedback response. As a counter phenomenon to all these increasingly many features and forms of media, some people have felt the pressure for continuous engagement exceeding their daily resources, thus looking for more tranquil content and patterns of use. For example, the recent emergence of ASMR (e.g., Barratt and Davis 2015), digital detox (e.g., Wilcockson et al. 2019), and mindfulness/meditation apps collectively speak for a need to "slow down," "quiet down," or just "calm down."

To make a cross-cultural and linguistic connection, we return to what Heidegger (1927) said about "ending," as it also applies to silence and explains the multisensory nature of *hiljaisuus*:

> Initially, ending means *stopping*, and it means this in senses that are ontologically different. The rain stops. It is no longer objectively present. The road stops. This ending does not cause the road to disappear, but this stopping rather determines the road as this objectively present one. Hence ending, as stopping, can mean either to change into the absence of objective presence or, however, to be objectively present only when the end comes.
>
> (p. 227)

Sonic silence, too, is defined by stopping. Silence starts when sonic ends; and yet, silence ends when the sonic returns. Ontologically, silence is more complicated: because it consists of nothing, it never ceases to exist, but rather hides itself, until resummoned. On the other hand, there is rarely absolute silence, but rather a lowering of noise or voice—silence enables us to hear things, like a drop of water, that we would not hear otherwise. In this sense, silence is relative and always present to some degree; in one sense, dependent on a subjective threshold.

Finnish *hiljaisuus*, when understood by its parallel meaning as slowness of movement and progress, operates with the same principle. Unlike the absence of sound that is associated with sonic silence, slowness, by definition, cannot be perfect immobility but always involves some movement, however minimal. In the same way as silence opens a possibility to hear what is not hearable otherwise, slowness enables seeing what is not seeable otherwise. Ontologically, again, there is no stopping but slowing down; unlike the rain that disappears and the road that emerges present, both silence and slowness—*hiljaisuus*—make it possible for other entities to come into existence in the subjectively experienced world. This accurately describes what the recent "slow media" trends represent (Rauch 2018), in other words, using media *hiljaa*.

Enactive Agency

Husserl famously considered human time-consciousness to operate by experiencing the past, present, and future simultaneously: to be able to hear a melody as *a* melody, we cannot merely "remember" the past notes and "think" of the future ones, but we must somehow experience them at the same time by cognitively processing three parallel temporal domains. More recently, Gallagher and Zahavi (2014: 16) have suggested the very basic human experience to be embodied in the same way, as "nothing is an affordance for my enactive engagement if it is presented to me passively in a knife-edge present." This enactive account helps contextualize the experience of *hiljaa* in media use.

With the increasing number of daily technological devices that all include numerous applications, some people have started to worry about their decreasing time left for other life activities. At the same time, the frequent distractions that these media yield in the form of audio, haptic, and visual alarms—let alone the future-oriented anticipation to frequently "check" updates—have been considered intrusive enough to produce various regulatory actions around the world, limiting the use of such technologies not merely on the subjective level but throughout entire societies. As individual differences regarding the "right" amount and way of use will remain vast, it makes sense to conceptually identify the experience of use not merely as "time spent" but, rather, the *given attention at a certain pace*.

For any person, comfortable use of media allows them to direct attention to meaningful content in frequency and style, which does not disable them from meaningfully existing and perceiving the rest of the world. With respect to *hiljaisuus*, as a multisensory notion connoting "silence," "slowness," and "calmness," using media *hiljaa* is an act relative to sound, space, and time; a subjectively experienced comfort in using media in a way that is not obtrusive in any sensory form, but tranquil in relation to one's cognitive and emotional resources in the lasting context of use. The tranquility in question does not imply a lack of meaning or passion in one's interactions; rather, it is relative to them—being able to focus attention to media content that matters at the right time and in the right place, "silently" and "slowly" enough to not take over one's overall enactive agency.

The very function we wish to convey by *hiljaa*—silently, slowly, calmly—can be associated with the Finnish proverb *hiljaa hyvä tulee*, literally translated "the good comes slowly." The moral is that being able to produce or enjoy something of meaning and quality entails a time of waiting, which cannot be shortened. Instead, the time of waiting *certifies* the quality of the outcome, which can easily be undermined by haste and lack of patience. In this meaning, using media *hiljaa* is to optimize one's media use—not to maximize the consumption of content, but rather to get the best out of the content by maintaining a healthy relationship to it. This relationship is "silent" in the sense that it does not overflow one's multisensory capacities, and it is "slow" in the sense that it does interfere with one's daily pace as an obtrusively distractive need.

Conclusions

In this chapter, we have suggested the Finnish adverb *hiljaa* as a term for describing media use that is simultaneously "silent" and "slow" in a positive sense, thus producing a phenomenology of usage that is "calm" or "tranquil" subjectively. Using media *hiljaa* does not deprive one of their enactive agency. Following the Finnish cultural history of "silence" and "slowness," both sides of *hiljaisuus* have been treasured as valuable human characteristics. *Hiljaa* emphasizes the quality of experience in an ascetic philosophical sense, where less becomes more.

Notes

1 Acerbi's "Travels through Sweden, Finland and Lapland to the North Cape in the years 1798 and 1799" has been archived by Oulu City Library. https://digi.kirjastot.fi/items/show/120926.
2 The cultural history of *hiljaisuus* has been explored in several Finnish journal articles and books, but one of the most versatile ones is the one edited by Kaartinen (2015). In their *Hiljaisuuden kulttuurihistoria* [The Cultural History of Silence] Kaartinen (2015: 9–10) and her associates approach the history and cultural understanding of *hiljaisuus* as an endogenous part of Finnish self-understanding.
3 The relations of silence, listening, and "idle talk"—or in German terms the tensions between "Rede" and "Gerede"—are well-known among media scholars. The distinction in relation to media technology has been elaborated, for example, by Gradinaru (2018).

Work Cited

Aho, J. (1911), *Juha*, Otava.
Barratt, E. L., and Davis, N. J. (2015), "Autonomous Sensory Meridian Response (ASMR): A Flow-like Mental State," *PeerJ*, 3: e851.
Berry, M. (2011), "Communicating the Cultural Richness of Finnish Hiljaisuus (Silence)," *CercleS*, 1 (2): 399–422.
Englund, P. (2005), *Hiljaisuuden historia*, [The History of Silence], Helsinki: WSOY.
Gallagher, S., and Zahavi, D. (2014), "Primal Impression and Enactive Perception," in V. Arstila and D. Lloyd (eds), *Subjective Time: The Philosophy, Psychology, and Neuroscience of Temporality*, Cambridge: MIT Press, 83–99.
Gradinaru, C. (2018), "Small Talk in Our Digital Everyday Life: The Contours of a Phatic Culture," *META: Research in Hermeneutics, Phenomenology, and Practical Philosophy*, 10 (2): 459–72.
Heidegger, M. (1927/1962), *Being and Time*, trans. J. Macquarrie and E. Robinson, New York: Harper & Row.
Kääpä, P. (2010), *The National and Beyond: The Globalisation of Finnish Cinema in the Films of Aki and Mika Kaurismäki*, Oxford: Peter Lang.
Kaartinen, M. (ed.) (2015), *Hiljaisuuden kulttuurihistoria*, [The Cultural History of Silence], Turku: University of Turku.
Larkin, W. J. (2003), *Culture and Biblical Hermeneutics: Interpreting and Applying the Authoritative Word in a Relativistic Age*, Eugene: Wipf & Stock.
Luukkanen, T. L. (2015), "Kansankielestä yliopisto-opintojen kieleksi, Suomen kielen alkuvaiheista Helsingin yliopiston teologisessa tiedekunnassa [The Rise of Finnish Language in the Faculty of Theology at the University of Helsinki in the 19th Century]," *Faravid*, 40: 133–47.

Oxford English Dictionary (2021) "Silence," in *Oxford English Dictionary* (online). Oxford: Oxford University Press.

Peltola, R. (2018), "Being Perceptible: Animacy, Existentiality and Intersubjectivity in Constructions with the Finnish Verb kuulua 'to be perceptible (through hearing)'," *Nordic Journal of Linguistics*, 2018–05, 41 (1): 39–74.

Puro, J. P. (2002), "Finland: A Mobile Culture," in James E. Katz and Mark Aakhus (eds), *Perpetual Contact: Mobile Communication, Private Talk, Public Performance*, Cambridge: Cambridge University Press, 19–29.

Puro, J. P. (2009), "The Silence of Finnish Sauna," in Richard Wilkings and Pekka Isotalus, (eds), *Speech Culture in Finland*, Lanhan: The University Press of America, 139–49.

Rauch, J. (2018), *Slow Media: Why Slow Is Satisfying, Sustainable and Smart*, New York and Oxford: Oxford University Press.

Wilcockson, T. D., Osborne, A. M., and Ellis, D. A. (2019), "Digital Detox: The Effect of Smartphone Abstinence on Mood, Anxiety, and Craving," *Addictive Behaviors*, 99: 106013.

Filmography

Kaurismäki, A. (1999) *Juha*.
Särkkä, T. (1956) *Juha*.
Tapiovaara, N. (1937) *Juha*.

12

kō kō kà, the Sound of Colonial Shoes: Forgotten Words of a Yoruba Song of Success

(Origin Yoruba)

Babson Ajibade

There are no doubts at all about the industrial revolution's huge impacts on the histories of the world's peoples including, of course Africa—whose interior rivers opened to the aggressive extraction of international trade steamboats (Stearns 2020; Acan and Aygenc 2021). While the industrial revolution started in Britain, a chunk of its financing came from inflows of cash from the disruptive slave trade (Clark 2010; Northrup 2011; Erenze 2016), making Africa somewhat a "financier." Unsparingly, Williams (1944) reminds us that Britain's ending of the slave trade was because it ceased to be economically viable and not so much because of abolitionist pressures. When European colonialism commenced in Africa, it transcended the politics of disruptive material extraction (Morgan 1959; Engelbert 2000a&b; Bortolot 2003; Lange 2004; DeCorse 2013) because there was a missionary branch of it that sought to "civilize" the natives by "conversion" to Christianity. In an alternative way, the colonial missionary objective to convert the natives was also "extractive." This time, however, what was "extracted" was not material, but religious servitude in "winning" them for a new God. To achieve the objective, the missionaries sought to replace informal traditional educational systems of apprenticeships, oral traditions, and the Koranic recital system practiced by various peoples of Nigeria with Western formal education.

As part of their activities, missionaries like the Church Mission Society (CMS), Baptist, Catholic, Presbyterian, Wesleyan, and Methodist (Amadi 1977; Bassey 1991; Okoye and Pongou 2014) built churches, schools, trained catechists, and sent many on scholarship to school. However, between the north and south of Nigeria, there was disparity in both the uptake of missionary activities and the development of education generally. From as early as 1914, 1,100 primary schools existed in the north, as against 37,500 that were in the South (Csapo 1981). While it is believed that the missionaries' mandate for the so-called four R's: religion, reading, writing, and arithmetic put the northern society off (Ajayi 1965), Okoye and Pongou (2014) show that exposure to missionary activity in Nigeria was a vital determinant of the relative ethnic prosperity upon European contact. Since scholars agree that "ethnic characteristics and the willingness to accept missionary activity" (Oyeniyi 2013; Okoye and Pongou 2014) factored in the inauguration of educational disparities between the north and the south of Nigeria, this chapter sought to explore how the sociocultural dimensions of a popular song, kō kō kà ..., of the colonial times helped dispose the ethnic Yoruba to colonial missionary education and, by it, create generations of educated manpower that survive to this day.

Singing the Colonial Shoes

In colonial times, the only lucrative jobs available were those that required reading and writing abilities in the English language (Ugboajah 2008). Dressing in western attires was not negotiable for natives working for the institution, which give socioeconomic becoming a western coloration. The colonial missionary did cloth the people's bodies in European attires in the "new moral economy of mind and body," making dress become a marker of power, status, class, and labor-value (Martin 1994; Roche 1994; Panikkar 1998; Hansen 2010; Mitchell, Shibusawa and Miescher 2014). Among the Yoruba of the time, the western-style heel shoe was the icon of this becoming. But, in popular imagination, it was not the shoe itself that was the icon of this modernity and success; it was the "authoritative" sounds—kō kō kà—made by the shoes' heels, as the white man walked by. Whether it was in the church auditorium, classrooms, or at the colonial residences, the shoes make *the* sounds on the floor, announcing presence, long before the colonial wearer came into view. It was made into a song that parents sang and children learnt and recited:

Bàtà rẹ̄ á dún kō kō kà	Your shoe will sound kō kō kà
Bàtà rẹ á dún kō kō kà, bí ō bá kàwé rẹ	Your shoe will sound kō kō kà, if you study
Bí òò bà kàwé rẹ, bàtà rẹ á dún ṣẹrẹrẹ ní lẹ̄	If you don't study, your shoe will sound ṣẹrẹrẹ on the floor

The sound, kō kō kà, is the equivalent of wearing a strong heeled shoe and taking three steps, from a station point, as shown in Figure 12.1. In this song, the coveted modernity of kō kō kà is contrasted with the backwardness of the sound ṣẹrẹrẹ (akin to one made by a flip-flop, dragged on the floor). This agrees with Zachernuk's (1994) assertion that western-educated Africans of the mid-nineteenth century often re-worked European ideas into distinctive

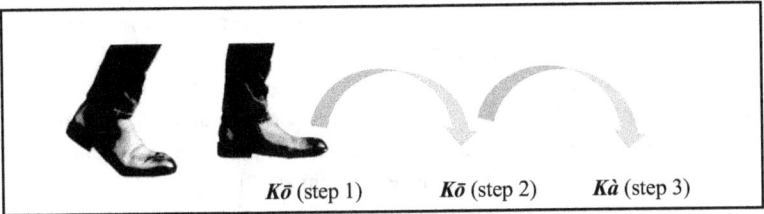

Figure 12.1 An illustration of how the kō kō kà sound is produced.

"hypotheses" suited to their colonial location. Suited to the Yoruba social and cultural location, the *kō kō kà* song therefore represented the ostensible Yoruba proletarian hypothesis, in which education was perceived to open the futuristic gateway to better lifestyles and desirable consumption practices.

From the belief that success in colonial life was tied to living like *àwón òyìnbó* (the white people), parents pursued the injunction in the *kō kō kà* song by either sending their wards to study hard at mission schools (Oyegbile 2020) or embedding them to live with and serve missionaries. Through this embedded servitude to missionaries, many young people got scholarships to study abroad, to triumphantly return at a later date. The song was further popularized by a singer known as Princess Bunmi Olajubu in the 1980s when Nigeria's petrodollar boom was declining. I recall kids my age singing it at school and in our play times in the 1970s to the 1980s. By the end of the 1980s decade when there was a structural adjustment and the economy collapsed (Maier 2000), popular cultures such as film fizzled out (Haynes and Okome 1997; Samuel et al. 2018), as well as the song also. As the famed promises in the *kō kō kà* song no longer could be realized, and education could not lift masses out of the structurally adjusted economy, the song gradually faded from public memory.

Pragmatic Cosmology

The Yoruba-speaking people, bonded by cultural commonalities, are spread in the west coast of Africa, between southwestern Nigeria and the Republics of Benin and Togo. Dislocated by the slave trade, Yoruba descendants are also to be found in the Americas. Originally, the Yoruba comprised several independent, thriving kingdoms that later declined due to forces such as wars with one another and with other ethnic kingdoms, and also the effects of the slave trade. Among several strands of the Yoruba creation myths, the names, *Ōdùdúwà*, and *Ife*, are ubiquitous features. *Ōdùdúwà* is the name of the progenitor of the Yoruba-speaking peoples, while *Ife* is the cradle of the culture's religion and civilization, with hundreds of representative terracotta, bronze, and iron artifacts surviving to this day. According to oral tradition, Ōdùdúwà had sixteen sons who became kings of ancient Yoruba kingdoms, and todays' monarchs are believed to be direct descendants of the ancients (Forde 1951; Ojuade 1992; Mullen 2004; Ellis 2007). The term, Yoruba, refers to both the people and their language (Olateju 2005).

In traditional Yoruba cosmology, the world is made up of two connected realms, the visible world of the living (called *Ayé*) and the invisible world of the heavens (called *Òrūn*) where ancestors, spirits, and deities live, ruled by *Ōlódùmārè*, the Supreme God (Idowu 1962). God is also called *Ōlórūn*— loosely translated as "one who owns the heavens." In one of the Yoruba creation myths, *Ōlódùmārè* gave a chain, some soil, a five toed chicken, and a snail shell to *Òrìsànlá*, one of the gods, and instructed him to go create the earth. On the way to execute the errand, *Òrìsànlá* fell asleep because he got distracted and drunken with palm wine. His brother, *Ōdùdúwà*, then took all the creation props that *Ōlódùmārè* gave, and proceeded to create the earth. He climbed down from heaven with the chain, poured the soil unto the water, and released the chicken to use its *ésè* (feet) to spread the earth in all directions, till all the terra firma was formed. *Ōdùdúwà* let a chameleon step upon the earth to test stability before he came down to settle in. There was a confrontation with *Ōdùdúwà* when *Òrìsànlá* came out of his drunken stupor. But *Ōlódùmārè* granted settlement to *Ōdùdúwà*, since it was he that created the earth.

From this beginning mythology, the iconography of the feet seems to have been firmly established in Yoruba thought. For, as Abimbola (1971) notes, the Yoruba conceive the human personality as having three key elements, *èmí* (soul) *ōrí* (head source) and *ésè* (leg/feet). While the literal translation means "leg," within human personality contexts, *ésè* would also mean "self-agency" or "hard work" or "struggle" (Olateju 2005). In the manner in which Abimbola (2006) structures it, *ésè* outlines the principle of individual effort or struggle that must precede the actualization of human potentialities. *Ésè* is then a Yoruba symbol of activity, mobility, and power in physical and spiritual personality terms. And, if the leg is the symbol of mobility, self-agency, and achievement, then the feet, being the part that makes actual contact with the floor during activities, are the embodiment of self-agency, self-development, and social elevation. To underscore the importance of *ésè* (the feet) in Yoruba systems of thought, we need only look at two popular proverbs:

1. Òlè l'ómo ésè ólè tọ lórí àkpātá (It is a thief that can trace the footsteps of a thief on a rocky surface)
2. Ēni bá fẹ tẹ'lẹ tútù, yò dōmi tútù si'wájú (anyone wishing to step on a cold floor has to first pour cold water ahead of the walk)

The first proverb encapsulates a social drama in which a thief makes his getaway via rocky grounds, upon which footprints will not show. In order to understand and successfully track the thief, the Yoruba insist that the tracker needs have the deft skills of a thief. The lesson here is that, prior to any gainful activity, a person must imbibe the inherent capacities needed for the quest. The second proverb has an even more relatable social drama, based on the high temperatures the earth can sometimes get, under the scorching African sunshine. Since many walked barefoot in traditional Africa, the parable advices that, on a hot day, anyone wishing to walk barefoot on a cold floor needs to first pour cold water on the ground. Again, the lesson here is a simple but logical one. Anyone wishing to have comfort must first use his/her own agencies to make the necessary modifications required for bringing the comfort into being.

Put together, these two parables underscore the pragmatism in Yoruba thought systems. The Yoruba believe very much in destiny and predestination. Òrí is the head source that controls àyànmó (destiny). The Yoruba believe that Ólódùmàrè predestinates all humans before they are born, and man's duty is to fulfill that destiny, which is out of his control (Hospers 1981; Oladipo 1992; Balogun 2007). However, Yoruba fatalism is very pragmatic. For, in Yoruba belief systems, while òrí is the bearer of destiny and also the essence that guides, rules, and controls human personality, traditional religion allows and enables individuals to find ways to change unfavorable destinies (Idowu 1962). In this, self-agency is key, as the parable, "ojú ni àlákàn fi n sọ òrí rẹ̀"—the crab watches its own head with its own eyes. With its unique anatomy, the crab has two independently moving compound eyes on stalks above, making it able to literally look down upon its own head. In the context of this parable, "òrí" refers to the head as a part of the body, and as controller of destiny. And, just as the crab is able to watch over its own head, in Yoruba thought, man is also able to watch over and direct his own destiny. Thus, when events are unfavorable in people's lives, and when negative events are foretold through dreams or through traditional clergies, the Yoruba go about finding ways including supplication, sorcery, and sacrifices to change things (Idowu 1962). In essence, like other African cultures, the Yoruba believe that, regardless of destinies and bad situations, man can, like the proverbial crab, "watch" over his own head and change unpalatable situations. In appropriating and using the sound of colonial shoes to engineer ethnic educational change, the Yoruba "watched its own head" and derived phenomenal impacts that could not have been envisaged. And, using colonial artifacts such as shoes to symbolize economic evolution is rooted in what Zachernuk (1994) terms "the complexities of West Africa's traditional dialogues with European ideas." Essentially, while the shoe was just an item of clothing for the colonialists, it became an icon of economic independence and social becoming—a sort of lived hypothesis that pushed people to higher echelons of the emerging social order. This new order of things—different from the traditional one in which kings and chiefs dominated—overturned previous *status quos* and opened up new spaces for self-remaking.

From Shoe Songs to Educational Revolution

By 1955, the Western Region government of Nigeria had galvanized the mantra of *kò kò kà* and introduced the free primary education program, laying the foundation for drastic educational change within its own ethnic geography (Ajayi 2008). In the years leading up to this, the Action Group Party (and later the Unity Party of Nigeria) led by Chief Obafemi Awolowo, increased expenditure on services that tended to the people's welfare, health, and education as much as possible, at the expense of all other subheads (Awolowo 1960). They introduced extensive teacher-training programs, including secondary technical education and secondary modern schools, which resulted in a phenomenal educational development. From 3,550 primary schools in 1952, the number rose to 6,274 in 1954 and 6,670 by the end of 1958 (Ajayi 2008). By the 1970s, "free education for all" had become the main objective of Awolowo's Unity Party of Nigeria. The methods were simple, including constructing half-walled classrooms (that many people scorned, at the time), providing free text/exercise books and reading resources, and ensuring that all schools offered arts, science, and commercial subjects. All of these granted education to millions of children from poor and low-income families, who would not have gone to school, otherwise. The number of schools built in Lagos State between 1979 and 1983, for example, is more than the total number constructed by all other governments of that state from 1983 until today (Fawehinmi 2021). This educational revolution ran across the Yoruba states well into the 1980's decade of despair, when Generals Buhari and Idiagbon's military coup of 31 December 1983 took place, and dealt a fatal blow to free education, and to the nation's educational development generally (Maigida 2017). However, spawned by the old colonial song of success, *kò kò kà*, the legacy of free education in the Yoruba states of southern Nigeria lived on and manifests even today. It positively affected several generations of critical intelligentsia and motivated many into careers in national development and politics (David 2020).

Nunn (2007) has provided an explanation in which the "stability of low production equilibria" continues to trap the colonized society in "suboptimal equilibrium" long after, making "Africa's past events continue to matter today."

It may be true that the colonial shoe—with the sounds it made on the floor—is a representation of Africa's colonialists' authority that has helped trap the Yoruba society in certain "equilibrium." However, unlike Nunn's suboptimal notion, this unique trap has led to social and educational optimization that continues to matter today, in the lives of the Yoruba of southwestern Nigeria. For those many children schooling in the pre-1986 Yoruba land, who sang the many versions of *kō kō kà*, colonialism and free education may have become bygone, to be relished with nostalgia. However, the song's richness sustainably impacted their lives because their own shoes sound "*kō kō kà*" today, referencing the success(es) made in their various walks of life. In Kofo Adeleke's recent 233-page biography of the Nigerian artist, Oyenike Okundaye, aptly titled, "*Bata Mi A Dun Ko Ko Ka*" the author analyzes the artist's works and traces her life's journey from the small village of Ogidi-Ijumu in Kogi State to the revered artistic personage she has become. Much rooted in eternal elements of her culture's mythology and worldview, the artist and her life keenly represent the fundamental Yorùbá song of success, *kō kō kà*, which translates "education is important in life" (Anazia 2021). In the song, *kō kō kà*, the fundamental Yoruba principle is that man can change his future, better his lot, and succeed in life's journey, by educating himself in the advantages of the here and now, no matter how difficult things may seem.

Transcending the politics of material and religious extraction, the British colonial enterprise pursued its own subjectivities, without recourse to the affectations of the colonized. Unknowingly, however, behind the back of the colonial gun-and-bible establishment, popular Yoruba imagination had reached back to the subtleties of its cultural mythology and, by it, crafted a motivational song of success for its own salvation. Created out a social artifact as obscure as the sounds colonial shoes made on the hard floor, this song could not have attracted more than a laugh from a colonial officer that hears it. Yet, this laughter would have been a response as naive as can be, oblivious of the serious cultural politics of social engineering that the song signified. While the colonial enterprise was content with material and religious extraction, Yoruba popular imagination worked out its own colonial gratuity and made cultural heroes (of an educated kind) out of its youths, using a seemingly insignificant archetype of British colonialism. In a way, therefore, against the ambiguous colonial conditioning, the *kō kō kà* song represents Yoruba cultural counter-positioning using an imagery of futuristic cultural heroes. Psychological studies have suggested that hero images can help uplift young people, inspire hope, and comfort (Kinsella et al. 2020). Thus, in using the song, the Yoruba were able to create subtle hero imageries that inspired and ensured a realignment of children toward self-improvement through education (Brown et al. 2016; Beggan 2019), and against the stereotypical cataloging that accentuated otherness, cultural difference, and racial superiority (Hansen 2010). In that sense, the West may be termed an unwitting "voyeur," in the construction, circulation, and reinforcing of negative *otherness* in (and about) the colonized. However, this is only one side of the *otherness* of the colonial "cultural voyeurism" coin—the more visible side. There is yet another, a less visible side, in which the local popular intelligentsia upturns, thwarts, and uses an ostensibly insignificant aspect of the colonialist's constructed *otherness* to reimagine and reinvent a positive new futuristic self. This is precisely what the Yoruba popular minds did, in using the sounds of colonial shoes as motivation and symbol of salient self-elevation. In doing this, it is not that the Yoruba "advocated the adoption of Western dress for their local subjects" (Hansen 2010); it is that the people's traditional pragmatism took hold, making them see the unique advantages in appropriating and using colonial categories in new ways of self-remaking. Thus, under the watchful eyes of the "oppressor," Yoruba popular imagination created a song—a mantra, so to speak, that glossed over the pain of colonialism itself and, instead, projected the unique subversive advantages of tapping into the colonial educational system.

There was certainly a heightening of identity politics leading up to Nigeria's independence in 1960 (Zachernuk 1994). But by the time Nigeria arrived as a nation-state, it was not just a question of various political and ethnic actors seeking personal space(s) in the new configuration but, more specifically, it was one in which individuals questioned their own possibilities and identities in the anxious new social economy. Swiftly appropriating and turning the essence of the *kō kō kà* song into an ethnic development agenda, the Yoruba political leadership under the direction of Obafemi Awolowo, created an impact far beyond what could have been envisaged.

With a gun in the right hand and a bible in the left—so to speak—the colonial enterprise certainly thrived in Nigeria among the Yoruba. Of course, none can wish away the incongruous moral dilemma of combining forced economic extraction with pious religious emancipation, on the same targets, by the same colonial inhumanity. If the choicelessness of the Yoruba was exemplified in their servitude to the colonial order, then the *kō kō kà* song and the decades of educational benefits it has given the people, is more than enough. For, not only was the first Nigerian university, the University of Ibadan established in 1948, even today, thirty-five of ninety-nine private universities in Nigeria are located in that ethnic geography. There is then a clear link between economic collapse in the 1980s Nigeria, the dearth of *kō kō kà* in Yoruba popular culture and the severe decline in educational development. Thus, if decades later the Yoruba continue to enjoy remnants of the educational revolution kindled by the *kō kō kà* song, then the cultural gamble of the colonial times has paid off, far beyond what could have been conceived. Not having benefited directly from the industrial revolution itself and, coupled with the disarray of British indirect rule, nonetheless, at least they have been able to create an educational revolution within their ethnic constituency, using the obscure sounds made by the shoes of their colonizers. How long the remnants of this ethnic educational revolution will sustain, the directions it will take, and whether the song's forgotten words will again rise in the emerging Nigerian economy of the post-covid era, remains to be seen.

Works Cited

Abimbola, K. (2006), *Yoruba Culture: A Philosophical Account*, Birmingham: Iroko Academic Publishers.

Abimbola, W. (1971), "The Yoruba Concept of Human Personality," in *La Notion de Personne enAfrique Noire. Collogues Intemationaux de Centre National de la Recherche Scientifique*, Paris: Centre National de la Recherche Scientifique, No. 544, 73–89.

Acan, V., and Erdal, A. (2021), "Changing Portrayal of Women during the Late Modern Period in Regard to Visual Communication Design," *Visual Studies*, (June 2021): 1–13, https://doi.org/10.1080/1472586X.2021.1950046 Retrieved October 1, 2021.

Ajayi, J. F. A. (1965), *Christian Missions in Nigeria, 1841–1891: The Making of a New Elite*, Ibadan history Series, London: Longmans.

Ajayi, S. A. (2008), "The Development of Free Primary Education Scheme in Western Nigeria, 1952–1966: An Analysis," *OGIRISI: A New Journal of African Studies*, 5: 1–12.

Akerele, K. (2020), *Bata mi A Dun Ko Ko Ka: A Biography of Nike*, Ibadan: Bookcraft Publishing.

Amadi, L. E. (1977), "Church-State Involvement in Educational Development in Nigeria, 1842–1948," *Journal of Church and State*, 19 (3): 481–96.

Anazia, D. (2021), "Bata Mi A Dun Ko Ko Ka launch, Soyinka, Onobrakpeya Celebrate Okundaye," *The Guardian*, January 17, https://guardian.ng/art/at-bata-mi-a-dun-ko-ko-ka-launch-soyinka-onobrakpeya-celebrate-okundaye/ Retrieved September 20, 2021.

Awolowo, O. (1960), *Awo: The Autobiography of Chief Obafemi Awolowo*, Cambridge: Cambridge University Press.

Balogun, O. A. (2007), "The Concepts of Ori and Human Destiny in Traditional Yoruba Thought: A Soft Deterministic Interpretation," *Nordic Journal of African Studies*, 16 (1): 116–30.

Bassey, M. O. (1991), "Missionary Rivalry and Educational Expansion in Southern Nigeria, 1885–1932," *The Journal of Negro Education*, 60 (1): 36–46.

Beggan, J. K. (2019), "On the Downside of Heroism: Grey Zone Limitations on the Value of Social and Physical Risk Heroism," *Heroism Science*, 4 (2): 1–35.

Bortolot, A. I. (2003), "Trade Relations among European and African Nations," in *Heilbrunn Timeline of Art History*, New York: The Metropolitan Museum of Art.

Brown, B., Nasiruddin, M., Cabral, A., and Soohoo, M. (2016), "Childhood Idols, Shifting from Superheroes to Public Health Heroes," *Journal of Public Health*, 38 (3): 625–9.

Clarke, C. (2010), "Fuelling the Machine: Slave Trade and the Industrial Revolution," *Constellations*, 1 (2): 26–41.

Csapo, M. (1981), "Religious, Social and Economic Factors Hindering the Education of Girls in Northern Nigeria," *Comparative Education*, 17 (3): 311–19.

David, P. (2020), "UPN Manifesto Attracted Me to Politics—Ize-Iyamu," *The Punch*, https://punchng.com/upn-manifesto-attracted-me-to-politicsize-iyamu/ Retrieved September 28, 2021.

David, S. L. (2003), *The Unbound Prometheus: Technological Change and Industrial Development in Western Europe from 1750 to the Present*, 2nd edition, Cambridge and New York: Cambridge University Press.

DeCorse, C. R. (2013), *Postcolonial or Not?: West Africa in the Pre-Atlantic and Atlantic Worlds*, Ibadan: Institut français de recherche en Afrique, Nigeria.

Ellis, A. B. (2007), *Yoruba-Speaking Peoples of the Slave Coast of West Africa: Their Religion, Manners, Customs, Laws, Language, Etc*, London: Forgotten Books.

Englebert, P. (2000a), "Pre-colonial Institutions, Post-colonial State, and Economic Development in Tropical Africa," *Political Research Quarterly*, 53: 7–36.

Englebert, P. (2000b), "Solving the Mystery of the African Dummy," *World Development*, 28: 1821–35.

Erezene, H. B. (2016), "European Influence in Ijo-Itsekiri Relations in Nigeria," *African Research Review*, 10 (1): 104–15.

Falola, T. (1986), "Missionaries and Domestic Slavery in Yorubaland in the Nineteenth Century," *Journal of Religious History*, 14 (2): 181–92.

Fawehinmi, Y. (2021), "Lateef Kayode Jakande: A Model of Excellence in Leadership," *The Cable*, February 19. https://www.thecable.ng/lateef-kayode-jakande-a-model-of-excellence-in-leadership, Retrieved September 28, 2021.

Forde, C. D. (1951), "The Yoruba-Speaking Peoples of South-Western Nigeria," in *Ethnographic Survey of Africa*, vi.102. London: International African Institute.

Hansen, K. T. (2010), "Colonialism and Imperialism," in Valerie Steele (ed.), *The Berg Companion to Fashion*, Oxford: Bloomsbury Academic, 155–9.

Haynes, J., and Onookome, O. (1997), "Evolving Popular Media: Nigerian Video Films," in Jonathan Haynes (ed.), *Nigerian Video Films*, Jos: Nigerian Film Corporation, 21–44.

Hospers, J. (1981), *An Introduction to Philosophical Analysis*, London: Routledge and Kegan Paul.

Idowu, E. B. (1962), *Ọlọ́dùmàrè: God in Yoruba Belief*, London: Longman.
K., N. P. (1998), "The 'Great' Shoe Question: Tradition, Legitimacy and Power in Colonial India," *Studies in History*, 14 (1): 21–36.
Kinsella, E. L., English, A., and McMahon, J. (2020), "Zeroing in on Heroes: Adolescents' Perceptions of Hero Features and Functions," *Heroism Science*, 5 (2): 1–45.
Lange, M. K. (2004), "British Colonial Legacies and Political Development," *World Development*, 32: 905–22.
Maier, K. (2000), *This House Has Fallen: Nigeria in Crisis*, London: Penguin Books.
Maigida, A. Y. (2017), "A Review of Nigeria's Universalization of Education and the Perceptible Analysis of Universal Basic Education as a Concept and Phenomenon," *International Journal of Academic Research in Business and Social Sciences*, 7 (7): 693–706.
Martin, P. M. (1994), "Contesting Clothes in Colonial Brazzaville," *The Journal of African History*, 35 (3): 401–26.
Michele, M., Shibusawa, N., and Miescher, S. F. (2014), "Introduction: Gender, Imperialism and Global Exchanges," *Gender and History*, 26 (3): 393–413.
Morgan, W. B. (1959), "The Influence of European Contacts on the Landscape of Southern Nigeria," *The Geographical Journal*, 125 (1): 48–64.
Mullen, N. (2004), *Yoruba Art and Culture*, ed. Liberty Marie Winn and Ira Jacknis, Berkeley: Phoebe A. Hearst Museum of Anthropology & University of California at Berkeley.
Northrup, D. (2011), "Africans, Early European Contacts, and the Emergent Diaspora," in Nicholas Canny and Philip Morgan (eds), *The Oxford Handbook of the Atlantic World*, Oxford: Oxford University Press, 1450–850.
Nunn, N. (2004), "Slavery, Institutional Development, and Long-Run Growth in Africa, 1400—2000," in *International Trade 0411007*, Germany: University Library of Munich.
Nunn, N. (2007), "Historical Legacies: A Model Linking Africa's Past to Its Current Underdevelopment," *Journal of Development Economics*, 83: 157–75.
Nunn, N. and Wantchekon, L. (2011), "The Slave Trade and the Origins of Mistrust in Africa," *American Economic Review*, 101 (7): 3221–52.
Ojo, O. (2008), "The Organization of the Atlantic Slave Trade in Yorubaland, ca.1777 to ca.1856," *The International Journal of African Historical Studies*, 41 (1): 77–100.
Ojo, O. (2017), "The Slave Ship Manuelita and the Story of a Yoruba Community, 1833–1834," *Revista Tempo*, 23 (2): 360–82.
Ojuade, J. S. (1992), "The Issue of 'Òdùdúwà' in Yoruba Genesis: The Myths and Realities," *Transafrican Journal of History*, 21: 139–58.
Okoye, D. and Pongou, R., "Historical Missionary Activity, Schooling, and the Reversal of Fortunes: Evidence from Nigeria (August 20, 2014)." Available at SSRN: https://ssrn.com/abstract=2484020 or http://dx.doi.org/10.2139/ssrn.2484020

Oladipo, S. (1992), "Predestination in Yoruba Thought: Philosopher's Interpretation," *Orita: Journal of Religion*, XXIV (1&2): 34–51.

Olateju, A. (2005), "The Yorùbá Animal Metaphors: Analysis and Interpretation," *Nordic Journal of African Studies*, 14 (3): 368–83.

Oyegbile, O. (2020), "Bata Mi a Dun Ko Ko Ka … Graceful Journey of Nike Okundaye," *NijaTimes*, December 19, https://www.naijatimes.ng/bata-mi-a-dun-ko-ko-ka-graceful-journey-of-nike-okundaye/. Retrieved September 23, 2021.

Oyeniyi, B. A. (2013), *Internal Migration in Nigeria: A Positive Contribution to Human Development*, Report, Brussels: ACP Observatory on Migration.

Roche, D. (1994), *The Culture of Clothing: Dress and Fashion in the "Ancient Regime,"* New York: Cambridge.

Samuel, U. E., Udo, B. E., and Imolemen, K. I. (2018), "The Implication of Naira Devaluation to the Nigeria's Economic Development," *Business and Economics Journal*, 9 (1): 1–6.

Stearns, P. N. (ed.) (2020), *The Industrial Revolution in World History*, 5th edition. New York: Routledge.

Ugboajah, P. K. N. (2008), "Culture-Conflict and Delinquency: A Case Study of Colonial Lagos," *Eras*, Edition 10. https://arts.monash.edu/__data/assets/pdf_file/0007/1670623/ugboajaharticle.pdf Retrieved September 20, 2021.

Williams, E. (1944), *Capitalism and Slavery*, Chapel Hill: University of North Carolina Press.

Zachernuk, P. S. (1994), "The Historiography of Origins in West Africa," *The Journal of African History*, 35 (3): 427–55.

13

L'Implèxe: What's in a Situation?

(Origin French/German)

Holger Schulze

What will be happening? Or, more precisely: can one know from the circumstances of a current situation how this situation will turn into another, a future situation? Or, even simpler: can we know the future and its dynamics of how it will unfold? One might be inclined to outright decline such questions. No one knows the future. And even if so, wouldn't that be horrific? Yet, we all make certain assumptions about the foreseeable future or some future far away—actually, we do assume such trajectories incessantly so. You might already have planned what you will do tomorrow. Some people even booked their holidays for next summer. Other people made contracts for a book to be published in the next two or three years. And not too few people have plans for their retirement, for when their kids left their home, for where they wish to be buried, how to be cremated, and whom to give their record collection or hand over their online archives and accounts.

Some of these future scenarios are clearly extrinsically motivated, but for others one can find an intrinsic motivation. I feel like going for a long walk in the woods tomorrow. I need to take a bath right now. For now, I've read enough; I need to listen to some music. I feel like watching a 1980s blockbuster movie now, what about you? Oh, I need a snack, something spicy, sour, maybe crunchy, hmmm … I wanna scream at something. I need to rehearse now to play my part in that piece a bit better. I am tired. I need to sleep. I want to come.

So, how can one conceptualize future developments starting out with a currently present situation, including your and my inclinations and all of their potential trajectories? On the following pages I wish to explore this question with a concept that was originally invented by a poet and essayist. The invention of this concept itself mirrors already the poetic and artistic research of its author. Since 1894 Paul Valéry used a huge number of notebooks, the famously erratic *Cahiers*, to note and to organize, to think with and to be inspired later by all the momentary ideas, inspirations, impromptu theories, sceneries, observations, and self-reflections on all areas of his life. Among other aspects of his life, his literary practice, and his everyday experience and thinking, he also explored the manifold sensibilities and their minuscule transformations and transmutations he experienced, sensed, and reflected. Valéry's *Cahiers* are a true chaosmos, if you will, of his reflections, his ruminations, and associative thinking, his sensibilities, the volatility of his sensibility and thinking. The *Cahiers* are the material situation out of which Valéry's thinking and writing did emerge. They are the fertile ground on which his poems, plays, and essays grew—and a concept like *l'implèxe*, or: *the implex*. So, what does the concept of the implex actually mean—and how can we use it as a term, a word, a conceptual tool?

What Is the Implex of this Situation?

The implex of a situation can be understood as an assortment of dispositions, determinations, trajectories, inclinations, and implications that structure tangibly what *lies* in this moment. The metaphor of *lying* is in this case remarkable: the phrase actually says that there is something to be found in the complete set of constituents of this very situation, in all its objects, their positioning, their activities, in the agents, and their positioning, their activities, their intentions, their previous experiences, apparent inclinations, their tendencies, and desires, even in the environmental conditions, the materials, their ongoing transformations, the climatic and pervasive weather of this situation that might lead to one or the other subsequent result. Wow, such an exhaustive inventory sure must sound either like some confused, alchemistic rambling or like some poetic incantation, carefully rehearsed, in order to conjure the hitherto unexpected apparition of a ghost, a ghoul, or even a *Weltgeist*? Indeed, all of this can be found in the concept of the implex.

The word implex can be unfolded into a much longer phrase. One might silently, implicitly hear, when reading or hearing the word implex at the same time a much longer explication such as: an *implied complexity* or a *complex of implications*? The word implex signifies a hidden entity, hidden in a materially compressed and folded structure that does not allow to recognize or to understand all its implications right away. But it is not invisible to gain access: it just needs the right technique, the right way to unfold it, the right skills and sensibility for doing so. Sensibility, indeed, is key here. If one can employ the right way of sensibility one might arrive at a correct assessment of a given situation: one arrives at a comprehensive and explicit result of the implex of this situation. In 1940 Paul Valéry notes in his *Cahiers*, under the moniker *Sensibility*:

> Implex, is basically what is implied in the notion of person or self, and is not of the present moment. It's the potential of general and specialized sensibility—of which the present is always a matter of chance. And this potential is conscious.
>
> (Valéry 2007: 221)

The *virtual* and the *potential*, these are highly abstract and complex categories—more often than not hard to imagine, to understand, and almost impossible to materialize, to visualize or to exemplify in a simple way. Baudrillard's and Virilio's concepts of the virtual still suffer today from misunderstandings and folk etymologies attached to their original concepts that were further developed from their origins in Deleuze's and Bergson's writings (Bergson 1991; Deleuze 1991; Virilio 1994; Baudrillard 2000; Shields 2002). Valéry now employs such an abstract concept to explicate his even more abstract concept. It evaporates before our eyes. But the implex has a truly corporeal and precise meaning, it can be explicated in thoroughly material terms.

Let's unpack it: "It's the potential of general and specialized sensibility—of which the present is always a matter of chance" (ibid.). An implex refers therefore to some sort of sensibility, to a corporeal and trained, a refined and personal sensorium of a particular person. It is an activity. This sensorium serves as a way to understand a given, material situation or context. This personal and active sensibility that you or I might be able to refine and develop over time understands *the present*—as in: *the present situation*—as a *matter of chance*: it is not a matter of fact, a matter of a finite and determined end of a development. It is the start of a further development, its *potential start*.

The implex takes the present situation as a starting point for further developments: it recognizes, through its active sensing, foremost its possibilities, its potential future trajectories and options, its spaces of possibility. One might argue that Valéry's term of the implex hereby comes asymptotically close to Robert Musil's *sense of possibility* or *Möglichkeitssinn* (Musil [1930] 1978: 16–18; Marquez 1991; Bauer and Stockhammer 2000)—and even to Virilio's aforementioned concept of the *virtual*. All three terms struggle in different ways with the potential but not yet actualized, the imminent and tangible, but still absent, still inexistent in the narrower sense. But whereas Virilio's term is strictly focused on technology's potential to at least intermittently actualize this potential; and whereas Musil's term is focused on a more psychological capacity to imagine and to outline potential scenarios and futures as if they were explicit as in Porphyrian Trees; the term by Valéry indeed implies an almost compelling (if not compulsive) direction of development. It is not an arbitrary option as in Musil's thinking and it cannot be operationalized through technology as in Virilio's thinking.

The implex is indeed a property of a particular person and her or his elaborated sense for such a development: "Implex, is basically what is implied in the notion of person or self, and is not of the present moment" (ibid.). Moreover, this sense is not habitual or obscure, it is not hermetic or stylized as some form of performance, magic spell or poetic, artistic demonstration: "this potential is conscious" (ibid.). It is a conscious sense for future trajectories and potentials that allows for self-reflection, for doubt and falsification, for confirmation an actualization. It can be observed and affirmed if an implex indeed unfolds in the way a person had already had a sense that it would.

What Is Implied in a Person?

The implex as a comprehensive and explicit result is explicating the potential developments starting from a given situation. However, the implex as an activity, as a capacity or skill, maybe even a competence pertains to a particular person. It is a personal skill. It is not the property of a situation or the skill of a situation. It is a person's skill to interpret, to understand, to sense, and to project the future trajectories of this situation. It is implied in this person: the future trajectory is not an impersonal, anonymous, or abstracted one. It lies in your or my or her or his sensibility and activity. This is the harshly and stunning anti-structural, the highly affectively loaded and intensity-filled economy within Valéry's thinking of the implex. The implex is a sense, a capacity to feel, or even to sensate. It is not some apersonal form of knowledge, not an epistemological practice and neither an anthropological model that could be operationalized. The implex as an activity of sensing is in a particular person and it is personal. In *Idee Fixe*, a so-called "A Dialogue at the Seaside," first published in 1932, Valéry lets one protagonist say:

> The implex ... is [our] ability to feel, react, do, understand—individual, variable, more or less perceived by us—and always imperfectly, and indirectly (like the sensation of fatigue),—and often misleading.
>
> (Valéry 1965: 56)

The implex is a way of sensing or feeling, Valéry is pretty clear in this passage. It is precisely this drawing together, this bundling, this multiplexing in one person that is the activity of sensing the implex: it is an activity of *implexing*. As an activity the word implex refers to this bundling and assessing of all the vectorial energy from all the potential trajectories in this very situation—as it is sensed, as it is felt and experienced by one person. This person, capable of sensing the implex, is the actual arena in which the implex materializes: it is, apparently, the best way in which the implex can find an actualization— where it actually unfolds. Your sense of something, your capacity to assess this situation, and its potential actualize at the same time the implex of this situation. It is in your sensibility.

What is implied in a person is a materially, a corporeally actualized assessment of this given situation now. The person is understood by Valéry if you will as a node, a zone of interaction and fusion, a burning glass of a situation's characteristics, its vectors. This understanding is not too far away from the expanded notions of agency that Bruno Latour and even more so Karen Barad and other scholars propose within the field of New Feminist Materialism. Here the collective and processural character of actions, sensations, impressions, and assessments is equally important. Though Valéry writes apparently about one subject and its sensations, its proprioceptive experiences as separated from others, this separation is only a functional one in order to analyze in more detail how all the properties, trajectories, ferments of a situation actually are realized within this person. Whereas Barad or Latour would never put so much emphasis on one subject as Valéry does, they as well account more for the situation and its constituents, their "intra-action" as agents as for one person (cf. Barad 2007: 141). In a sense Barad, Valéry, and Latour are actual *situationists* in a strictly non-Debordian and a highly relational and contextual understanding. They all favor and focus on *situated knowledges* (Haraway 1988) or even *situated generativity* (Schulze 2018: 212-31).

Valéry though, indeed, stresses not so much the collective emergence, but the inherent sense for something, the vectorial energy in all the sensibilities present in a person. This is his sensualist background. But he connects this to the issue of how the scientific knowledge and concept of a human being, of man, and of self had changed recently in the twentieth century—and how this might or might not have affected one's actual self-reflection. What kind of person are you if you consider yourself being a swarm of vectors, a node of connectivities, a medium, and material in midst of a situated constellation instead of the one and only acting subject?

What Is the Implex of These Events?

The situated and personalized aspects are just the most obvious approaches to understanding or analyzing an implex. However, these might not be the most consequential approaches for theory, epistemology, even politics, and all sorts of thinking, arguing, and writing. In 2012 Dietmar Dath and Barbara Kirchner published a large volume of over 800 densely set pages in German that focuses under the title of *Der Implex* on the aspects of social progress also inherent in this very concept. Dath and Kirchner take Valéry's concept of an intrapersonal sensation of situated knowledge or generativity and expand it into a sociological or even historical figure of thought. In *Der Implex* they investigate the dynamics, obstacles, and successful strategies when struggling with social progress. In eighteen sections they scrutinize the documented histories of Marxist and other projects of social transformation in a sort of inspired timetraveling. They review in their analysis the predetermined situations of these projects, their potential, and their actual effects on people's everyday life—all in light of the implex.

This reviewing starts with the assumption—in a simple but thoroughly bureaucratic, German phrase—that "bestimmte nicht unwahrscheinliche Folgelagen seien der Implex einer spezifische Ausgangslage gewesen" (Dath and Kirchner 2012: 44). They assume that *certain, not improbable subsequent situations were the implex to a specific starting situation*. Therefore, if these consequences are implied complexly, as an implex, in the starting situation, then one could already start reflecting on the implex in any present and given situation. One could ask right now: what will have been the social and political, the economic, and technological implexes of this very situation right now? How will the present constituents of this situation predetermine future developments—though not in a linear manner, but in a more implied, indirect, dialectical way that might even seem unlikely, self-contradictory, or paradoxical right now? Or: what hidden potential to social change lies in the events these days?

For Dath and Kirchner social transformations rely to a large degree on particular scientific discoveries. They provide the potential to pave the way for subsequent inventions effectively then driving social change that might lead to a revolution. Political transformations are—following Dath and Kirchner—equally implied in scientific discoveries as in social transformations (Dath and Kirchner 2012: 42). This is exemplified in *Der Implex* by their main example of the Industrial Revolution. This revolution provided on the one hand the technical means for an accelerated capitalization and exploitation of workers and lower classes—but on the other hand it also offered the tools for new and much more powerful forms of workers' associations than ever before. The Industrial Revolution promoted factually the following political revolutions—a genuinely dialectic and Marxist *Denkfigur*.

From this prime example, Dath and Kirchner unfold a series of comparable cases to exemplify the analytical strength and the future prolificness of the implex. They assume for instance that contemporary transformations regarding globalization and digitalization might have in the near future similarly dialectical effects as the Industrial Revolution: the revolution of computerization, digitization, automation, and globalization might promote in the end an even more substantial political uprising, a societal, institutional, and economical reversal, a larger revolution than ever before. Dath and Kirchner see the implex at play in all of these cases—and they use their analysis to try to understand better what makes social and political change possible at all? What are the prerequisites that distinguish potentially futile endeavors from more promising and hopeful ones? In contrast to Valéry's largely introspective, essayist, and poetic understanding they propose a revolutionary interpretation of the implex. Therefore, they do not focus on effects on a person, but effects on a situation. The implex of a situation or a series of events is in their understanding therefore defined as an inclination toward a certain direction of further development or action, implying—if not demanding—a collective or individual generativity. Cautiously enough, though, Dath and Kirchner reject all teleological or even eschatological determinism in this process. Still, it is required for all actors involved to actually respond to and to deal with the manifold coincidentalities affecting it. An implex is not unfolding and realizing itself without our action. More precisely it realizes itself through us. It is a generative and transformative understanding of the potential in societies and cultural developments—not their determinist structure.

They document this, most convincingly, it seems to me, by referring to the everyday examples of the washing machine or the dishwasher. Historically, both of these machines apparently had the potential function to overturn the heteronormative power structures of the bourgeois family and its gender roles. In the end, it can be observed actually:

> The washing machine or the dishwasher have knocked a few weapons out of misogyny, however, this was nowhere and never sufficient for corresponding social changes; this detailed observation already contains everything one should know about the chances of any further elimination of the division of labour as a breeding ground for hierarchies, exploitative conditions, exclusion, etc.
>
> (Dath and Kirchner 2012: 808;8 translated by Holger Schulze)

It is instantly clear that the implex in a situation is never a thoroughly determining force toward future developments. It is a potential that can be actualized, that might indeed be actualized—but maybe even in a different way with more and different problems arising from its unfolding. Events that carry an implex can always turn out this or another way. And neither a progressive and reflected consciousness of its actors nor the most advanced material or technological tools will safely determine a desired outcome.

This is the complex dialectics of an implex: from hindsight it might seem even too simple to analyze: it might even look like some historical logic just resulting in their unavoidable consequences. Yet, in the moments just before the unfolding of an implex this result is neither trivial nor obvious. The implex is a thorough volatile and malleable quality in society: it desperately needs the action, the activism, the intervention, also the protest and the critical, the vital, and truly innovative and revolutionary agency of many protagonists. Only these actors on the stage of politics and of social protest can indeed, following Dath and Kirchner, transform a still imaginary constellation of an implex into some actual social progress. They materialize an implicit inclination of a situation, a complex set of implications, their potential inherent to a given situation, and its events into political action and social progress. The implex is real, it is material and existing—yet it remains a mere potential if no one cares to contribute to it, to actualize it, to bring it into existence by one's own energy and political agency.

The Implex of This Chapter

Right now, just before handing in this chapter to the editor of this volume, the concept of the implex is not a widely used or even known one. To most of the readers this is surely a new concept. However, one can envision a future boom, a wider spreading of this concept, surely supported by the writings in which Dietmar Dath and Barbara Kirchner expanded on this concept—but maybe also, because this concept meets contemporary thoughts and needs in regard to transforming societies and economies in various directions: to decolonize and to decarbonize them, but also to care for a more equal distribution of wealth on a planetary scale and to address, to attack, and to eradicate injustices within societies from the sides of racism, sexism, ableism, classism, or ageism. The concept of the implex might help in all of these cases to strategically work with existing inclinations to reach this goal.

However, this is just some speculation, a particular vain one in my case of this chapter here. It is more realistic, it seems to me, to focus on the rather individual if not personal reactions, the sensing thoughts, the thinking sensations, or *Denkempfindungen* that some of the readers might experience along the way of joining me here in this chapter. "Memory operates in terms of a similar virtuality, beginning with a virtual state and leading step by step up to the point where it gets materialized in an actual perception" (Ansell 2005: 1117). I sense that the events unfolding from reading such a chapter, maybe remembering some observations or thoughts or references later on, in another context of academic work, research or publishing could indeed contribute to a wider debate around the issues raised with Paul Valéry's concept of *l'implèxe* and how authors like Dietmar Dath and Barbara Kirchner recently worked with it. How could it be possible for you and for me to refine our collective *Implexaufmerksamkeit—our sensibility for implexes*? Can we train our sense for *specific starting situations that might result in desired, future situations as their implex?*

Works Cited

Ansell, K. (2005), "The Reality of the Virtual: Bergson and Deleuze," *MLN—Modern Language Notes*, 120 (5): 1112–27.

Barad, K. (2007), *Meeting the Universe Halfway: Quantum Physics and the Entanglement of Matter and Meaning*, Durham: Duke University Press.

Baudrillard, J. (2000), *The Vital Illusion*, New York: Columbia University Press.

Bauer, G. and Stockhammer, R. (eds) (2000), *Möglichkeitssinn. Phantasie und Phantastik in der Erzählliteratur des 20. Jahrhunderts*, Opladen: Westdeutscher Verlag.

Bergson, H. (1991), *Matter and Memory*, trans. N. M. Paul and W. Scott Palmer, New York: Zone Books.

Dath, D., and Kirchner, B. (2012), *Der Implex. Sozialer Fortschritt: Geschichte und Idee*, Frankfurt am Main: Suhrkamp Verlag.

Deleuze, G. (1991), *Bergsonism*, trans. H. Tomlinson and B. Habberjam, New York: Zone Books.

Haraway, D. (1988), "Situated Knowledges: The Science Question in Feminism and the Privilege of Partial Perspective," *Feminist Studies*, 14 (3): 575–99.

Márquez, César Moreno (1991), "The Sense of Possibility: On the Ontologico-Eidetic Relevance of the Character (the Experimental Ego) in Literary Experience," *New Queries in Aesthetics and Metaphysics: Time, Historicity, Art, Culture, Metaphysics, the Transnatural – BOOK 4: Phenomenology in the World Fifty Years after the Death of Edmund Husserl*. Edited by Anna-Teresa Tymieniecka, 329–42.

Musil, R. [1930] (1978), *Der Mann ohne Eigenschaften*, Reinbek: Rowohlt Verlag.

Schulze, H. (2018), *The Sonic Persona. An Anthropology of Sound*, New York: Bloomsbury Academic.

Schulze, H. (2020), *Sonic Fiction*, New York: Bloomsbury Academic.
Shields, R. (2002), *The Virtual*, London: Routledge Publishing.
Valéry, P. (2007), *Cahiers/Notebooks 3*, trans. Norma Rinsler, Paul Ryan, Brian Stimpson, based on the French Cahiers edited by Judith Robinson-Valéry, Frankfurt am Main: Peter Lang.
Valéry, P. (1965), *The Collected Works of Paul Valéry—Part V: Idee fixe. A Duologue by the Sea*, trans. D. Paul, preface by J. Mathews, introduction by Philip Wheelwright, Princeton, NJ: Princeton University Press.
Virilio, P. (1994), *The Vision Machine*, Bloomington: Indiana University Press.

14

Ljom—A Meditation

(Origin Norwegian)

Erik Steinskog

I only remember very indistinctly from an academic conference many years ago discussing terminology related to sounds. More specifically, it was about echo, and relations between English and German. In addition to echo, other words in the conversation were reverberation and resounding, as well as *Widerhall*, *Nachklang*, and *Hall*. Neither English nor German is my language, and the conversation was about different connotations of these words that are often lost on me. Working primarily in English, the constant attempts to understand nuances in language, so as to describe what I am writing about as good as possible, are a necessary part of my everyday life. While that episode from many years ago is almost forgotten, the feeling of not quite having the words available needed for my writing, as well as a constant feeling of not having enough nuances in my language, is still with me.

In this article, I will give a different take on questions of language and sound, although the echo will come back. It is a constructed take, in the sense that I am forcing myself to think with, around, and in continuation of a term from my own language: the Norwegian word *ljom*. I am trying to unfold the word's meanings and connotations, trying to explicate nuances that word have for me, to see how a different perspective is opened up for me by forcing myself to think in one language and write in another. In one sense, then, a meditation on a word. This context also leads to a text being more personal—subjective or idiosyncratic—than I prefer. But it seems to me inevitable that not least the associations of the term *ljom* as well as the attempt to write about them in English are situated in me as a writer. In *Monolingualism of the Other; or, The Prosthesis of Origin*, Jacques Derrida writes that "One cannot speak of a language except in that language" (Derrida 1998: 22), and still I am trying to do just that. There is, though, and following from Derrida's sentence, a distinct possibility that I will fail. But perhaps there is still something to be learned from such a failure.

One of the consequences of this attempt, one of the results I strive for is a reflection on what happens for my thinking when working with a different vocabulary. Trying to write about sound, however, reflection might not be the best word, given the visual connotations. A literal understanding of reflection would be to seeing oneself in a mirror, and thus an event of doubling taking place almost instantaneous. Trying to think something similar in the aural or acoustic domain, it would seem that the echo is the aural parallel of reflection. But then a different temporality is at stake, as the echo takes a bit of time to come back. The resounding takes more time than the reflecting. While the optical and the acoustic may point to a similar analogy, the movement from the reflection to the echo, implies both temporal and spatial relations, as well as different relations to the senses.[1]

Thinking about sound depends upon the language available for conceptualizing sound. The sounds may be "the same," but the language is more and different than just a neutral description. What we hear is dependent upon the words we can use to describe what we hear. Listening is not just taking in sounds, it is not just a passive reception, and this despite the often-repeated claim that the ears are always open to receive sounds, that we have no "earlids." R. Murray Schafer writes, in *The Soundscape* (originally from 1977), that "The sense of hearing cannot be closed off at will. There are no earlids" (Schafer 1994: 11), whereas Marshall McLuhan and Quentin Fiore state, in *The Medium is the Massage* (originally from 1967), that "We can't shut out sound automatically. We simply are not equipped with earlids" (McLuhan and Fiore 2001: 111). I find it of interest in both Schafer and McLuhan, that any distinction between listening and hearing is not referenced. To me, the reference to the missing earlids rather points to how the sense of hearing is differently organized than the sense of seeing, that the ears are open. Thus, the ear will filter out parts of the sounds around the listener. As Schafer writes: "The ear's only protection is an elaborate psychological mechanism for filtering out undesirable sound in order to concentrate on what is desirable" (Schafer 1994: 11). So while Jean-Luc Nancy, in *Listening*, makes a sharp distinction between listening and hearing, there is also a possibility that this distinction is more a question of filters, where hearing is toward the unfiltered side whereas listening is toward the perfectly filtered. Schafer's psychological vocabulary obviously moves in a different register than Nancy, making the comparison of the two difficult. But there is also the possibility of insisting on the distinction between listening and hearing: "If 'to hear' is to understand the sense [...], to listen is to be straining toward a possible meaning, and consequently one that is not immediately accessible" (Nancy 2007: 6). But in Nancy's discussion this distinction is understood differently in the case of listening to language on the one hand and listening to music or sound on the other. "In the latter case, that of music, it is from sound itself that sense is offered to auscultation" (Nancy 2007: 6).

As someone writing my research in a second language thinking of the relation between vocabulary and what can be thought, is in one sense also an everyday experience. I am a Norwegian citizen living and working in Denmark, but the biggest part of my research is written in English. And while my English vocabulary is getting bigger and better, the experience of not quite having the words to be precise is well-known. In addition, when teaching in a language that is slightly different than my mother tongue, I also at times feel a distance to my own language, as if I need time to re-enter the space for thinking that my mother tongue establishes. And, to go into even more minute details, the first language I learned to write in school was *nynorsk* ("new Norwegian"), the smallest of the two official Norwegian written languages (the largest being *bokmål*) two different languages with different histories, different geographies, different ideologies, and thus different associations for the language users.

Thus, when I hear the word *ljom*, the word this article is centered around, I firstly hear it in *nynorsk* (even more precisely I hear it in my spoken dialect, but for the sake of argument I simplify to written language right here), and that even if the word is found in both *nynorsk* and *bokmål*, and there is no difference of meaning in the two. In that sense the word is Norwegian (beyond the division of *nynorsk* and *bokmål*). The word also has an Old Norse etymology. It comes from *hljómr*, which is also one of the etymologies for the English word "loud." The Norwegian word is both a noun ("ljom") and a verb ("å ljome"), and as such describes both a sonic phenomenon and perhaps better phenomena in the plural, but it also describe the making of said phenomena. It would, however, be a mistranslation to simply say that "ljom" is equivalent with "loud." Rather, translating *ljom* one needs access to a number of concepts of sound: echo, reverberation, arguably noise, as well as "sounding" or "to sound." It is this movement from one word—in both its versions as noun and verb—to a multiplicity of words for sonic phenomena, that this article circles around, as both a point of departure and a line of flight. What happens, one may ask, when trying to think a cluster of words and terminology, with a foreign vocabulary, a vocabulary where the relations between the different terms are reshuffled or imagined differently?

Ljom means a (distant) rumbling sound, as well as resound. I want to spend some time breaking down these different components. The different features inherent in a "(distant) rumbling sound" also mean that dimensions of time and space are at stake in the meaning of the word. On the one hand, the distant dimension that can be found related to *ljom*, points out that as listeners we hear differently whether the sounds are close or distant. The sounds are—or may be—the same, but our position in relation to the sounds makes them different.

The term "rungende" is often used in describing the kind of sounds called *ljom*. It signifies resounding as well as rumbling and could also be translated as swelling. Here a distinction to echo comes into play. Echo could be seen as the most literal understanding of "re-sound." A sound that is heard again, softer or more distant, than the first time it was heard. Not least in nature is this how an echo works. One could easily take a stereotypical, almost national romantic, view of making a noise along a Norwegian fjord or between mountains and hearing how the sound comes back as an echo, resounding back to the sound-maker. This making, however, is not necessarily the result of human agency, as the *ljom* can also come from nonhuman actors and be used to describe natural sounds. The Norwegianness of the term *ljom* also opens for a renegotiation between so-called natural sounds and cultural sounds, that is, *ljom* can also be used to describe echoes and reverberations as they are heard between mountains or across fjords, and while this use could be seen as (hopelessly) nationalist and/or romantic, in this article this will rather be used as a way to question how one might think about "natural" sounds (or sounds in nature) as cohabiting how sounds found in "culture"— from cityscapes to music—are interpreted.

With the addition of "distant" as a description of *ljom*, one possible way of understanding it is as a "field of sound" taking time as well as working in space, where volume and clarity may change, although it is "the same" sound that is heard over time. An echo is kind of the same, although the second time we hear the echo is slightly different than the first (often it is softer). Thus, the meaning of the word implies that the particular sounds of *ljom* are perceived differently according to the listeners' positionality. Hearing a rumbling in the distance may imply an indistinct sound, almost a noise, as if different sounds are superimposed on one another and where, perhaps due to distance, it is difficult or impossible to make distinctions in the sound. Listening to a concert from another place than the concert venue may be one example. Because one is at the wrong place, the sounds one hears are not the same as the audience. One could also think of sounds in the environment as rumbling, where the sounds from a distant highway may be in the background if one is not paying attention, and gradually becomes a rumbling if one tries to listen. This rumbling sound, however, cannot be the same as background noise. At least not if one follows how Michel Serres writes about background noise in *Genesis*: "The background noise never ceases; it is limitless, continuous, unending, unchanging" (Serres 1995: 13). Serres also writes that "we never hear what we call background noise so well as we do at the seaside" (Serres 1995: 13), but the indistinct dimension of background noise in Serres's understanding, means that it must be something different *ljom* is referring to. The rumbling sound, the re-sound, the reverberation—what sticks out as something that *ljomar* is not unending and unchanging. It is something we can hear. So if "background noise is the ground of our perception, absolutely uninterrupted," as Serres writes (Serres 1995: 7), then *ljom* is something, an object—sound-object—that can be distinguished from an overall rumbling.

That *ljom* is etymologically related to the English word "loud" is of interest as well. Even if I said that it would be a poor translation to say that the *ljom* and loud is equivalent, the question about volume is of interest. As a "(distant) rumbling sound" one must in a sense imagine the volume of what is heard. Listening at a distance means that one can add to the sound the most likely volume the sound has at its origin. If a distant sound is perceived as loud, this must mean that the perception of loud is not reduced to volume alone. Perhaps this is easiest discussed in relation to an echo. As resounding one is used to the second sound—the echo—being softer than the first, thus the echo is not only taking place later in time, but also in a process of decrescendo. The temporality of the echo is thus at the same time a change in volume, or loudness. But the former loudness is in a sense still inscribed in the sound. The sound will have been loud even if it is not still loud. This part of the conversation, however, also indicates that "loud" is not necessarily a dimension of the sounds. It can also be a dimension of the imagination. I have some reservations about the term imagination in writing about sounds, as the image in imagination makes it too much into a term of visuality. I am not saying that music cannot in some sense produce images in the mind of a listener. That is too well known to argue against and can be seen as a way of codifying music over time, so that certain figures, sounds, orchestrations, and so on, are given associations that listeners use in their listening. In that sense, for example, we may as listeners share some common ground in how we would expect the sounds of an open landscape to be in a film score. Listening to similar sounds without visuals—say in a concert hall—may then bring back the same kind of associations. In that sense music can be given a more concrete "content" that just being abstract sounds. And in this particular sense, the term imagination is probably the right one. What I am thinking about in relation to loudness, however, is slightly different. How do we hear volume? And not least, how do we hear volume in the combination that something distant is at the same time loud? Playing a LP of music one knows is "loud" at a low volume does not take away the "loudness." There is something in the texture and timbre of the sounds that still communicates the loudness. This banal fact is of interest in understanding *ljom* as well, in particular in the sense of a distant sound.

I am not saying that all sounds I would describe as *ljom* are loud, but to me at least the loudness is implied in a lot of the sounds where I would use *ljom* to describe them. But due to the distance, the sounds can still be perceived at a lower volume, but the loudness is implied. Does this mean that I only imagine the loudness? Is it my imagination that is adding more volume to the sounds that there actually is?

In addition to "distant" and "rumbling," *ljom* also means sound. It is a particular sound, but is a sound, nevertheless. Thus, *ljom* is also related to "lyd" as well as to "ljod" (both terms for sound), a word which is found in Icelandic (as *ljóð*), but also in Norwegian dialects. It is not a word I use—when writing Norwegian, I use *lyd* instead (which is "the same" word). Given that the l in *ljod* is silent—*(l)jod*—for me at least the relation or similarity between *ljod* and *lyd* are less clear. It is not that I need writing to see the relations, but simply that thinking about the etymology of everyday words, is not something I do except when doing research (where I also forget from time to time), and I am not doing research in my mother tongue. But here, in the midst of writing about *ljom*, as a particular kind of sound, the relation to *lyd*, and thus the "master-concept" sound comes into play. Thus, not only is *ljod* or *lyd* two versions of the same word, but they are also overall terms that in an everyday sense cover or subsume *ljom* as a subcategory. Trying to think the relation between these two words, however, leads to me questioning my own sense of hierarchies. While it is obvious that "sound" is the universal concept and *ljom*, as defined above, is a particular concept, there is something about the experience of sounds where one could say that the experience always is particular. It is not that I question grammar, it is more that the relation between *ljom* and *lyd/ljod* gets me to think about my experience of sounds, not least of different sounds, and how the minor differences in words are attempts to describe differences in sounds, even if both the two terms under discussion can be translated as "sound." Is it that the differences are untranslatable? I do not necessarily think so. Rather, thinking in Norwegian gives me a different sense of nuances than I am capable of communicating in English. I am convinced that a native speaker of English will have similar experiences with words used to describe sounds, perhaps not identical, but similar. And perhaps this is the most important thing I have learned from forcing myself to think about *ljom*, that some experiences of the sonic, some ways of thinking nuanced about sound, is influenced by those tiny changes in vocabulary that follows from an intimate life with a language.

I cannot quite help also thinking about the Norwegian term "klang" in this context. As in German it is translated as sound, but is also related to terms like tone, sonority, and note. I would also say that it is closely related to timbre. In German one may also relate to "Ton," "Schall," "Geräusch," and "Laut" again in a context where different nuances of sound are at stake. Whereas *klang* is a noun, a related verb is also found: *klinge* (to sound). And I again get into a challenge when trying to describe the differences between *ljom* and *klang*. But perhaps *klang* is closer related to tone and implies something closer to harmony. Not that *ljom* is disharmonic, at least not by necessity, but both the loudness and the rumbling dimensions of *ljom* make it easier to think these sounds on the side of the non-harmonic.

The Norse etymology of *ljod* or *lyd* is *hljóð*, a term used to describe sound and noise, music and cries, but also, perhaps more surprisingly, silence. Thinking about sound and silence related to the same term might feel paradoxically at first. To me, however, this opens a possibility for thinking silence not as the absence of sound, but as a certain space of sonority. It is not, though, that sonority is easy to think. As Jean-Luc Nancy writes, in *Listening*: "The sonorous present is the result of space-time: it spreads through space, or rather it opens a space that is its own, the very spreading out of its resonance, its expansion and its reverberation" (Nancy 2007: 13). The relation between space and time, which Nancy even compares with the famous line from Wagner's *Parsifal*—"Here, time becomes space" (Nancy 2007: 14)—is also used to discuss listening. In the act of listening, and, "as soon as it [the sonorous] is present, the sonorous is omnipresent," Nancy writes, and in these complicated reflections on sound, the sonorous, and listening/hearing there is something between one element and the other, "in such a way that sound sounds or resounds always beyond a simple opposition between consonance and dissonance, being made of an intimate harmony and disharmony among its parts" (Nancy 2007: 15). This is of course not something Nancy relates to the etymology of *hljóð*, but I reference it here more to illustrate how my meditation on the Norse terms gives me an opportunity to rethink Nancy's discussions differently. And expanding on the "return from one element to the other," that Nancy discusses, I also include with *hljóð* also sounds and resounds beyond the opposition of sound and silence. I am not saying that Norse etymologies and John Cage's thinking are pointing in the same directions, but there are interesting parallels.

In a sense, then, *ljom* and *ljod* mean almost the same. Why do two words have the same meaning? And here comes one of those passages I am unable to write in English. As a language-user I know the different nuances between *ljom* and *ljod* if I were to use them in my own language. But I am unable to translate that difference into writing in English.

Note

1   This discussion of reflection and echo is inspired by Philippe Lacoue-Labarth's *Typography* (Lacoue-Labarthe 1998: 165).

Works Cited

Derrida, J. (1998 [1996]), *Monolingualism of the Other; or, The Prosthesis of Origin*, Stanford: Stanford University Press.

Lacoue-Labarthe, P. (1998), *Typography: Mimesis, Philosophy, Politics*, Stanford: Stanford University Press.

McLuhan, M., and Fiore, Q. (2001 [1967]), *The Medium Is the Massage: An Inventory of Effects*, Corte Madera, CA: Gingko Press.

Nancy, J. L. (2007 [2002]), *Listening*, New York: Fordham University Press.

Schafer, R. M. (1994 [1977]), *The Soundscape: Our Sonic Environment and the Tuning of the World*, Rochester, VT: Destiny Books.

Serres, M. (1995 [1982]), *Genesis*, Ann Arbor: The University of Michigan Press.

15

Māya: A Measured Response in and to Cinematic Virtual Reality

(Origin Sanskrit)

Soudhamini

Introduction

There is a certain mysteriousness associated with the Indian philosophic notion of *māya*, that defies capture by reason alone and must be apprehended creatively. First mentioned in the *Vedas,* an oral-aural tradition of epiphanic verse, compiled into text between 1500 and 1800 CE, it later becomes a foundational term in *Advaita Vedanta*, a philosophical system predicated on nonduality (*dvaita*—duality, *advaita*—nonduality) that emerged at/as the culmination, both historical and teleological, of the *Vedas* (*veda + anta*: end). Together they constitute a complex discourse distributed over multiple treatises, as well as an unbroken spiritual tradition that continues till today. My approach to it is limited and minimalist, as I look at one particular aspect of it, viz. the poetic act as philosophical enquiry, and the onto-cosmology—notion of self in the world—that it is predicated upon. Cinematic Virtual Reality and VR in general are micro-cosmologies that the audience inhabit from within, and I believe the Vedic vision can provide an aesthetic, ethical, and ecological model for this immersive habitat.

Māya in the Vedas

For the Vedic *Kavi*—poet-seer, *māya* is that mysterious power of manifestation by which the living universe comes into being ceaselessly as an emergent cosmos. Grounded in a dynamic order *māya* is the revelation of the universe as an integrated, self-emergent, and self-organizing whole, that inspires the *Kavi's* rapturous verse in response. Refusing the modest comfort of either religion or science, these verses seek to apprehend reality on its own terms, as mystery and as epiphany and polyphony, to be apprehended directly through poetic and philosophical intuition.

> Where was this creation born? Where did it come from?
> The gods were born after the creation of the universe
> Who then can know whence it comes?
>
> (*Ṛgveda* 10:129)

> Where is the breath and blood and soul of the earth?
> Where can one go to ask this of someone who knows?
>
> (*Ṛgveda* 1.164.4)

Participating actively in *māya*, not simply as beholders but as active *mayins* in their own right through their verse, the origins of which are equally unknown, the Vedic *Kavi* wonders too and often in the same breath, about the *māya* of the self, and what it is grounded in.

> How does the wind not cease to blow?
> How does the mind not rest?
> Why do the waters ...
> never ever stop flowing
>
> (*Atharva Veda* 10:7:37)

> Searching within their hearts with wisdom
> Poets found the bond of being within nonbeing
> Their ray extended light across the darkness
>
> (*Ṛgveda* 10.129)

> My ears unclose to hear, my eyes to see,
> the light that harbours in my spirit broadens
> Far roams my mind, its vision extending into the distance
> What shall I speak, what shall I now *imagine*
>
> (*Ṛgveda* 6.9.6, emphasis mine)

The senses including the mind are precision instruments, sensitive antennae that probe and scan both inner and outer universes. Faculties focused within, they study the act of knowing even as it differentiates itself from non-knowing—how knowledge comes *to be*—leading to the recognition that order and being—the ontological state—occurs from within. This shapes their understanding of the universe too as being internally originated and ordered, and they align the rhythm of their verse to the rhythms of this universe as a living presence. Day, night, the seasons, the sound, touch, sight, and feel of water, as well as its absence in drought, its excess in floods, its celebration in rain, and in similar fashion the dynamic being of fire, air, earth, ether, the sun, dawn, thunder, lightning, bandits, rivalry, hunger, fear, joy, awe, need, gratification—everything comes within the purview of these verses. And even as the attention spirals within and without, the sense of unbroken continuity between self and universe, sharing the same experiential registers and grounded in the same dynamic order, arises as the first intimations of nonduality. Self::verse::universe—"There is a structural and qualitative connection here between a hidden truth and the way that truth is expressed" says William Mahony (1998: 64).

Prabhu Dutt Shastri (1991) among others, traces the etymology of the term *māya* from the Sanskrit root √*ma*: to measure, to show, to form, to know. Betty Heimann refers to these "manifold implications of the verbal root" as a word's original "material" meaning (1964: 172). Drawing on this range of meanings, "the measurer," suggests Jan Gonda, is the one who possesses "true knowledge" (1959: 180) operating as "a limiting or determining principle" (1959: 192).

> The hypothesis may be ventured that *ma* expressed the sense of realising in the phenomenal world – and this implies in three-dimensional space – what was mentally conceived, converting an idea into dimensional actuality.
>
> (Gonda 1959: 168)

This includes for Gonda the process by which thought is converted, "through the arrangement of words, adapting them to definite schemes and metres ... into a poem" (1959: 169) indicating a close relationship and parallel between imagination and cosmogony. "The same expressions may apply to the production of handicraft, the generation of offspring, the performance of beneficent or maleficent deeds and the creation" says Gonda (1959: 167).

Similarly, for Mahony the ambit of *māya* includes "*áma* – to build, construct, *nima*—to shape, form, *parima* – to fashion, *vima*—to arrange and *sanma* – to bring together" (1998: 244)—all of which can moreover be understood and employed both physically and figuratively. Poetry is *praxis*, and the poets weave their poem—"let not my thread be severed as I weave the song" (*Ṛgveda* 2.28.5) or fashion and carve it like a sculptor—"I have imagined a thought like a skilled workman" (*Ṛgveda* 1.38.1) and steer it like a charioteer—"As a wheelwright bends a chariot seat, so I turn the verse in my heart" (*Ṛgveda* 10.119). The Universe itself is therefore seen as an "artefact"(Mahony 1998: 35), an "image" (37), and a "poem" (37). "The power of sound, vision and thought capable of producing concrete phenomena—these are summed up in the word *Māya*," says Jeannine Miller, "and show *Māya* as that mental power capable of producing or shaping things at the phenomenal level" (1985: 117).

The Sanskrit root √*vid*, from which the term *Veda* is derived, is equally—"to know, perceive, understand" as it is to "experience, make-known, teach," clarifies Mahony (1998: 235). Aligning themselves with the universe, the *Kavi* makes it known by precept, invoking it *in like measure*, in the scale and cadence of their verse, emulating and invoking its dynamic rhythms not simply through words but as living form. Even today the recitative meters—*chandas*—of the *Vedas*, with their precisely staggered aural rhythms, are deemed more significant than their meaning. Meaning is always emergent and experiential, the words being merely the spur and residue of the Vedic recitative act.

Māya in Advaita Vedanta

In the *Vedantic* discourse that follows historically and is compiled as the *Upanishadic* treatises between 700 and 500 CE, the philosophical insights of the *Vedas* are sought to be elaborated into a schema. There is a compulsion now to *establish* foundational terms rather than know them imaginatively and poetically alone. The *brahman* as formless ground now becomes the focus rather than *māya*. But the self is still the instrument of knowledge, providing the epistemological framework by which "to know." The *Mandukya Upanishad* thus defines the *brahman* as that universal continuity of consciousness, that persists beyond our sleeping, dreaming, and waking states, and the *atman* as its embodied presence in the individual self. *Māya* now becomes a veil that obscures rather than reveals. In the phenomenology of *Advaita Vedanta*, argues Sankara, *māya* is a critical fallacy, a delusion of the mind that through projection (*vikshepa*) and superimposition (*āvriti*) obscures true reality (1921: 46–7)—but dissolves when recognized as such. To ascribe ultimate value to the visible universe, without realizing that it is mere appearance and true reality lies behind it, is like mistaking a rope for a snake, says Sankara (1921: 45–6). When one realizes one's error, the snake disappears, it simply ceases to exist like a mirage. And a mirage, says Sankara elsewhere, does not wet the desert sands (1921: 177).

The power that the *Vedic Kavi* ascribed to *māya*, Sankara seems to deny, in the service of establishing the *brahman* as the only true reality. Even so the notion of *Māya* is retained as a paradox within the *advaitic* schema. Frithjof Schuon thus exclaims—"*Māya* may be likened to a magic fabric woven from a warp that veils and a weft that unveils" (1965: 89). Raimondo Panikker refers to it as "the most *powerful* and *elusive* of terms of Indian *wisdom*" (1983: 461, emphasis in the original). The eighth-century Sankara's vision is a worldly and theological one, compared to the Vedic cosmic and poetic vision. Yet it has critical value. Patriarchy itself can today be considered *māya in* this wordly sense of the term, a fabricated system so pervasive in its structuration of every system and institution we live by, that it passes for reality. The Vedic poet would recognize it as *dur māya*—the harnessing of *māya* to harm, rather than *su māya*—for good. Many such instantiations can be cited, as indeed Barthes (1972) does in the name of myth, that he first debunks then re-mythologizes, a mode that Chela Sandoval then commandeers for "meta-ideologizing" her "methodology of the oppressed" (Sandoval 2000).

The elegance of *Advaita* as a philosophic schema, lies in its integrity of organization around the principle of nonduality, never splitting into binaries. It is able to do this because resolution always takes place within the self. The *atman* is the central node of *advaitic* intuition, where inside and outside, formlessness and form, meet and get resolved. It is the primary relationality of *māya: atman* that I will now carry over as an organizing principle into the CVR cosmo-ecology.

Māya—Atman in Cinematic Virtual Reality

Not much work has been done yet to theorize Cinematic Virtual Reality in light of western philosophical notions of the virtual, particularly in the work of Pierre Levy and Gilles Deleuze. I have found it extremely useful to explore this in two previous essays (Soudhamini 2020, 2021). In this chapter, I extend that study further to look at the resonances between Levy and Deleuze's notion of the virtual, and the notion of māya. Both philosophically and in the "apparatus" of VR, i.e., technology + ideology, such resonances abound, and my hope is that through such an intercultural cross-fertilization, I may be able to propose a paradigm of practice for CVR, that is both creative and critical, aesthetic and ethical.

Pierre Levy derives the term virtual from the Latin *virtus* meaning strength or power. "The virtual, strictly defined has little relationship with that which is false, illusory or imaginary," says Levy.

> On the contrary it is a fecund and powerful mode of being that expands the process of creation, opens up the future, injects a core of meaning beneath the platitude of immediate physical presence.
> (Levy 1998: 16)

Closer to the Vedic *Kavi's* invocation of *māya* than to Sankara's, Levy is also less invested in establishing "true reality," seeking to understand the virtual on its own terms. "The virtual is that which has potential rather than actual existence. The virtual *tends* toward actualization, without undergoing any form of effective or formal concretization" he says (1998: 23 emphasis in the original). And once actualized, the actual does not resemble the virtual. Rather it is a response to it. The virtual's mode of "expanding the process of creation" is thus formal and evolutionary.

> The virtual is a kind of problematic complex, the knot of tendencies or forces that accompanies a situation, event, object or entity, and that invokes a process of resolution: actualization.
>
> (Levy 1998: 24)

With Deleuze the virtual achieves an even fuller articulation. Raising the fundamental question, "What is the nature of the virtual?" Deleuze replies, "the characteristic of virtuality is to exist in such a way that it is actualized by being differentiated and is forced to differentiate itself, to create its lines of differentiation in order to be actualized" (Deleuze 1991: 96–7). Most interestingly this process of differentiated actualization is for Deleuze too an act of "measuring."

> Virtual time itself determines a time of differenciation, or rather rhythms or different times of actualisation which correspond to the relations and singularities of the structure that, for their part, *measure* the passage from virtual to actual.
>
> (Deleuze 1994: 211, emphasis mine)

Actualization comes about in and as duration, in and as a continuous process of formation and transformation of the virtual into the actual. "Evolution takes place from the virtual to actuals. Evolution is actualization, actualization is creation (1991: 98)." Actualization is thus "an immanent event ... actualized in a state of things and the lived that make it happen" (Deleuze 2001: 31). Levy's virtual as problematic, becomes with Deleuze, "a state of the world, a dimension of the system, and even its horizon or its home" (2004: 280). "It is not immanence to life, but the immanence that is, being in nothing, is itself a life" (2001: 27). It is in other words a "pure immanence" (2001).

To me Deleuze reads like a contemporary scientific-philosophical formulation of the Vedic *Kavi's* poetic intuition. One could even call it scientific intuition, for intuition is indeed a "method" for Deleuze (1991: 13). It would be (literally) counter-intuitive, to look for one to one correspondence between the two, for they are independent frames of reference and epistemologies, far apart in space-time. One is expressed as discourse but with the precision of poetry. The other is expressed as poetry but is also tacit discourse. Rather than argue the connection I suggest that we simply pay attention to it, embracing both epistemologies and allowing them to inform, inspire and nuance our understanding and practice in CVR.

Cinematic Virtual Reality itself, I propose, is a mode of actualizing VR technology, by responding to its affordances creatively. But to do that, the field or "the state of things or lived that make it happen" must first be cleared. VR's chief affordance according to techno-ideologists, is a deep spatial and sensorial immersion referred to as "presence." Mel Slater and Sylvia Wilbur define it in the following terms, and as a foundational definition I quote it at length:

> Immersion is a description of a technology and describes the extent to which the computer displays are capable of delivering an inclusive, extensive, surrounding, and vivid illusion of reality to the senses of a human participant [...] The fundamental idea is that participants who are highly present should experience the VE [Virtual Environment] as the more engaging reality than the surrounding physical world, and consider the environment specified by the displays as places visited rather than as images seen.
>
> (Slater and Wilbur 1997: 606)

Loosely translated as the sense of "being there," presence is technically defined as "an illusion of non-mediation" (Lombard and Ditton 1997)—and valued as such. The success of a VR experience is calibrated by how well it manages to sustain an illusion of presence. For Michael Abrash, chief scientist at the Facebook owned Oculus, "Presence is an incredibly powerful sensation and its unique to VR ... most people find it to be kind of magical, and we think that once people have experienced presence, they'll want it badly" (Abrash 2014: np). Presence is thus VR's ideological fulcrum, and with VR we are truly privy to a technology that "engineers" response rather than simply evoking it, tapping into what Abrash gleefully calls our "lizard brain."

What must be immediately apparent from the above discourse is that VR technology is an attempt to create a "limited" version of Sankara's *māyā* as illusion, but for diametrically opposite ends. If Sankara's *māyā is* a critical fallacy, VR attempts to induce rather than dispel it. As technology, VR is an undeniable achievement in terms of how completely and credibly it manages to create its own virtual and illusory reality. But audiences are nowhere as gullible as this discourse anticipates, and despite what the market may salivate for, it is not with our lizard brains that we respond. Far from being an "illusion of non-mediation," the wonder and admiration is precisely *for* the mediation. The technology *is* the message, so to speak.

For Jeremy Bailenson, technological presence is the seat of empathy, rendering VR as Chris Milk famously put it, "the ultimate empathy machine" (Milk 2015). Any number of films from Milk's own "Clouds over Sidra" (2015) to Alejandro G. Inarritu's "Carne e Arena" (2017) are predicated on heightening a sense of presence to create empathy—facilitating audiences to walk in another's shoes, inhabit another's world, even become another. For Bailenson "VR is far more psychologically powerful than any medium ever invented [...] When done right, VR experiences [...] will feel so realistic and immersive they will have the potential, similar to experiences in the real world, to enact profound and lasting changes in us" he says (2018: 2–4). Bailenson in other words seeks to harness the illusion for good, as the means to an end.

In another direction, media art theorist Oliver Grau, locates VR within a long tradition of "illusion spaces" all of which attempt to "integrate the image and the observer" (2003: 14). This "illusion of integration," warns Grau, is inevitably characterized by "diminishing critical distance" (2003: 13), radically affecting "the institution of the observer" (2003: 10).

> My contention is not that virtual art from the computer is always directed at maximising illusion. However, it must be said that it does operate within the energy field of illusion and immersion – the paradigm of this medium. Whether the individual artists are critical of this aspect or implement it strategically, nevertheless, it remains the foundation on which this art operates.
>
> (Grau 2003: 9)

While Grau unlike the others, seems to be resisting VR's power of illusion rather than celebrating it, he too seems to share the (mis)conception that the virtual, the digital, nay the image itself, is ontologically flawed with the "original sin" of illusionism.

In both cases, the medium is conflated with the technology, the same nomenclature—VR—being used for both. The filmmakers who create an illusion of "being there," also create an illusion of alterity—being someone else—toward creating empathy in the experience, and behavioral change beyond. In Grau's case the ontology of the virtual is itself illusory, being non-material (arising as it does from the computer) hence any medium predicated on it can only be illusory whatever strategy an artist might employ.

This pervasive association of the virtual with illusion is Sankara's "shadow" uncannily inverted!

If one could flip the paradox, and understand the virtual as the Vedic *māya*, and virtuality itself as generative and creative, as Deleuze and Levy propose, an altogether different paradigm opens up. Howard Rheingold, one of the first to track the development of VR across small university hubs and entrepreneurial start-ups across the globe recognized early that with this technology

> Our most intimate and heretofore most stable personal characteristics – our sense of where we are in space, who we are personally, and how we define 'human' attributes – are now open to redefinition.
> (Rheingold 1991: 46)

Jaron Lanier, credited with naming VR, admits the technology's considerable sense of presence when he says "Once your nervous system adapts to a virtual world the most ordinary surface, cheap wood or plain dirt, is bejeweled in infinite detail for a short while. To look into another's eyes is almost too intense" (Lanier 2017: 54). But he goes on to insist

> It is not just the world external to you that is revealed anew … For who is the VR experience for if not for you … There you are the fixed point in a system where everything else can change … Virtual Reality is the technology that exposes you to yourself … [It] peels away phenomena and reveals that consciousness remains and is real.
> (Lanier 2017: 55–6)

This is the paradigm of *māya-atman*, the relationality of the self with a technological presence that is simultaneously vivid and insubstantial, full and empty, presence and absence, in response to which one is stripped to one's essence, as the "phenomena" of our everyday selves is peeled away, and one is pure consciousness, a virtual self. Both aspects of *māya* coalesce here as one continues to wonder and marvel at what the laser described beam reveals, even while stepping back and watching oneself watch. The *atman*, I propose, is the formal definition of the self in CVR. One is a self *as* consciousness. Every aspect of the technology, from image, sound and their space-time co-ordinates in the narrative mise-en-scene, can be designed and choreographed to invoke not the lizard brain, but the evolutionary, virtual self of the audience. This is the problematic, potential and promise of CVR as a medium.

Works Cited

Abrash, M. (2014), "What VR Could, Should, and Almost Certainly Will Be within Two Years," *Steam DEVDAYS*, http://media.steampowered.com/apps/abrashblog/Abrash%20Dev%20Days%202014.pdf

Bailenson, J. N. (2018), *Experience on Demand: What Virtual Reality Is, How It Works, and What It Can Do*, New York and London: W. W. Norton and Company.

Barthes, R. (1972), *Mythologies*, trans. Annette Lavers, New York: The Noonday Press.

Deleuze, G. (1991), *Bergsonism*, trans. Hugh and Barbara Habberjam Tomlinson, New York: Zone Books.

Deleuze, G. (1994), *Difference and Repetition*, trans. Paul Patton, New York: Columbia University Press.

Deleuze, G. (2001), *Pure Immanence. Essays on A Life*, trans. Anne Boyman, New York: Zone books.

Deleuze, G. (2004), *Desert Islands and Other Texts. 1953–1974*, Los Angeles and New York: Semiotext(e).

Gonda, J. (1959), *Four Studies in the Language of the Veda*, The Hague, Netherlands: Mouton & Co.

Grau, O. (2003), *Virtual Art: From Illusion to Immersion*, trans. Gloria Custance, Cambridge, MA: MIT Press.

Heimann, B. (1964), *Facets of Indian Thought*, London: Allen and Unwin.

Inarritu, A. G. (2017), *Carne Y Arena*, Fondazione Prada, http://www.fondazioneprada.org/project/carne-y-arena/?lang=en.

Krishnananda, S. (1968), *The Mandukya Upanishad, Rishikesh*, India: The Divine Life Society.

Lanier, J. (2017), *Dawn of the New Everything*, New York: Henry Holt and Company.

Levy, P. (1998/1956), *Becoming Virtual: Reality in the Digital Age*, trans. Robert Bononno, New York and London: Plenum Press.

Lombard, M., and Ditton, T. (1997), "At the Heart of It All: The Concept of Presence," *Journal of Computer-Mediated Communication*, 3 (2): 321.

Mahony, W. K. (1998), *Th Artful Universe. An Introduction to the Vedic Religious Imagination. SUNY Series in Hindu Studies*, ed. Wendy Doniger, New York: State University of New York Press.

Mcluhan, M. (1964), *Understanding Media: The Extensions of Man*, Canada: McGraw-Hill.

Milk, C. (March 2015), "How Virtual Reality Can Create the Ultimate Empathy Machine," https://www.ted.com/talks/chris_milk_how_virtual_reality_can_create_the_ultimate_empathy_machine?language=en. and Gabo Arora. 2015. Clouds over Sidra. URL: https://www.unicefusa.org/stories/clouds-over-sidra-award-winning-virtual-reality-experience/29675

Miller, J. (1985), *Vision of Cosmic Order in the Vedas (Vedic Doctrine of Cosmogony)*, London: Routledge and Kegan Paul.

Panikker, R. (1983), *The Vedic Experience Mantramanjari: An Anthology of the Vedas for Modern Man and Contemporary Celebrations*, Pondicherry: All India Press.

Rheingold, H. (1991), *Virtual Reality*, New York: Simon and Schuster.

Sandoval, C. (2000), *Methodology of the Oppressed*, Minneapolis and London: University of Minnesota Press.

Sankaracharya. (1921), *Viveka Chudamani. Text with Translation and Notes*, ed. Almora Swami Madhavananda, The Himalayas: Advaita Ashrama.

Schuon, F. (1965), *Light on the Ancient World*, London: Perennial.

Shastri, P. D. (1911), *The Doctrine of Maya in the Philosophy of the Vedanta*, London: Luzac and Co.

Slater, M., and Wilbur, S. (1997), "A Framework for Immersive Virtual Environments (FIVE): Speculations on the Role of Presence in Virtual Environments," *Presence: Teleoperators and Virtual Environments*, 6 (6): 603–16.

Soudhamini. (2020), "The CVR Narrative as a Moebius Strip," *Journal of Screenwriting*, 11 (2): 175–89. doi: https://doi.org/10.1386/josc_00024_1

Soudhamini. (2021), "Theorizing the Virtual: An Unfinished Conversation with Thomas Elsaesser," *Quarterly Review of Film and Video*, 38 (7): 676–93. doi: 10.1080/10509208.2021.1945399

16

Mediataju: A Sense of Media

(Origin Finnish)

Jukka Sihvonen

The entitled word *sense* is translated into Finnish as *taju* (pronounced **ta'you**), and *a sense of* media becomes one word: *mediataju*. However, the scope of *taju* is a bit different from what *sense* is in English (or *sens* in French). The expression of *not* having sense (that is, being *senseless*) is in Finnish the same as being *unconscious* (*tajuton*). The difficulty to define *taju* in any explicit way is evidence of the conceptual nature that I want to emphasize in this chapter: sense is an effect engendered by a machinery. Therefore, in order not to be unconscious (*tajuton*) of what media is, one should become aware of the ways in which media not just exemplifies but even cherishes its own function as a machine producing sense (*taju*). Later in the chapter Paul Auster's *The Inner Life of Martin Frost* (2007) is discussed as an example of attaching *mediataju* to the relationship between literature and cinema.

In this chapter the notion of sense is discussed on the basis of Gilles Deleuze's *Logique du sens* (1969). *Mediataju*, as a neologism rather than a word used in everyday speech, has been developed in following the various modes of sense discussed by Deleuze. Thus, *mediataju*—a sense of media—can be an example of experimental concept creation and as such it should be understood in an active way referring to the infinitive verb (*to sense*) and the participle (*sensing*) modes rather than just the noun *sense*. Furthermore, the notion of *mediataju* also aims at expanding over to other modes of media besides language, most of all, the audio-visual realm.

Mediataju also aims at re-evaluating terms such as *literacy*, a widely and consistently applied notion especially in the circles of media education.[1] The argument here is that media education needs learning skills not only to *produce and consume* media (a particular literacy) but also, if not above all, to *sense* media; not only ways to evaluate various media "texts" critically but ways to enhance methods to diagnose the mechanisms with which media is aiming at effects.[2] There already exists an amount of literature on the applicability of Deleuze's concepts in the areas of both media and education.[3] These treatments, however, have concentrated quite rarely on the notion of sense in particular. The standard way to deal with *sense* in this respect has been to concentrate on the cognitive notion "to make sense."[4] *Logique*, discussed by Deleuze as a problematic, however, implies a much more complex way of sensing.

The Bridge Connecting Two Worlds

One of the abstract questions of *mediataju* as a sense of media concerns the way in which two worlds are bridged together: the world of reality and some other world of fantasy and fiction. A premature answer would indicate that the bridge is but an illusion because the worlds are intertwined through and through. In his *Logique du sens* Deleuze deals with this connection for example by making references to both Lewis Carroll and the Stoic philosophy.[5] Lewis Carroll deals with a similarly dual setting by concentrating on the other- and outer-worldly adventures of Alice, the ones that take place "in the wonderland," and the ones visited after having gone "through the looking glass."[6] In these respects the field in which the point of connection between worlds becomes investigated is the realm of language.

The notion of *sense* becomes discussed all over *The Logic of Sense* but especially in its fifth (and concerning *nonsense* in its eleventh) series. As has been pointed out by several writers already, this notion is a tough one to define in a simple way.[7] In Deleuze's hands it refers to something that can be called as common (*le sens commun*), to something that can be said as good (*le bon sens*), to something that can mean something quite different at the same time (*deux sens à la fois*), to something that can be asked in which sense it has to be understood (*quel qu'un sens*), to something that can be unidirectional (*le sens unique*), and so forth. Likewise, when translated into English the word becomes utterly flexible: a *sense* of rhythm, a *sense* of direction, a *sense* of achievement, a *sense* of humor, a *sense* of hearing. The Finnish versions of these idioms include meanings referring to a vast variety of terms: consciousness, reason, instinct, feeling, sensation, direction. What perhaps unifies them all—and therefore is also evidence of the concept's usefulness—is that *taju* implies the issue of learning and possessing a *skill*. Sensing (*tajuaminen*) is a creative act of capability to become aware of something.

In an interview that was published in the spring 1968 and entitled "On Nietzsche and the Image of Thought" Deleuze talks about the philosopher as one of those to have re-evaluated notions such as "sense" and "value" offering even a short definition: "sense is not a reservoir, not a principle, or an origin, not even an end, it's an 'effect', an effect produced [*un effet produit*], whose laws of production must be uncovered; [–] the idea of sense as an effect produced by a specific *machinery*, a physical, optic, sonorous effect, etc." (Deleuze 2004: 137, emphasis added).

Furthermore, in his article "How Do We Recognize Structuralism?" (written during the same period in 1968, but published not until 1972) Deleuze again underlines the notion of sense as an effect: "sense is always a result, an effect: not merely an effect like a product, but an optical effect, a language effect, a positional effect" (Deleuze 2004: 175). Then he defines the negative term "nonsense" as referring *not* to a lack of meaning but quite the contrary, the excess of sense (*l'excès de sens*).

In *The Logic of Sense* these ideas become expressed (again with a nod to Nietzsche) in this way: "[–] sense is never a principle or an origin, [–] it is produced. It is not something to discover, to restore, and to re-employ, it is something to produce by a new machinery" (Deleuze 1990: 72). Bernd Herzogenrath (2012: 3) combines this idea with the media; they "are nothing but these machineries of sense-production, and the rhizomatic interconnections among the various media are what constitute the field of intermedia[lity]." In this sense, intermediality could be one form of a sense of media. Finally, Deleuze ends the "Eleventh series of Nonsense" even in a programmatic way: "Today's task is to make the empty square circulate and to make pre-individual and nonpersonal singularities speak—in short, to produce sense" (Deleuze 1990: 73).

The Empty Square and the Square Circle

How does sense become produced? This is the problem Deleuze discusses, among other issues, in *The Logic of Sense* through the bipolar binoculars of Stoic philosophy and Lewis Carroll. The shared linguistic model is *paradox* and the way in which its effect leans on the borderline, the surface dividing (but also joining) *doxa* with paradox. Etymologically "paradoxical" refers to something that is against expectations. Furthermore, it is the power of the paradox to generate thought that connects Stoic's theory of λεκτα ("the expressed") and Deleuze's notion of sense. Deleuze has the same impulse as the Stoics had when they "saw logic as pedagogical in nature and purpose" (cf. Johnson 2020: 148; 177).

"In its sense-producing function, media thus belong to (or are nothing but) a surface effect" (Herzogenrath 2012: 2). The *surface* is the site of sense and as such always already something unclear, hazy and out of focus, questionable, wavering, obscure, in a word, *dodgy*. In French and in English the term often used in these contexts is *ambiguïté/ambiguity*. The word stems from the Latin *amb-* ("both ways") and *agere* ("to lead, drive") and it can be used in referring to several meanings: something being obscure, vague, nonspecific, applicable in multiple ways, and potentially metaphorical (Johnson 2020: 161–2).

Consider an absurd paradox and the fundamental quality of it to define one thing and another completely different thing simultaneously: a square circle. It exists only in the realm of language. There are no square circles in the real world. The square circle is a sign that exists, but without an object. Take another example, the one Lewis Carroll writes about in *The Hunting of the Snark* (1876). This something (Carroll names a "snark") potentially exists, but it does not have a real name, therefore it does not exist in the realm of language, or more precisely, it exists not just, but only in an *ambiguous* way as a hybrid. The hunting of snark ends up becoming a hunt for an ambiguous sign of an ambiguous referent.

The empty square that Deleuze writes about refers to an impossible object that denotes events, not things. On the one hand there is a homeless without a home (in the real world), on the other hand there is only the home, but nobody (real) living in it. Now, to sense this paradox requires understanding the unbroken nature and mutual co-dependence and—presence of these two figures, the home and the homeless person, or the empty square and "the occupant without a place" (Deleuze 1990: 47). An embodied example of the "occupant without a place" is Claire (played by Irène Jacob) in *The Inner Life of Martin Frost*, whereas the inner life of Martin (played by David Thewlis) is "the empty square." The story circles around the magical fact that Martin's writing attributes Claire's existence in the sense that when he stops doing it, Claire, as a kind of muse, begins to vanish. Therefore, in order to keep his muse alive Martin has to write, that is, to stick to the event of writing (with the machine).

Truc, thingy, snark, Boojum … These are some of the invented words created to deal with the task of describing ambiguous ways of being. One of Carroll's methods has been simply to combine two existing words in order to create a new one, such as *snail* (or *snake*) and *shark* to build *snark*. The problem becomes excessively interesting when translators have tried to translate this word into different languages. It is surprising (and to say the least, somewhat illogical considering the origin of the word) how often *snark* has been left untouched or translated more or less directly as for example by Ivan Riaboff who translates it as *scrapquin* into French (perhaps wanting it to rhyme with *baragouin*, "gibberish"). A notable exception is Alice Martin who translates *snark* into Finnish as *krauki* (see Carroll 2013). Her translation adopts Carroll's portmanteau-method,[8] but with the Finnish words *krapu* ("crab") and *hauki* ("pike"). These make together *krauki*—though "literally" this would be back in English, of course, *crike* or *crake,* not *snark*.

The capability to understand, enjoy, and play with paradoxes is fundamental in a surface-intensive logic of sense especially when the media in question concerns language. Deleuze already offers several examples from both the Stoic philosophy and Carroll's works. The pedagogical impetus, however, also concerns training skills of thought. Could it be possible to detect similar phenomena as verbal paradoxes also in the field of audio-visual media?

On *mediataju* and Paul Auster

Concerning the thin line, flat surface, or the interface between different media modes, Paul Auster might be considered as an apt expert in producing effects following the logic of sense.[9] Of the two films written and directed by Auster, *The Inner Life of Martin Frost* is basically about writing (as are many of the novels written by him): "A story about a man who writes a story about a man who writes a story—" (Auster 2007: 19). The act of writing (as seen on the screen) can be tedious, but on the other hand, there can be a certain mystery to it. The *Martin Frost*—film focuses on this haunting aspect.

In *The Book of Illusions* (2002), which is one of the "original" sources of the film, we get the written form of it in the mode of a story, a sort of *cinekphrasis*: the first-person narrator of the book, the film-scholar David Zimmer describes in detail what he sees and hears when viewing the film called "The Inner Life of Martin Frost." In its fictional world covered in that book, the film exists as one of the films directed by Hector Mann whose films have been the object of Zimmer's research project. Through the eyes and ears of David Zimmer Auster then describes what the film is all about. The next step takes place when Auster rearranges this story into an actual film-script and then finally re-creates it as an actual film.

The story travels from a written book in which it was an event of viewing a film, into a film in which the event of writing (and not writing) becomes the central issue. However, as we learn from Auster (2007: 7–8; 12), the first version of "The Inner Life of Martin Frost" really was a film-script intended for a compilation film (starring Willem Dafoe and symptomatically called *Erotic Tales*) that, however, never came out as planned. So, here we have a story told first in the mode of a film-script for a short film (that was not made); then in the mode of a story about seeing a film described in a novel; and finally in the mode of a feature-length film released. All these different modes of expression (λεκτα) are embedded in the final film, and the capability to experience their machinery, for example their intermediality, requires a particular sense of media.

Could it be possible to argue that Auster makes films, but he just publishes them as books? If so, then *The Inner Life of Martin Frost* could be a proof of the reverse: it is a book that just happened to come out as a film. In this respect it might be helpful to follow Auster's own thought when he comments the *Martin Frost*-film to his interviewer, Celine Curiol:

> I'm not a full-time filmmaker, after all, and I tend to think of my occasional forays into the world of movies as an extension of my work as a novelist, as a storyteller. Not all stories should be novels. Some should be plays. Some should be films. Some should be narrative poems. In the case of *Martin Frost*, it was conceived as a film from the start—just as *Smoke* and *Lulu on the Bridge* were.
>
> (Auster 2007: 14–15)

In *The Inner Life of Martin Frost* the tangible machine is the typewriter, the medium of producing words.[10] However, the word *producing* is not quite correct here. Recall the quote from Deleuze earlier: "sense is always a result, an effect: not merely an effect like a product, but an optical effect, a language effect, a positional effect" (Deleuze 2004: 175). Effects imply to questions of creating expressions. All these examples seem to underscore a similar viewpoint: they emphasize the way in which change and the unexpected, that is, *becoming* exists inside the persistent frame of the constant. This does not mean that cinema for Auster would be an answer to the yearning for immediacy, as Timothy Bewes (2007: 275) has suggested. Rather, it is a *problematic* constantly explored by Auster with the various means of storytelling machines. One can make sense of an Auster-story if one can read, but it is impossible to read his way of telling the story without a sense of media.

The Potential Learning Curves

Mediataju would refer to all the listening, reading, viewing, writing, and playing skills required when dealing with the media. Not just being competent in reading media messages (as texts), not just being skillful in knowing how media operates with its different modes, not just being critical enough to resist media messages, and/or curious enough to enjoy media in its various new ways. But all of these. And the notion of owing a sense of media—having something like *mediataju*—is meant to cover the entire field.

These ideas can be linked with Deleuze's long-time project of writing "critical and clinical essays" on literature.[11] Perhaps the idea of a critic and a clinic was launched by reading closely Nietzsche's ideas about value and sense. To put it simply in these terms, their inter-relatedness might be expressed thus: evaluation (*critique*) concerns the will to power that delivers values, and diagnostics (*clinique*) concerns the forces that deliver sense. Whereas the core field in media literacy seems to be learning the meaning of media messages as texts, *mediataju* concentrates more on the machinery in and with which media effects become produced as effective and sense-driven (*sense* understood here in its multiple meanings): "Subjectivity, a collective assemblage of enunciation, indeed any assemblage, is an ongoing production, an ongoing arrangement of relations" (Harper and Savat 2016: 22).

Mediataju aims at supporting the coexistence of all these connotations rather than forcing the notion to a unanimously shared understanding such as the willingness to become *literate*. In this respect and in relation to the traditional ways in which for example language has been taught at schools, there is a sense of resistance in *mediataju*. Rather than emptying itself to a principal relationship between a word (say, "a tree") as a stand-in for and an object (say, an image of a tree), it works in an opposite direction opening a wider field of references. The task that *mediataju* sets for education is willingness to acknowledge this multiple nature and the rebellious energy it may welcome.

In this respect *mediataju* would follow with Deleuzean concepts such as assemblage, becoming, diagram, event, and rhizome. Assemblage instead of proposition, becoming instead of being, diagram instead of dialectic, rhizome instead of tree, event instead of representation, and finally *mediataju* instead of media literacy; floating as "the promise of all revolutions" instead of signification (cf. Deleuze 1990: 49–50).

Notes

1 Among the mass of literature on this topic, suffice it to mention but one example, Renee Hobbs' book *Digital and Media Literacy* (2011). In a telling way the book sets up its two major tasks in the mode of these two questions: "How can educators make sense of popular culture, mass media, and digital technologies to help students develop *critical thinking skills*? How do students learn to be *responsible and effective communicators* with an appreciation of the human condition in all its complexity?" (Hobbs 2011, viii; emphases in the original.)

2 As a term within media education discourses there is a somewhat similar— or, perhaps, even a wider as it concentrates broadly on the area of digital

media—suggestion (to replace print-dependent "literacy"), and that is Gregory Ulmer's (2003) neologism "electracy." I have published a book (in Finnish) with the title *Mediatajun paluu* (2004)—"The Return of a Sense of Media"—in which some of the notions concerning the concept itself have been discussed before.

3   Excellent guides in this respect are *Media After Deleuze and Education* (Semetsky and Masny 2013).
4   See note 1 here and the way in which Hobbs uses the phrase in the first question.
5   This point of contact has been emphasized by Ryan J. Johnson in such a way that he was able to entitle his book as *Deleuze, a Stoic*: "Although he does not explicitly translate the term, what Deleuze means by 'sense' (*sens*) in *Logic of Sense* corresponds to the Stoic λεκτόν, along with an intimate connection between sense and the event (*l'événement*)" (Johnson 2020: 108). Sense, as a concept in connection with the Stoic notion λεκτόν ("what is said"; "the expressed" and derived from "to speak"), would simply refer to the way in which something has been selected (cf. Johnson 2020: 108–9). In terms of expression this, however, is not a reference to the act of expression, but rather, to what is expressed. This "what is expressed" on the other hand, as Deleuze explicates, is an "extra-being" because it is something and somewhere *between* being and nonbeing (see Deleuze 1990: 31). This mode of "being" is *subsisting*: "Bodies exist and λεκτα subsist as their surface [–]" (Johnson 2020: 112).
6   These of course are the titles of the famous *Alice*-books written by Lewis Carroll: *Alice's Adventures in Wonderland* (1865) and *Through the Looking-Glass and What Alice Found There* (1871).
7   See for example Lecercle (1985: 96–117); Williams (2008: 3–7); Bowden (2011: chapters 1 and 4); Palmer (2014: 90–104); Lapoujade (2017: 131–54); Johnson (2020: Part II); Newland (2021: 114–15).
8   Portmanteau is a "method" that Humpty Dumpty explains to Alice in *Through the Looking-Glass*: "Well, 'slithy' means 'lithe and slimy.' 'Lithe' is the same as 'active'. You see it's like a portmanteau—there are two meanings packed up into one word."
9   A certain sensitivity about the duality and the surface there in-between is a mark openly admitted by Auster himself: "Life is both tragic and funny, both absurd and profoundly meaningful. More or less unconsciously, I've tried to embrace this double aspect of experience in the stories I've written—both novels and screenplays" (Auster 2007: 19).
10 This "aspect" of the machine, and the option to study Auster's work as "a mode of writing" also within cinema, is discussed further in Trofimova 2014.
11 This project, mentioned here and there in various interviews already in the 1970s finally materialized as a book *Critique et Clinique* in 1993 (see Deleuze 1997).

Works Cited

Auster, P. (2007), *The Inner Life of Martin Frost*, London: Faber.
Bewes, T. (2007), "Against the Ontology of the Present: Paul Auster's Cinematographic Fiction," *Twentieth-Century Literature*, 53 (3) (Fall): 273–97.
Bowden, S. (2011), *The Priority of Events: Deleuze's Logic of Sense*, Edinburgh: Edinburgh University Press.
Carroll, L. (2013), *Kraukijahti, suomentanut Alice Martin, kuvittanut Tove Jansson*, Helsinki: WSOY (*The Hunting of the Snark*, 1876).
Deleuze, G. (1990), *The Logic of Sense*, trans. M. Lester, New York: Columbia University Press.
Deleuze, G. (1997), *Essays Critical and Clinical*, trans. D. W. Smith and M. A. Greco, Minneapolis: University of Minnesota Press.
Deleuze, G. (2004), *Desert Islands and Other Texts 1953–1974*, ed. D. Lapoujade, trans. M. Taormina, New York: Semiotext(e).
Harper, T., and Savant, D. (2016), *Media after Deleuze*, London and New York: Bloomsbury Academic.
Herzogenrath, B. (2012), "Travels in Intermedia[lity]: An Introduction," in B. Herzogenrath (ed.), *Travels in Intermedia[lity]: ReBlurring the Boundaries*, Hanover New Hampshire: Dartmouth College Press, 1–14.
Hobbs, R. (2011), *Digital and Media Literacy: Connecting Culture and Classroom*, Thousand Oaks, CA: Corwin Press.
Johnson, R. J. (2020), *Deleuze: A Stoic*, Edinburgh: Edinburgh University Press.
Lapoujade, D. (2017), *Aberrant Movements: The Philosophy of Gilles Deleuze*, trans. J. D. Jordan, New York: Semiotext(e).
Lecercle, J. J. (1985), *Philosophy through the Looking-Glass: Language, Nonsense, Desire*, La Salle: Open Court.
Newland, J. (2021), *Deleuze in Children's Literature*, Edinburgh: Edinburgh University Press.
Palmer, H. (2014), *Deleuze and Futurism: A Manifesto for Nonsense*, London and New York: Bloomsbury Academic.
Semetsky, I. and Masny, D. (eds) (2013), *Deleuze and Education*, Edinburgh: Edinburgh University Press.
Trofimova, E. (2014), *Paul Auster's Writing Machine: A Thing to Write With*, London and New York: Bloomsbury Academic.
Ulmer, G. L. (2003), *Internet Invention: From Literacy to Electracy*, New York: Longman.
Williams, J. (2008), *Gilles Deleuze's Logic of Sense*, Edinburgh: Edinburgh University Press.

Myslet médii. Thinking in, With, or Through Media: Images, Interfaces, Apparatuses

(Origin Czech)

Vít Pokorný

The aim of this essay is to think about thinking, to think about what thinking is and how it is. I start from the assumption that thinking is always somehow connected with the medium, that is, that it always operates through some perceptible means of expression and that it is inseparable from the practices and techniques of its expression. Miroslav Petříček bases his analysis of what it means to *think through images*[1] on the fact that an image is not a representation of reality and that it does not relate to it from outside, but from inside. Bernd Herzogenrath, in his project of *practical aesthetics*, claims that practical aesthetics does not want to think about art, but through art, which means that it understands "the practice of the artwork not as its object of analysis, but as its own modus operandi: not thinking about art according to external (mostly rational, propositional) categories that more often than not follow the logic of the 'written word,' but thinking with art, thinking with images, thinking with sound, and so on" (Herzogenrath 2021: 1).

Thinking here means thinking through/in/with something, that is, not only through speech and text and not only through images, but generally through any means of expression (artifact—interface) in which thinking can manifest (dance, ritual, mask, technique, ornament, sound modulation, text, film, etc.). We want to understand the artifact that becomes the place of expression of thought here as an *interface*, as generally defined by B. Hookway (see Hookway 2014), that is as a relational system emergent to its constitutive parts. Related to this general notion of interface is the belief that thinking is never tied to just one sensory modality of its expression. Thinking as an embodied and relational activity of a living organism performed through some interface is not limited only to the visuality of the text or the vocality of the speech. Therefore, it is necessary to thematize other than sound and visual forms and to deal with the multisensory nature of thinking in general.

Thus, not only does thinking always operate through something, it is always mediated, as well as mediating, but it also always takes place somewhere, that is, as an embodied and situated activity of the organism in the environment. In this context, we want to interpret the concept of thinking in light of Deleuze's text *Proust and the signs* (Deleuze 2000) according to which we seek the truth not because we want to, but because the violence of signs forces us to do so.

However, thinking through, with, or in something also means that we, as the authors, are not fully autonomous. Thinking does not originate from within the free, disembodied will. It depends on the interface of its action by whose possibilities it is limited. In her chapter "On the practice of theory" (Krtilova 2021), Kateřina Krtilová, therefore, asks, on the one hand, how to accept the technological or media determination of thinking and, on the other hand, how to think thinking as a free activity that is able to exceed each of its technological determinants. In the background of this text there is the belief that thinking is not an entirely transparent activity and additionally that the concept of thinking is not simple, does not indicate something uniform and closed in itself, and is not a single category with a clear meaning. Instead, we want to open access to the plain of thinking, to the topology of thinking as the plain of diverse socio-culturally and historically situated processes and relationships.

Thinking in Images

Petříček's guide to contemporary thinking, which is the subtitle of his book *Thinking in Images*, can be read, among other things, as an interpretation of McLuhan's sentence: "*the medium is message*" (McLuhan 1964). This sentence can be read in the context of the problem of "image" as follows: Thinking finds its expression in the way it can communicate something. However, this way is tied to the capabilities of the medium used. Meaning cannot be communicated otherwise than through some means of expression—through text, image, music, dance, or gesture. Acknowledging that, Petříček also emphasizes that *thinking in* texts and *in images* are mutually nontransferable activities. Image comprehension is irreducible to the problem of reading texts because these different ways of grasping or expressing meaning are not interchangeable. Therefore, Petříček asks what may be the essence of being an image in the sense of this non-reducibility and mutual non-transferability. With this problem, two questions arise. Firstly, the question of translation, that is, the question about the possibility of transferring meaning between different media, between different means of expression. Secondly, the question of the relationship between image and reality.

If we start in the middle, that is, with the problem of translation, Petříček holds as extremely naive the idea that when translating from one language or medium to a different one, there is an object, some content or meaning that is independent of the medium, which it is possible to separate and grasp in a pure and unmediated form. However, we can identify a similar problem already at the level of perception. Our perception does not convey a meaning independent of how we perceive it. The world is present to us through the medium of our corporeality, already in perception. In other words, perception as an image is never a representation of a reality that exists independently of it. Reality thus appears to us through the image, which acts within the real as a part of it. The perceptual image, therefore, does not relate to reality from outside, from some independent, unmediated, or zero position. Petříček even claims that, in his interpretation, the sentence *the medium is message* refuses to acknowledge the difference between the image and the reality, and leaves the question of whether the image is true to reality, and whether it represents it accurately aside. The image does not depict reality but instead creates or modulates it. It is an active reconfiguration of the relationship between someone who expresses or understands something and the environment to which he or she relates through images. Indeed, the reality is not something that could be achieved or is impossible to achieve with images, but something that forces us to change the strategy of description or action. Just as reality is not independent of the image and appears only through it, the image is not a passive and neutral reflection of reality. Petříček hence claims:

> If we understand reality based on the essence of what being an image means, which is the exact opposite of the case when it is understood as a representation of reality that does nothing to it and that is not its internal feature because it is neutral to it, so if we understand reality based on the essence of what being image means, then reality is nothing given and motionless, but always in motion, a becoming.
>
> (Petříček 2009: 16)

Image thereby does something to reality, and reality is not a neutral content of an image. It is not some unchanging meaning transmitted by a medium. A concept expressed through text, for example, is not an objective representation, but a specific gesture. It is a node in the hunting network of the language. It is a means of communication that does not convey content independently on the expression but performs a specific activity, namely, it connects people who speak to each other, who use the conceptual sign to mark and record something to which they can relate. The painted image of the sea is not the sea, it is not a copy of the sea. It is neither a copy of the seascape nor is there a sea in it. It is an interplay of colors and shapes on the canvas, which somehow encodes the relationship to the reality of the experienced sea. The image is consequently a translation of experience into a conveyable form, which functions as the means of transmission on the one hand and its content on the other. Words do not convey some hidden and invisible content, but only themselves. They act as signs that can activate cognitive processes and practical actions. The image is a particular movement of reality, a temporary crystallization of the relations between the image users. Petříček explains the becoming of reality through an image as follows:

> Within the becoming, every autonomous perspective or projection is a state that can be explained either as an event on the surface of the becoming or, more simply, as one of the possible cuts through it. So, the essence of being image would indicate how to conduct the cut. At the same time, it is crucial to acknowledge that each cut somehow changes the picture of reality.
>
> (Petříček 2009: 16)

The image, and in a general sense, every communicable and communicative expression of thought, is, therefore, a movement within reality, one of the ways reality appears. So, the image does not relate to the immobile reality as its neutral clone and does not stand against it as its pure reflection, but it unfolds within it as a performative communication relationship. As such, image is, according to Petříček, of dual nature. We can interpret it as an *event on the surface of becoming* or as a possible *cut through reality*. What does it mean to be an event on the surface of becoming? As an event, it is always an active communication relationship—statement, announcement, symbolic sign, or dance. It takes place on the surface, meaning that the becoming of reality consists of nothing but multiple surfaces, so there is no hidden depth to it that would hide behind, below or above images, words or gestures. Reality is present in every autonomous perspective in which it manifests itself, in every cut that is made through it.

What does it mean to be a cut through reality, then? Petříček undoubtedly takes the concept of the cut from film language. In film language, cut means a transition between scenes or individual images, while the transition involves the alternation of singular scenes. Even on the level of perception, reality appears to us as a set of various cuts embedded within the environment. We never see things from all sides, we never hear all the sounds at once, and we have only different perceptual cuts at our disposal, connected within the continuity of our bodily presence in the environment. The medium's activity consists of coding the perceptual diversity of the experienced reality into an image (concept, gesture) which records and distributes information in the form of a new sign body, and materialized as a graphic, acoustic, gestural, or tactile cut.

The Violence of Signs: Hunting the Real

When trying to comprehend the meaning of the phrase to think with something (with images, with music, or with text), our answer is the following: It means to create an event—an active cut—within reality. Petříček understands the medium in which something is expressed, in a critical commentary to McLuhan, as a new organ that we create to grasp or display reality, to position it in front of us so that we can relate to it. Thus, for him, the medium is not a simple extension of the sense organs, as it is for to McLuhan, but a construction of a new organ that makes it possible to perceive and think differently, to make a different cut in reality. Such a new organ consists of materiality and functionally different from our original embodied relation to the world. The materiality of that organ is the materiality of extension, which has the character of an interface. Yet, what does it mean that medium is a new organ and an interface? To answer the first part of the question, I will employ Deleuze's concept of thinking developed in the book *Proust and signs*. In his interpretation of Proust, Deleuze raises strange although fundamental questions: Why do we search for truth? Why do we want to know something? Why do we think at all? Thinking, or in Deleuze's Proust, searching for truth is not an activity of the pure spirit that desires knowledge motivated by its inner spontaneity, nor is it an original part of our nature, as Aristotle would suggest. Deleuze, in this respect, claims:

> Proust does not believe that man, nor even a supposedly pure mind, has by nature a desire for truth. We search for truth only when we are determined to do so in terms of a concrete situation, when we undergo a kind of violence that impels us to such a search. Who searches the truth? The jealous man, under the pressure of the beloved's lies. There is always the violence of a sign that forces us into the search, that robs us of peace. The truth is not to be found by affinity, nor by good will, but it is betrayed by involuntary signs .... We must first experience the violent effect of a sign, and the mind must be "forced" to seek the sign's meaning.
> (Deleuze 2000: 15–23)

The search for truth means to attempt to know, to try to understand, explain, conceive, and express one's understanding. Also, thinking is not a pure theory but a practical activity performed in the world. What, then, is the violence of a sign and how do we respond to it? We don't try to comprehend things just for fun, because we have to, because we have to. We attempt to know because a sign forces us to do so by its particular type of violence. We think when something concerns us, urges us, and demands our answer. By signs, we do not mean symbolic characters, but signs in the sense of indexes. By signs, we mean the traces transmitted by things, beings, events, and situations to which we somehow react and respond. Thinking is an activity, a responsive reaction. It is performative and pragmatic, not receptive. However, when discussing thinking in images, we usually utilize the notion of thinking based on a specific conception of visuality—visuality understood as nonparticipatory and detached observation from a distance. A different idea of visuality renders visual perception as an active participatory process that involves looking around, focusing attention, turning the head, searching, the kinaesthetics of the eye, and a complex of neural and cognitive processes such as identification or recognition. Therefore, thinking cannot be defined only based on distant visuality, but based on perception in general, that is, also on hearing, touching, sniffing, and tasting, if we would take into account only the five traditional senses, and finally on the responsive activity of our enactive bodily presence in the environment.

In this respect, we don't define thinking as an internal process, combinatorics of internal representations, or an observation from a distance. Instead, thinking means a situated and responsive activity of an organism in the environment. As such, thinking is not exempt from the general conditions of the human situation. It is a purposeful activity of the corporeal being in its environment. It is an activity that allows it to orient itself in a milieu, to know what to do and how to act toward it. Thus, thinking is not a pure activity occurring in the dimension of pure disembodied concepts. It is a situated communicative performance of a living organism in an environment realized through the materiality of a medium.

Thinking does not necessarily need to use a concept or an image. Initially, it begins to acquire a form on a corporeal level, for instance, with growl. Growling is the dog's response to a threat. The dog understands the gesture of the outstretched hand as a threat and responds by creating a sound sign. He expresses the idea of readiness to attack with an intimidating attitude and angry growl. His body, considered to be a medium, a means of expression, turns into a sign sent to the threatening hand. The growl sound is also part of the whole repertoire of dog sound signals which together form a sound interface that serves as a means of communication always at hand because its materiality is the dog's body itself.

Hence, thinking realizes in some system of means of expression or artifacts, which operates as an interface. According to B. Hookway's general definition, the concept of interface consists of two parts—*inter* and *face*. *Inter* connotes what happens between, in a relationship, in interaction—activity of sending and responding, receiving and reacting. *Inter*-face is what divides and connects at the same time, creating the space in-between. What thus stands as an intermediary between the two communicating entities is the *face*—the shape and the form, perceptible and understandable appearance of the interface itself constituted as a system of acoustic, graphic, gestural, or other types of signs (or a system of tools such as the dashboard of a car) that transmit information. The information here is certainly not some neutral content of the message, but the activity of mutual in-forming, a mutual transformation of the relationship between two or more entities via the interface. According to Hookway, the interface is primarily a type of relationship and thus a means of communication. It exists only as a relationship and only if that relationship is active. In its perceptible form, the interface establishes the connection between the members of the relationship, and simultaneously the distance between them, separating them from each other into a shared interspace. Consequently, the interface allows the transfer of forces and information within the relationship. The inseparability of the division and augmentation processes is a constituent of the overall interface system. The interface fundamentally is a relationship that separates in the interconnection and connects in the separation. These dynamics create a new entity with its own properties that are irreducible to the properties of its constitutive components. The interface becomes an artifact that acts as a threshold for transition, transmission, and transaction, and the exterior of the interface can be controlled by controlling the relationship.

The interface is thereby a technology which allows to control the environment and simultaneously becomes a part of this environment. It defines and transforms members of the relationship it has established by its own activity. The interface is an extension in the sense of a new organ and in the form of an artifact. As an extension, it changes the behavior of those who use it and thus also changes the shape of the environment where the action takes place. As an artifact, it is a set or system of objects that work together as a threshold between the interface users and the environment. Under certain sociocultural conditions, a simple interface can merge with other interfaces to become an apparatus with all its social, cultural, and political consequences.

So if we understand the media as interface for thinking, we can also briefly describe the path that leads to the emergence of the apparatus. The initial question is: How is information transmitted through a communication interface such as language or image? By information transfer I mean the transformation of the relationship between those who use the interface for some purpose. Alongside that, we identified violence as the initial motive for thinking, as a source that originates in the environment that somehow urges us, concerns us and requires our response.

To explain the concept of apparatus, let's take a hunter's experience as an example. Hunting experience requires that the hunter understands the signs that lead him to a prey—the sounds that prey makes, the paths it travels, the food it consumes, and similar ones. Successful coordination of hunting then requires a common understanding of all these signs and, if necessary, some way of preserving and communicating them. Hunting groups gradually develop a system of signs and turn them into a hunting interface. Given the notion of thinking developed in this text, we can then claim that the hunter thinks through this interface. He does not initially think about the animal using words. He or she thinks according to the animal according to whose signs he forms his own artificial gestures-sounds-signs system, the interface. Besides signs, the hunting interface comprises other parts, such as the hunting tools, weapons, or traps, which are evenly expressions of the hunter's thinking and are constructed according to the prey that must be caught. By merging hunting and communication technologies, a hunting group establishes a system of artifacts, thus constituting a hunting interface.

To explain the process of origination of the communication interface, we need to determine its crucial elements. I consider a rhythm in the sense of regular repetition to be one of the decisive elements of such a process. The sign indicating the arrival of prey, a hand gesture, or a call must repeat many times to become an independent reference for the incoming prey. In this example, thinking does not work purely linearly or causally, but in circles or in loops, or perhaps in spirals, which surround the signs transmitted by the environment. If thinking is not a representation, but a specific cut within reality, an activity that causes something to appear, then we can conceive of it as treading a new path and as an unique performance. In this context, Petříček claims that we cannot say that "we recognize things as events, because they always appear before us differently or only once. Rather we always uniquely grasp them. What we call recognition, identification, is always the result of a certain, even minimal abstraction, reduction, deceleration" (Petříček 2009: 24–5). However, grasping requires some means—a hand, a word, or an image. In this respect, a hunter's image of the animal results from repeated hunting experiences, which transforms into a transferable, reproducible, and recognizable feature via the processes of abstraction, reduction, and deceleration. The image of the animal becomes a reservoir of such experience and evokes them when used. Hence, the thinking in images in the sense of creating and using a communication interface establishes through the processes of sedimentation, repetition, imaginative transformation, and reactive evocation. From this perspective, we can comprehend the medium as an active interface, as a transformation machine that concentrates sedimented experiences that can always be recalled.

The medium as a new organ is always a social organ, not an individual one. As a social organ, it stems from shared experience and a common need for action. When established, it becomes an essential part of the environment where both the action and the experience occur. And, if the assumption that we always think with something, that we always think through some medium is valid, then we must also consider the materiality of this organ (or machine). We can, for example, compare thinking to cross country skiing. Riding in freshly fallen snow is an analogy to the uniqueness of each act of thinking. When riding I set up the boundaries within a space and determine the path by going through it. Over time, when the landscape is traversed many times by many people, recurring tracks emerge, that is, the paths that best travel through the landscape or that lead to significant places. It is therefore not necessary, or even desirable, to create new routes all the time. It is enough to repeat those already traveled. Thanks to this repetition, we gain stable and lasting control over the environment in which we operate. The stability and control that the interface of repeated tracks establishes are important because they represent the basis of the functionality of such interface.

In general, each sign system ultimately works by regularly repeating a set of the same characters. By disrupting this repetition, we can reach the boundaries of the system and thus be able to transform and expand it. Thanks to the constant process of repetition and expanding disruption, the system grows and transforms into an apparatus, as Agamben (see Agamben 2009) or Flusser (see Flusser 1997) would describe it. However, the route from the hunting interface described above to an apparatus is quite complicated, so we can only briefly indicate it here. First, a system must reach a certain level of complexity. Then, the need for a general interaction and communication system must arise, and only in such case a simple hunting interface may develop and transform into an apparatus. The apparatus then includes not only the specific materiality of technologies but also specific narrative and epistemic strategies and social and power relations such as the division of roles within the hunting system, or a myth of a Big Hunter. According to Flusser, a once-established apparatus controls and programs its participants, turns them into programmable units, and distributes their roles within a wider system.

Institutionalization or the establishment of the apparatus is associated with the emergence of artifacts and technologies that become independent of their physical origin and create their own emergent structure, which itself becomes a new actor within the entire social domain. Hookway argues that interface operations consist of interactions in the sense of a transactions. The interface users and developers invest energy into building and operating the interface. In return, the interface enriches their capture and control capabilities. At the same time, Hookway claims that learning to use the interface is a kind of subjectivation. Augmentation through extension is a type of subjectivation, in the sense of Foucault's techniques of subject formation. We can become subjects only as members of communication communities that use communication interfaces. Therefore, we become our social selves by using these interfaces which consequently determine who we are and how we think and act.

New Media and the Autonomy of Thinking

In her essay "On the practice of theory," Kateřina Krtilová does not focus on the practical thinking embodied in action, creation, and control of the environment through interfaces but on the theoretical thinking, namely on the methods in humanities. The humanities traditionally think in specific text genres, whose scope tends to be stable and limited. They also operate within specifically organized scientific and academic institutions, within the scholarly apparatus with all its material, social, and power aspects. The practical turn that Krtilová advocates involves modification of the interface and, consequently, alteration of the operation of various elements of an apparatus. Crucial is Krtilova's question about what happens when we accept Kittler's technological determinism, namely the idea that when media determine our situation, they also regulate our intellectual operations. In other words, if we think in texts, we must follow the logic of written language and cannot think outside the rules of the scientific genre. In this respect, other media present a challenge: How to think differently than with texts? How to think with photography, film, television, or comics? How do we combine different ways of thinking and connect divergent means of expression.

Following Kittler and Flusser, Krtilová also considers the transition from a universe of texts to a universe of computers or technical images. Digital information processing and the whole set of digital interfaces, among other things, bring the need to think differently than just in text, to detach from the domination of text, and reflect on the possibilities of digital media. In this context, however, it is also necessary to mention McLuhan's principle, namely that the emergence of a new medium does not mean the complete disappearance of previous media but the reconfiguration of the overall media situation. Such principle raises the following questions: What does it mean to think with the computer and the internet? How does instant online communication determine our intellectual operations? Or, to put it differently, what does it mean to live in the current media-sphere dominated by new media, that is, by network and digital media, within which we all operate only as parts of different configurations and actor-networks? Or also, what does it mean when our thinking runs through a machine that can read symbolic characters, that can analyze its own operations and learn from its own mistakes? And then again, what is, for us as users of digital interfaces, the significance of machine code autonomy, which operates in the background of our own symbolic operations, is controlled by algorithms, and is performed by autonomous operations in various planes and areas of code? Or, what does the ability of artificial intelligence to process, sort, and analyze large data sets unprocessable by humans and generate its own images, videos, and texts mean for the human agency?

Such questions opens the problem of the autonomy of thinking. Indeed, the nature of thinking includes freedom, the possibility of distance, the possibility of imagination and free association. However, if our thinking is only a set of operations within some interface, if we can only think of something or through something, the question arises, who controls what, who is an autonomous actor, and in what sense? Given our reasoning in this text, there are then three possible ways of addressing such problems. First, if thinking involves the possibility of distance, then it does not mean distancing to some zero point, to some meta position, but only the understanding that a given cut of reality is insufficient and that another needs to be conducted. The reality, as Petříček puts it, appears to us as a resistance that forces us to change our description strategies, and alter our cutting techniques. Second, from the perspective of interface theory, the search for an absolute autonomy of thinking does not make sense, because interface is always a relationship of mutual dependence and belonging. What matters is not who controls what, whether the user controls the interface, or the interface controls the user. It is more important that the user-interface relationship constitutes the ability to control the environment, where the interface operator uses the inferface-generated capabilities. Third, together with Krtilová and the German *Medienwissenschaft*, we can assume that no predefined media actually exist because anything can become a medium if it is used within a functioning interface, if it acts as a medium in the sense of a mediating interface between us and the environment.

The first and second answers give rise to the following humble claim: thinking with/in/through something requires understanding interface in which we operate, comprehending how specific apparatuses and interfaces work, what they allow and, most importantly, what they do not. The third answer implicates that every interface and every apparatus is something that we created ourselves and that we use based on some transaction costs, and therefore we can also not use it, respectively. We can transform it and reinvent the necessarily limited new strategies of responding to the violence of the world's signs.

Note

1   Petříček's book is available only in Czech, see Petříček 2009, all translations mine.

Works Cited

Agamben, G. (2009), *What Is an Apparatus and Other Essays*, trans. D. Kishik and S. Pedatella, Stanford: Stanford University Press.
Deleuze, G. (2000), *Proust and Signs. The Complete Text*, trans. R. Howard, Minneapolis: University of Minnesota Press.
Flusser, V. (1997), *Nachgeschichte. Eine korrigierte Geschichtsschreibung*, Frankfurt: Fischer Taschenbuch Verlag.
Herzogenrath, B. (2021), "Introduction. Toward a Practical Aesthetics: Thinking with," in B. Herzogenrath (ed.), *Practical Aesthetics*, London: Bloomsbury, 1–24.
Hookway, B. (2014), *Interface*, Cambridge: MIT Press.
Krtilová, K. (2021), "On the Practice of Theory. The Technological Turn of Media Theory and Aesthetic Practice of Media Philosophy," in B. Herzogenrath (ed.), *Practical Aesthetics*, London: Bloomsbury, chapter 2, 35–44.
McLuhan, M. (1964), *Understanding Media: The Extensions of Man*, New York: McGraw-Hill.
Petříček, M. (2009), *Myšlení obrazem. Průvodce současným filosofickým myšlením pro středně pokročilé*, Praha: Herrmann a synové.

18

Naqqāli: Iranian Storytelling in Two Films by Ali Hātami

(Origin Iranian)

Behrooz Mahmoodi-Bakhtiari

Among the Iranian filmmakers, Ali Hātmai is regarded as the "most Iranian" one. A filmmaker with very strong ties to the Iranian traditional lifestyle of the nineteenth century, he was highly interested in classical methods of Iranian storytelling, and started two of his initial movies with *naqqāli*, a specific one-man show presenting the epic or the religious stories by the help of accompanying pictures. This article makes a very quick overview of *naqqāli*, and introduces the films in which Hātami has made use of it.

Naqqāli (lit. "Recounting") is an Iranian storytelling tradition. It is the art of narrating episodes of Persian folk epics and popular romances. In this "secular type of entertainment related to the performance of plays" (Mahdavi 2007: 490), heroic and religious narratives are presented in written and spoken form (Yamamoto 2010: 240). It is a one-man show encompassing pantomimic gestures and vocal modulations which can move an audience either to tears or to laughter (Chelkowski 1984: 46). The stories performed by this storyteller (*naqqāl*) are either the heroic adventures of a religious hero, or a secular one. This specific performance is sometimes carried out according to the texts known as *tumār*s, manuscripts, or booklets constituting a mnemonic aid for the storyteller's performance[1] (Marzolph 2015: 272) and illustrates *naqqāli* as a text-dominated Iranian performing tradition (Page 1979: 201). It is because of this written-oral nature of *naqqāli* that it is regarded as a solid basis for Persian oral studies, as well as having an important role in transmitting the Persian epics and popular romances in the course of a long time (Yamamoto 2010: 240).

In his anthropological classification of the genres of theater and spectacle, Beeman (1993: 382) notes three items, and names the Iranian *Naqqāli* and the Rajastani *Jester* among the examples of less thoroughly codified forms of *Textual theater*. The other types are *Music-text dance* (MTD) *theater* (like Iranian *ta'ziya*, Japanese *Kabuki*, and Indian *kathakali* as the codified forms, and Turkish *orta-oyunu*, Japanese *kagura*, and Mexican *Pastorella* as the less thoroughly codified ones), and Dance theater (with Indian *nautunki* and Bolivian *diablada* as the less thoroughly codified ones). According to Mahdavi (2007: 490), *naqqāli* is correctly a type of performing arts it is a form of dramatic monologue with various characters, and requires a certain amount of acting ability on the part of the *naqqāl*, who should illustrate his narrative through skillful mime, hand and body movement, and change of pitch in voice.

Historically, *naqqāli* is an ancient and very refined art in Iran, whose roots may be traced back to the pre-Islamic traditions of Iran and the Parthian gosans (Chelkowski 2010: 261). The reputation of this tradition is so long and fascinating that several narrative collections of the world literature owe their mediation into world literature to pre-Islamic and early-Islamic Iran (Marzolph 2015: 271). However, written accounts of this method of storytelling appeared much later in Iran. The earliest references to the Iranian professional storytellers appear in the monumental work of the historiographer Abol-Fazl-e Bayhaqi (AD 995–1077), and the most extensive discussion of storytellers as a class, along with their different groups and various props, is found in the book *Futuwwat Nāme-ye Soltāni* ("The Royal Book of Futuwwa") by Mullā Husayn-e Kāshefi (d. 1504–05), also known as Wāʿez. In this book, Kāshefi distinguishes three groups of narrators-performers in sixteenth-century Iran: (1) storytellers *(hekāyat guyān)*, (2) narrative verse singers *(afsāne khānān)*, and (3) lyric verse reciters *(nazm-khānān)* (see Omidsalar 1984: 205–8).

Although there are documents about storytelling since the sixteenth century, we may say that the Qājār period (1779–1925) was the golden age of oral tradition in Iran, during which about 6,000 to 10,000 dervishes practiced storytelling, and other verbal art forms (Yamamoto 2010: 245). According to Marzolph (2015: 271), in no other period of Iranian history, we may command such a wealth of information about storytelling and storytellers. This tradition was so strong that it also passed the Iranian borders, and was practiced in places such as India as well (see Khan 2019).

The professional storytellers often accompanied their performance by large illustrative paintings on canvas known as *Shamāyel* or *parde*, which represented the characters and the events of the story they narrated, mostly the fate of the martyrs of Shiism. Therefore, the performer of *naqqāli* is also known as *shamāyel gardān* or *parde-dār*. In this respect, *naqqāli*, according to Marzolph (2015: 275), is comparable to the performance of the European ballad-monger or Bänkelsänger.

Naqqāli: *Iranian Storytelling*

Figure 18.1 A typical *parde* used for a one-man show (https://www.iranhotelonline.com/images/EditorUpload/502202.jpg).

The size of *parde* is around 150*300 centimeters, and portraits on it are of two sorts: the portraits of the protagonists or the holy characters are often magnified and illustrated with elegance in the center, while the wicked are ugly and monsterlike. The sequence of events in these paintings is haphazard (Chelkowski 1989: 101), and perspective does not make much sense, as they are these two-dimensional illustrations. Also, the pictures are intertwining and no blank space remains between the scenes, which means there is no pause during the narration (for a detailed discussion, see Lashkari and Kalantari 2015: 248).

The storyteller usually stood beside the screen and pointed to different parts of it, in order to make his presentation more visual and delightful. Making different voices for the different characters and even depicting the sounds of the scenes are among the other talents that a *naqqāl* should have for his career.

Naqqāli took place in both public and private locations, but the best-known place for this performance was the *qahve khāne* or coffee house (Martin and Mason 2006: 244). The content of *naqqāli*s differed according to the time of the year (if it were the mourning times or the feasts), and the taste of the audiences, and could range from the tragic story of the martyrdom of Imam Hussein in Karbala, to the entertaining books such as *Iskandarnāme* and *Chehel Tuti* ("forty parrots"); and from *A Thousand and*

Figure 18.2 A *Parde-dār* and his screen (http://radiofarhang.ir/NewsDetails/?m=060001&n=684754).

One Nights to folk stories such as *Amir Arsalān*, and *Husayn-e Kurd*, mostly popular picaresque romances. For the more learned audiences, stories from *Shāhnāme* by Ferdowsi or *Khamse* of Nizāmi would be presented (see Mahdavi 2007: 490). A *naqqāli* performance usually closes with a "cliff-hanger," or an unresolved situation (Yamamoto 2010: 254), in the sense that the storyteller stops at a point where the protagonist is yet to experience new events, and the story is literary in suspense. This paves the way for the next performance.

In the twentieth century, *naqqāli* which was certainly a craft practiced for centuries in Iran, rapidly started to fall off. Its decline was expedited during the Pahlavi régime (1925–79), when *naqqāl*s were accused of instigating members of guild organizations in the late 1920s, and their activities in coffeehouses were forbidden. Yamamoto (2010: 246) notes that around 1935 coffeehouses were temporarily closed down, and after they improved their conditions, only a few capable *naqqāl*s were licensed to recite Ferdowsi's *Shāhnāme*. The penetration of the mass media into the Iranian society was another major threat to the *naqqāli* tradition. With the beginning of radio broadcasting began in Iran in the 1940s and in the wake of the Second World War, coffeehouses were no longer guaranteed places for *naqqāli*. Rapid modernization and the emergence of radio, television and cinema in the 1950s forced many storytellers out of their jobs (Yamamoto 2010: 246). The popularity of different types of *naqqāli* quickly waned, and activities such as *pardeh khāni* were largely forgotten by the late twentieth century (Lashkari and Kalantari 2015: 256). The decline of this art and its activists was so prompt that, according to Page (1979: 196), in 1974–5 in the city of Shiraz, there were only four full-time active storytellers. Other traditional activities such as *Ta'zieh* and *Ruhowzi* (the traditional Iranian passion play and comedy) did not die out but moved from their natural urban surroundings to the rural areas, where they still continue their existence in a modified, less glamorous form (Martin and Mason 2006: 246).

However, the Pahlavi regime tried to make up for this gradual death during its final decade in power. A major effort made in this respect was the foundation of *Jashn-e Honar* (Festival of Arts) in Shiraz (1967–77), which concentrated mainly on theater and music, and acclaimed theatrical artists such as Tadeusz Kantor (1915–90), Jerzy Grotowsky (1933–99), and Peter Brook (1925–) regularly attended it from 1967 to 1978 (Talajooy 2011: 499). The festival of Arts also organized two other festivals in Tus and Esfahan. The former was devoted to oral and written epic and heroic literature, and the latter was concerned with "Popular Traditions" (Gaffary 1984: 380–1). In recent years, some efforts have been made to revive this verbal art and its major arena: the coffeehouses, and the audiences (as opposed to the previous times) are no longer purely male, and women and children may also attend them (Marzolph 2015: 280). The training and emergence of some female *naqqāls* are also another totally new happening in this field. Also, some theatrical artists made conscious use of *naqqāli* in their plays.[2]

What we noted so far, dealt with the narration of the religious or epic stories with the aid of specific screens. Another method of narrating stories dealt with the folk stories and a device known as *Shahr-e Farang* (lit. "City of Europe"). Being a replica of the peep show or *la vue d'optique* in eighteenth-century Europe, *Shahr-e Farang* consisted of a large brass-bound box standing on legs with three viewers of thick lenses. People would sit cross-legged on the ground and watch several pictures through those lenses and enjoyed the amusing and colorful commentary of the *Naqqāl* of *Shahr-e Farang* (Gaffary 1984: 364). According to the tastes of the viewers, the pictures shown in *Shahr-e Farang* were either the European cities, the holy Islamic shrines, or the pictures related to folk stories of foreign cities. With the advent of cinema and television, *Shahr-e Farang* disappeared, and some traces of it were left only in some films and shows, such as those by Ali Hātami, as we will see later on.

Ali Hātami

'Abbās-Ali Hātami (1944–96) was in Iranian filmmaker, mainly known for his clear inclination to the Iranian traditions in general, and the Qājār lifestyle in particular. Being born and raised in the old, classical downtown of Tehran, he illustrated a nostalgic sense about the methods of living in nineteenth-century Iran in most of his movies, and made use of many performing features of that era. He made his directing debut with the film *Hasan Kachal* ("Hassan the Bald" 1970), which is based on a famous Iranian folk tale about a lazy bald boy, who finds himself in the face of problems and grows wise and brave to reach the girl he loves. This film starts with the image of a *Shahr-e Farang*, and the viewer of the film watches the first minutes of the movie through this traditional storytelling lens. The *naqqāl* of *Shahr-e farang* starts the narration, and after some general remarks, he starts the story of Hasan Kachal. The narration is almost entirely rhythmic, and the whole movie is also regarded as the first musical Iranian film. The film shows several paintings, in the form that a *naqqāl* may point on his screen, and the narration goes as follows:

> shahr, shahr-e farang-e. khub tamāshā kon, siyāhat dāre. Az hame range. Shahr, shahr-e farange. Tu donyā hezār shahr-e qashange.
>
> shahr-hā ro bebin, bā gonbad o menār. shahr-hā ro bebin bā borj-e zang-dār. shahr-hā ro bebin bā mardom-e mu talā. shahr-hā ro bebin bā mardom-e cheshm-siyāh. ke hame yek jur mikhandan o hame āsun del mibandan. Va tuye hame-ye shahr-hā hanuz gol dar miyād. āsemun ābiye hame-jā, ammā āsemun-e un vaqtā ābitar bud. ru bumā hamishe kaftar bud.

Narrator: The city is the foreign city (*Shahr-e Farang*). Watch well. It deserves sightseeing, it is of all colors. The city is the foreign city. There are a thousand beautiful cities in the world. Watch the cities with domes and minarets. Watch the cities with bell towers. Watch the cities with blond people. Watch cities with black-eyed people, who all laugh the same, and all fall in love easily. And

Figure 18.3 *shar-e farang*, and the images of the story of Hassan the Bald.

flowers are still growing in all these cities. The sky is blue everywhere, but the sky was bluer then. There were always pigeons on the roofs.

Hayāt-ā bāq budan, ādam-ā sardamāq budan. Bache-hā chāq budan, javun-ā qolchomāq budan. Dokhtar-ā bā-hayā budan, mardom-ā bā-safā budan. Howz-e por ābi bud, mard-e mirābi bud. shab-ā mahtābi bud, ruz-ā āftābi bud. hāli bud, hāli bud. nuni bud, ābi bud. chi begam, nun-e gandom māl-e mardom age bud, nemiraft az galu pāyin be khodā, agar ham moshkeli bud, ājil-e moshkel goshā halesh mikard.

Bache-hā bāzi mikardan tu kuche. 'jomjomak, barg-e khazun', 'hamumak murche dāre', bāzi-ye 'mard-e khodā' ... kojāst mard-e khodā?

Salām-i bud, 'aleyki bud, hāl-e javāb salāmi bud. age sorkhāb-sefidāb ru lopp-e dokhtar-ā nabud, lopp-e dokhtar-ā mes-e gol-e anār goli-moli bud.

Sofre-hā gar hame haft-rang nabud, hame āshpazkhune-hā dud mikarad. Khrus-ā khorus budan, hāl-e āvāz dāshtan. Rowqan-ā rowqan bud, gusht-i bud, donbe'i bud. Ey, shab-e Jom'e-i bud.

The yards were gardens; the people were cheerful. The children were fat, the youth were robust. The girls were modest; the people were friendly. The pond was full of water, there was a man who distributed water in houses. The nights were moonlit, the days were sunny. It was a nice feeling, a nice feeling. There was bread, there was water. In case the wheat bread belonged to the other people, it would not be swallowed, I swear. If there was a problem, it would be solved by the problem-solving nuts. The children played in the alley, played the games named "the moving autumn leaves," "the public bath has ants," "the game of the man of God" ... But where? Where is the man of God?

Once there were greetings, there were responses to greetings, there was a mood to answer the greetings. If the red cosmetics were not on girls' cheeks, girls' cheeks were naturally red like pomegranate blossoms. In case the tablecloths were not decorated with several types of foods, at least all the kitchens worked and let out the smoke. The roosters were real roosters. They were in the mood for singing. The types of oil were real types. There was meat, there was a tail. Oh, there were also weekend nights.

barekat dāsht pul-ā. Pul be jun baste nabud.
Ādam az dast-e khodesh khaste nabud.
Nuni bud, paniri bud. peste'i bud, qesse'i bud, qesse'i bud.
Qesse-ye kak be tanur, Nushāfarin, Hoseyn-e Kord, qesse-ye Hasan Kachal.

Figure 18.4 The beginning of the story of Hassan the Bald.

Narrator: Money was blessed.
Money was not as dear as life. People were not tired of themselves.
There was bread, there was cheese. There was pistachio, there was a story, there was a story.
The story of flea in the oven, [the story of] Nush Āfarin, [the story of] Hossein the Kurd, the story of Hassan the Bald.

Qesse ha chi ke shenidi pāk farāmush bokon, biyā va be qesse-ye Hasan kachal gush bokon.

Tu-ye yek bāq-e bozorg, ke hame dor tā doresh golkāri bud, yek 'emārat budesh. Tu hame 'emārat-ā, in 'emārat shāhkār-e me'māri bud. dowr tā dowr-e 'emārat chār tā estakhr-e bozorg, ke tushun lab be lab az māhi bud. hame ruz tang-e qorub, ke āb-e favvāre-hā vā mishodan, mahi-hā-ye qermez-e yek vajabi, be bolandi-ye āb-e favvāre-hā mipparidan.

In khune ke tu-ye shahr negin-e angoshtar bud, māl-e sheypur zan-e mard-e bolandakhtar bud.

Āqā sheypurchiye to meydun-e mashq hamishe mārsh mizad. Sheypur-e ist khabardār mizad.

Forget all the stories you have heard. Come and listen to the story of Hassan the Bald.

In a large garden, surrounded by flowers, was a mansion. In all the mansions, it was an architectural masterpiece. All around the mansion, there were four large pools, which were full of fish. Every day at dusk, when the water of the fountains was opened, the goldfish jumped to the height of the water of the fountains. This house, which was like a jewel of the ring of the city, belonged to the trumpet player of the army. Mr. Trumpeter played in the training field, he was always marching, and played the alerting tunes.

Figure 18.5 The story of Hassan the Bald continued.

Vali shab-hā tu khune hāli dāsht, hāli mikard. Vāse-ye ahl-e khune āhang-e hāldār mizad.

'adas polo, reshte polo, reng-e khāle rowro mizad. Chon zanesh Bibi khānum, noh māhe hāmele bud. Āqā seypurchi ārezu mikard, ke zanesh pesar bezād. Ye pesar, kākol zari. Ammā az bakht-e badesh, bache bi-kākol shod. Kachal o kuchel o ham kāchel shod.

Sar nagu, āyne begu. Sar mesāl-e kaf-e dast. Vāse darmun ye dune mu nadāsht.

Jāliz-ā sabz shodan, bute shodan, seyfi dādan, ammā yek mu ru sar-e Hasan kachal sabz nashd. Bābā deqmarg shod o mord.

Narrator: But at nights, he was in a good mood in the house. Enjoyed himself, and played funny melodies for the people of the house.

He played rhythmic melodies, because his wife, Mrs. Bibi, was nine months pregnant. Mr. Trumpeter wished that his wife would give birth to a son. A son of golden forelock. But unfortunately, the child was without a forelock. He turned out to be totally bald.

That was not a head, it was actually a mirror. Just like the palm of the hand, without a single hair for a remedy.

The weeds grew green, turned into bushes and melons, but not a single hair grew on Hassan Kachel's head. The father died of grief.

khune nun-darār nadāsht, khune mard-e kār nadāsht, bibi ham fekr-e shohar tu sar nadāsht. Ganj-e Qārun ham migan tamum mishe. Az tu in bāq-e bozorg, ye khune mund be qadd-e qarbil. Qāli hā hasir shodan. Bibi āshpazi mikard, bibi khayyāti mikard, jāru mikard, pāru mikard. Vāse-ye kharj-e khune, band-andāzi mikard. Hasanak bāzi mikard, tāb mikhord. Chon ke hambāzi nadāsht, ye ruzi raft tu kuche. Raft o bargasht tu khune. Dige pā az khune birun nagzāsht. Mesl-e inke bache-hā Hasani ro how karde budan. Yā behesh gofte budan 'kalle-kadu'. Hasani tu khune mundegār shodesh. Bibi did tu khune mundan vāse mard kār nemishe. Fekri kard, chāre'i kard. Ye shabi ke Hasanak khāb budesh, khāb-e haft tā pādeshāh, Bibi jun in kār-o kard:

Narrator: The house did not have a person to earn the living, the house did not have a working man, Bibi also did not plan to have a new husband. Qarun's treasure is also said to be finished someday. From this large garden, a house the size of a sieve remained. The carpets turned into mats. Bibi did cooking, Bibi did sewing, sweeping, and rowing. She made up others to pay for the expenses of the house. Hassanak kept playing and swinging. Because he did not have a teammate, one day he went into the alley and went back home. He did not leave the house anymore. It was as if the children had booed Hassani, or called him a "pumpkin head." Hassani stayed at home. Bibi realized that it does not make sense for a man to stay at home. She thought and made a choice. One night when Hassanak was asleep, he was dreaming of seven kings, Dear Bibi did this:

From this time, the titles of the film get started and the rest of the movie is in the form of moving pictures. Hassan's mother tempts her lazy son to go out of the house by placing fragrant apples from his bed to the doorway, and sends him out of the house to find his fortune.

Hassan Kachal was a box office hit in its time, and Hātami was greatly encouraged to experience the folk stories and musical movies again. So he made his third film, *Bābā Shamal*[3] (1971) with almost a similar formula. *Bābā Shamal* again starts with a *naqqāli* about the beauties of the older times and the grace of the older people, and narrates the story of a local water reservoir in which something unethical takes place, and the main movie starts from that point. Like the former example, the narrator says the famous sentence: "Forget all the stories you have heard. Come and listen to the story of *Bābā Shamal* (Hassan the Bald in the former)."

Figure 18.6 Prologue for the story of *Bābā Shamal*.

Mardomā, be-gush! Mardomā, be-hush!
Shahr, shahr-e āftāb! Shahr, shahr-e mahtāb! Shahr, bā mardom-e sefid o
  siyāh. Shahr, bā mardom-e boland o kutāh!

Listen, people! People be vigilant!
[Look at the] the City, city of the sun! The city, is the city of the moon! The city, with its white and black people. The city, with tall and short people!

In āqā salmuniye, bā hame khodemuniye.
In bābā dallāke, mige dast o del pāke.
Dāre dandun mikeshe, engāri ādamo bā zanjir-e zendun mikseshe!
Āqā ro karde tu-ye lab, goli be jamāl-e mirqazab!

Agar-am nāluti'i peydā mishod, mizad kalak, un bud o chub o falak.
  Agar-am adab nemishod bā chub, āqā ro dodasti injuri mibastan-esh
  be tup. Bāz-am be qwl-e rendun, goli be jamāl-e zendun!

Inā nokarāsh budan. Inā dokhmarāsh budan. Inā farrāshāsh budan. Inā
  darvishāsh budan. Inā hamrishāsh budan. Inā ādamāsh budan. Inā
  biqamāsh budan. Inā khub khubāsh budan. Inā motrebāsh budan.

Hama ro beriz tu hashti, goli be jamāle Mashti.

This man is a barber, he is friendly to everyone.

This man is a bathroom masseur, and claims that he is a nice, decent man.
He is pulling a tooth, as if he is pulling a person with a prison chain!
He has placed the man in misery, the executioner is worth of praise here!

If there was an evil who wanted to deceive, he would face punishment and the carousel. In case he would not learn a good lesson, he would be held tied up before a cannon like this. According to the hooligans, (in comparison) the prison was worth of praise.

Figure 18.7 The story of *Bābā Shamal* continued.

[Of the city], these are the servants. These were the chiks. These were the officers. These were the dervishes. These were the relatives. These were the people. They were the carefree people. These were the good ones. These were the singers.

Throw everyone on the porch, Mashti is worth of praise.

Age howz-e meydun-ā yek dune favvāre nadāre, del-e mardom mesāl-e daryāst. Age ru-ye āsemun tayyāre nist, gāhi vaqt-ā kalāqi mibini. Age shahr-ā hame golkāri nist, tu-ye har kuche ye bāqi mibini. Ruz-e chārshanbe-ye mā, age mesl-e shomāhā, ruz-e khoshbakhti nist, shabā-ye jom'e hekāyat-hā dāre. Sobh-e jom'e hammum-ā qowqā mishe. Jā-ye shab-zende-dār-ā unjā mishe. Mosht-e mardom pish-e mardom vā mishe.

Gusht o piyāz o donbe, goli be Jamāl-e jom'e.

If the pool of squares does not have a fountain, the hearts of the people are like the sea. If there is no plane in the sky, sometimes you see a crow. If cities are not all decorated with flowers, you see a garden in every alley. Although Wednesdays are not days of happiness like your time, there are hot stories about Thursday nights. On Friday mornings, the public baths become very crowded. There is a place for those who enjoy the nights. People's secrets are revealed to other people.

Meat, onion and tail, Friday is worth of praise!

Āre, dowre-ye shomā nāmarde. Dige dard-e del faqat del-darde. Āh-e mardon sarde.
Deliye, deldāriye. Rumi o Zangebāriye.
Nuniye, paniriye. Qesse'iye, Qesse'iye, Qesse'iye.
Qesse har chi shenidi pāk farāmush bokon. Biyā o be Qesse-ye Bābā Shamal gush bokon.

Yes, your period is a cruel one. Now opening one's heart means having belly pains. People take cold sighs.

There is a heart, there is a beloved. There is Rome, there is Zanzibar (Tanzania).

There is bread, there is cheese, there is a story, there is a story, there is a story.

Forget all the stories you have heard. Come and listen to the story of Baba Shamal.

Tu-ye in shahr-e qashang, shahr-e rang o vārang, ye gozar hast ke tu nāf-e gozar, ye āb-anbāri hast. In āb-abnbār negin ast o gozar, angoshtar.

Figure 18.8 The story of *Bābā Shamal* continued.

Shikamesh daryā va āb-e khosh-khorāki dāre. Āb-e khosh-ta'm va pāki dāre. In gozar rāh-e miyunbor-e do tā mahalle hast. Tu-ye hich kodum az in do tā mahalle ham āb-anbāri nist. Zan-ā bā kuze vo mard-ā bā dalv. Darvish-ā bā kashkul, saqqā-hā bā kise, bache-hā āb mibaran, āb mikhoran. Gedā vo 'a'yun o ham pir o javun, zan-ā-ye bache-baqal, do'ā mikonan hamashun be āb-anbār-e mahal.

In this beautiful city, this colorful city, there is a passage. And in the very center of this passage, there is a reservoir. This reservoir is a jewel, and the passage is a ring. It contains a sea in its belly and has fresh water. It has tasty and clean water. This passage is a shortcut between two neighborhoods, and there is no water storage in either of these two. Women with jugs and men with buckets, dervishes with bowls and water sellers with bags take water from there. Children take water and drink water. Beggars and nobles, as well as the old and young, women with their children in their arms, all pray for the maintenance of the local reservoir.

As opposed to *Hasan Kachal*, the film *Bābā Shamal* was a total flop, and Hātami could not find any other producer to make similar movies. It seems that the time of such methods of storytelling was over, and the rapidly modernizing Iran of the 1970s was no longer interested in what Hātami fancied. Hātami's cinema was an original of his own and was terminated with his untimely death in 1996.

Notes

1 For an English translation of a *tumār*, see Page (1979).
2 For example, Bahram Beyzaie and Pari Saberi have made use of *naqqāli* and some other Iranian traditional plays in their plays. Also, Mohammad Rahmanian's *Amir* (2000) and Hamid Amjad's *Mehr va Aiynehā* (Mehr and the Mirrors, 2000) are clearly concerned with *naqqāli* (see Talajooy 2011: 501–14).
3 For a detailed study of this film, see Khanjani (2012).

Works Cited

Beeman, W. O. (1993), "The Anthropology of Theater and Spectacle," *Annual Review of Anthropology*, 22: 369–93.
Chelkowski, P. (1984), "Islam in Modern Drama and Theatre," *Die Welt des Islams*, 23 (24): 45–69.
Chelkowski, P. (1989), "Narrative Painting and Painting Recitation in Qājār Iran," *Muqarnas*, 6: 98–111.
Chelkowski, P. (2010), "Kāshefi's *Rowzat al-Shohadā*': The Karbalā Narrative Underpinning of Popular Religious Culture and Literature," in Philip G. Kreyenbroek and Ulrich Marzolph (eds), *Oral Literature of Iranian Languages: Kurdish, Pashto, Balochi, Ossetic, Persian and Tajik*, London: I. B. Tauris, 258–77.
Gaffary, F. (1984), "Evolution of Rituals and Theater in Iran," *Iranian Studies*, 17 (4): 361–89.
Khan, P. M. (2019), *The Broken Spell: Indian Storytelling and the Romance Genre in Persian and Urdu*, Detroit: Wayne State University Press.
Khanjani, R. S. (2012), "Animating Eroded Landscapes: The Cinema of Ali Hatami," MA Thesis of Film Studies, Carleton University.
Lashkari, A., and Kalantari, M. (2015), "Pardeh Khani: A Dramatic Form of Storytelling in Iran," *Asian Theatre Journal*, 32 (1): 245–58.
Mahdavi, S. (2007), "Amusements in Qajar Iran," *Iranian Studies*, 40 (4): 483–99.
Martin, W. H., and Mason, S. (2006), "The Development of Leisure in Iran: The Experience of the Twentieth Century," *Middle Eastern Studies*, 42 (2): 239–54.
Marzolph, U. (2015), "Professional Storytelling (Naqqāli) in Qājār Iran," in Julia Rubanovich (ed.), *Orality and Textuality in the Iranian World: Patterns of Interaction across the Centuries*, Leiden and Boston: Brill, 271–85.
Omidsalar, M. (1984), "Storytellers in Classical Persian Texts," *The Journal of American Folklore*, 384: 204–12.
Page, M. E. (1979), "Professional Storytelling in Iran: Transmission and Practice," *Iranian Studies*, 12 (3–4): 195–215.
Talajooy, S. (2011), "Indigenous Performing Traditions in Post-Revolutionary Iranian," *Iranian Studies*, 44 (4): 497–519.
Yamamoto, K. (2010), "Naqqāli: Professional Iranian Storytelling," in Philip G. Kreyenbroek and Ulrich Marzolph (eds), *Oral Literature of Iranian Languages: Kurdish, Pashto, Balochi, Ossetic, Persian and Tajik*, London: I.B. Tauris, 240–57.

19

肉声: The Fleshly Voice

(Origin Japanese)

Gretchen Jude

nikusei: the "raw voice" that comes out of the human throat and reaches the ears directly, as opposed to a voice that passes through devices such as microphones, telephones, speakers, and megaphones.[1]

Body and Voice

I am in the kitchen, washing dishes after a dinner party. Since I had a few glasses of wine over the course of the evening, I am singing to myself quite freely. When I go back into the other room to join some close friends who have stayed late, one exclaims warmly yet with some surprise: "Oh, was that your voice singing? I thought you were a CD!" Although pleased at what is clearly meant as a compliment, I am left speechless. Is sounding like an audio recording something I aspire to? If my voice is a CD, where does that leave the rest of me?

Live or Memorex?

In a classic advertising campaign of the 1970s, audio cassette manufacturer Memorex featured aging jazz legend Ella Fitzgerald in a series of television commercials to illustrate the power and fidelity of their product. The ads show Fitzgerald scatting a melody topped by a high note that dramatically shatters a wine glass. The subsequent shot demonstrates that a recording of her performance sounds so similar to the diva's voice that it also breaks the glass.

While these advertisements create an equivalence between a living voice and its technological reproduction, Mercer points out that the image of Ella

Fitzgerald as an embodied person—"in the living, singing flesh"—is another key component in the equation:

> Just as critical to Fitzgerald's authenticity in the campaign is her unreconstructed middle-aged appearance: her wig, round body — and in some spots, cataract-correcting eyeglasses — lend warmth and conviction to her televisual style. The iconic Fitzgerald comes across as so *real* in the commercials that her mere presence authenticates the ad's claim of a Memorex cassette recording breaking a glass. "Is it live or is it Memorex?" the ads ask. What matters is that it's Fitzgerald onscreen.
>
> (Mercer 2019)

In one iteration of the ad series, Fitzgerald's friend and long-time collaborator Count Basie is shown in a recording booth, listening to both live and recorded Ella through studio monitors. "I can't tell!" he exclaims. The trick, of course, is that both voices come to him through the audio system. Here, even Ella "live" is Ella through speakers. The audiovisual reconstitution of her living body singing for machines somehow creates a persistent sense of her human presence, even after her passing.

The challenges to understanding **what a voice is** in this age beyond mechanical reproduction have exponentially increased in the fifty years since the Memorex tape campaign. Telephony, digital processing, and vocal synthesis have become ubiquitous across cultures. In previous writing, I have attempted to come to grips with our current sonic scenario, suggesting the term "plasmatic voice" to describe the new normal (Jude 2018; Jude 2019). This term indicates a globally distributed assemblage that is both relational and transformational, entailing flows of affect and information between people and machines. Plasmatic voice shows the electrified potential for myriad transformations of vocal movements into the vibratory fullness of air. Plasmatic voice is complexly embodied, with its materiality multiplied through by repeated transductions and transmissions, dispersed through non/human realms. Under conditions of plasmatic voice, I can, at the touch of a button, hear hundreds of other voices from the furthest corners of earth in an instant. Conversely, my singing can be heard by people I will never met.

However, as I explore in this essay, English has no word to indicate a voice specifically **without** the electrical interventions normalized by the expansion of plasmatic voice. "Fleshly voice" functions as counterpart to plasmatic voice — not in binary opposition, but as two regions on a spectrum of (post) human sounding. "Fleshly voice" originates from the Japanese term *nikusei*, which I examine as an alternative to articulations of the human voice found in contemporary Western theory and philosophy.

Voice, (Dis/Re)Embodied

Common to Euroamerican and Japanese conceptualizations of voice is the persistent yet problematic relationship between the body and its inherent sonic potential. The human voice evolved as a relational phenomenon, signaling to others (both human and nonhuman) and sounding out proximal environments. As Cavarero suggests, the voice remains intimately tied to corporeality, in, for example, the mutual recognition between mother and infant, which "represents the communication of a corporeality that, because it is unique and irreplaceable, is expressed vocally" (2012: 80).

Before the technologies that brought about the condition of plasmatic voice, human voices emerged and faded from bodies within human physical scale. Vocalization techniques and knowledge of the reflective acoustic properties of materials and spaces (mountain valleys, caves) allowed some voices to travel locally and reverberate hauntingly (rural Bulgarian women's vocal traditions and Tuvan throat singing spring to mind). Yet human voices remained inextricably tied to individual human bodies living in specific times and places. When a person died, so did their voice.

Since the invention and development of audio devices over the past 150 years, however, the situation has changed drastically. A sounding body had always held acousmatic potential—the possibility of the voice being heard while its physical source remained out of sight, invisible. But the spread of sound technology has exploded this rare and magical event into dull ubiquity, as Dolar points out:

> Radio, gramophone, tape-recorder, telephone: with the advent of the new media the acousmatic property of the voice became universal, and hence trivial. They all share their acousmatic nature, and in the early days of their introduction there was no shortage of stories about their uncanny effects, but these gradually waned as they became common, and hence banal. It is true that we cannot see the source of voices there, all we see is some technical appliance from which voices emanate, and in a *quid pro quo* the gadget then takes the place of the invisible source itself. The invisible absent source is substituted by the gadget which disguises it and starts to act as its unproblematic stand-in. The curious remainder of wonderment is the dog intently inspecting the cylinder of a phonograph.
>
> (2006: 63)

More and more, the vocalizing human body disappears, only to be replaced by a speakers and earbuds.

For Chion, the technological disembodiment of a voice in film is a symbol of power. What he calls the *acousmêtre* speaks with god-like powers far beyond those of any normal human, who is visibly linked to a corporeal (and thus limited) source. Because it is not seen as coming from a particular body, the *acousmêtre* represents a being that exists everywhere. In contrast, the (sounding) body, once rendered visible onscreen, is effectively disempowered—even when its same voice is heard subsequently from offscreen (1999: 24). In the process of de-acousmatization which follows "from finally showing the person speaking," the all-powerful unseen speaker is captured on film and rendered visible, causing their panoptic powers to quickly dissipate (1999: 23): "*Embodying the voice* is a sort of symbolic act, dooming the acousmêtre to the fate of ordinary mortals. De-acousmatization roots the acousmêtre to a place and says, 'here is your body, you'll be there, and not elsewhere'" (1999: 27–8, italics and quotes in original).

It goes without saying that such dis/re-embodiment of a voice occurs only through audiovisual technology. Voice, if examined solely as sound waves, propagates immediately outward and away from its vibratory source, the sounding body. So, by definition, a voice cannot be strictly located within an embodiment—that is, it must leave the sounding body's position. We know that a voice originates in a human(-sounding) body, even if that body is not visibly/tangibly in proximity to the listener. Thus, human voices are **both** embodied in origin **and** disembodied as sound. Further, since vocal sound by definition is physically perceptible as vibrational patterns in air molecules between (and within) human bodies, a voice never loses its materiality—whether as buzzing larynx or vibrating air, or even as a signal chain in the process of transduction. Our perception of any voice is inextricably tied to bodies: others' and our own.

Electrified Voices, Machinic Bodies

Yet, as LaBelle points out, our experiences of these sounding processes radically change depending on context: "Shifts in technology bring with them new configurations of embodiment, and in addition, resituate how voicing comes to make incarnate a sense of self" (2010: 147). Sterne examines how the history of audio technology is also a history of discursive changes. With audio, the premodern senses and actions were abstracted into mechanical processes (2003: loc. 1651):

> In the logic of automata, sounds are the result of sound-production devices such as mouths. For tympanic machines, frequencies were

frequencies — to be heard by ears; speech and music became specific instances of sound, which was itself a reproducible effect.

(2003: loc. 1431)

Human vocal utterance was similarly abstracted into pure sonic content, as "voice becomes vocalization" (2003: loc. 2351). The sounding body was primed for subordination to electroacoustic devices and technological processes.

A century after the tympanic revolution, Barthes (1977) famously christened as "the grain of the voice" the sonic presence of a singer's corporeality heard through audio recording.[2] Just as the grain of a piece of wood (appearing on a polished surface to be merely a peculiar pattern) evidences the living processes and structures of a tree, the grain of the voice traces the unique individual embodiment of a singer, in excess of the song's signification. The voice's origin in the body persists through transductions, to affect another's embodied ears.

Perceptualizing a Vocalic Body

Conner and Fales variously account for the relation between voices and their bodies of origin by foregrounding the role of the listener. Introducing the notion of the vocalic body, Connor asserts, "Voices are produced by bodies: but can also themselves produce bodies" (2000: 36). The existence of the vocalic body springs from the urge of the listener to more fully encounter the human source of a vocal sound: "[I]t is we who assign voices to objects; phenomenologically, the fact that an unassigned voice must always imply a body means that it will always partly supply it as well" (2000: 36). Simply put, in hearing the complex and shifting frequencies of a voice's unique timbre, we construct an aural image of a particular body that is resonantly formed and actively vibrating.

Fales posits that human perceptual/cognitive systems reflexively attribute every sound to a physical source. The term perceptualization refers to a listener's identification, creation, and combination of "necessary interpretive elements … with acoustic properties of the environment to create auditory percepts" (2002: 63). Because "sound is a moving phenomenon, its processing is necessarily interpretive and time-dependent" (2005: 163), which necessitates speed. The preconscious nature of perceptualization enables humans' rapid response to sonic input from our surroundings. Our perceptual systems evolved to know immediately that the sound of a snarling dog means existential danger.

Much of the information key to such identifications revolves around timbre (2002: 59). Fales points out that perceptualization is exponentially stronger in the auditory processing of formant-based vocal sounds than of harmonically structured frequency patterns (2002: 72). That is, human listeners are most perceptually active when processing a human voice[3] because perceptualization favors the fusion of complex vocal sounds (i.e., the formant bands typical of the vocal tract) into a single auditory percept that we can then identify as a human voice.

In short, when listening, we inherently seek salient objects—and human perception of sound events is particularly adept selecting out other human voices from the vast vibratory world that surrounds us. Embodied relationality is built into aural perception, so to accurately discuss the human voice, it is essential to have terminology that can foreground the inescapability of bodies and bodily processes in both vocalizing and hearing voices.

Meat Voice

If the vocalic body is the function of a listener perceptualizing a body through their experience of a voice's sounding, how can we speak of that voice which sounds directly, immediately, through a **particular**, proximal body? The grain of the voice (emerging inextricably from the grain of the apparatus) and the *acousmêtre* of cinema are both plasmatic—cyborg creations that can exist only in the connection of human bodies to electrical technologies. In contrast, the Japanese term *nikusei* denotes a voice free of technological trappings, although the term is often used to describe recorded or otherwise electronically mediated voices which nonetheless retain a sense of the vocalist's intimate physical presence. Hereafter, I discuss examples of the term as well as various translations into English that, I argue, retain more visceral and corporeal qualities than Barthes' *grain*, for example.

Nikusei is a compound word consisting of two Sino-Japanese *kanji* characters. The first character is the word *niku*, meaning "meat," while the second character denotes "voice." *Niku* also occurs in many compound words emphasizing corporeality and physicality, including the words *nikutai* (body, flesh, physicality) and *nikuhitsu* (handwriting, literally "meat inkbrush"). In the second instance, the character *niku* indicates the immediacy of the physical gestures of writing, a sense of human presence transmitted by the marks of the writer's own body.

Kahn's notion of the deboned voice echoes the viscerality of *nikusei* in an unintentional yet evocative parallel:

> While other people hear a person's voice carried through vibrations in the air, the person speaking also hears her or his own voice as it is

conducted from the throat and mouth through bone to the inner regions of the ear .... [A]t the same time that the speaker hears the voice full with the immediacy of the[ir own] body, others will hear the speaker's voice infused with a lesser distribution of body because it will be a voice heard without bone conduction: a deboned voice.

(1999: 7)

The term "deboned voice" shorthands the technical explanation for the jarring sensation of hearing one's own voice recorded and played back. What sorts of conceptual heavy lifting might the concept of **fleshly voice** achieve?

A Natural Voice

Japanese folk singer Tomokawa Kazuki titled his second album *Nikusei*, glossing the title as "A Natural Voice." This album, released in 1976 by the so-called screaming philosopher, performs an emotional rawness that resonates with the artist's regional, working-class roots. Born in Japan's rugged, impoverished far north in 1950, Tomokawa writes songs imbued with a post-war international sensibility: acoustic and electric guitars, drum kit, piano, and female backing vocals all support Tomokawa's powerfully expressive vocals. His freely visceral singing style on the first track ("Ojiccha" [Grampa]) about Tomokawa's grandfather's impending death—replete with choked screams, fluttering howls, and manic laughter—strongly conveys the meaning of its lyrics, even without translation. Here, *nikusei*, used to describe a recorded voice, emphasizes the hard-working singer's authenticity as an embodied being—the voice of one who feels and who calls forth others' emotions in response to his sounding. The naturalness of this connotative use of *nikusei* can be likened to hearing the voice of a loved one who has passed away, not with fear or haunting, but rather with a sense of being touched by sound, echoes of a beloved body's absence.

Actual Voice

A similar use of the term describes historical recordings that evoke a visceral sense of history's continuity with the present. In 1909, General Nogi Maresuke recorded a speech for Kaikosha, an elite military club, which Victor Japan acquired and released to the public in 1931, as 78 rpm discs under the title *Nogi shōgun no nikusei to sono omoide*. Commentary provided by the

Director of the Kanazawa Phonograph Museum translates this as "General Nogi's Natural Voice and His Recollections," describing the recording as "a record of the actual voice of General Nogi Maresuke" (Yokaichiya 2018: n.p.). Struggling to convey in English the lode of connotations provided by *nikusei*, Yokaichiya translates:

> Though a single voice states, "I am Nogi Maresuke," its dignified tone stiffens one's spine right up. The physical sensation of hearing a live voice[4] strikes one completely differently to that one reads silently from the pages of a book.
>
> (2018: n.p.)

Both the singularity of the speaker's authoritative voice and the sensation of the listener's sudden proximity to that vocal personage can be conveyed by Japanese terms such as *nikusei* in a way that seems to elude English. Most strikingly, the choice of the English term "live voice" in reference to a recorded voice indicates the need for a **fleshing out** of the concept of voice in relation to audio technology.[5]

Own Voice: The Shared Moment of Speech

Strikingly, *nikusei* is also used in Japanese media analysis and critical theory to indicate Saussure's *parole* (as opposed to *langue*). Nakahira Takuma, an influential photographer and leftist theorist active in the 1960s and 1970s, utilizes the term in his commentary on Enzenberger's media theory. A founding member of *Provoke*, a short-lived yet pivotal photography journal, Nakahira attempted to radicalize Japanese photography with a visual language of blurry, grainy, unfocused images—a suite of techniques which, at *Provoke*'s height of influence, extended even into the mainstream advertising of the time. Nakahira describes this impulse to "challenge the dominant regime of vision" as an instance of the photographer's *nikusei*—what Yoda translates as "corporeal voice" (2017: loc. 4409).

In Sass's translation of the same article by Nakahira (1973), she emphasizes the collective aspect of *parole*, defined as "intervention of a momentary instance selected from within" the structured system of *langue* (2017: loc. 3848). In English, Nakahira's *nikusei* becomes **our voice**: "What exactly is our voice? It is something which has rather nothing to convey — it is just our silence directed towards the dismantlement of all existing things: this is what our paradoxical language is" (2017: loc. 3842). In discussing an article by *Provoke* cofounder Taki Kōji critiquing *Life* magazine as a "monolithic and homogenizing media structure" (2017: loc. 3855), Sass also glosses *nikusei/parole* as both **moment of speech** and **raw voice** (2017: loc. 3855).

The nuanced linguistic triangulations necessitated by transcultural theorization of collective expressions of human resistance indicate both universality and variability of forms of utterance which are embodied and situated, even those located beyond a single individual's vibrating body. For what is voice if not a relational phenomenon that is inescapably contextual?

Fleshly Voice: Voice in the Raw

Expressing the deep-seated emotions intimately connected to the human voice calls for a word of Germanic origin more direct, more visceral than the Latinate "corporeal." Indeed, during the global pandemic, vocalizing with others in the flesh has proven to be one of the riskiest activities we can undertake. Even before physical distancing measures, in many social settings, acoustic singing face-to-face was an increasingly rare occurrence. One effect of mediatization is the sense of boldness, even presumption, that burdens an ordinary person casually singing in the most mundane situation. The friend who, years ago, complimented me on my thoughtless, solitary song seemed equally impressed at my apparent lack of self-consciousness—a freedom from restraint.

Whether my real-life voice measured up to the exigencies of recording standards is not the crux of the matter. It was the shock of my naked voice reverberating off the enamel sink, my body shamelessly presencing itself through sound—not just live but **in the raw**. A fleshly voice still carries a strong yet subtle affective charge—now more than ever, as expanding conditions of plasmatic voice make young people, singing alone into their camera phones to produce performances for TikTok, into legatees of Fitzgerald's voice on Memorex.

Notes

1 *Daijisen Digital Dictionary*, translation from Japanese by author.
2 Sterne additionally posits "the grain of the apparatus" (2003: loc. 4838), perhaps most iconically exemplified by the scratch and hiss created by the physical contact of an amplified needle with a rotating LP's vinyl groove.
3 Or more accurately, sounds that have spectral qualities like those of a human voice.

4 *raibu kankaku*: lit. "live feeling," that is, the sensation of a live performance as opposed to a recording.
5 See Auslander (1999).

Works Cited

Auslander, P. (1999), *Liveness: Performance in a Mediatized Culture*, London: Routledge.
Barthes, R. (1977), *Image–Music–Text*, trans. S. Heath, New York: Hill and Wang.
Cavarero, A. (2012), "The Vocal Body: Extract from a Philosophical Encyclopedia of the Body," trans. M. Langione, *Qui Parle*, 21 (1): 71–83.
Chion, M. (1999), *The Voice in Cinema*, trans. C. Gorbman, New York: Columbia University Press.
Connor, S. (2000), *Dumbstruck: A Cultural History of Ventriloquism*, Oxford: Oxford University Press.
Dolar, M. (2006), *A Voice and Nothing More*, Cambridge, MA: MIT Press.
Fales, C. (2002), "The Paradox of Timbre," *Ethnomusicology*, 46 (1): 56–95.
Fales, C. (2005), "Short-circuiting Perceptual Systems: Timbre in Ambient and Techno Music," in P. Greene and T. Porcello (eds), *Wired for Sound: Engineering and Technologies in Sonic Cultures*, Middletown, CT: Wesleyan University Press, 156–80.
Jude, G. (2018), "Vocal Processing in Transnational Music Performances, From Phonograph to Vocaloid," Unpublished Doctoral Dissertation, University of California, Davis.
Jude, G. (2019), "Vocal Performance through Electrical Flows: Making Current Kin," *Performance Philosophy*, 4 (2): 393–409.
Kahn, D. (1999), *Noise, Water, Meat: A History of Sound in the Arts*, Cambridge, MA: MIT Press.
LaBelle, B. (2010), "Raw Orality: Sound Poetry and Live Bodies," in N. Neumark, R. Gibson and T.van Leeuwen (eds), *Voice: Vocal Aesthetics in Digital Arts and Media*, Cambridge, MA: MIT Press, 147–71.
Mercer, M. (2019), "The Voice That Shattered Glass: How Ella Fitzgerald's Cassette Campaign Fueled a Late-Career Renaissance," on *NPR's All Things Considered*, Online Edition, September 3, 2019.
Nakahira T. (1973), "Nikusei no kakutoku wa kanō ka: Media-ron hihan e mukete," *Nihon Dokusho Shinbun*, March 19, 1973: 1.
Sass, M. (2017), "The Culture Industries and Media Theory in Japan," in M. Steinberg and A. Zahlten (eds), *Media Theory in Japan*, Durham, NC: Duke University Press, 151–72. Kindle Edition.
Sterne, J. (2003), *The Audible Past: Cultural Origins of Sound Reproduction*, Durham, NC: Duke University Press. Kindle Edition.
Tomokawa, K. (2021), Website: http://kazukitomokawa.com

Yoda, T. (2017), "Girlscape: The Marketing of Mediatic Ambience in Japan," in M. Steinberg and A. Zahlten (eds), *Media Theory in Japan*, Durham, NC: Duke University Press, 173–99. Kindle Edition.

Yokaichiya, N. (2018), "Historical Recordings Collection: Commentaries," *Rekion: National Diet Library, Japan*, Website: https://rekion.dl.ndl.go.jp/en/ongen_shoukai_03.html

20

OTKA3 (OTKAZ): From Expressive Movement to a Figure of Thought

(Origin Russian)

Julia Vassilieva

OTKAZ is a Russian term which was deployed in a specific way in relation to aesthetics, film, and philosophy of art by revolutionary director Sergei Eisenstein. Often translated as *recoil*, a term borrowed from theater studies, in the first instance OTKAZ denotes a particular trajectory of stage movement—a zigzag line, a spiral, or a semi-spiral, each of them recording the movement toward the aim in a roundabout way. Yet, in Russian, OTKAZ also means refusal, denial, and negation. In his unique mobilization of the term, Eisenstein activated a range of meaning and made the term reign supreme in his theory and practice. More and more often, Eisenstein scholars opt for using the Russian term to preserve the original conceptual richness and polysemy of Eisenstein's thought. This entry outlines various ways in which Eisenstein used the term OTKAZ and places this notion within a broader context of psychological and philosophical inquiry. OTKAZ is crucial not only for understanding Eisenstein's view on the relationship between actor and space, *mise en scène* construction, and expressivity but goes to the core of his theorization of cinema by defining the unique function that this medium can perform in relation to movement—movement of bodies, movement of time, and movement of thought.

In a received account of Eisenstein's intellectual trajectory, his early years are most often associated with the much-celebrated notion of montage—which he carried from theater, as "the montage of attractions," to cinema, as "the montage of film attractions." Yet, Eisenstein's montage proves to be inextricably connected with the discussion of movement, a category that cuts through the Eisenstein's entire oeuvre. Eisenstein's interest in actors' movement and its expressive potential emerged when he was working in theater in the early 1920s and was fueled by Eisenstein's engagement with diverse sources such as Russian discourse and practice of biomechanics, elaborated on in two different ways by theater director Vsevolod Meyerhold and physiologist Nikolai Bernstein, studies of movement by English physician and physiologist William Benjamin Carpenter, the contribution to the German body culture of Rudolf Bode, the psychological and philosophical ideas of Ludwig Klages, and Heinrich von Kleist's discussion of the marionette theater. But it was Eisenstein's engagement with cinema that allowed him to expand his interest in expressive movement toward broader issues of aesthetics and philosophy. After moving to cinema in the mid-1920s, Eisenstein (2002: 170) wrote: "Practice in cinema helped me to expand issues of expressive movement to the issue of expressivity as a whole, as the same laws determine phenomena which represent the basic form of such manifestations—expressive movement—and, simultaneously, the highest form of the system of image production."

Eisenstein saw the essence of the expressive movement in OTKAZ, "that movement which, when you wish to make a movement in one direction, you initially make in the opposite direction (in part or completely) [...] This is one of the fundamental laws inevitably met at all levels and in all varieties of expressive movement" (quoted in Law and Gordon 1996: 192). Initially, Eisenstein posited OTKAZ as the formula of expressive movement because its trajectory presents a physical outline of conflict, it stages the dynamic of two opposing forces or motives—away and toward the aim of movement; and the notion of conflict was paramount for early Eisenstein. He wrote: "The most interesting case in terms of its [expressive movement's] motor formation is the case of a psychologically expressive movement that represents a motor exposure of the *conflict* of motivations; and instinctively emotional desire that retards the conscious volitional principle" (Eisenstein 2010: 52).

In 1928 Eisenstein went on to test this hypothesis experimentally, capitalizing on his emerging collaboration with Russian psychologists Lev Vygotsky and Alexandr Luria, which he started three years earlier. Engaging the help Luria Eisenstein conducted a series of experiments that explored what trajectory the movement would follow if the subject faces a situation of conflict. In these experiments, the subject, a woman referred in protocols as "M," was placed under hypnosis and given the instruction to move toward a highly desirable object (a bouquet of flowers, a plate of fruit) while at the same time facing a threat from the location of this object—a snake lurking between the flowers, a wasp hovering over the fruits. The experimental protocols produced by Luria contained the description of experimental conditions, the set of three various instructions to the subject and also—the diagrams of the movements. Confirming Eisenstein's hypothesis, the woman moved toward the goal along the trajectory of spiral, enacting the conflict engendered by the presence of two objects—one generating desire, another—fear. These diagrams also made visible another aspect of OTKAZ movement—namely, that it entails the change in point of view, taking in the scene in a panoramic, 360-degree way, the fact made even more prominent by the instruction to the subject to imagine that she is walking in the garden of Allupka's Palace in Krimea—the location where Eisenstein filmed his famous roaring lions for *Potemkin* three years earlier (Vassilieva 2019).

Eisenstein later saw another demonstration of circular movements in psychological experiments conducted by eminent German psychologist, Kurt Lewin. Lewin's distinguished contribution to Gestalt psychology related to his theory of field forces and the notion of living space, comprising what he defined as topological psychology (1936). Eisenstein met Lewin on Luria's recommendation in Berlin where he stayed on the way to the United States in autumn 1929 and where he also delivered a lecture on expressive movement. From 1923 to 1924 Lewin had been using cinematography to record his experiments which he showed to Eisenstein to share his findings as well as to seek the director's advice on using the medium. Among Lewin's films was a short film depicting an eighteen-month-old girl, Hannah who was trying to sit on the stone. Having approached the stone, in order to sit on it the girl had to turn 180 degree and face away from the stone—and that action the girl was not able to perform, as she could not take her eyes away from the stone. As a result, she would circle around the stone repeatedly. Lewin explained the child's movement through his theory of field forces—the stone has a strong positive valence, yet because the child is too young, she is not able to restructure the field successfully to organize her movements within it (Bulgakowa 2014).

Yet, the notion of the field of forces was criticized by Eisenstein's Russian collaborators, Luria and Vygotsky for its mechanism and lack of attention to purely human ways of interacting with the environment. Instead of Levin's field of forces Vygotsky introduced an alternative notion—the field of meaning, or the field of significance. Unlike the field of forces, the field of significance is an inner field which emerges in human consciousness and is mediated by words and other signs. Vygotsky's field of significance encompasses not only the topology of the visually observable space, but also—the universe of human meanings, values, strivings, ethical and conceptual commitments which provides a broader context for human actions. The field of significance addresses not only the connection between movements and emotions, but also the connection between movements and thought—the key objective of Eisenstein. The introduction of this inner field further allowed Vygotsky

(2018: 336) to approach the most crucial aspect of human behavior, free will, and self-determined actions:

> We are powerless to change the field of forces and external *Aufforderungscharacter*, but by changing the *inner field*, we can change the influence on us from outside. By creating inner fields, which is only possible with the help of rational speech, *the problem of will is moved from outside to inside*, from the plane of behaviour onto the plane of consciousness.

Eisenstein's engagement with Luria's and Vygotsky's work in the area of motor control and regulation, as well as the relationship between movement, emotions, and thought reveals a complex set of interconnected ideas bearing on different aspects of the problematic that Eisenstein termed "expressive movement." These problematics can be divided into two broad parts: first, how an emotional state (e.g., of an actor) or an idea (of an author) can be expressed in movement; and second, how an observed movement can produce an emotional and intellectual response in the viewer. Eventually, Eisenstein would bridge these two aspects with the notion of an "image" (*obraz*, in Russian). He notes in his diary: "Perhaps we should say not 'expressive movement', but image-based movement. The image of action, the image of thought. Images in these *locutions* are understood dialectically both as a *modus* of expression, and as an object of apperception from outside" (Eisenstein 1928). Now, in such an approach a movement itself seems to turn into a sign which on the one hand, gives an expression to, on the other—produces thought and feeling. If Vygotsky and Luria place sign at the center of volitional, goal-oriented organization of movement and actions, Eisenstein extends these considerations into the realm of aesthetics, arguing that movement itself can take on signifying functions, can become a complex sign, and, by the same token, become a means of organizing an aesthetic response, encompassing both emotional and intellectual components. Eisenstein's use of his epitome of expressive movement, OTKAZ, and his sustained media-archaeological analysis of OTKAZ in various cultural and historical traditions demonstrate how he put such an understanding in practice.

In Eisenstein's theoretical writings detailed discussion of OTKAZ can be found in his numerous analyses focusing on *mise en scène* and trajectories of movement on stage. He praises Chinese director Mei Lanfang and Japanese kabuki theater for their skillful mobilization of OTKAZ; he refers to Lessing's notes on hand movements; and he highlights the exaggerated use of OTKAZ movement in the ritual dancing of North American indigenous people. And in his cinematic work Eisenstein insists on the necessity of breaking down the movement into two phases—the initial one, away from its aim, and the amplified second phase, toward the aim—to achieve maximum expressive effect. He uses OTKAZ in all his films—from *Strike* (1924) and *The Battleship Potemkin* (1925) to *Ivan the Terrible* (1943–7); it can be observed at the level of individual actors and in the collective movement of Eisenstein's famous invention, the "mass protagonist."

The most celebrated sequence in Eisenstein's oeuvre, Odessa steps sequence in *Potemkin*, uses OTKAZ to stage the central conflict of the film in the most dramatic way: as it is well known, the oppressive brutal force of Tsarist military machine is placed above the innocent armless people below, and the soldiers' advance toward the people is rhythmically punctuated and reinforced by the close-ups of their feet on the steps of the stairs. Yet, in the climax of the scene the soldiers' movement is interrupted: the mother of the little boy, who was rushing down ahead of her son, turns around and notices that her child is wounded. She takes her son in her arms and reverses her steps back—now toward the soldiers, in a slow, measured, and deliberate manner, performing a poignant OTKAZ. She stops before the soldiers and demands justice for her son only to be shot in a summary execution style seconds later, exposing the depth of the conflict which goes beyond the class struggle, but rather—threatens youth, innocence, and as such—life itself with—annihilation.

Another example of an effective use of the OTKAZ is found in the finale of *Ivan the Terrible, Part I*. The finale is a "turning point" in the film's narrative: it depicts Ivan retreating outside Moscow to Alexandrova Sloboda to test his supporters and to compel people to pledge their loyalty and to beg for his return, which will give him an opportunity to reaffirm and consolidate his power. In terms of the *mise en scène* though the finale is staged like a sequence of ballet movements each of them representing an instance of OTKAZ. It starts with the Tsar siting in the armchair, contemplating his decision to retreat, visibly tortured by doubts. The distant singing becomes audible, and as Ivan registers the singing and his demeanor changes from tortured to hopeful, Eisenstein cuts to the long shot of the crowds of Tsar's supporters approaching his residence and crossing the snowfield in a zigzag trajectory (an OTKAZ performed by mass protagonist). Ivan rises, turns 180 degree, and walks toward the background of the shot, where his servants place a heavy fur coat on his shoulders and give him his scepters, after which Ivan makes an abrupt turn to face the camera, and the window through which the crowds can be seen and toward which he starts walking. However, upon reaching the window the Tsar makes another 180 degrees turns in the opposite direction, his approach toward the spectacle of the pleading crowd becomes interrupted for a moment by Ivan throwing his body away from it; as if the doubts are still lingering in his mind and he is yet no ready to face his people. At this point the camera shows the crowds of Ivan's supporters now immobilized as a zigzag and framed by the similarly jagged contour of the window. But the Tsar only glances at the crowd before making another 180 degree turn, which places him on a decisive trajectory toward meeting the people outside, which he does upon descending few steps and reaching a landing, where he bows to his people and waits till the crowd starts kneeling. He then makes another 180-degree turn and starts ascending, the movement interrupted by yet another turn timed to coincide with the crowd getting of the knees, before finally reaching back the window through which we see the crowd once more.

As Joan Neuberger (2019) stresses, the central theme of the film is power and Ivan's questioning of its legitimacy, limits, and price is the central vector of the film dramaturgy. The finale of Part I is crucial in Ivan's quest—from now on he would assume an unlimited power and would place himself above religious, legal, and human law. Part II would unveil the tragedy of power turning on itself, of sovereignty drowning in violence, of Ivan taking on the right to kill and disregarding the value of human life. The finale of Part I foreshadows this development by mobilizing the possibility of OTKAZ movement to stage the dialectical movement of thought.

The carefully choreographed movements of multiple OTKAZs in this scene are instrumental in performing Ivan's decision-making: from doubt, through temporarily pause in thought, through considering and retreating from an initial possibility to the confirmation of his decision. But Eisenstein does not only aim to "stage" the movement of thoughts of Ivan, he also effectively provides a script for the reciprocal movement of thought in the audience, who can experience and derive the sense of Ivan's ambivalence, questioning and final resolve not only from the dialogue—every word Ivan utters in this scene has been carefully weighted, selected, loaded, not only from the sequence of changing moods on his face: pain, desperation, hope, anticipation, fear, deliberation, concentration, confidence, determination, but with equal force—from his movements. The development of abstract thought is disaggregated into these visual and embodied components, disarticulated into a chain of movements and gestures, each of them though representing a complex, semantically rich sign.

The figure of Ivan also holds key to Eisenstein's understanding of the relationship between the body and the "Urphenomen" of cinema—its ability to disarticulate objects and figures into their parts, and then reintegrate them within the image on screen. Eisenstein aimed to render the figure of Ivan in such a way "as to try to capture the marks of tragic majesty in his historical role" for which he drew inspiration from his analysis of Shakespeare's tragedies, including *King Lear, Coriolanus, Macbeth*. Both for Shakespeare and Eisenstein the body of the ruler serves as a metaphor for the state, the danger of its disintegration and the necessity of its unity. For instance, Eisenstein (quoted in Lary 2021: 223) stressed the connection between the images of dismemberment of the body and disintegration of the state in *King Lear*:

> Shakespeare turned to this theme at the very moment when the dismemberment of England was a possibility [...] From this point of view, *Lear* is opposed to the division of the state, as is shown by the folly of this division here.[...] In *Lear* there is the theme of disastrous partition. The basic situation in Shakespeare is the division of the state and ruin. In no other tragedy is there so much injury to the body parts and destruction of the human organism as in this piece.

It is precisely against this threat of annihilation of the state that the ruler's torn body should be reintegrated into one—the strategy that Eisenstein (2000: 245) identifies at the heart of the imagistic structure of Shakespeare's tragedies which reveals "that same mark of a human body torn into parts and gathered into one." Eisenstein (2000: 243) further suggests that since the body occupies such a central place in Shakespeare's creative work "we are bound to wonder whether in his methods of work there is a distinctive refraction of the resurrected '[Dionysius and Osiris method.'" The Greek myth of Dionysius (which reworks an earlier Egyptian myth of Osiris) articulates the powerful trop of God's dismemberment and death followed by his resurrection and reintegration. In Eisenstein's (2000: 247) reading, the Dionysius-Osiris myth speaks not only to death and resurrection, but also to movement, change, and becoming and as such forms a basis of the "imagistic structure" predicated on the understanding of the body as ultimately constructed and synthetic phenomenon:

> In the imagistic structure there is a transition from the assembly and collocation of dispersed limbs into a new proto-image—the assembly or collocation of the same limbs under the conditions of the sequentially changing positions of a body that has not been torn apart, a body that breaks the static collocation of its parts as it passes from phase to phase of its movement.

Even more significant though, is that for Eisenstein (2000: 247), "the Osiris-Dionysus method" of disassemblage and reassemblage does not only relate to the representation of body and its movements on screen, it captures the essence of cinema as Eisenstein understood it—its assembled, montaged nature.

> As regards Shakespeare's imagistic structure it could be said to be a move from the gathering and assemblage of scattered limbs into a different proto-image—to an assemblage of the same limbs under the conditions of sequentially changing positions of a body that is not torn apart—a body that breaks the static assemblage of its parts as it passes from one phase of motion to another. The transposition of this to a series of concrete images is not just one of a number of film methods, it is our basic phenomenon of film.

What is at stake in "our basic phenomenon of cinema" is not only movement, but also the issue of unity and division, the issue so powerfully encapsulated in the figure of OTKAZ. For Eisenstein, as Luka Arsenjuk (2018) stresses, OTKAZ is not only an epitome of expressive movement in its ability to dramatize conflict, it is also, and more importantly—a figure of thought, that takes physical movement as a point of departure for a new, purely cinematic dialectics, dialectics arising from the fact the cinema is an art of the moving image. As such it is only cinema that can realize the full potential of OTKAZ as an instrument of thinking. Arsenjuk (2018: 6) suggests that OTKAZ enacts the synthesizing possibility of cinematic thought by dramatizing splitting of (apparent) unity and the overcoming of this splitting through the dialectical logic of "negation of negation." Arsenjuk (2018: 7) writes:

> Movement toward an object can be realized only after it finds its orientation in a moment of OTKAZ. It is only in the abandonment of the aimed-at object that this object can appear as the aim of movement. Which is to say that the concretely realized outcome of the process needs to be grasped not simply as a positive result but through the instance of a self-relating negativity (negation of negation), which provides the process with its dynamism.

Following Yuri Tsivian, Arsenjuk (2018: 8) argues that unity for Eisenstein is always already divided and the potential of cinema as a new form of thought lies precisely in its ability to grasp and model this division:

> Strictly speaking, unity in Eisenstein is and is not. As such, it is certainly nothing conciliatory. In place of the stereotypical image of the dialectical doxa (overcoming of division in unity, triumph of synthesis

over moments of nonsynthesis), one finds in Eisenstein the contours of another, more critical dialectic, which we may call the dialectic of division. The dialectic of division considers division (or self-division) the primary and irreducible moment of thought, whose movement must for this reason be seen as simultaneously destructive and constructive of unity.

And if in its full measure OTKAZ for Eisenstein is no less than an embodiment of a unique potential of cinema, its capacity to engage with division and alienation, and a possibility to overcome this division.

Works Cited

Arsenjuk, L. (2018), *MOVEMENT, ACTION, IMAGE, MONTAGE: Sergei Eisenstein and the Cinema in Crisis*, Minnesota: University of Minnesota Press.

Bulgakowa, O. (2014), "From Expressive Movement to the 'basic problem,'" in A. Yasnitsky and R. Van Der Veer (eds), *The Cambridge Handbook of Cultural-historical Psychology*, Cambridge: Cambridge University Press, 423–48.

Eisenstein, S. (1928), *Diary*, Moscow: Russian Government Archive of Literature and Art (RGALI, 1923-2-1108).

Eisenstein, S. (1964), *Izbrannye proizvedeniia v 6-ti tomach* [Selected works in 6 volumes], ed. Pera Atasheva vol. 1, Moscow: Iskusstvo.

Eisenstein, S. (2000), *Montazh*, Moscow: Muzei kino.

Eisenstein, S. (2002), *Metod, tom 1*, ed. N. I. Kleiman, Moscow: Muzei kino/Eizenshtein-tsentr.

Eisenstein, S. (2010), *Sergei Eisenstein, Selected Works, Volume 1, Writings, 1922–34*, trans. R. Taylor, London and New York: I.B. Tauris.

Lary, N. (2021), "Ivan The Terrible in the Context of Shakespearean Tragedy," in I. Christie and J. Vassilieva (eds), *The Eisenstein Unvierse*, London: Bloomsbury, 423–48.

Law, A. H., and Gordon, M. (1996), *Meyerhold, Eisenstein, and Biomechanics: Actor Training in Revolutionary Russia*, Jefferson, NC: McFarland.

Lewin, K. (1936), *Principles of Topological Psychology*, New York: McGraw-Hill.

Neuberger, J. (2019), *This Thing of Darkness: Eisenstein's Ivan the Terrible in Stalin's Russia*, Cornell: Cornell University Press.

Vassilieva, J. (2019), "The Eisenstein-Vygotsky-Luria Collaboration," *Projections*, 13 (1) (March 2019): 23–44.

Vygotsky, L. (2018), *Vygotsky's Notebooks: A Selection*, ed. E. Zavershneva and R. Van Der Veer, Singapore: Springer.

رند, or Rend

(Origin Persian)

Mohammad Hadi

مصلحت نیست که از پرده برون افتد راز
ورنه در مجلس رندان خبری نیست که نیست

If translatability is defined based on a superfluous linguistic and cultural communicability, the aim of this article is to unveil and emphasize the untranslatability of رند or Rend as a conceptual persona. رند is not a figure gratified or even untroubled with communicating. It does not have it that we are going to elevate Rend to a transcendent, mystic figure beyond human reach, nevertheless رند as an unequaled, unparalleled figure in Persian is presented as a person who leaves language and correct communication to زاهد Zahed, or ascetic and chastises زاهد for his arrogance covered under his plain and unadorned appearance. رند is even reluctant to make things clear in her language as her archenemy, زاهد is a worshiper of imparting or exchanging rules and communicating them in an *apparently* bashful and self-deprecating manner. رند is not, by nature, against communication, yet she is skeptical of زاهد and the way he communicates things, rules, and norms, in a word, morality. رند observes a large degree of hypocrisy in زاهد but this is not only a moral hypocrisy but also a communicative one. زاهد's communicative hypocrisy is, in effect, rooted in sticking to text and overlooking the context as much as possible. Therefore, this paper places emphasis on a figure who is hard to translate in the original language, let alone into other languages. Through the notion of "cultural translation," introduced by Homi Bhabha, we have been shown that translation no longer implies the overcoming of existing differences between cultures, a process that initiates cultural differences. In this regard, cultures are conceived as hybrid phenomena and in-between fields. Therefore, this article does not aim to make رند translatable, rather it provides some diffused aspects of how it functions in Persian language and literature.

concepts

Deleuze and Guattari coined the term "conceptual personae" in *What is Philosophy?* (1991). Gilles Deleuze and Felix Guattari dedicate a chapter to "conceptual personae" as living embodiments or illustrations of philosophers' key ideas. رند can be seen as one main conceptual persona in Persian language and culture which seems enormously challenging to translate. It is no exaggeration to say that رند is "the most evocative symbol of the indefinable ambiguity of the Persian character" (Daryush Shayegan, in Gray 28). Hafez as the poet who, like many other Persian poets, uses this figure in his poems, has been regarded as the source of the analysis of this conceptual persona. رند can be understood as, reveler, drunkard, social outcast, and outlaw. Yet this figure does not remain in the realm of literature and finds its way into everyday language as a form of theo-political opposition.

رند's Elusive Evolution

In Persian, رند is a rather common and quite widespread everyday word. Although its everyday usage implies deception, mischievousness, or slyness, interestingly enough it is a key to gaining a major insight into a large part of Iranian mysticism. Contemporary commentators go that far to say that رند bears an indefinable ambiguity, yet what it signifies can prove particularly difficult to negotiate. The sense of the ineffable in the concept of رند, reinforces a further characteristic which makes the translator's task much more daunting. One can highlight three different periods in the evolution of رند. And such shifts in meaning is regarded here as yet another sign of vehemence, elusiveness, and always-on-the-move character of رند.

In the first phase, رند is regarded with a negative connotation as a lout, pervert, and even libertine. One who is subordinate to her passions and is unable to master them. In the second phase, رند is depicted as a positive figure imbued with honor and dignity; the one who does not care about fame and wealth, mainly valorous and gallant. In the third phase, رند is again seen in a negative sense, an unreliable trickster and one who is self-important, untrustworthy, unscrupulous, and mainly unprincipled. Accordingly, in the first phase in its literary history, the word رند had a negative meaning. In the second phase, it takes a relatively positive meaning and again in the new Persian, it bears a negative meaning at least in everyday usage of the word. This paper does not look for a semantic thread which connects and explicates the linguistic changes, but it aims to utilize this constant shift in the meanings attributed to the Word رند as an indication of the untranslatability of the word even in its origin, namely Persian, which makes any semantic seizure or apprehension nearly impossible.

In Hafiz's ontology, which is ironically not far from that of the Book in Islam, angels are lower than humans. In other words, due to the freedom and the possibility to commit sin, humans are attributed much more value than the angels who are doomed to remain innocent. This can be reflected in the dichotomy of زاهد -رند, where ascetic's hope to be elevated to the level of innocent angels and in doing so he hides his sins and keeps his face clean, رند admits her imperfection and even uses this imperfection as a weapon against the pretensions of the ascetic.

رند even seeks notoriety, as she is convinced that fame is defined for the ascetic. Yet she is not intentionally looking for notoriety. رند's proximity to other figures such as fool or yurodivy in Russian literature. Yurodivy or the fool in Russian literature acts intentionally in a provocative and foolish way, in the eyes of men and triggers shock and even indignation. It can clarify the way رند prefers being ridiculed than being celebrated. So, it is no wonder to see that رند has restored its notoriety in contemporary Persian language. رند evades morality in the common established sense of the word. To رند, morality is but a product, a text disengaged with reality. That is exactly why رند is able to criticize and mock values which hide their temporariness or evanescence. رند stands in sharp contrast to زاهد. زاهد is ascetic and preaches mainly what he does not practice. With his ascetic ideals, زاهد strives to find an absolute morality which is beyond time and place. زاهد is the symbol of duplicity, desiccation, or bitterness. He is against life simply because he regards life as a moral project. زاهد aims to shrink life to a system of morality. That is precisely why زاهد can even be applied to secular modes of morality which are happy with defining values once and forever. On the other hand, رند is a parodist of established values and that should not come as a surprise that in contemporary Persian رند associates negative meanings such as rake, ruffian, or debauchee. She stands against the sanctimonious self-righteousness of the religious authorities but also the secular self-evident values.

It should be emphasized that any attempt to translate رند or yet better to say, any attempt to overlook the hardship in its translatability is doomed to remain in a superficial exchange of concepts without implicating their territories. After all, رند is the one that deterritorializes morality and in the absence of that morality it will be reduced to an abstract tool. رند, in this sense, triggers the processes of deterritorialization and reterritorialization which designate both the status of the relationship to a group, state, or religion or to herself and within a psychological individual. Therefore, رند is not only a result of reacting to the hypocrisy in doxa but also an affirmation of life in her own deeds. All these lead to the becoming minor of رند as she is constantly undergoing new forms of ethics which are neither religious nor secular.

رند and Safety in Translation

رند stands in opposition to زاهد who does things in an enforced way. رند makes it hard to translate because she is hard to communicate based on the norms that the settled norms or religion have implemented in the society. رند withstands sheer safety that Zahed appreciates and marvels in, yet she promotes a safety which goes hand in hand with infamy. While زاهد or ascetic believes that almost everything has a rule and this rule can be applied in every context, رند is aware of such moral safety which can ultimately result in her own infamy and زاهد's fame. And that is no wonder رند in contemporary Persian conveys a negative connotation. But which kind of safety can be an infamous one? How can you feel safe while you're infamous? رند is sure that pursuing her eros stigmatizes her. Like the impoverished beggar in the road, رند has nothing to lose and her "nothing to lose" makes her the best property. Something that might remind us of a form of poverty which is different from those of ascetics. رند's poverty is social or even political poverty, whereas زاهد's poverty is a pretentious one in order to sustain religious belief and organizations. رند is able to transform this poverty into a capital in order to not bow the knee to hypocrisy. Ascetics' poverty, in this framework, is simply two-faced poverty.

رند and Vulnerability

فرصت شمر طریقه رندی که این نشان
چون راه گنج بر همه کس آشکاره نیست

زاهد's approach to peace is teleological, namely, peace is unattainable and hence must be abandoned in this world. Despite its challenging lifestyle, رند lives in harmony and equilibrium with her passions while ascetic condemns passions as bearing sin and causing a vulnerability. Vulnerability is for رند, not a state of weakness but a genuine path to her power. She does not lament for her vulnerability, nor does she feel lacking something. رند does not fall in the trap of perfection that pious religious or biased secular depict, for she believes that such a state of purity and perfection simply does not exist. Therefore, either it is a lie or it pretends to be perfect. رند's approach to her sinfulness does not lead to expressing regret and remorse, rather her need for drinking more and living joyfully. As Davis puts it, we see in رند, the "forbidden intoxications of mysticism by alluding to the forbidden intoxications of wine" (Davis 2004: 310–18).

Translating زاهد is much easier simply because زاهد is defined based on an original purity which can be applied to its translation from one language to another. One can dare to say that رند's untranslatability is made up of the dialectic between innocence and sinfulness. If a formal and widely acknowledged translation is possible it is only because of the illusion of purity. Texts and concepts in their purity can be easily translated from one language to another simply because the moral norms are taken universal and can be transformed from one language to another. But once the text commits sin or it disrupts our communicability, translation becomes a constant ethical endeavor. Such untranslatability should not be seen as a mystical obstacle, nor a linguistic barrier, rather as a stubborn resistance done in the becoming which aims to attribute a difference to a language-culture and evades all attempts in assimilating a culture to others.

رند and Stimmung

راز درون پرده ز رندان مست پرس
کاین حال نیست زاهد عالی مقام را

It is very important to note that the basis of poetry in Iran and to some extent in Iranian logic is not communicability. It seems quite universal that the basis of human communication is mutual comprehensibility, but in fact, it is not, and in Persian poetry and language communication has an important precondition, and that is being affected. In fact, the basis of communication is *the present*. In Persian, the word Haal حال has two meanings. On the one hand, it means the present time and yet it also means the current feeling or Stimmung. رند is a figure who prioritizes Stimmung to communication, or at least, tries to figure out the Stimmung prior to communicating her message. Communication in the absence of Haal or Stimmung is to رند, nothing but a lie or an egoistic ambition which can certainly be justified under common morality. In the absence of Stimmung or attunement (Stimmen or abstimmen), communication yields nothing but hypocrisy and violence.

In effect, it can be argued that one of the main differences between زاهد and رند lies in the fact that the زاهد is content with the appearance-transparence of language and mere morality and complying by defined norms is enough for him, while for رند no moral principle and value is accepted without being sufficiently attuned. Otherwise, it is all waste and lies. So even the simple translation as obedience to the rules and norms or regulations is questionable for رند simply because transparency should not preclude the Stimmung.

رند is a happy character, yet the reasons for her joy are unclear. رند's appreciation of life and joy rejects any kind of blind faith and as a result any sort of slavish submission. If health and sickness for Nietzsche are characterized through active and reactive forces, which represent two different ways of appraising life, زاهد is the one who has already interpreted life and is now, sadly and desperately at the work of implementing the norms and values. For Spinoza, this is the typology between good and bad. For the زاهد, good and bad are already *clearly* distinguished in the book, so he is in charge of taking care of his principles. As Deleuze writes, "The individual will be called good who strives ... to organize his encounters, to join with whatever agrees with his nature," and, the bad is one who "lives haphazardly, who is content to undergo the effects of his encounters, but wails and accuses every time the effect undergone does not agree with him and reveals his impotence" (Deleuze 1988: 22–3).

Yet beyond this genealogy of Morals, this paper claims that رند's joy is rooted in taking affects into account. In other words, while زاهد is a person who precludes mood and Stimmung and sticks to the text, the رند is a figure who by taking Stimmung seriously can elevate to joy. If the ascetics forbid love, wine, and other elements, رند condemns such strict dogmas as pure hypocrisy. Zahed or the sanctimonious hypocrite sits in opposition to رند who is indicative of highlighting an unaligned function in portraying the real situation of society or Stimmung. That is why the Stimmung of رند does not only embrace the present feeling but also the common Stimmung in the society, sometimes close to Zeitgeist, whereas to the ascetic the text, morality and regulations transcend time and place. One can mention Robin Hood as the Western counterpart for the Hafezian رند and describes him as the generous and courageous free-spirit, who had no respect for established norms. In this regard, رند is the Persian criterion for distinguishing preordained morality from genuine ethics.

According to Kalatehseifary, Hafez writes himself as a member of his imagined society, and takes the role of رند, the liberal-minded freethinker. He shows his hatred of Zahed and portrays his affection for his physical and spiritual beloved. Zahed embodies the sanctimonious hypocrite, who upbraids Hafez, a رند, for his pagan belief. Hafez's role as رند is indicative of two things: through the role of a freethinker, Hafez highlights his unaligned function in portraying the real situation of society and leaves it up to his audience to distinguish between good and evil. Hafez's رند, furthermore, is someone who does not involve himself in extremes, and believes in enjoying every minute of life through the blessings of love and wine. Hafez' رند deviates from the norm in a disguised, camouflaged manner. She makes her blend in with surroundings while she is perpetually breaking faith with them.

Works Cited

Benjamin, W. (2012), *The Task of the Translator*, Chicago: University of Chicago Press.
Bhabha, H. (1994), *The Location of Culture*, New York and London: Routledge.
Davis, D. (2004), "On Not Translating Hafez," *New England Review* (1990-), 25 (1/2): 310–18.
Deleuze, Gilles. (1988) *Spinoza: Practical Philosophy*. San Francisco: City Lights Books.
Deleuze, G., and Félix G. (1994), *What Is Philosophy?*, New York: Columbia University Press.
Elizabeth T. G. (1995), *The Green Sea of Heaven: Fifty Ghazals from the Diwān of Ḥāfeẓ*, Ashland, Ore: White Cloud Press.
Kalatehseifary, M. and Joseph, v. (2009), "Hammer Purgstall's German Translation of Hafez's Divan and Goethe's West-östlicher Divan," MS thesis. University of Waterloo.
Koen, B. (2009), "Hafez," 'Erfan and Music: As Interpreted by Ostad Morteza Varzi, Margaret L. Caton, Costa Mesa, CA: Mazda Publishers, 2008, ISBN 978-1-56859-248-0, viii 261, *Iranian Studies*, 42 (5): 784–9. doi: 10.1017/S0021086200018478
Iranica, Encyclopedia, "Encyclopedia Iranica," *Center for Iranian Studies-Columbia University*, 7 (08) (1985): 2019.
Ivanov, Sergey A. (2006), *Holy Fools in Byzantium and beyond*, Oxford and New York: Oxford University Press on Demand.
Lewis, F. (2002), "Hafez viii. Hafez and Rendi," Encyclopedia Iranica Online.

22

Sankofa—A Synthesis

(Origin The Twi Language of the Akan People of Ghana)

Didi Cheeka

The concept of Sankofa approximates Hegel's approach to history and philosophy—not as a series of accidental, unrelated events and ideas, but as an organic whole, which developed through a process of dialectical contradiction. If we accept the above approach, in the sense, for instance, that how we got to where we are at the present depends on that already past, and apply this to Sankofa, we begin to see how the term could be translated beyond its traditional concept to embrace practices related to, say, a specifically philosophic field. Sankofa—which could translate as, It is not taboo to return to the past—is a concept taken from the Akan people of Ghana. A question that arises, in this essay, is how to theorize this concept in philosophical terms. Perhaps, to frame the question precisely: how do you deploy the concept of Sankofa dialectically, in a field of discourse whose most prominent thinker, Deleuze, finds nothing more detestable than "Hegelianism and the Dialectic"? The above question indicates my attitude in this essay—my approach is at once political-historical, rather than academic.

Theses

To proceed with a question. What is philosophy? The need to pose this question arises from the dominant trend among post-modern thinkers to treat (real) philosophy with contempt, to dismiss and label it as "metanarratives" to be consigned without second thought to the dustbin of history. Philosophy emerged from the quest for a rational, scientific understanding of the world—that is, without recourse to mysticism. To respond to the question: philosophy, therefore, is an attempt at grappling with the big questions of life and death, the world around us, the nature of ideas and matter, as well as the concept of what is good and what is bad. It is, I think, a telling statement on the state of decay of intellectual life and what passes for philosophy today that, in seeking to apply the concept of Sankofa philosophically, this writer is forced to return to Hegel. Most, if not all, of what passes for philosophy today is mere pseudo-philosophical pretensions—as evidenced by Sokal and Bricmont's Intellectual Impostures.

Hence the return to Hegel—and this, too, is in the spirit of Sankofa: being that the word itself implies a return. Sankofa is proof that, without reading Hegel, Twi language was familiar with the idea of dialectics developed by the philosopher. The interconnection between things and between thought—as revealed by the development of Marx's dialectical materialism from Hegel's idealist materialism—is contained in the idea of Sankofa: the past is negated by the present which in turn is negated by the future and this is expressed in the charged symbol of a backward-looking, forward-flying bird. The past is negated by the present, while preserving, in the process, all that is essential and progressive within it. In approximating Sankofa to dialectics, therefore, I adopt a consistent materialist approach—in the sense that Marxism negated Hegel's idealist method, while simultaneously preserving all that was progressive and revolutionary in his dialectical method.

However, whatever shortcoming, given his idealist approach, is inherent to Hegel's History of Philosophy, what is of undeniable importance is the dialectical method that saw—not a mass of unconnected ideas, accidents, and individual geniuses—but, rather, an organic process with a law and an inner logic of its own. Commenting on Hegel's Philosophy of History, Engels said this method represented a colossal step forward and "was the first to try to demonstrate that there is development, an intrinsic coherence in history." Hegel's presentation of the history of philosophy as a process that evolved through series of contradictions, in which one set of ideas apparently negates a previous one, leading to an endless spiral of development of human thought is in striking consonance with the concept of Sankofa.

Usually depicted by a bird flying forward with its head turned backwards, reaching with its open beak an egg poised on its back, could the concept of Sankofa be put to use to rethink and reactualize a traumatic past using [visual] memorial materials—a sort of coming to terms with the past? In this regard, the translation I prefer, which I use for my artistic curatorial practice is: In order to go into the future, we must return to the past. In his introduction to the History of Philosophy, Hegel referenced nature, "the bud disappears when the blossom bursts forth," being thereby negated by the blossom which is, in turn, negated "when the fruit appears," and "replaces the blossom as the truth of the plant." In the Sankofa symbol, the bird is flight-poised carrying the egg, delicately balanced, on its back. The egg, symbolizing the past, disappears when the chick bursts forth, being thereby negated by the chick which, in turn, is negated when the adult bird appears.

As the one supplants the other in their necessary stages, what is revealed are stages of organic unity in which the one could not come into being without the other already being and going out of being. The one flows into and out of the other, in their different forms, and their shared necessity is the real meaning of the Sankofa concept. You cannot have the one without the other. Just as Hegel saw not merely a negative process whereby a set of ideas vanquished another in the development of philosophy, the Sankofa symbol expresses the need for the preservation of all that is necessary, in order to go forward, in the past. Hegel referred to this process as sublation. The bird, rooted in the present, carrying the past, precariously balanced on its back, into the future, expresses dialectics which Engels says, "takes things and their perceptual images essentially in their interconnection, in their movement."

Perhaps, having arrived at an interpretation of Sankofa, before we proceed further, we might consider the meaning of dialectics. The term comes from the Greek dialektike, derived from dialegomai, which translates as, to converse, or discuss. In its original meaning, it signified the art of discussion, evident in Plato's Socratic dialogues. Dialectics has its real beginnings in Heraclitus' brief aphorisms, viz., "each changes place and becomes the other"—described by Jung as the "most marvelous of psychological laws: the regulative function of opposites." Dialectics holds that "sooner or later, everything runs into its opposite," that all things and phenomena in nature has a past and a future.

Antithesis

The past is negated by the present. Conceived by post-modernists, this negation signifies the "end of history"—in the sense that the past is essentially a meaningless series of random events or accidents, governed by no definite laws and unconnected to the present, therefore, trying to study or preserve it would be a pointless exercise. The past, in its negated state, appears as "just one damn thing after another," or, following Gibbon, "little more than the register of the crimes, follies and misfortunes of mankind." Citing Jung confront us with the possibility of applying Sankofa, beyond a specific philosophic field, to a specifically psychoanalytic study. What can this concept say about historical amnesia? Is there a point of convergence between philosophy and psychoanalysis—in the sense of the ways in which the latter could speak, through the dialectical contradiction of memory and amnesia, of the repression of traumatic experience out of which arise the need to negate the past?

Because the symbol of Sankofa is extremely important to understanding the term, it is necessary, in order to understand the possibility and importance of extending the concept beyond the field of philosophy to the psychoanalytic study of social life, that is, drives and impulses, to conduct a semiotic analysis of the Sankofa symbol so as to better apply it beyond philosophy to psychoanalysis. Given the initial acceptance, in the application of the Sankofa concept to philosophy, of the connection and interdependence of phenomena even in their contradiction and opposites, then the Sankofa symbol is a natural semiotic representation, in psychoanalysis, of the contradictory process of going away from the past and returning to the past, of the contradictory process of remembering and forgetting, of the contradictory interaction of the conscious and unconscious. In this regard, the egg, representing the past, becomes symbolic, for me, of an archive.

Memory is capricious and arbitrary, and tends to suppress, to drive into a dark corner events that the mind is cognitively unable, or unwilling to grasp. Still, these memories do not entirely disappear, for they tend to leave their ghostly presence in the archive. Locating forgetting as arising from traumatic history means that the performative possibilities offered by the process of restoration and digitizing become the only way to grasp, to access an otherwise inaccessible history. Official history encourages collective forgetting, collective migration from memory. This imposed forgetting and enforced migration position history, to quote Cathy Caruth, as an "Unclaimed Experience." But, does the refusal to acknowledge memory mean the nonexistence of memory? Does merely refusing to gaze into history's abyss, for fear of being unable to tear oneself afterwards from history's gaze, erase history?

The avoidance of reconciliation with history means that the past is not talked about and is gradually repressed. But the wounds from this repressed past do not go away, do not heal. They return in repeated acts of violent conflicts within the society. History comprises events of which the full facts have never been made public—the temptation, naturally, is to infer that it is not in the interests of the state to analyze these atrocities and seek closure for those affected. It is in this sense that it is possible to speak of society as a post-traumatic space. If this is so, then what form should return, in Sankofic term, to the past take?

Synthesis

There is, in recent times, a growing memory boom in cinema as, utilizing the rich resource of history, filmmakers actively seek to engage with, to return to a violent past. It is possible that this interest is informed by the fact that a new generation is only now awakening to its own history and the need to tap the memory of the last surviving witnesses to this history. One thing seem certain: the possibility—in light of everything that had gone before—of navigating the future, using memory practices to trace trauma, to make sure it does not repeat itself, by revisiting its hurts, its hidden places appear less the preserve of politicians. There is, for instance, Inadelso Cossa's *A Memory in Three Acts*, that explores, through the story of survivors, the decade-long bloody struggle of Mozambique to free itself from Portuguese colonialism: a former prisoner revisits the dilapidated building, preserved as a monument to what took place within its walls, where he was tortured; the daughter of a former agent of the secret police tells how her father was murdered in her presence following the fall of the Portuguese dictatorship. These accounts offer multifaceted testimony to a brutal colonialism whose wounds are still fresh. There is a sense, then, in which it is correct to say that we remember differently.

Here, especially from the point of view of cinema's potential to memorialize, I'm reminded of Ruy Guerra's Mueda, Memoria e Massacre, when the filmmaker returned to Mozambique to film the yearly re-enactment of the Portuguese massacre of civilians in Mueda. By this I mean that the act of dealing with an illegitimate past, so to say, that is violently repudiated demands more than a judicial, political process—reconciliation committees and constitutional proceedings are not enough, and have proved incapable, especially concerning inherited acts of hatred, anger in which the state is implicated. If it is true that the abandonment of Nigeria's historical memory was rooted in the trauma of war, then rescuing the national audio-visual archives contains the possibility of a re-encounter with trauma, as well as an attempt to understand it—archival practice, thus, becomes a witnessing, an excavation of memory, a shattering of silence.

I had visited the "Topography of Terror" Nazi Forced Labor Documentation Center in Berlin—the city where the so-called scramble for Africa was decided—and indeed, in the center of Berlin you keep coming across monuments to national trauma. In this, especially among other colonial powers, Germany is unique: hardly any other country has made a memorial to the darkest period of its history—the Nazi era/Holocaust and East Germany under Stasi Terror. The British Empire, on the other hand, is still actively refusing to make public, archival materials on its history of slavery and colonialism. The restlessness and unease apparent in attempts to evade, silence, and deny the past are evidence that the past is still present, still lying in the future. The obsessive pursuit of memory—increasingly evident in historiography, psychoanalysis, cinema, performance, public art etc.—is indicative that it has become a modern marker of culture.

It is true that every society has to find its own way of dealing with a difficult, dark past and what worked somewhere might prove problematic elsewhere, still, societies, where the past still holds the present and future hostage, could learn from others' earlier efforts. Perhaps, to cite Indonesia, which had initiated a political process of coming to terms with its dark, violent past. In 2016, the Indonesian government, which had campaigned on a promise to examine the country's past, held a symposium in Jakarta to discuss the murderous events of 1965. Successive governments had spent the past fifty years denying the murders, but awareness of the events had been gathering momentum, in Indonesia and abroad, especially, following filmmaker Joshua Oppenheimer's documentaries, *The Act of Killing* in 2012 and *The Look of Silence* in 2015. In *The Act of Killing*, Oppenheimer—unlike Chris Hilton's *Shadow Play* or Robert Lemelson's *40 Years of Silence: An Indonesian Tragedy*, leads the audience through the executioners' everyday lives through glimpses of individual people involved in the atrocities rather than a historical overview of Indonesia's past.

As the opening images of the film Independencia, directed by Mario Bastos, unfolds—deserted fields, rivers, bushes, a bare room—a narrator wonders what vestiges of the country's liberation struggle still exist in the collective memory. At one point in the narrative, a former guerilla commander laments, "I don't know how we forgot that," as he recalls the intense racism and exploitation in colonized Angola. This collective work comes some forty years after Angola's independence and is the result of monumental research by Associação Tchiweka de Documentação (Tchiweka Association for Documentation)—a nonprofit association that supports activities dedicated to the preservation of memory and knowledge about the struggle for independence of Angola—and film production outfit, Geração 80 (1980s Generation). Angola's history is marked by thirteen years of anti-colonial war (1961–74) and twenty-seven years of civil war (1975–2002). Interweaving fragments of memory and archival material, Independencia presents a not-so-distant past—but so foreign and strange to the present—to instigate dialogue and remembrance of things forgotten.

For the past twenty years or so, Nigeria has been a formal democracy, but, in reality long years of military dictatorship still exert its hold: the state still conceals quite a lot and keeps many things secret—above all else it seeks to conceal national history from its people and nowhere is this apparent as in academic history books and the fact it once banished history as a stand-alone subject from the classrooms. Academic discourse tends to reference the postcolonial as the core of Nigeria's history and, given its dominance in discourse, there is always the tendency to foreground the [post]colonial experience and render all other national pasts insignificant or nonexistent. As a consequence, Nigeria's past continues to hold its present and future hostage: the Biafran war, the most traumatic event of the Nigerian experience seems to belong to a distant, foreign past. The question of traumatic events has been widely discussed in psychology, psychoanalysis, and literature, but has never been applied to Nigerian history in a scholarly study. However, it's not possible to understand modern Nigeria without engaging with the war of 1967–70s. This is the meaning of the Sankofa concept: to come to terms with the past—it's the Achebean dictum of knowing "where the rain began falling on us."

Works Cited

Achebe, C. (1964), "The Role of the Writer in a New Nation," *New Nigeria Magazine* No. 81.

Caruth, C. (1996), *Unclaimed Experience: Trauma, Narrative and History*, Baltimore: Johns Hopkins University Press.

Deleuze, G. (1977), "I Have Nothing to Admit," *Semiotext(e)*, 2 (3): 111–16.

Engels, F. (1859), *Marx: Critique of Political Economy*, Review by Frederick Engels, Das Volk, Nos. 14 & 16.

Engels, F. (1855–56), "Marx & Engels Collected Works," Vol. 14.

Field, A.N. (2014), "To Journey Imperfectly: Black Cinema Aesthetics and the Filmic Language of Sankofa," *Framework: The Journal of Cinema and Media*, 55 (2): 171–90.

Gibbon, E. (1777), *The Decline and Fall of the Roman Empire*, London: Strahan & Cadell.

Hegel, G. W. F. (1902), *Lectures on the Philosophy of History*, London: George Bell & Sons.

Jung, C. G. (1967), *Two Essays on Analytical Psychology*, UK: Routledge.

Woods, A. (2021), *The History of Philosophy: A Marxist Perspective*, London: Wellred Books.

23

Saudade: (De)mythologizing a Portuguese Concept*

(Origin Portuguese)

Susana Viegas

The Myth of a Concept

In recent years, *saudade* has become a brand. Across Portugal (and abroad, in countries with large Portuguese-speaking emigrant communities), it is not difficult to find shops and marketplaces devoted to the sale of original Portuguese brands, or copies of iconic traditional products, along with regional food products. This phenomenon has come to be known as the "Mercado da Saudade," or the *saudade* market, popular among the enthusiasts of a "genuine" or "authentic" lifestyle.[1]

The *nostalgic* feeling associated with this kind of phenomenon is far from being unique to this locale, however. Who hasn't wanted, at some point in their lives, to rediscover a favorite childhood toy? The basic sense of the word *saudade* may be understood as something akin to this feeling, in particular when it is used as a synonym for nostalgia for the past or simple homesickness.

This is its primitive, vernacular sense, later transformed into a depurated literary and cultural practice, which was at the basis of what became a philosophical concept. More than the nostalgic feeling of a past to be recovered, *saudade* becomes a *melancholic* feeling.[2] It was precisely in this sense that *saudade* was evoked in Dom Duarte's work, *Leal Conselheiro* (*Loyal Counselor*). King of Portugal from 1433 until his death in 1438, Duarte was one of the first to define *saudade* in paradoxical terms, in an

---

* This work was funded by national funds through the FCT-Fundação para a Ciência e a Tecnologia, I.P., under the Norma Transitória-DL 57/2016/CP1453/CT0031 and UIDB/00183/2020.

attempt to conceptualize and bring to a rational level awareness of this peculiar state of mind, defined as a mixed *feeling* of pleasure *and* pain (Dom Duarte 1982).

Saudade became a sophisticated, complex concept, crucial to understanding Portuguese culture and thinking, the idea being that this state of mind was (allegedly) typically Portuguese. One first myth surrounding the concept derives from this assumption, its *territorial* demarcation, its Homeland, thus corresponding to its *untranslatable* quality. Indeed, philosophers have long considered the concept of *saudade* untranslatable (Vasconcelos 1914), only fully understood in the Portuguese-speaking world, although it is a word of Galician-Portuguese origin that is also present in contemporary Galician culture and philosophy (Piñeiro 1984).

From a Deleuzian-Guattarian perspective, it is possible to deterritorialize, and then reterritorialize, this concept. *Saudade* may function as an outsider concept, as the involuntary origin of thought, thus marking philosophy's own heterogeneity. Philosophy needs non-philosophy. For Deleuze and Guattari, "[p]hilosophy is a constructivism" (1994: 35–6), as in the Russian art movement, meaning that it is a rhizomatic practice of thought akin to a concept-creating machine, always connected to other machines or different forms of thinking (all sorts of disciplines and fields of study). Within this Deleuzian-Guattarian perspective, philosophy regains new breath as an inventive way of thinking: "Philosophy is the art of forming, inventing, and fabricating concepts" (1994: 2).

As a philosophical concept, *saudade* brings about new thoughts and new ways of experiencing the world, opening up its processual nature, as well as new ways of thinking about subjectivity and temporality. All philosophical concepts, for their own central complexity, must have an endo-consistency compatible not only with an exo-consistency with other concepts but with a necessary *internal variability*—or, as Daniel W. Smith states, "the aim of the analytic is to insert into concepts a structure that is problematic, differential and temporal" (2012: 69). This problematic, differential, and temporal structure moves philosophy away from its traditional task, seen as a privileged way of engaging in truthful "contemplation, reflection, or communication" (Deleuze and Guattari 1994: 6), and approaches philosophy's concerns with the self-positing nature of its toolbox concepts.

So what happens when we bring *saudade* into deeper reflection on the world's mediatization and intercession and on related media epistemological questions? How does it impose a new way of thinking of media, of problematizing it, in the sense of thinking *with* the medium itself (as opposed to applying philosophy to the medium)?

Eduardo Lourenço's Saudade

The Portuguese philosopher and essayist Eduardo Lourenço argues that *saudade* is not representational because of its mythical proportions. In *O Labirinto da Saudade* (The Labyrinth of Saudade) (usually translated as *The Labyrinth of Longing*), Lourenço designs a Portuguese imagology (that is, the image that the Portuguese have made of themselves, equivalent to *autognosis*) through the analysis of literary and cultural discourses.

In consequence, he arrives at a psychoanalytical reading of *saudade* by highlighting three major traumas of Portuguese identity (the 1140 Foundation of the Kingdom of Portugal, the Portuguese dynastic crisis of 1580, following the disappearance of the Portuguese King D. Sebastião in the battle of Alcácer Quibir, and the 1890 British Ultimatum), wavering between a divine and miraculous foundation and the subaltern and inferior nature of the Portuguese nation. Either way, it creates the idea of an unstable subjectivity. Defying its historical, ephemeral being, as if this complex of simultaneous superiority (being "blessed" by the gods) and inferiority (being predestined, dependent on fate) was a way to *"hide from ourselves our own authentic situation of being historical on an intrinsically fragile state"* (Lourenço 2005: 25).[3]

This intricate concept is thus entangled with a metaphysics of the subject, by fragmenting its identity, and a metaphysics of time, with a twofold movement between the past and the future, with the consciousness of a collective resistance to denying the transient nature of things: "Unhappy with the present, dead as immediate national existence, we have begun to dream of the future and the past simultaneously" (Lourenço 2005: 28).[4] In this way, *saudade* leads to consciousness of an *ahistorical* and *achronological* temporality, of an everlasting present between an *imaginary* past and future.

Directly related to a philosophy of *saudade*, *Saudosismo*, a "sublime metamorphose" of a world *conceived* and experienced as unreal, is also critically examined by Lourenço (2005: 31). Saudosismo is a literary and mystic cultural movement headed by the poet Teixeira de Pascoaes, and as Lourenço observes (2005: 31), it is a consequence of the British Ultimatum of 1890's being expressed in ultranationalist movements. We can see that this movement toward the past (on the part of a person, an object, or a country) may be more than a mere affectionate evocation. It may be the praising of authenticity, originality, in a soul or a national identity.

But the ontological paradox of combining presence and absence, past and present, and contentment and discontent only discloses its central *hopelessness*. According to Carolina Michaëlis de Vasconcelos, the word "saudade" became popular in the sixteenth century, following the disappearance of the Portuguese King D. Sebastião in the battle of Alcácer Quibir, a loss that gave rise to a paradoxical *collective* mourning of his disappearance combined with the expectation of his return (Neto 2014: 930). These are irreconcilable feelings—mourning someone's death and expecting a miraculous comeback—as is the temporal dimension involved, between memory and desire, past and future, driven by a desire that cannot be fulfilled.

Pascoaes (1988) gave the word "saudade" an undoubted existential, messianic, and religious dimension, equating it with what was considered to be the unique spiritual feature of the Portuguese soul. By contrast, Lourenço criticizes *saudade*'s idiosyncrasy in precisely these terms. For him, a consequence of this idiosyncrasy was the creation of the myth of the supposed untranslatability of the word, as if only a Portuguese soul could understand and live it. Thus the word became synonymous with a country, although one that was much in need of regeneration, of a return to its previous glory. By rejecting all foreign cultural and philosophical influences, *Saudosism* was characterized as a traditional, nationalistic, and xenophobic movement, committed to looking back to the past and avoiding future innovativeness, as Fernando Pessoa and António Sérgio would later argue (Neto 2014: 754).

From its established literary and cultural sense, *saudade* developed into a philosophical and existential conception of being lonely, this time within a cosmic and transcendent consciousness of *ontological absence*. It reminds us not only of the personal feeling of missing someone or something that no longer exists, but of the sense of the collective's own isolation from others and from the world. The traumas that Lourenço recognizes as lying at the origins of a *Hyper-identity* lead him to compare the *Portuguese colonizer* to the *Portuguese emigrant* (2005: 119), as both conceive of their own existence as superior once abroad, far away from their homeland. In this way, *saudade* also embodies the imagined and dreamlike image that such characters have constructed of themselves.

De/reterritorializing *Saudade*

Even if the analysis of a metaphysics of time seems to be logically guided by hopeless and vain longings, we find it to be a very effective concept, since its power lies not in its logical mode of thought but in what we can do with it. What are the existential and cultural problems that lie at its origins? And how are we to deal with illusory expectations? One possible answer turns out to be a reactionary and retrogressive effect, against difference and innovation. If, for example, following Walter Benjamin's ontology of images, we think of images as being dialectical, doubles by nature—past and present, mobile and immobile, part and whole—we realize that *saudade* persists by restraining its true progress into something faultless and improved. It has a messianic nature, but not in a dialectical (historical) way. As will become evident in the following analysis, taken in this sense *saudade* creates more obstacles than developments.

For Deleuze and Guattari, a concept is a territory, with its own intensive connections, its double movements of de- and reterritorialization. *Saudade* has been deterritorialized from its primeval literary sense and reterritorialized as a philosophical concept. Philosophically examining media using the concept of *saudade* illuminates the meaning of the conceptual thinking that defines media philosophy. It continuously questions its pragmatics and the conservative and repetitive sense of mediation; that is, *saudade* may be seen as a fundamental concept in understanding the ideology behind, and guiding, mediation.

This peculiar perspective on *saudade* has unconsciously shaped a conception of national historical power and greatness which, in Lourenço's view, has given rise to a collective delusion with visible effects on both political and economic decisions, as well as on cultural and social movements. Media philosophy of cinema, the news, advertising, and social networking, for example, explores how these movements are represented and mediated. Lourenço outlines his imagology through literature, but the image the Portuguese have constructed of themselves can easily be completed through other types of media, such as films and moving images.

How does film contribute to this imagology? The history of cinema reveals how some genres may contribute to a reflection on the medium and its influence, as in the case of Westerns: these films demonstrate deep nostalgia for a past era, as expressions of an inherently conservative genre that creates an image of a mythologized historical space and time, the expansion to the West, reinforcing the importance of the individual's efforts and lifestyle and perpetuating stereotypes that we find questionable today (Slotkin 1992). The problem is far from being limited to film and is indeed also present in fashion and music, testifying to the (re)cyclicality of pop culture. How ought we to distinguish what is a mere representation from what has critical significance?

Cinema has always had the ability to represent the masses, a collective or a people, or in its absence, to invent it. As Deleuze says, in the movement-image regime the people are present, and the individual, the hero, embodies the collective's aspirations and ideals. There, the people are present as *Dividual*, that is, the mass which is individuated as such "instead of leaving it [mass] in a qualitative homogeneity or reducing it to a quantitative divisibility" (Deleuze 2008: 157). In this way, the people are present in Eisenstein, Dovjenko, Vidor,

Capra, and Ford. However, *"the people are missing"* (Deleuze 2008: 208) in the second regime of images, the time-image. Its absence marks cinema's political assignment, toward a future of inventing peoples: "Not the myth of a past people, but the story-telling of the people to come" (Deleuze 2008: 2015).

In Portuguese cinema, Manoel de Oliveira and Miguel Gomes, directors from very different generations, are paradigmatic cases of an imagology performed with moving images. As Iván Villarmea Álvarez observes, memory is an important subject in some of Oliveira's films, understood as "an uncontrolled source of inspiration for exploring his [Oliveira's] self, his past and the historical imaginary of his country, reaching the point of faking it when necessary" (2015: 158).

Manoel de Oliveira's work raises important questions about a mediated world. Nostalgia for one's past—as in *Viagem ao Princípio do Mundo* (Voyage to the Beginning of the World) (1997) and *Porto da Minha Infância/Porto of My Childhood* (2001)—and for one's country's past—as in *Non, ou a Vã Glória de Mandar* (No, or the Vain Glory of Command) (1990), *Palavra e Utopia* (Word and Utopia) (2000), and *O Quinto Império: Ontem Como Hoje* (The Fifth Empire) (2004)—has always haunted Oliveira. The director noted in an interview (1991–2) that his famous shots of the sky and clouds are an attempt to bring the viewer closer to a historical time; although everything else can be lost, the sky will always remain. But what stands out in Oliveira's attempt is an awareness of an ontological impossibility, of an insurmountable transcendence, which reduces memory's efforts to a vain hope of bringing a lost past back to life, reinforcing the sense of *saudade* as opposed to common nostalgia or longing. We are dealing with feeling an absence that is not just the absence of something or of someone but rather an ontological absence.

Miguel Gomes's films are also narratives about an imagined Portuguese identity. *Tabu* (2012) has as its background the colonial war and the process of decolonization, but the film's focus is an overly romanticized, impossible love story. As Carolin Overhoff Ferreira suggests, Gomes "permits the feeling of nostalgia for the colonial past, camouflaged as the longing for one's youth, as post-colonialism's insistence in its most negative side, explicitly the master-servant relationship towards contemporary African migrants" (2014: 19). *Aquele Querido Mês de Agosto* (Our Beloved Month of August) (2008), a film about the annual return of thousands of Portuguese emigrants to small, poor, rural Portuguese villages for their summer vacations, likewise raises central epistemological questions about a mediated world.

The emigrant's annual return transforms the country into a place of entertainment, pleasure, and music, a hyperbole of normal happiness (which they *really* feel when abroad the rest of the year). Although it embodies film's aesthetic tendency to present itself as truthful, as spontaneous, *Our Beloved*

Month of August reproduces a fictionalized reality, a fairytale of homesickness and foreign professional success, thus raising relevant epistemological and ethical questions about its documentary character. The impossibility of a true documentary film hinges on the ontological status of the portrayed, fictionalized reality. Ironically, this myth contaminates the story created around the film's production, a tripartite narrative structure that is itself seen as the work of Chance, as if the director were stripped of his freedom or efficacy and dependent on divine, miraculous forces.

These directors fail to establish a critical perspective on their own imagery self-knowledge (*autognosis*), at its unrealistic and oneiric origins, as if it were a mere monologue with themselves, a preservation of myths of their country's past as a community of colonizers and emigrants.

Conclusion: (De)mythologizing a Portuguese Concept

The commonsensical approach to thinking about *saudade* may lead us, in a first moment, to the universal and empirical experience of recalling a lost object or a faraway place that has personal significance. The Portuguese concept of *saudade*, however, similar to the German *Sehnsucht*, is not merely a synonym for a nostalgic feeling. Unlike grief or sorrow, it does not suggest exclusively sad or depressed feelings for the one or the thing that is absent. *Saudade* evokes pleasure, not just pain, as we can presume from its nostalgic consciousness.

It is in this usual, paradoxical sense that we can deduce new ways of thinking of subjectivity and temporality. *Saudade* has shaped the way a people look at their own past and their own history, as individuals and as a society: by unconsciously *mythologizing* (Lourenço 2005). Thus, the concept has unconsciously shaped an idea of historical power and the development of greatness that has real effects both in political and economic decisions and in cultural and social movements.

Media philosophy explores how these movements are represented and perceived. Recent conservative political and social movements may also be clarified through this concept, since critical thought of this nature is relevant, for example, to postcolonial visual studies, such as critical thought on how the colonies are represented, either in cinema, the news, advertising, social networking, or mass media in general. But who mediates? For Deleuze, "mediators are fundamental" (1995: 125); that is, each "discipline" or domain needs the creativity of mediators in order to express itself, which led Réda Bensmaïa to state that Deleuze created a new type of philosopher: the philosopher as "stalker" (2017: xi).

As a speculative concept, *saudade* may be of interest to media philosophers since it helps us to understand temporality and modern modes of media perception and reception. More than a Portuguese feeling, *saudade* is a universal experience of time, a time that seems not to pass. Considered within this conceptual framework, the experience of time is thought as an eternal present moment, taken as an everlasting moment: it remains between a past that is remembered and a future that is desired. In Deleuzian terms, we can always "put concepts in motion," as Paul Patton reassures us (2010: 23); we can put the concept of *saudade* in motion, that is to say, by admitting the concept's impreciseness and opening it to thinking the world's new movements.

It is interesting to note its non-representability, or capacity to be an inventive, processual, and rhizomatic way of thinking anew. Rather than giving us an image of the world which we simply recognize or not, it leads us to new paths of thinking, created by an encounter with a specific, unintelligible, and perplexing ontological and temporal experience. The concept gives body to a sense of lack that will never be fulfilled, persisting as a problem, forever unresolved. Thus, returning to the initial cases of the trend of *saudade* marketplaces, we see how to sell an idea that really suits any marketing department's purposes, since *saudade* begins with a sense of incompleteness and ends with the same feeling. As Tauel Harper and David Savat point out, "advertising works by construing desire as generated by lack" (2016: 126).[5]

Thus, because it is never complete, this desire, or expectation, is destined to fail, or at least to be postponed indefinitely. Again, the sense of incompleteness is present in Eduardo Lourenço's notion that we dream of the future and the past at the same time. Thus, *saudade* is not only a conceptual expression that explains this kind of confusing phenomena but a way of questioning the mediatization/intercession of such phenomena and related media epistemological questions. Moving images do not merely copy reality; they are driven by sensations, by creating new thoughts and new experiences of the world that the viewer cannot simply recognize. Thus the importance of philosophically investigating the epistemological question of how the world is mediated and the role of mediators.

Notes

1 See, for example, Ribeiro (2008).
2 Melancholy, nostalgia and *saudade* have different relationships to temporality. Melancholy situates the past as definitely past and, as such, is the first and most acute expression of temporality. Nostalgia is strongly focused on a given past or a given object out of our reach, which can be

imaginary or real and recoverable. *Saudade* is a complex paradox, sharing some similarities with both melancholy and nostalgia.

(Chagas 2016: 10)

3 "*Esconder de nós mesmos a nossa autêntica situação de ser histórico em estado de intrínseca fragilidade.*" All translations into English are mine.
4 "Descontentes com o presente, mortos como existência nacional imediata, nós começámos a sonhar simultaneamente o futuro e o passado."
5 Contrary to Deleuze and Guattari's view that what is important is to see what comes out of that desire since desire is a process, a positive flow, a *desiring production*.

Works Cited

Bensmaïa, R. (2017), *Gilles Deleuze, Postcolonial Theory, and the Philosophy of Limit*, London: Bloomsbury.
Chagas, P. (2016), "Mirrors of Melancholy: Lourenço on Music and Musical Understanding," *Portuguese Journal of Musicology*, 3 (1): 5–34. http://rpm-ns.pt/index.php/rpm/article/view/286/404 (accessed May 3, 2021).
Deleuze, G. (1995), *Negotiations 1972—1990*, trans. M. Joughin, New York: Columbia University Press.
Deleuze, G. and Guattari, F. (1994), *What Is Philosophy?*, trans. H. Tomlinson and G. Burchell, New York: Columbia University Press.
Deleuze, G. (2008), *Cinema 2*, trans. H. Tomlinson and R. Galeta, London: Continuum.
Dom, D. (1982), *Leal Conselheiro*, Lisboa: Casa da Moeda.
Ferreira, C. O. (2014), "The End of History through the Disclosure of Fiction: Indisciplinarity in Miguel Gomes's *Tabu*," *Cinema: Philosophy and the Moving Image*, 5: 18–45. http://cjpmi.ifilnova.pt/5-contents (accessed May 3, 2021).
Harper, T. and Savat, D. (2016), *Media after Deleuze*, London: Bloomsbury.
Lourenço, E. (2005), *O Labirinto da Saudade*, Lisboa: Gradiva.
Neto, V. (2014), "Saudosismo," in coord. M. F. Rollo, *Dicionário de História da I República e do Republicanismo, Volume III: N-Z*, Lisboa: Assembleia da República.
Oliveira, M. de (1991–92), "Le ciel est historique," *Chimères*, 14: 131–56.
Pascoaes, T. de (1988), *A Saudade e o Saudosismo*, Lisboa: Assírio & Alvim.
Patton, P. (2010), *Deleuzian Concepts: Philosophy, Colonization, Politics*, Stanford: Stanford University Press.
Piñeiro, R. (1984), *Filosofía da Saudade*, Vigo: Editorial Galaxia.
Ribeiro, D. (2008), "Ultrapassar o 'mercado da saudade'," *Expresso* (11 setembro). https://expresso.pt/economia/ultrapassar-o-mercado-da-saudade=f403393 (accessed May 3, 2021).
Slotkin, R. (1992), *Gunfighter Nation: The Myth of the Frontier in Twentieth-Century America*, New York: Athenaeum.

Smith, D. W. (2012), "The Nature of Concepts," *Parallax*, 18 (1): 62–73.
Vasconcelos, C. M. de (1914), *A Saudade Portuguesa*, Porto: Renascença Portuguesa.
Villarmea Álvarez, I. (2015), *Documenting Cityscapes: Urban Change in Contemporary Non-Fiction Film*, New York: Columbia University Press.

24

Schalten und Walten: Toward Operative Ontologies in the Digital Iconosphere

(Origin German)

Lorenz Engell

Introduction

Although the language of this volume is English, my title has kept the German wordings of *Schalten* and *Walten*. These terms could appear as rather Teutonic and certainly are very difficult to adequately translate into English. The literal translation of *Schalten* into "switching" is not so much a problem, but *Walten* would translate as "ruling," which is close to what is meant here, but not the very same. And in English, the two terms do not rhyme and, which is more, do not, as far as I know, form an overall colloquial expression or idiom. "Ich kann *Schalten und Walten*" in everyday German means: "I can do whatever I want or decide" in a given institution, organization, or milieu which I more or less dominate. He or she who is able to execute *Schalten und Walten* is sovereign, has agency, the will and power to act, disposes of possibilities of decision and powers of ordering.

What I want to develop here, though, is *Schalten und Walten* as a media philosophical and more closely as a media ontological concept. This is promising since *Schalten und Walten* comprehends and complements terms of the operative (or practical, or empirical: the ontic, that which is) and the ontological (or principal: being) which are thought of as mutually exclusive within traditional philosophical ontology (Siegert 2017). Especially with regard to the mediasphere of electronic pictures that marks and demarcates (Debray and Merzeau 2005: 162–4, see also Debray 1991) that makes up our world today, I shall show that and how these images are to be defined as (techno-ontic) switch images which through their switching produce and reproduce their (ontological) rule.

What makes of *Schalten und Walten* a media philosophical concept only comes out, though, if the two terms are looked at not as one, but in their complementarity. *Schalten* is a technique. It refers to management skills and technical knowledge of administration, governance, and control, and of its tools. It is associated with technical operations, early on with the pushback of a ship from the pier when casting off, today of pushing buttons and flipping switches (*Schalter* in German). It relates to "how to," and to execution and the executive. It is more about the practices and procedures and measures of power than about power itself. *Schalten* intervenes and goes along with cause-and-effect relations. According to Charles Sanders Peirce's list of categories, that which is produced by *Schalten* or is activated through it, would be *secondness* (Peirce 1868: 292; see also Peirce 1998). In short, it is operative. The English equivalent *switching* reflects this more or less adequately.

Walten, on the other hand, is lasting, and connected with stasis, not action. It does not make a difference and is no difference. It does not articulate, nor act, and not even decide. It is, it is there, it is out there, it is being, dominating and more or less insensible for us and non-recordable for machines, this is all. It has no parts or steps. It is not operative in the sense of interventions. It is not divisible, is not based on distinctions or decisions and does not come in the form of interventions or distinct operations. It is not technical. In Charles Sanders Peirce's logics of categories, it would figure as firstness, that what is since it is, without any difference or relation to something else, not even causes nor tangible or addressable effects (Peirce 1868: 294). *Walten* implies power in the sense of dominance as a given state of being, or atmosphere, or milieu. It is not operative, but ontological. The English "ruling" translates this in a way, but it constantly connotates the exact complement, namely *Schalten*, ruling by rules and playing rules. *Walten* in contrast knows no rules.

Schalten und Walten, therefore, is a very traditional expression for what I want to explore here, namely the project of drawing together the *operative* and the *ontological*. In a more or less traditional ontology, this would simply not be possible at all. Traditional ontology would collapse if it turned out as operative as would, as we will see, the core assumption of the ontological difference between *being* (*Sein*) and *that-what-is* (*Seiendes*) (Heidegger 1993: 1998).

Max Bense's Dream

To explore this more closely, I would like to take a little detour via a quotation. In 1969, German philosopher of science, semiotician and aesthetician Max Bense wrote:

> Civilization is not a state, but a process. A process we prefer. It shifts the world from a metaphorical state to a mathematical one, and it will

not stop transforming problematic realms into calculable ones. Only worlds that can be anticipated are programmable, only those that can be programmed are constructible and habitable in a human way.

(Bense 1969: 7, my translation)

Even if not referring explicitly to it, the quotation brings in what we here call *Schalten und Walten*. We can read what Bense captures with the "metaphorical state" and the "problematic areas" as what we mean by *Walten* here. On the other hand, according to Bense, the state that can be calculated, anticipated, programmed, and constructed would be the opposite or complement, in short: *Schalten*. By the way, concepts, conceptual thought, and the conceptual world, are to be included into Bense's mathematical state, in so far as they are *clara et distincta concepta*, logically sharp and precisely operable concepts, the p and q of analytical philosophy, for example. What Bense then stipulates is nothing more than the displacement of *Walten* to the benefit of *Schalten* as the very mega-program of modernization as such. The *Walten* of nature as well as the *Walten* of the social shall, according to Bense, more and more reside under the command of technology, which more than ever in an increasingly digitized world technology is obviously and not only metaphorically based on switching operations, *Schalten*.

Through modernization and digitization, the world has since got under a mode of switching, and everything that is has increasingly been brought about and into being by operations of switching. Whatever is, is more and more a result of switching operations in a digitizing world. This of course gives rise to concern oneself with the operative ontology of switching. But it is precisely here that the more complementarizing or integrative concept of *Schalten und Walten* diverges from what Bense is proposing. Drawing *Schalten* und *Walten* together in order to elaborate on Operative Ontologies does not to exclude or overcome what is metaphorical for Bense, that is, the problematic, the contingent, the historical, and, in short, the material, but, on the contrary, to integrate it (Krämer 2017).

For the operations of switching can by no means be done without *Walten*. In order to be effective in the world, operative, they must be implemented into the world. Bense's construable worlds must first be built, erected, and even furnished. They are literally contaminated with the material and metaphorical worlds. And when viewed in light, the mathematical state of the world itself or the programmable, switchable, is also by no means a bodiless and immaterial one. Calculation, programming, and anticipation themselves require an apparatus, material devices with physical bodies. They depend on instruments and tools, on computers, for example. They remain attached and even stuck on the res extensa. That is exactly the difference between traditional ontology and operative ontology as we imagine it (Engell, Hartmann and Voss 2013: 7–8).

For Bense, aesthetics (and of course anthropology) are undoubtedly metaphorical undertakings. In relation to the human body as a carrier of philosophical operations, however, aesthetics and anthropology have already made extensive efforts to promote and research the body of thought, the bodily, physical conditions of thought—the bodily physical *Walten* behind the brain's *Schalten*. Their investigations focus on the material conditions and the interactions between philosophical and organic operations. Media philosophy now adds to this the consideration of the technical and medial bodies.

I would like to show this briefly on a very simple and everyday object (Engell and Wendler 2009: 42). Logically or conceptually, one could say that the venetian blinds make a distinction between inside and outside, which embodies themselves at the same time. The venetian blinds are also a switch; they let the light in or out, make the outside visible from the inside or not. They regulate the access to what we see or do not see through it. And to the extent that access to something determines its state or mode of being—also a basic conviction of media philosophy—the venetian blinds thus also transform the world, namely the world of the visible, from a simply given state into a regulated state. The venetian blinds would be a very simple Bense apparatus.

The Return of *Walten*

And it would be all the more so as the venetian blinds repeat the regulation that they impose on the world of light and visibility. They make their own function, which they perform in the medium of light, visible precisely in light. They make visible the invisible, the medium (Luhmann 2000: 102–32), namely light (McLuhan 1964: 10–12). On the inside of the distinction (Spencer Brown 1969), in the space in which we find ourselves and which they delimit from the outside, venetian blinds create light and dark stripes. In this way they repeat and show the binary distinction between the visible and the invisible, and the inside and the outside, which they themselves implement. In this respect, the venetian blinds are not only a recursive, but to some extent a reflexive, a logical-philosophical machine in the realm of *Schalten*.

In fact, however, the highlight of the venetian blinds lies precisely in the fact that they are not just this, but a metaphorical and problematic machine in the sense of Bense as well. The nice thing about the venetian blinds is that they know intermediate states between open and closed. The stripes of visibility and light are changeable, manipulable (Engell and Wendler 2009). Exactly this change between the states is what the venetian blinds, in contrast to a simple window shutter, executes. Thus, the venetian blinds also generate a time of their own, which is more and different than the mere, sharp, reversible and even expansionless distinction between before and after. The adjustment of the venetian blinds, like any operation, for example that of the departure of a ship, has a course. It takes hold of time and costs time. The venetian blinds do not simply implement the logical operations of separation, differentiation, and repetition, but the aesthetic operations of coupling and transition between states or even transmission. They are, in short, a metaphorical machine, and yet and at the same time still a switch, technical and, if you like, mathematical and logical in character and function.

In addition, of course, the venetian blinds themselves have a body that extends in space. This is shown by the fact that it wears and wears out: time rules and takes its toll, *Walten*. The handling lines can tear, the lamellas can bend and must be cleaned regularly, physically. The venetian blind is also directed at our biological bodies, it requires a certain handling, *Schalten*. Only these transfers and overlaps of different bodies and materials, *Schalten und Walten* make the venetian blinds a philosophical apparatus in the sense of media philosophy (Engell 2003).

What applies to the venetian blinds probably applies to all switches. They all consist of something material, metal, plastic, semiconductors, or other materials. They belong to *physis*, and *physis*, as Heidegger put it, means *Walten*: "*Die Natur waltet*" (Knowles 2013; see also Derrida 2011). They produce not only mathematical distinctions, logical negations, but also metaphorical contacts, touches, and transitions, but also heat and sometimes noise. They generate the *Eigenzeit*, which they need for their execution, and reach out into space. If complex semiconductor circuits can finally take over thought processes such as arithmetic or even speech, then they are still bodies of thought and hence linked to *Walten*.

In this sense, the entry or implementation of the mathematical (or conceptual) world into the metaphorical (or material, physical) world is not the replacement of the one by the other that is our topic, but rather their coupling with each other. Thus we would perhaps formulate that some *Walten* always prevails in all *Schalten*. If only what is switchable can exist, then all *Schalten* requires a *Walten* which it itself generates (Kittler 2017: 182).

The Switchable Picture

I want to further explore *Schalten und Walten* through a case study of one of the most important products of recent media technologies, namely the electronic picture (Engell 2021: 3–6). Switching is the *conditio sine qua non* of the electronic picture. From early on, the television picture is first and foremost a switchable picture, and everything else follows literally after it and exactly from it. In the evolution of technical images, other types of images have succeeded television in its switchability, such as video images and digital images. But the television picture is the prototype of the switchable picture—and vice versa: switching is the prototype of all televisual operations. Hence, it is worth concentrating on the television picture here.

The television picture, along with its sound, derives from its switchability and defines itself through it. It does not, on the other hand, ground in its visibility and audibility, like other pictures do, nor in its frame, nor in its duration, like for instance film.

There are three reasons for this extraordinary position of switching for television. Firstly, switching relates the tv picture and its user, that is, switching determines the practice of television. Secondly, television pictures are set off against one another by switching processes (instead of editing, montage, or collage techniques). Switching discerns them and relates them at one time so that they even touch one another, in a technical and literal sense. Finally, switching works also in the micro-technical processing of the images themselves. Even the infinite, volatile flow of electromagnetic signals, which the screen converts into optical signals and to which the image owes its existence, is regulated, controlled, articulated, and structured by switching processes. The television picture emerges from its switchability as an entity that is contoured at all and thus observable for us as well. Friedrich Kittler's above quoted famous dictum: "Only what is switchable is at all" (Kittler 2017: 182) definitely applies to the television picture.

In order for television pictures to pass through on the surface of the tube screen, the television set must be connected to the world outside television in two ways: it requires physical contact firstly with the electrical power supply and secondly with the flow of electromagnetic signals. All visible and recognizable images that television will then circulate are conversions and complications of the two streams into which television switches on. They form the primary technical or physical environment, milieu or *media sphere* of television: *Walten* (Debray, Merzeau 2005: 162–9; see also Debray 1991).

In terms of technical history, the picture tube is actually an electrographic device at first. It serves to make visible what is there but cannot be seen, that is: electricity as *Walten*. It optically manipulates and measures electrical currents and signals, comparable to an oscillograph or a radar screen (Abramson 1974: 65–9). The television picture is thus an interconnection of the current and the signal circulation, second, its product and, third, its visual trace. It indicates the currents to which it owes itself and of which it is a part.

The image is not split off the signal and does not belong to some completely different order, but it emerges from the signal and couples itself to it. Again, Schalten und Walten are drawn together operatively and ontologically in the picture tube.

The Emergence of *Flow*: *Walten* from *Schalten*

So *Schalten* on its turn brings with it *Walten* like its own shadow, and, of course, media theory is interested in this remaining ontological shadow of digitization and of mediatization in general. But there is even more than the necessary pertinence of *Walten* even under digital conditions. *Walten* is not only the unavoidable substrate of *Schalten*, it can also emerge from it. One striking example can be seen in what Raymond Williams called the *flow* (Williams 1992: 85–112). The flux of images on tv is, due to the switchability of the screen picture, continuously and constantly interrupted in a most abrupt way by switching over to other images, mist heterogeneous image types, tv genres, broadcast formats. They interfere with each other in a way to only leave caleidoscopic meaningless fragments, tiny bits and pieces of what used to be for instance, news, advertising, weather forecasts, sports, shows, episodes, fictions, live transmissions, announcements, wrap ups, and so forth. There is no coherence of whatsoever quality, especially if it comes to semantics, to meaning, or to any form of Gestalt. The term of coherence (or of interruption) loses any significance. Switching operates, as Hartmut Winkler once put it, an operation directed against any kind of context and hence of text (Winkler 1991: 59–61, 106).

But, Williams observes, a strange kind of rhythm, or of surfing on the surface of the fragmented sequence of distinctions and of switching operations, comes into being (Williams 1992: 85–7). Based on highly frequent interruptions, a *flow* of plasticity and viscosity arises, a state of experience or even existence, a mode of being which integrates viewers, images, switchable pictures, sounds, and the world beyond. *Flow* is a bodily and hence physical, material phenomenon, not just a structure or a sequence of otherwise disembodied distinctions (Czsikszentmihaly 1985: 38–40, 123–5). It hence brings *physis* back into the game. *Flow* emerges from switching, *Schalten*, but it rules in the sense of *Walten*.

What can be found in the switchable picture may also emerge elsewhere. The Maltese Cross in the movie camera (and projector) could also be addressed here, or, even more general, language. In what André Martinet called *la double articulation du langage*, the articulation or segmentation of what has already been articulated or fragmented, the coherent dominion of sense emerges as both an artifact, and hence on the side of switching, and an unavoidably and unquestionably ruling condition of existence (Martinet 1980). Signals, discernible and switchable entities, as they emerge from ruling noise may on their turn, if sequenced, generate a kind of second-order flow-like noise and as such turn into given conditions of existence. The cloud, or looped CCTV Systems, or the pervasion of the habitat with computers, and hence switches, may be regarded in a comparable way as modes of turning *Schalten* into *Walten*.

In this sense *Schalten und Walten* describes not only Bense's entry or implementation of the mathematical, switchable (or conceptual) world into the metaphorical, ruling (or material) world. It is not the replacement of the one by the other, but rather their coupling and their turning into each other. Thus we have to state that some *Walten* always prevails in all *Schalten*. If only what is switchable can exist, then all *Schalten* requires a *Walten* which it itself generates.

Walten by *Schalten* in the Digital Iconosphere

In the course of the further evolution of television, this entanglement of *Schalten und Walten* which in the end *is* tv transforms and enhances. I will only briefly mention three phases of this evolution. First, with the remote control, the operation of switching extends and intensifies. More than ever, watching television means switching and hence the tactile character of the medium comes to the fore. The course of a television evening in the sense of *Walten* is widely detached from the program offer and from preset structures in the sense of *Schalten,* although switching is the core operation of generating a television evening. Via switching and the remote control, the tv experience acquires the qualities of navigation on a surface where nothing is fixed or repeatable. The striated space—to quote Deleuze's and Guattari's famous dichotomy from A Thousand Plateaux—created by switching turns again into a smooth space (Deleuze and Guattari 1987: 474–500).

Second, with the introduction of the flat LCD display, the pixels of the screen themselves become switches (Engell 2021: 230–2). Where the pixels of the traditional cathode ray tube had been luminescent dots that were activated or not, now, the pixels are individually addressable switches which let the light pass or not. The light does no longer come from the pixels, but from the background LED, and is continuously on, but does not pass to the screen if not allowed by a pixel cell which opens or closes according to the signal it receives. The screen itself has become a thousand switches and the picture is a complex switching operation. The picture is hence an articulation of its own being a switch image. But literally behind the switch image foil of the LCD resides the light, the lamp which is constantly radiating with light, the LED. The LED behind of the LCD screen backs *Schalten* with *Walten*.

And third, we have the increasing interference between the tv screen and the multiple other screens that surround it, the so-called "second screens" such as laptop computers, tablets, and mobile phones that are active alongside and synchronized with the regular tv screen. On the other hand, we have the huge screens of all kinds of public viewing *dispositifs*, from bars, lounges, and lobbies to stadiums and open places. Together, they form the pervasive and permanent, the lasting (and hence ruling) iconosphere of the digital picture which has no outside and knows no articulation as such. They address each other, they refer to each other, they even reduplicate and incorporate each other. Touch screens and remote control complement each other, and all images run on and across all screens. If there is a tv screen at all—for instance for reasons of its pictorial and perceptive qualities and its huge dimension—then the tv screen might be seen as nothing but a second screen to the other second screens, even if empirical research has shown that for so far the tv offer on the large screen is still the focus, the reference horizon and the overall background lighting of the whole iconospheric configuration of screens.

Markus Stauff, though, has convincingly suggested to look at television now as a configuration of screens and screen operations (Stauff 2015). Television is not a specific type of program or of images or technical picture. It is a permanent and always performative operating in and on constellations of images on and across multiple screens. Television is having pictures run while other pictures run. Its main feature is, as from its earliest beginnings in the nineteenth century, synchronization and simultaneization in short: its liveness. Via the switch, the television picture synchronizes images and events and users and the multiple screens in the world and at hand of users. Its mode of being is hence even more *Walten*, an omnipresent, ubiquitous one, it is all there, and always, and always already. It can permeate and pervade the world through all the ubiquitous and omnipresent screens which constitute our habitat and our way of being in the world, the world's *Walten* by our *Schalten*, that is: the operative ontologies of the electronic image.

Works Cited

Abramson, A. (1974), *Electronic Motion Pictures*, New York: Arno Press.
Bense, M. (1969), *Einführung in die informationstheoretische Ästhetik*, Reinbek: Rowohlt.

Brown, G. S. (1969), *Laws of form*, London: Allen and Unwin.
Csikszentmihaly, M. (1985), *Beyond Boredom and Anxiety: The Experience of Play in Work and Games*, San Francisco and London: Jossey-Bass.
Debray, R. (1991), *Cours de mediologie generale*, Paris: Gallimard.
Debray, R., and Merzeau, L. (2005), "Mediasphere," *Medium*, 4 (3): 162–9.
Deleuze, G., and Guattari, F. (1987), *A Thousand Plateaus* (1980), Minneapolis: Minneapolis University Press.
Derrida, J. (2011), *The Beast and the Sovereign*, vol. II, Chicago: University of Chicago Press.
Engell, L. (2003), "Tasten, Wählen, Denken. Genese und Funktion einer philosophischen Apparatur," in Stefan Münker, Alexander Roesler and Mike Sandbothe (eds), *Medienphilosophie. Beiträge zur Klärung eines Begriffs*, Frankfurt/M: Fischer, 53–77.
Engell, L. (2021), *The Switch Image. Television Philosophy*, London, Dublin and New York: Bloomsbury Academic.
Engell, L., Hartmann, F., and Voss, C. (eds) (2013), *Körper des Denkens. Neue Positionen der Medienphilosophie*, München: Fink.
Engell, L., and Wendler, A. (2009), "Medienwissenschaft der Motive," *Zeitschrift für Medienwissenschaft*, 1 (1): 38–49.
Heidegger, M. (1998), "On the Essence of Ground" (1929), in William McNeil (ed.), *Martin Heidegger, Pathmarks*, London and New York: Cambridge University Press, 97–135.
Heidegger, M. (1993), "What Is Metaphysics," in David Farrell Krell (ed.), *Martin Heidegger Basic Writings*, New York: Harper Collins, 307–41.
Kittler, F. (2017), "Real Time Analysis. Time Axis Manipulation," *Cultural Politics*, 13 (1): 1–17.
Knowles, A. (2013). "Towards a Critique of Walten. Heidegger, Derrida and Henological Difference," *Journal of Speculative Philosophy*, 27 (3): 265–76.
Krämer, S. (2017), "Die Rettung des Ontologischen durch das Ontische? Ein Kommentar zu, operativen Ontologien," *Zeitschrift für Medien- und Kulturforschung*, 8 (2), Operative Ontologien: 125–42.
Luhmann, N. (2000), *Art as a Social System*, Stanford: Stanford University Press.
Martinet, A. (1980), *Éléments de linguistique générale* (1960), Paris: Armand Colin.
McLuhan, M. (1964), *Understanding Media. The Extensions of Man*, London and New York: Routledge.
Peirce, C. S. (1868), "On a New List of Categories," *Proceedings of the American Academy of Arts and Sciences*, 7: 287–98.
Peirce, C. S. (1998), "A Syllabus of Certain Topics of Logic," in *The Essential Peirce: Selected Philosophical Writings*, Vol. 2, Bloomington: Indiana University Press, 258–99.
Siegert, B. (2017), "Öffnen, Schließen, Zerstreuen, Verdichten. Die operativen Ontologien der Kulturtechnik," *Zeitschrift für Medien- und Kulturforschung*, 8 (2): Operative Ontologien, S.: 95–113.

Stauff, M. (2015), "The Second Screen. Convergence as Crisis," *Zeitschrift für Medien- und Kulturforschung*, 6 (2): 123–44.
Williams, R. (1992), *Television as Cultural Form* (1973), Middletown: Wesleyan University Press.
Winkler, H. (1991), *Switching—Zapping. Ein Text zum Themas und ein parallellaufendes Unterhaltungsprogramm*, Darmstadt: Häuser.

Seken: Webs and Networks of In-Betweenness

(Origin Japanese)

Sebastian Kawanami-Breu and Shintaro Miyazaki

Etymologically, *seken* 世間 consists of two characters. 世 (se, YO) can roughly be translated as "becoming" of living beings and as generations. It combines a pictographic component, which looks like three leaves or branches sprouting from a main branch forming a simple network, with an ideographic component, which triplicates the character for "ten" 十 into "thirty" 卋 (one generation of people lasted for about thirty years). The English term "generation" actually catches both temporal nuances quite well.[1] 間 (kan, ken, MA), in the old writing style not in use anymore, inserted the character for "moon" 月 in between the characters for "gate" 門. Moonlight falling in through an open gate means "space," "in-between-ness," or "opening," understood both in a spatial and temporal sense, as it could also depict the moon passing by the opening.[2] These two characters were combined into *seken* 世間 as a translation of the Buddhist term *loka* from Sanskrit, a term referring to the world of ephemeral beings, both living and nonliving, whose spiritual transcendence (出世間 *shusseken*) was the goal of the Buddhist doctrine. Buddhism arrived in Japan via China and Korea around the sixth century BCE, but it is difficult to trace an exact point of origin for *seken*, as we encounter the word only sporadically in ancient poetry and Buddhist folktales (where the exact date of composition is unknown). It is probably safe to say that *seken* is co-original with Buddhism in Japan, which was first adopted by warriors and aristocrats since the Nara period (710–94) and later spread into a popular belief system after the Muromachi period (1336–1573).

We propose to translate *seken* as "the relational web of human affairs," an invisible web that surrounds and involves us in a larger community of human beings. *Seken* is grown like the branches in the image above and this generative force creates *relations of networked In-Betweenness*. As the cultural historian Abe Kinya writes, "*seken* is a strong bond that binds each person to the other, even though there are no explicit rules of membership. But individuals do not

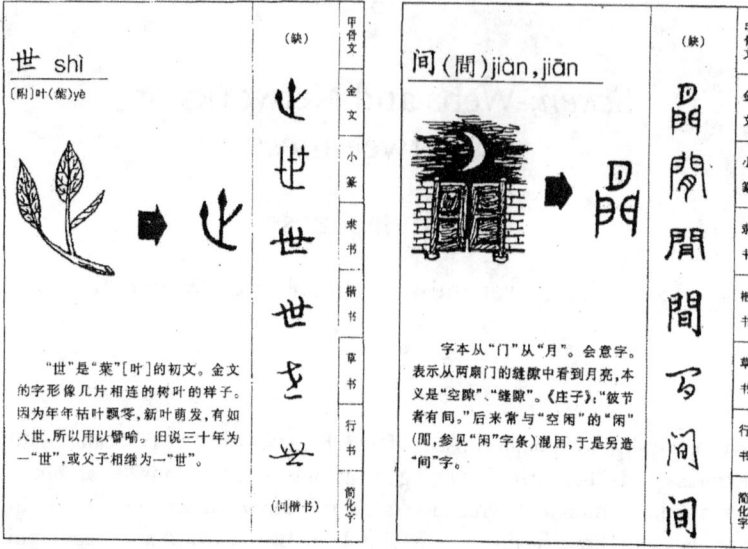

Figure 25.1 Etymological illustrations of the characters *se* (shi) and *ken* (jiān) in Chinese handwriting. Images reproduced from *Zìyuán cháxún* (Etymological Sources for Chinese Characters) http://qiyuan.chaziwang.com.

voluntarily create this web of affairs by themselves. They live in it, as if their place was given to them somehow inside it" (Abe 1995: 16). Thus, we would argue that seken has a different structural articulation from *loka*, which is formed, as mentioned earlier, as an onion-like construction of circles in circles. What we would also suggest de-emphasizing are the semantics of "immanence," which were implied in the Buddhist origins of *seken*. The duality of the "transient human world" and the "afterworld" beyond death disappeared slowly, the more the word became rooted in a stable society and no longer just a term used in the writings of monks and warrior aristocrats (those "specialists of impermanence"). Instead, what became stronger after the Edo period (1603–1868) was the connotation of a social web of affairs—and "affair" can be understood quite literally here, as we encounter the term very often in the context of human love affairs which confront the unwritten rules of *seken* or fall apart because of them. This connotation also applies to "monetary affairs" and other kinds of "affairs" where human action is socially enmeshed and mediated.[3]

One reason for this transformation is the increasing stability and complexity of "human affairs" vis-a-vis the earlier periods of violent domination, war, and scarcity. But we could also follow the ideas of Hannah Arendt and add that what gives *permanence* and a thing-character to the immaterial "world of human affairs" (expressed in speech, action, and thought) are media environments. As media of social exchange (the introduction of currencies) and of anamnesis, memory, and storage (an ever-growing collection of images and texts) allow to materialize traces of the human world into artefacts, the human world itself loses its fleeting and transient character. As a result, *seken* as a term begins to revolve around matters of "immanence."[4] Historically speaking, this connotation of *seken* as a "worldly space of affairs" is established and remains largely constant since the Edo period. It seems that here probably not for the first time, but still significantly, the previous onion-like cosmogeometrical architecture of *loka* slowly transformed into a more web-like understanding of worlds.

Unlike the more abstract and systemic term "society," *seken* refers to the web and network of human affairs that immediately surround us, in which our actions are inserted and valued. It is noteworthy that *seken* has many sensual and aesthetic qualities, expressed through terms like *seken no me*, *seken no mimi*, the eyes and ears of *seken*. *Seken no kaze wa tsumetai* 世間の風は冷たい, "the human world is indifferent to me/us" literally means "a cold wind is blowing at me/us in *seken*." *Seken-shirazu* 世間知らず (one that has no idea of *seken*) is somebody who steps on the toes of others, in other words, someone who is ignorant of invisible rules and workings of a specific human web, someone operating outside the protocols of a social network. Indeed, Japanese society is often regarded as unique when it comes to the effort that goes into the non-violation of such protocols. But instead of making essentialist claims, we prefer to say that the Japanese language, in some of its traditional components, has a well-developed feeling and well-established names for forms of tacit knowledge and implicit social dynamisms that are equally at work within other cultures as well. *Seken* refers to the *web of surrounding presence* of others, without which the things we say or do lose their reality. This presence does not have to be "there" literally, it is a potentiality, not unlike what Lacan (1988: 235ff) called the "Big Other," an instance that "listens to" and "knows" what we say and do and thereby mediates our subjective experience with imagined expectations of the social order. However, the Lacanian term is an anthropomorphism and does not necessarily express the *web of surrounding presence of others*, which has become a general and global condition after the dawn of mediated environments, social networks, instant messaging, internet of things, ubiquitous computing, and more. Therefore, we suggest, that *seken* might actually be a better way to express the relationality and sensuality implied in the sociotechnically mediated life forms of our current digital condition. Instead of sticking with the supposed "uniqueness" and "intranslatability" of the Japanese conceptual heritage, it could be fruitful to include such non-Western ideas in our philosophical toolkits, for example to explore dynamisms of inclusion and exclusion in social webs and networks from this perspective.

Meiji "Society" and Seken

The introduction of the term "Society" to Japan, as a modern concept to describe human relations, which happened in the early Meiji Period, after the country was more or less forced to open its borders and participate in the modern world economy, reveals more pertinent aspects. When Amane Nishi, a leading Japanese intellectual of that time, eventually coined the word *shakai* 社会 as the Japanese translation of society in 1877, the term was still unheard of. According to Abe Kinya, its creation followed after forty different attempts to find a good expression that caught the essence of the word. (Abe 1995: 175) Another genealogy of *shakai* traces its origins back to a term used in Middle Chinese for ritual gatherings for offering to the God of Earth, which Fukuchi Gen'ichirō adopted in 1875 as a translation for "society." The older term *seken* was also among the candidates. But in the end, Nishi and his contemporaries chose a neologism instead of a traditional concept, above all, because *seken* was not centered around the human individual and its dignity as the smallest denominator of social life. In the Meiji-Era, when Japan aspired to leave the heritage of its feudal class system behind, cultural translation and social engineering were intrinsically bound to each other: to coin a new word also meant to forge a new form of human relations, often one that was diametrically opposed to tradition. Even after Nishi had translated "society," the so-called modern, liberal individual citizen, which was a conceptual prerequisite for the thinking of society, still had no particular roots in Japan. Only in 1884, around seven years later, one can find sources that translate the modern person as kojin 個人. This once again illustrates how foreign the concept of the individual liberal person was.

While the Meiji technocracy succeeded in installing a new operating system on top of an old one in politics and governance, language could not so easily be engineered: *Seken* disappeared from official language in science, politics, and education. But no one could stop people from navigating their daily lives still in terms of *seken*. As a scholar or a journalist, one could split roles and use "objective" Western terminology during work (writing about "society" in a newspaper, for instance), only to switch back to the embodied concepts of tradition later in the evening. Some aspects of that bifurcation and dialectics still remain intact today in the different connotations of *shakai* and *seken*. While the former is primarily used when speaking about abstract or systemic components of political life (economy, law, democratic institutions), the latter is used more in speaking about the concrete, non-formalized, and often relatively small networks of human relations in which one has a "place" and one's actions have meaning and value.

Just like the term "society" could not be easily transplanted into the Japanese microcosm of *seken* at the end of the nineteenth century, it is equally questionable whether the term *seken* could actually be used outside the context of Japanese social relations today. The problem of translatability here is not one of referential relations of words to each other, but of the different forms of life (Wittgenstein) implied in the concept. But while it certainly cannot simply "replace" our existing concepts of social relations, it might still have some validity on the level of a phenomenological or media theoretical thought experiment about how we can describe non-modern or networked forms of intersubjectivity. Despite concerns about the "intranslatability" of concepts, one should not forget how much the creativity of earlier philosophical attempts to describe intersubjectivity and the human lifeworld itself was bound to the introduction of ruptures into consciousness by inventing a new, sometimes "foreign" language.

Instead of a Conclusion

Looking at contemporary digital society through the lens of *seken* may allow us to speculate: in how far did the patterns of social relations, which we still tend to describe in traditional terms of a "society" built from atomic "individuals," which then leads up to a hierarchy of "nation states" and a "world society"—in how far did these things, which we still frame in terms of a modern, liberal society, maybe already morph into something else, which the Japanese term *seken* actually could offer a better grasp of?

This is certainly not meant to reactivate older stereotypical views on the degree of (non)existence of individualism in or outside Japan, or to make grand claims whether the Japanese view of society is modern or not. It rather leads to the point that inside the thinking of *seken*, there are forms of tacit knowledge to be unraveled, which may be rooted in their own local history, but which also show parallels to the ways of worldmaking and living within the new forms of relationality that emerged through social media and networked computing—a space which media theorists of the recent years no longer characterize as an object outside us, but as an "environment" that entails, entangles, and defines our subjective experience. When human relations become enmeshed in a space of micro-relations, of little, globally connected neighborhoods which all have their own rules of inclusion and exclusion, then maybe the generalized internet condition is a condition that amplifies the *seken*-character of intersubjectivity vis-a-vis other forms of organization, such as the family, the state, and so on.

Once more, it is interesting that the Japanese *seken* is always also something sensual: as in expressions like "*seken no me*" or "*seken no mimi*," it has "eyes" that see what you do and "ears" that hear what you say. For instance, when somebody faces *instant-excommunication* in a SNS shitstorm, she or he falls from grace not in the eyes of "society," but in the eyes of *seken*. *Seken-shirazu* (one that has no idea of *seken*) could be somebody who steps on the toes of others, in other words, somebody who is environmentally challenged. Is Japanese society really that "unique" when it comes to the effort that goes into the non-violation of social etiquette and norms? Couldn't it also be that the introduction of a mediated space of instant communication has led to the emergence of similar phenomena in the West as well? There is a not-only-human "Big Other" now that listens to what we say, and whose feelings we better not violate. In a world that has become more complex through the constant networked presence of others, and where community can have a stronger normativity than society, *seken*, as a term for the *surrounding presence of others*, maybe does catch some of the aspects of our current human condition a bit better than our inherited and seldom questioned Universalist concepts of "mankind" and world "society." It may help to address, visualize, and problematize hidden discourses, rules, and protocols and thereby offer glimpses into possibilities to change and transform our "web of affairs" into more desirable, friendlier, and solidarity-oriented forms of in-between worlds.

Notes

1 This term was particularly used for the becoming and succession of "dynasties." The expression "yo" in the Japanese national anthem *kimi ga yo* 君が代 in fact denotes the emperor's "reign" and could equally be written as 世 in ancient terminology.
2 Both are pictographic elements; "moon" 月 was replaced by "sun" 日 during the modernization reforms of Japanese Kanji in the early twentieth century.
3 Before the literature of the Edo period, the world-denying connotation of Buddhism is relatively strong, that is, the meaning of *seken* revolves around the ephemeral, the fleeting, the existence beset by sin and lack. A world-affirming connotation, which gradually became visible in and after the Edo period, presupposes various historical developments (economic stability, urban culture, new social strata, etc.). In certain respects, it is in the culture of the *Chōnin* (the merchant class) of the Edo period that the more modern Japanese view of *seken* first appears: it is now oriented more toward interpersonal relations than toward the difference between this world and the otherworld. The literary characters of Ihara Saikaku (1642–93),

for example, are people who ignore the opinion of the "world" (*seken*) and enter into forbidden queer love relationships within it. They are, as Abe (1995: 134) writes, prototypes of alternative lifestyles outside the social mainstream.

4   Arendt doesn't use the term "environments," but she writes about the connection between worldliness and mediality: "The reality and reliability of the human world rest primarily on the fact that we are surrounded by things more permanent than the activity by which they were produced, and potentially even more permanent than the lives of their authors. Human life, in so far as it is world-building, is engaged in a constant process of reification, and the degree of worldliness of produced things, which all together form the human artifice, depends upon their greater or lesser permanence in the world itself" (Arendt 2018: 94–6).

Works Cited

Abe, K. (1995), *Seken to wa nani ka?* 世間とは何か (What Is *Seken*?), Tokyo: Kodansha.

Arendt, H. (2018), *The Human Condition*, Chicago and London: The University of Chicago Press.

Lacan, J. (1988), *The Seminar. Book II. The Ego in Freud's Theory and in the Technique of Psychoanalysis, 1954–55*, trans. Sylvana Tomaselli, Cambridge: Cambridge University Press.

"Zìyuán cháxún," (Etymological Sources for Chinese Characters), http://qiyuan.chaziwang.com/etymology-14367.html (last checked September 15, 2021).

26

Tathāgatagarbha: Translating the Untranslatable

(Origin Chinese)

Victor Fan

In comparative literature and philosophy, translating concepts that are deemed untranslatable is often necessary for the purpose of enabling scholars from different linguistic and cultural perspectives to access and partake in a discourse. Nonetheless, as Lydia Liu ([2004] 2006: 12–13) argues, in an act of translation, signs that have different values in their respective languages are often "thrown together" into a "super-sign." The result is a new system of differences that does not help readers of the target language to interpret directly the sign originated in the source language. Rather, this super-sign constitutes a new discursive space that often takes an established discourse originated in the target linguistic sphere to a new direction.

In this chapter, I use the historical conversation between Buddhism, Taoism (Daoism), and European philosophy on the meaning of Tathāgatagarbha as a case study to scrutinize what it means by translating the untranslatable. The Sanskrit term Tathāgatagarbha literally means the *grabha* (womb) from which Tathāgata (a being/non-being that is neither coming nor going, neither not coming nor not going) is generated. This "womb" is considered by many Buddhist scholars as the meontological ground of all interbecomings and interdependent relationalities. The concept itself is regarded as inarticulable in and untranslatable into language. This case study, I argue, demonstrates that by enabling two different, but mutually relatable, philosophical systems to talk to one another, scholars can foster a potentiality of translatability from the untranslatable. Such an act can also inspire scholars from different linguistic and cultural ecologies to rewrite their own epistemes, based on a new *topos* reconfigured by the act of translation itself.

Existence and Emptiness

The debate on the Tathāgatagarbha is founded upon two concepts in Buddhism: existence and emptiness. In Theravāda Buddhism (early sectarian Buddhisms), what we take for granted as existent beings and objects are in-formed out of dependent originations. SA-298 of the *Saṃyuktāgama* [Connected discourses] defines dependent originations as such: "The existence of a consequent depends on the existence of a cause-condition; the origination of the consequent depends on the origination of that cause-condition" (Huang [1999] 2017: SA-298 (178); Yen [1981] 1997: 34). Therefore, what we call a being or object is a form that does not have—or is empty of—any essence, nature, or what Fyodor Stcherbatsky ([1930–32; 1933] 2008: 1:119–45) would call, existential value. It is originated and extinguished from one *kṣaṇa* (moment or smallest unit of time) to another.

In Theravāda Buddhism, therefore, emptiness is transitive. Yet, in the earliest Chinese translation of Buddhist scriptures, the *Sishierzhang jing* [*Sutra of Forty-Two Chapters*] (1923–34: 2), first-century Yuezhi (Indo-Scyth) translators—some even say authors—Kasyapa Matanga and Dharmaratna borrowed two words from Taoism to replace these concepts: *hiŭ* (Middle Chinese)/*you* (modern Mandarin) (existence) and *khung/kong* (emptiness). According to the dualistic cosmology of the *Laozi* [*Tao Te Ching*, written or compiled from approximately sixth to fourth centuries BCE], Dao (Tao) is best understood as the pure potentiality from which creativity and stasis interact and in-form all processes of becoming. As a pure potentiality and the ontological ground of all interbecomings, Tao is meontologically empty (Chen 2020). As Thomé H. Fang (1899–1977) ([1974–7; 2012] 2014: 1:24–28) argues, it is unclear in the *Laozi* whether emptiness is to be considered transitive or intransitive. However, in the *Sutra of Forty-Two Chapters*, desire and other afflictions are compared to dirt that constantly conceals emptiness. For the two translators, *tathātā*—which they translate as Tao—is a *zhen* (truth) that a *samaṇa/śramaṇa* (ascetic practitioner) must disconceal and maintain (*Sishierzhang jing* 1924–34: 2).

Kasyapa Matanga and Dharmaratna's word choices might have been influenced by two discourses: (1) the ongoing debate among different Theravadin sects on the relationship between existence and emptiness in India, and (2) the scholarly debate within the imperial court of the Emperor Ming of Han (57–75) on the relationship between Tao and emptiness in order to institutionalize ancestral worship, Confucianism, Taoism, and Buddhism as a syncretic philosophy that could consolidate the emperor's authority (Puett 2002). In this sense, the two translators or authors were not borrowing terms from Taoism; instead, by throwing together linguistic signs that have different meanings in different bodies of knowledge, they actively contributed to the formulation of an emerging epistemic space.

The logical temptation to interpret (and translate) the transitive notion of emptiness as (or into) an intransitive one is in fact discussed in the *Connected Discourses*. For Sakyamuni (Pāli)/Śākyamuni (Sanskrit) Buddha, *tathatā/tathātā* (the way it is) is neither existent nor empty, neither not existent nor not empty (*Za ahan jing* 1924–34: SA-262 [143]). For existence and emptiness are both *papañcas* (perceptual-conceptual proliferations) (Bodhi 1995: 1204 n229; Ñaṇananda [1971] 2012). His logical formulation, known among scholars in India during his lifetime as *catuṣkoṭi* (four-cornered negation), is employed by Nāgārjuna (circa 150–250) in his philosophical treatise *Mūlamadhyamakakārikā* [*Fundamental Verses of the Middle Way*]. And the term *mādhyamaka* (middle way) has since then been used by Mahāyāna philosophers in their debate on how *tathātā* is to be defined (Yin Shun [1952] 2014).

Nāgārjuna's definition of *tathātā* is sometimes referred to as the *atyantaśūnyatā* (absolute emptiness). His definition was challenged in the fourth and fifth centuries by Asaṅga and his half-brother Vasubandhu, who initiated a debate that would later be called Yogachara/Yogācāra Buddhism. Theravādin scholars believe that *viññāṇa/vijñāna* (consciousness) is not a unified formational process. Rather, each sensory-perceptual domain (including sensory-perceptual organs and sense data, sensations and affections, perceptions, and a volition driven by ignorance) is a consciousness. Thus, there are consciousnesses of the eyes, ears, nose, tongue, body, and thought organs (Huang [1999] 2006: SA-293 [326–27], 296 [330–32], 300 [337–38], 364 [341–42], 373 [344–46], 388 [348], and 404 [353–54]; Stcherbatsky [1930–32; 1993] 2008: 1:119–45; Yen P'ei [1981] 1997: 1–32; Yin Shun [1949; 2010] 2016: 98–104).

Yogācāra scholars argue that these six consciousnesses are perceived and conceptualized as one because a seventh consciousness known as *manas* attaches itself to these six specific consciousnesses and the dispositions that underdetermine their formational processes. The operation of these six consciousnesses (unified by *manas*) is a manifestation or actualization of a subset of cosmically interrelated potentialities and causalities. These potentialities (called *bījas* or seeds) can be considered memories deposited from the past (within one's lifetime, from one generation to another, or even from one transmigration to another). This subset of seeds gives the illusion that there is a stable self (again, in one lifetime or from one transmigration to another) because *manas* perpetually attaches itself to these relationalities. This subset is called the *ālaya*-consciousness (or storehouse consciousness), which is open to seeds from other subsets.

At each point-instant, karma—a formational impulse underdetermined by those dispositions embedded in these potentialities—initiates the actualization of an avalanche of seeds and the virtualization of an avalanche of awarenesses into seeds.

Without any mindfulness of the operational principles of the *ālaya*-consciousness and karma, this process of actualization-virtualization runs on autopilot and produces afflictions such as avarice, anger and frustration, and a delusion that all states of beings exist with permanence. Mindfulness enables the *ālaya*-consciousness to let go of *manas*'s attachment to the self and let the operation of the formational process be as the way it is. By letting the formational process be, the *ālaya*-consciousness continues to operate according to the principle of dependent originations, but an awareness of the emptiness of the self transforms afflictions into detachments (a release from suffering) (Han 1998; Lo 2008; Yen 1971).

Potentialities do not exist until they are actualized. Hence, these potentialities exist in name only. Yet, their relationalities actually exist and the *sabhāva/svabhāva* (nature of their existence) is empty. Asaṅga considers this empty layout of relationalities a creative impetus, an idea rejected by Vasubandhu. For Vasubandhu, there is no monistic creative impetus; rather, this layout is best understood as a pure relationality and those creative impulses (karma) that drive––and are driven by––the formational process are immanent in the process itself. Dharmapāla (530–61), based on the *Saṃdhinirmocana Sūtra* [*Sūtra of the Explanation of the Profound Secrets*] calls this pure relationality the ultimate existence, whose nature is empty (of any nature) (Dharmapāla 1924–34: §6 [67–76]; Han 1998: §1 [28]; Yen 1971: §4 [2:514–25]; *Jie shenmi jing* 2010: §4 [138]).

Bhāviveka (circa 500–78) regards Dharmapāla and other Yogācāra scholars' effort to locate such ultimate existence as a roundabout way to refer to the absolute emptiness. For Bhāviveka, Nāgārjuna is unclear whether the four-cornered negation is meant to be *paryudāsa* (implicative) or *niṣedha* (non-implicative). In an implicative negation, absolute emptiness is at once existent and empty (the double negation returns to affirmation); in a non-implicative negation, the double negation must be taken as is. The former hints at a pure relationality that maintains the difference between substrate and form, whereas the latter hints at an undefinable *je ne sais quoi* that serves as the ultimate substrate (or the ultimate ontological ground). Bhāviveka argues that both conclusions maintain the perceptual-conceptual divide between substrate and form, which cannot be the way it is (Bhāviveka 1924–34: §2 [12]; Wan 1978: 1:252–53). This debate is known among Buddhist scholars as the Tathāgatagarbha.

Chinese Buddhism's Monistic Tendency

During the historical transition from Middle Way to Yogācāra scholarships in India (often known as the Six Dynasties in China, 220 or 222-589), many Buddhist texts were translated into Middle Chinese. Early twentieth-century scholars claimed that these texts were translated based on a standardized principle called *kakŋʸiɛ/geyi* (matching conceptually comparable terms between Buddhism and Taoism). Buddhist scholars today tend to argue that there has never been any standardized way to match concepts (Mair 2010: 227-64). On the contrary, the translations done by Kumārajīva (344-413), a scholar who was kidnapped from Kucha by a convoy sent by Emperor Fu Jian of Former Qin (r. 357-85), employed a vocabulary and syntactic structures that were more common in Chinese writing at the time, which in turn reconfigured the Chinese language and Taoist scholarship.

Although Kumārajīva was well-versed in the Yogācāra debate, his main output consisted of Middle Way *sūtras* and *śāstras* (treatises), which privilege the elaboration of the concept of absolute emptiness (Sharma 2011). His version of the *Vajracchedikā Prajñāpāramitā Sūtra* [*Diamond Sutra*] is still one of the most popular translations of the text today, even though his version is known for abbreviations and modifications for the sake of achieving syntactic and logical clarity.

For example, in the text's explanation of temporality, the original syntax (preserved by the Hwendzɑng/Xuanzang, 602-64, translation) is: "The awareness of the past is ungraspable; the awareness of the future is ungraspable; the awareness of the present is ungraspable" (Lo 2007:44). This original syntax conforms to the four-cornered negation process: (1) the awareness of the past is in-formed by dependent originations and is therefore impermanent; (2) since the future is an extension of the past and since the past is impermanent, the future--which is also informed by dependent originations--has no existent cause in the first place; it is therefore impermanent and nonexistent; (3) since the present is the interval between the past and the future, if both the past and the future are empty of existential values, the present is also empty of existential value (neither existent nor empty, neither not existent nor not empty) (Yin Shun [1952] 2004: §17 [280-83]). Kumārajīva modifies the syntax as: "The mind [consciousness] of the past is ungraspable; the mind of the present is ungraspable; the mind of the future is ungraspable" (Nan 2003: §18 [203]). Such a modification conceals the logical reasoning behind it; instead, it places the emphasis on the emptiness of the consciousness. Kumārajīva's modification is inflected by the Yogācāra belief that an ontological investigation and the meontology (the study of the emptiness of being) of such an investigation are ultimately a scrutiny of the formational process of the *ālaya*-consciousness and its ultimate existence. Thus, the Middle Way thinking that underlines the *Diamond Sutra* is translated into a Yogācāra one.

By the sixth to eighth centuries, Yogācāra thoughts became the mainstream of Chinese Buddhist scholarship. Duŏzhiın/Dushun (557–640), based on the *Avataṃsaka Sūtra*, argues that the Tathāgatagarbha is to be defined as *khungthiung mieuhiŭ/kongzhong miaoyou* (existence is initiated intricately out of the liminality between emptiness and existence) (Dushun 1924–34). Meanwhile, Th'iεngiĭ/Zhiyi (1924–34: §5 [71]) argues that the four-cornered negation should be considered as: neither existent nor empty, at once existent and empty. Both scholars conduct logical arguments of their own based on the Yogācāra Abhidhamma/Abhidharma (meta-discourses), and the core of their argument is that existence and emptiness are both perceptual-conceptual proliferations (Anālayo 2014). Yet, *tathātā* is not to be arrived at transcendentally through reason or transcendently on a metaphysical plane. Rather, *tathātā* is the empty relationality itself, which is immanent in our lived experience. Nevertheless, their culturo-linguistically translated definitions of *tathātā* resonate with the Taoist understanding of the relationship between emptiness and Tao.

Xuanzang, who studied with Dharmapala's student Śīlabhadra (529–645), summarized the key Yogācāra debate in the *Vijñapatimātratāsiddhi* [*Discourse on the Perfection of Consciousness-Only*]. This text, which serves as the foundation of subsequent scholarly debates in China and Japan, curiously omits the Tathāgatagarbha question. For Xuanzang (1924–34: §8 [56–63]), mindfulness enables the seeds to go through a process of *parāvrtti* (reversal). Reversal can be understood as a process of recodifying the relationalities between seeds, so that instead of producing attachment and afflictions, their actualizations can produce detachment and contentment. For him, as enough seeds are reversed or recodified, the formational process is no longer a consciousness that runs on autopilot, but a *paññā/prajñā* (insight into the process itself).

Thomé H. Fang (1978: 1:319–96) argues that Xuanzang's omission is poor scholarship. Yet, such an omission might have been a result of his resistance against the concept in the first place. For Xuanzang, if the nature of these relationalities is empty of any nature, their *vijñapati* (manifestation) as insight is ultimately empty. In other words, even though he had devoted his whole life to Yogācāra studies, his conclusion is closer to the Middle Way understanding of absolute emptiness. In fact, his last translation project was to restore the logical structure of the Middle Way classic *Mahāprajñāpāramitā Sūtra*, of which the *Diamond Sutra* is a part. However, Fang argues that in so doing, the *ālaya*-consciousness can be easily misunderstood as a monistic creative force.

During the same century, Hweinəng/Huineng (638–713), the Sixth Elder of Zen, proposed the concept of *dzıısieng/zixing* (self-nature). In the *Liuzu tanjing* [*Platform Sutra of the Sixth Elder*], a posthumous collection of his sermons, he claims that this idea was inspired by Kumārajīva's version of the *Diamond Sutra*. Huineng's notion of self-nature is attributable to the *Saṃdhinirmocana Sūtra*, which argues that every form has three self-natures: (1) *paratantra-svabhāva* or being initiated out of dependent originations, (2) *parikalpitaḥ-svabhāva* or being initiated out of the dependent originations between internal and external forms (i.e., the potentiality to sense and perceive and the potentiality to turn sense-perception into signs), and (3) *pariniṣpanna-svabhāva* or the nature of being empty of nature. Huineng's idea of the self-nature is the *pariniṣpanna-svabhāva*, but the employment of the terms *zi* (self) and *xing* (nature) persuades both scholars and casual readers to (mis)conceptualize the Tathāgatagarbha as a monistic stasis (Fok 2015: §1 [111]; *Jie shemi jing* 2010: §4 [138]).

The Tathāgatagarbha is often considered as inarticulable and untranslatable, and all these efforts of translation and articulation—that is, super-signs—are logically grounded. Nonetheless, if the Tathāgatagarbha is precisely a non-state of neither becoming nor not becoming, which cannot be logically deduced or induced, it is meta-logical (or what Charles Sanders Peirce would claim, only abduceable) (Peirce 1997: 199–201; 1998: 2:155, 191–95, 204–11, 226–42). Translating the concept of the Tathāgatagarbha and its scholarly discourse therefore always produces mistranslations. From the Song (960–1279) to Ming (1368–1644) dynasties, the imperial academy developed a syncretic philosophical discipline called *lixue* (neo-Confucianism), which sought to conceptualize ontological, epistemological, and ethico-political questions by reading Confucianism, Taoism, and Buddhism comparatively (Wu [1995] 1962). In such scholarship, Buddhism was often used as a supplement that corroborated Taoist ideas, which further contributed to the notion that *tathātā* was an intransitive and monistic concept.

Euro-American Episteme

This untranslatability problem remained largely unaddressed from the seventeenth to the nineteenth centuries, as Confucianism was privileged as the only legitimate and utilitarian academic subject in both the Qing empire (1644–1911) and the Tokugawa shogunate (1603–1868). When Paul

Carus (1852–1911) organized the World's Parliament of Religions (1893) in Chicago, the Qing government sent only Confucian scholar Pung Kwang Yu (Peng Guangyu) to attend, whereas Shaku Soyen (1860–1969) from Japan represented Zen Buddhism, assisted by his student Suzuki Teitarō Daisetz (1870–1966) (Seager 2009). Carus invited both Soyen and Suzuki back to the United States, and, according to Margaret Dornish (1970: 47–66), suggested that Suzuki compare Zen's understanding of self-nature with the philosophy of Baruch Spinoza.

Scholars today believe that Soyen asked Suzuki to mistranslate and reframe Zen concepts in Christian terms in order to reach his audience in Chicago and San Francisco. The three major super-signs created by Soyen and Suzuki continue to shape the way many Europeans and Americans understand Buddhism. First, according to Huineng, *tathātā* cannot be arrived at via logical reason. Rather, as the meontological ground of the *ālaya*-consciousness and its manifestation (i.e., the six consciousnesses), *tathātā* has always been the way it is, here and now, only that it has been concealed by forms and afflictions. One returns to *tathātā* not through gradual ratiocination or contemplation, but through a schizophrenic investigation into this inarticulable nothingness of nothingness, until it suddenly reveals itself. In the United States, Soyen argues that such a sudden disconcealment of the way it is a form of mysticism. He also argues that insight is a form of spiritual awakening, even though the concept of the spirit has been rejected by Buddhist scholars since the Buddha's lifetime. Finally, he discusses *tathātā* as a transcendental truth (Thompson 2005: 3–5).

Soyen's work in the United States and Suzuki's promotion of Zen in the academic circle initiated a debate among intellectuals in Kyoto around Shin Buddhism—a school of thought that believes that the Pure Land (a realm of absolute mindfulness) is not only immanent in one's lived experience, but also imminent in the here and now. For Suzuki ([1982] 2004: 6–7), the *amupalabdha* (Unattainable or *tathātā*) is "where zero identifies itself with infinity and infinity with zero …." For him, it is "not something that is imposed upon things stringing them together and holding them together from the outside. It is the principle of integration residing inside things and identical with them." For Suzuki, the Unattainable is Spinoza's ([1667] 2000: 3P1CP2 [165–66] and 3P8-12 [171–74]) understanding of God, the nothingness of nothingness that is the creative impetus, and all beings not only participate in this creative impetus, but also, the creative impetus is immanent in all beings. This view is shared by Nishitani Keiji (1900–90) ([1982] 2004: 125), who calls *tathātā* a "field of emptiness (*śūnyata*) or absolute nothingness … which enables the myriad phenomena to attain their true being and realize their real truth."

By grafting Judaic-Christian concepts and reasoning onto the Buddhist debate on existence and nothingness, Suzuki and Nishitani both lean toward a monistic understanding of *tathātā* as the creative impetus or truth. Tanabe Hajime (1885–1962) ([1946; 1986] 2016: 71–73), meanwhile, uses the Buddhist debate to push further Heidegger's notion of Dasein. For Tanabe, "Heidegger terms this sort of 'not' (Nicht) an 'existential nihility' (Nichtigkeit), and considers the nihility of the ground as the fundamental guilt (Schuld) of one's being (Dasein)." He argues that Schuld is best understood as a "fundamental misapprehension of emptiness at that which exists and questions Heidegger's definition of conscience" as the "awakening to consciousness of this guilt" and of "freedom of one's being" as the "resolve to preserve conscience." Tanabe argues that Heidegger "fails to recognize that absolute nothingness" is not an existential nihility, but a "layout of pure relationalities." Thus, Dasein is more properly understood as "being-qua-emptiness," which consists of *ōsō* (going toward) Pure Land (absolute mindfulness). Yet, this going-toward-ness is also a *gensō* (returning from) Pure Land, which has always been there and been concealed by a misrecognition of being as form. Thus, consciousness or *zangedō* (way of repentance) involves care-as-the-way-it-is: caring in form as in emptiness (Fan 2022: 207).

In Hangchow (Hangzhou), Yang Wenhui (1837–1911) (2000: 523–29) considered the Shin Buddhism debate as being founded upon a Euro-American notion of the emptiness of emptiness as a state to be attained or to which the consciousness returns, rather than a process of becoming. Based on the *Mahāyāna śraddhotpādaśāstra* [*Awakening of Faith in the Mahāyāna*, attributed to Aśvaghoṣa (c. 80–150 CE)], he argues that existence and emptiness are perceptually-conceptually different manifestations. When one observes the surface of a lake, one is engaged in movement, which is in turn a manifestation of the time it takes for an avalanche of awarenesses to be informed. Movement consists of originations and extinctions, and therefore, the surface of the lake takes the form of waves. Yet, the self-nature of these waves is water, which is neither becoming nor not becoming. Nonetheless, water (as a self-nature) has no form until it is manifested (as a consciousness)—as movement and time. *Tathātā* is neither existent nor empty, neither not existent nor not empty. In this sense, *tathātā* is not the emptiness of emptiness, but non-emptiness (the negation of emptiness).

Yin Shun ([1950; 2010] 2014: 54–57) argues that Yang's interpretation of the *Awakening of Faith* is based on a neo-Confucian divide between *ātmakatva* (self-nature or ontological ground)/non-emptiness, *lakṣaṇas* (forms)/the *ālaya*-consciousness, and the *adhyavasāya* (function)/the ability of the *ālaya*-consciousness to drive—and be driven by—the formational process. Yang's student Ouyang Jian (1871–1943) argues that such a neo-Confucian ontology in the *Awakening of Faith* proves that the treatise itself is not a translation from a Sanskrit original, but a neo-Confucian invention. For Ouyang, if the Tathāgatagarbha is manifested simultaneously as existence and emptiness, and if the relationality between existence and emptiness drives—and is driven by—karma, karma and the potentiality to generate afflictions must be generated from the Tathāgatagarbha. This means that the Tathāgatagarbha is afflictions-generating. Moreover, Ouyang accuses Yang and the Awakening of Faith of treating the Tathāgatagarbha as a monistic ground that is transcendental. Yang and his student Lü Cheng both argue that Yang's understanding of the Tathāgatagarbha is not only a Taoist inflection, but also a tendency of late-Qing and early Republican (1911–49) scholars' borrowing of Immanuel Kant's notion of the transcendental as a way to translate the untranslatable Buddhist concept into a term and within an epistemology that could converse with modern European thinking (Cheng 1992: 158; Lü 2005: 48:24241–44).

Although the Kyoto school and the Nanking school of debates remained separate, the two groups of scholars were informed about their ideas. The compilation of the *Taishō Tripiṭaka* (Chinese-language Buddhist canon) also enabled both groups of scholars to "rediscover" those original Chinese and translations of Sanskrit and Tibetan treatises on the Tathāgatagarbha that were not included in the 1733 *Qianlong Tripiṭaka*. Thomé H. Fang (argues that Xuanzang's omission of the Tathāgatagarbha debate and the subsequent disappearance of many Tathāgatagarbha texts contributed to an ongoing effort among Chinese-language Buddhist scholars (both in China and Japan) to rely on Taoist and then European knowledges to construct their own understandings of the Tathāgatagarbha (Fang 1978: 1:319–96).

Conclusion: Mistranslation as Production

Thomé H. Fang and many Buddhist scholars in twentieth-century China and Japan, and later on, Korea, Taiwan, and Hong Kong had a tendency to dismiss Chinese scholarship on Buddhism as a wasteful, roundabout, and inauthentic way to conceptualize the Tathāgatagarbha, based on an ignorance of that debate in India from the second to the sixth centuries, and in Tibet afterward. However, if the concept of Tathāgatagarbha is inarticulable and untranslatable into language in the first place, the attempt of Chinese-language scholars to employ super-signs constructed out of a comparative study between Buddhism, Taoism, Confucianism, and European philosophy suggests a potential of translatability for the untranslatable.

For Fang, the very untranslatability of the Tathāgatagarbha enables him to locate an aporia that is often overlooked by both Asian and European philosophers. In Zen, *tathātā* is instantiated as the here and now. The here and now is best understood as a zero point-instant: as the number zero is a sign that is something, which indicates nothing. But then, all points are precisely generated from an instant that is neither an instant nor not an instant, neither not an instant nor not a non-instant (*Lengqie'abaduoluo baojing* 1924–34: §4 [36–45]). Both Stcherbatsky and Fang observe that a comparative reading between Buddhism, Kant, Henri Bergson, and William James would yield a lot of similar conclusions. For Fang (1922: 30–33), Bergson's ([1896; 1939] 2019: 81–146) understanding of consciousness and time is remarkably similar to Buddhism's. However, for Bergson, the present is an instantiation of memories that are re-actualized from the past, and these memories continue to underdetermine the way the consciousness is informed in the future. This idea of the present does not account for, precisely, the meontological point-instant, from which the potentiality to inform is actualized, from one present to another. Fang argues that James's (1890: 2:611 and 629–30) notion of the specious present—a potential present that is actualized as the presentness in our experience—is supposed to address this omission. But James would still maintain that memories from the past will still affect—and be affected by—the future. This, for Fang, is a form of fatalism.[1]

Fang argues that both Bergson and James reduce the present to an interval that is protentionally overdetermined by the past and the retentionally overdetermined by the future, a notion that we can see in the philosophy of Bernard Stiegler ([1994, 1996, and 2001] 2018) today. For him, what is untranslatable in Zen is precisely the present as present (here and now), which is neither part of the flux we call consciousness nor not part of it, the very microperceptual and microtemporal point-instant that is not an instant, from which the potentiality of *tathātā* to disconceal itself is let be, as the way it is.

Note

1 William James refers to (Clay 1882: 151).

Works Cited

Anālayo (2014), *The Dawn of Abhidharma*, Hamburg: Hamburg University Press.

Bhāviveka (1924–34), *Dasheng changzhen lun* [On proving the emptiness of Madhyamaka], vol. 1, in the *Taishō Shinshū Daizōkyō* [*TSD*], ed. Takakusu Junjirō, et al., Tokyo: *Taisho Tripitaka* Publication Association, 30, no. 1578.

Bergson, H. ([1896; 1939] 2019), *Matière et mémoire. Essai sur la relation du corps à l'esprit*, Paris: Presses Universitaires de France.
Bodhi (1995), "Mahā Kaccāna: Master of Doctrinal Exposition," *Wheel Publication*, no. 405/406, Kandy: Buddhist Publication Society.
Chen, G. (2020), *The Annotated Critical Laozi: With Contemporary Explication and Traditional Commentary*, ed. Paul J. Dambrosio and Xiao Ouyang, Leiden: Brill.
Cheng, G. (1992), "Ouyang Jingwu xiansheng de shengping, shiye ji qi Fojiao sixiang de tezhi," [The Life, Career, and Characteristics of His Buddhist Thoughts], *Yuanguang Foxue xuebao* [The Yuanguang Journal of Buddhist Studies], 4 (December): 141–91.
Clay, E. R. (1882), *The Alternative: A Study in Psychology*, London: Macmillan and Co.
Dharmapāla (1924–34), *Dasheng guang* Bailun *shilun* [On the Interpretations of the *Śataśāstra*], in *TSD*, 30, no. 1571.
Dornish, M. H. (1970), "Aspects of D. T. Suzuki's Early Interpretations of Buddhism and Zen," *The Eastern Buddhist*, New Series 3 (1) (June): 47–66.
Dushun (1924–34), *Zhu* Huayan Fajie *guanmen* [Methods of Observing the Dharma Realms According to the *Avataṃsaka Sūtra*, with Annotations], annotated by Fei Xiu, in *TSD* 45, no. 1884.
Fan, V. (2022), *Cinema Illuminating Reality: Media Philosophy through Buddhism*, Minneapolis: University of Minnesota Press.
Fang, T. H. (1922), A Critical Exposition of the Bergsonian Philosophy of Life, MA Thesis, University of Wisconsin, Maddison.
Fang, T. H. ([1974–75; 2012] 2014), *Zhongguo Dasheng Foxue* [Chinese Mahāyāna Buddhism], Beijing: Zhonghua shuju.
Fang, T. H. (1978), "Jiu yuanqi lun tan Zhongguo dasheng Foxue sixiang yanbian guocheng zhong yanzhong de yinan," [On the Most Serious Conundrum in the Evolution of Chinese Mahāyāna Philosophy Based on the Theory of Dependent Originations], in Chang Man-t'ao (ed.), *Fojiao zhexue sixiang lunji* [Anthology of Critical Essays on Buddhist Philosophy], Taipei: Dasheng wenhua chubanshe, 1: 319–74.
Fok, T. (2015), *Liuzu tanjing* [Platform Sutra of the Sixth Patriarch], Hong Kong: The Dharmasthiti Group.
Han, Q. (1998), *Dasheng* Apidamo jilun *bieshi* [An Annotated Anthology of Discourses on the *Abhidharma-samuccaya* (Compendium of Abhidharma) of the Mahayana Faith], Hong Kong: Zhongguo Fojiao wenhua yanjiusuo, authorship attributed to Asaṅga.
Huang, J. ([1999] 2006), *Za ahan jing daodu* [*Saṃyuktāgama*: A Reading Guide], *suttas* trans. Guṇabhadra, Taipei: Buddhall.
Huang, J. ([1999] 2017), *Za ahan jing xuanji* [*Saṃyuktāgama*: A Selection], *suttas* trans. Guṇabhadra, Taipei: Buddhall.
James, W. (1890), *The Principles of Psychology*, New York: H. Holt.
Jie shenmi jing [Saṃdhinirmocana Sūtra, or Sūtra of the Explanation of the Profound Secrets] (2010), trans. Xuanzang, Putian: Guanghua si.

Lengqie'abaduoluo baojing [Laṅkāvatāra Sūtra] (1924–34), *TSD* 16, no. 670.
Liu, L. ([2004] 2006), *The Clash of Empires: The Invention of China in Modern World Making*, Cambridge, MA: Harvard University Press.
Lo, S. (2007), Nengduan jingang borë boluo miduo jing *zuanshi* • Borë boluomiduo xin jing *jianglu* [*Vajracchedikā Prajñāpāramitā Sūtra*: A Revised Edition with Interpretation • *Prajñāpāramitā Hṛdaya sūtra*: Lectures], Hong Kong: The Dharmalakshana Buddhist Institute.
Lo, S. (2008), *Weishi fangyu* [Introduction to Yogācāra Buddhism], Hong Kong: The Dharmalakṣaṇa Buddhist Institute.
Lü, C. (2005), "Qinjiaoshi Ouyang xiansheng shilüe" [A Concise Biography of My Dearest Teacher Master Ouyang], in China Inner Study Institute (ed.), *Ouyang Jingwu dashi jiniankan* [In memory of Ouyang Jingwu], repr. in Guojia tushuguan fenguan (ed.), *Zhonghua Fojiao renwu zhuanji wenxian quanshu* [Complete Collection of Biographies of Figures in Chinese Buddhism], Beijing: Xianzhuang shuju, 48, 24241–44.
Mair, V. H. (2010), "What Is Geyi, After All?," in Alan K. L. Chan and Yuet-Keung Lo (eds) *Philosophy and Religion in Early Medieval China*, Stony Brook, NY: SUNY Press, 2010, 227–64.
Nan, H. (2003), *The Diamond Sutra Explained* [Lectures Given in 1980; Transcriptions First Published in 2001], trans. Hue En (Pia Giammasi), Florham Park, NJ: Primordia Media.
Ñāṇananda, K. ([1971] 2012), *Concept and Reality in Early Buddhist Thought: An Essay on* Papañca *and* Papañca-Saññā-Saṅkhā, Sri Lanka: Dharma Grantha Mudrana Bhāraya.
Nishitani, K. ([1982] 2004), "Science and Zen," in Frederick Franck (ed.), *The Buddha Eye: An Anthology of the Kyoto School and Its Contemporaries*, Bloomington, IN: World Wisdom, 107–36.
Peirce, C. S. (1997), *Pragmatism as a Principle and Method of Right Thinking: The 1903 Lectures on Pragmatism*, Albany: State University of New York Press.
Peirce, C. S. (1998), *The Essential Peirce: Selected Philosophical Writings*, Bloomington: University of Indiana Press.
Puett, M. (2002), *To Become a God: Cosmology, Sacrifice, and Self-Divinization in Early China*, Cambridge, MA: Harvard University Press.
Seager, R. H. (2009), *The World Parliament of Religions: The East/West Encounter, Chicago, 1893*, Bloomington: Indiana University Press.
Sharma, N. (2011), *Kumārajīva: The Transcreator of Buddhist Chinese Diction*, New Delhi: Niyogi Books.
Sishierzhang jing [Sutra of Forty-Two Chapters] (1924–34), trans. Kasyapa Matanga and Dharmaratna, in *TSD* 7, no. 784.
Spinoza, B. ([1667] 2000), *Ethics*, trans. G. H. R. Parkinson, Oxford, UK: Oxford University Press.
Stcherbatsky, F. ([1930–32; 1993] 2008), *Buddhist Logic*, Delhi: Motilal Banarsidass Publishers.
Stiegler, B. ([1994, 1996, and 2001] 2018), *La technique et le temps*, in three volumes, as a single volume, Paris: Fayard.

Suzuki, T. D. ([1982] 2004), "Self the Unattainable," in Frederick Franck (ed.), *The Buddha Eye: An Anthology of the Kyoto School and Its Contemporaries*, Frederick Franck (ed), Bloomington, Ind.: World Wisdom, 107–36, 2–10.

Tanabe, H. ([1946; 1986] 2016), *Philosophy as Metanoetics*, trans. Takeuchi Yoshinori, Valdo Viglielmo, and James W. Heisig, Nagoya: Chisokudō, 2016.

Thompson, J. M. (2005), "Particular and Universal: Problems Posed by Shaku Soen's 'Zen,'" self-published PDF.

Wan, C. (1978), "Guanyu kong you de wenti" [On Emptiness and Existence], in Chang Man-t'ao (ed.), *Fojiao zhexue sixiang lunji* [Anthology of Critical Essays on Buddhist Philosophy], Taipei: Dasheng wenhua chubanshe, 1: 247–56.

Wu, K. ([1995] 1962), *Song Ming lixue* [Neo-Confucianism from the Song to Ming Dynasties], Taipei: Huaguo chubanshe.

Xuanzang (1924–34), *Cheng weishi lun* [Vijñapatimātratāsiddhi or Discourse on the Perfection of Consciousness-Only], in TSD 31, no. 1585.

Yang, W. (2000), *Chanjiao pian* [Interpretations of Buddhism], in *Yang Renshan quanji* [Complete Collection of Works by Yang Wenhui], Hefei: Huangshan shushe.

Yen, P'ei ([1981] 1997), *Fojiao de yuanqi guan* [On the Concept of Dependent Originations in Buddhism], Taipei: Tianhua chuban shiye.

Yin, Shun ([1949; 2010] 2016), *Fofa gailun* [A Basic Discussion of Buddhist Theories], Beijing: Zhonghua shuju.

Yin, Shun ([1950; 2010] 2014), Dasheng qixinlun *jiangji*, [Lectures on the Mahāyāna śraddhotpādaśāstra], *śāstra* Aśvaghoṣa (?), trans. Paramārtha (?), Beijing: Zhonghua shuju.

Yin, Shun ([1952] 2004), Zhongguan lunsong *jiangji* [Lectures on the Mūlamadhyamakakārikā], Taipei: Zhengwen chubanshe.

Za ahan jing [Saṃyuktāgama] (1924–34), in TSD 2, no. 99.

Zhiyi (1924–34), *Mohe zhiguan* [*Great śamatha-vipaśyanā*], in *TSD* 46, no. 1911.

27

Todetita: Facebook's Ontological Malady

(Origin Romanian)

Bogdan Deznan and Andrei Ionescu

Todetita is one of Romanian philosopher Constantin Noica's six "ontological maladies," which he first discusses in a volume published in Romanian in 1978, and translated in English by Alistair Ian Blyth in 2009. Noica distinguishes these maladies from both somatic and psychological pathologies, and describes them as "maladies of a higher order, of the spirit let us suppose."[1] According to him, no neurosis "can explain the despair of Ecclesiastes, the sentiment of exile on earth or of alienation, metaphysical ennui, the sentiment of the void or of the absurd, the hypertrophy of the I, rejection of everything, and empty controversy," just as no psychosis "can explain economic or political turmoil, abstract art, the demonism of technology, and the extreme cultural formalism that nowadays leads to the primacy of empty exactitude." And by contrast to somatic diseases, which have an accidental character, and psychological illnesses, which are "somehow contingent-necessary, because they arise from man's individual and social conditioning, both of which are still accidental," the maladies of the spirit appear to be *constitutive* (Noica 2009a: 29).

In order to define and analyze these "maladies of Being," Noica relies upon both Hegel and Aristotle. From Hegel, he takes an understanding of Being as not having a monolithic but rather a threefold or trinitary character. As Noica explains in what is considered his most important philosophical work, *The Becoming within Being*,[2] the first to fully understand this complexity at the heart of Being was Hegel, who "made avowed recourse to the trinitary model, when he condensed his dialectics, at base his speculation about Being, in triplicacy: *Allgemeinheit*, *Besonderheit* (which represents determinations), and *Einzelnheit*. For Hegel, everything is at base, which is to say in Being, the unfolding of this triplicacy (usually presented defectively as: thesis, antithesis, synthesis)" (Noica 2009b: 169).[3]

As Noica shows, these three fundamental terms of Being can often be unbalanced, leading to a certain "precariousness" of Being and to "great maladjustment[s] of the spirit" (Noica 2009a: 29), which he describes in terms of his six ontological maladies. In naming the maladies, however,

Noica relies on Aristotle's categories for the general/universal (*katholou*), the individual (*tode ti*), and the determinations (*horos*),[4] leading to the following six concepts: *catholită, todetită, horetită, ahoretie, atodetie*, and *acatholie*.[5] The first three maladies can be described in terms of a certain *lack, or deficiency* in achieving the fullness of one of the categories of Being. Thus, catholitis is characterized by a deficiency of the general, todetitis by a deficiency of the individual, and horetitis by a deficiency of determinations. By contrast, the last three maladies, which Noica calls "the maladies of lucidity" (Noica 2009a: 94), consist of *deliberate rejections* of the general (acatholia), the individual (atodetia), or the determinations (ahoretia).

In this article we will focus on *todetitis*,[6] and argue that this term could be fruitfully integrated into media philosophy, particularly in analyzing the nature, functions, and ontological status of social media platforms. We will take Facebook as a case study, and analyze it as a depository of ideality or a set of general determinations, which makes it particularly prone to be described through the concept of todetitis.

A Brief Overview of Todetitis

In *Becoming within Being*, Noica describes todetitis as a crisis of Individuality, caused by the precariousness of Determinations that elevate themselves to Generality (2009b: 270). Once stricken by todetitis, man

> will lack something which we realize from the outset will have to have an essential impact on full Being: the Individual. He will breathe the same air, but it will be an air which is conditional and general, not *this* air, the always particular air of earth; he will feed himself, but with universal substances; he will experience and know things, but these will be essences rather than particular realities; he will take pleasure in looking at a plant, but it will be a greenhouse plant.
>
> (2009a: 30–1; emphasis in original)

In other words, under this spiritual affliction, humans lose touch with concrete, individual realities, and tend to get stuck in abstract thoughts and processes that are increasingly uprooted from "the earth of immediate reality" (2009b: 273).

Noica initially describes todetitis as the "malady of perfection" and employs religion as a first "case study" for painting the "clinical file" of this ontological illness: "In the concept of divine perfection, man's religious awareness has often experienced the suffering caused by not being able to see this concept embodied in anything" (67).[7] But if in the distant past, todetitis emerged from "an awareness of the *incorruptible* and of supreme perfection," in the modern world it springs from "the fainter but much more rigid constancy of the need for rigour and *exactitude*" (80; emphases in original). It now becomes "the malady of the theoretical temperament" (2009a: 67) or "theoretical awareness" (71), which Noica associates "with the highest endeavours, primarily those of cognition" (68).

According to him, the primacy of the General over the Individual brings with it a "primacy of rigour, of exactitude, of mechanistic-rational perfection, beneath which the nonetheless natural being of man risks deregulation through an excess of regulation" (69). It is not surprising then that he draws his favorite examples of (modern forms of) todetitis largely from the sciences, including mathematics and logic (68–9), medicine (70), or biology and evolutionary theory (72, 76–8), and uses this concept to build a harsh critique of "the impasse of scientific culture" (70) that he considers to characterize his contemporary society: "Under the general meanings accredited by the knowledge which we have managed to acquire, the world today becomes one of the laboratory, of the retort, of the transplant, or of artificial satellites and man's colonization of the cosmos, it becomes a world of the planning, controlling and modelling of human destinies" (80). In such a world, humans become "caught up in statistics" and "the monotony of the General" which "transforms any individual endeavour into a general *case* crushes individual situations and destinies" (73; emphasis in original).

Yet, Noica acknowledges that the concept of todetitis should not be limited to images of divine perfection lacking individual incarnation that characterized many pre-Christian religions, or to the quest for rigor and exactitude afflicting the modern, scientific mind, and thus be seen to characterize solely the saint or the savant. In fact, this malady can easily emerge in "the common man" too, "due to the awareness of the *ideal*" (80; emphasis in original), which gives rise to "a condition of excessive ideality" (2009b: 273).

In the following section we will take the social media platform Facebook as a case study, and employ the concept of todetitis in order to describe this medium's nature, functioning, and ontological status. As we will argue, analyzing Facebook through Noica's conceptual lenses can offer us fresh insight into this medium, and open directions for further research about other forms of social media too.

An Analysis of Facebook by Means of Todetitis

With the above considerations in mind, it is now necessary to transition to an illustration of todetitis by means of a concrete example. For this purpose, we have chosen the social media platform Facebook. Noica's theoretical insights will provide the contours of our assessment of Facebook in terms of todetitis.

An initial and mandatory step that needs to be taken concerns the ascertaining of the ontological status of Facebook. This operation will be carried out within the conceptual framework provided by Noica's ontological presuppositions and will thus essentially be circumscribed by the binary opposites of individuality—generality. The goal will therefore be to highlight the peculiarities intrinsic to the mode of being proper to Facebook in order to account for the predominance of generality to the detriment of individuality in the case of this platform.

A defining feature of Facebook is that it is a medium. As such it facilitates the circulation, exchange, and proliferation of information on virtually limitless topics and under various forms. The latter part of this observation points toward a fact that must be readily recognized: Facebook, to the extent that it is a medium for social interaction, always presupposes a pre-given framework that enables and simultaneously determines and organizes this interaction. To be more precise, the medium sets its own bounds in imposing categories (man, woman, married, etc.) and proposing particular modalities of interaction (having to do with the technological support of the medium).[8] If in the former instance the pre-given of the medium was itself preceded by a pragmatic preoccupation with the sphere of the human in order to extrapolate a set of abstract determinations that account for order in the medium, in the latter, the conduits for socializing and communication imbedded in the platform at the same time rigorously establish the parameters for individuality within the horizon of Facebook. That we have considered these two aspects independently should not belie the fact that they presuppose each other and are inseparable, constituting the ultimate ground of possibility for the emergence and proliferation of identities.

Considering what has been stated so far, by employing the lens of Noica's ontology to the case of Facebook we can ascertain this medium's standing with reference to individuality and generality. It should be noted that a major premise of the Romanian philosopher's ontological system is a bifurcation of generality into *internal generality* (Gi) and *external generality* (Ge). For internal generality, Noica favors such synonyms as "structure," "code," "information" in order to convey the notion of a basic, immanent source of order and regularity that always determines the individual when the latter manifests itself. When utilizing external generality, what is meant is a *suspended world* that both precedes and exceeds the individual.[9] Crucially, individuality arises at the intersection of internal and external generality, and is predicated upon a compatibility between the two spheres of the general.[10]

Paradoxically, in the case of Facebook it is this compatibility between Gi and Ge that ultimately prohibits the individual. Yet, how is this interplay between individuality and generality to be construed when referring to Facebook? To begin with, it is worth recalling that Facebook is primarily a medium, and as such receives its intrinsic general determination at the nodal point between two exterior generalities. Indeed, on the one hand, the inner bounds specific to Facebook are set with reference to a pre-given, extra-individual external generality, which is the domain of human social interactions. From this area Facebook extrapolates its interior parameters in terms of identity formation, categorization, and modes of communication (here limitations are set also by the capacities of the underlying technology).[11] External generality functions as a reservoir of determinations that this platform sets for itself. Yet can there be talk of any traces of individuality at this level? The answer depends on what we are willing to assume as individuality. Certainly, to the extent that Facebook is defined by a specific set of parameters which filter and organize the input from the external world, it can be argued that the medium possesses individuality, albeit in a diminished sense. What grants particularity in this situation is the very matrix underlying the possibility, specificity, and functioning of Facebook. However, beyond such a view, it must be stressed that this medium, pregnant with vacuous patterns and categories, thus delimitations, as it is, engenders a virtually infinite number of individualities without ever reaching a definite and exhaustive fulfillment of one or more if its determinations. The medium abstracts its inner structure, thus its interior generality, from the sphere of life and subsequently applies this very framework back on to the world.

This brings us to the second pivotal aspect discernible in our Noician exegesis of Facebook along the lines of generality and individuality. We have already seen that Ge precedes and grounds Facebook in the sense that it provides the platform with an array of general characteristics that together form the very conditions of possibility for the medium. Now it is appropriate to enquire how Facebook, once constituted, interacts with external generality. Consistent with what we have surmised regarding the inner constitution of Facebook, it is rather apparent that in this interaction too, the general predominates. Once Facebook is constituted in its inner being as so many general determinations selectively drawn from the external world, what remains is to offer some clarification concerning the intersection of this platform (as possessing an internal generality) with external generality (potential users and members).

Facebook opens up an array of venues for articulating identities and conducting interaction that are configured in a given way. This internal order partially and mediately reflects an extrinsic order that also confronts Facebook following its inner-constitution. However, in the latter case it is no longer an issue of extrapolating general parameters, but of instantiating individualities. But what does this imply more specifically and what consequences does it entail for the individuality-generality relationship in the case of Facebook?

Firstly, individuality with regard to Facebook unavoidably presupposes an ontological deficiency. This is because regardless of the multitude of determinations and their crystallizations into individual entities, there is also an ontological rest that cannot be overcome. No matter how precise, up-to-date, suggestive a Facebook profile is, it will always fall short in its individuality of the amplitude and inexpressible concreteness of unmediated interaction. This is a border that excludes the possibility of a fully saturated individualization. Consequently, at this level as well, generality seems to come to the fore as most illustrative for Facebook. Individuality in the medium is subject to its strictures and rules, which it cannot exceed by drawing on additional layers of being. Generality on the other hand, seems to be the very condition for the realization of actual instances within the ontological horizon of Facebook, while also setting concrete bounds to what an individual must or can exhibit, thereby facilitating a mitigated notion of individuality.

Ultimately, the classification of Facebook as a concrete instance of todetitis with its corresponding failure to attain individuality also reveals a process of idealization at work within cases of this malady. According to Constantin Noica, idealization exhibits itself when the "reality" of a domain of being is overshadowed by its "potentiality."[12] This is certainly the case of Facebook, where, as we have seen, there is no individuality beyond the implicit general determinations of the platform.

Conclusion

In this article we employed Constantin Noica's concept of todetitis in order to analyze the nature, functionality, and ontological status of the social media platform Facebook. We argued that Facebook can be understood as set of general determinations that cannot find a proper individual fulfillment, and thus remain ontologically deficient. Our analysis has proven that ontological categories such as Noica's can fruitfully be employed in order to better understand not only traditional forms of media such as those discussed by Noica (including literature, painting, music etc.) but also new media such as Facebook.

More interdisciplinary research needs to be done in order to place our analysis into dialogue with contemporary anthropological and sociological discussions of Facebook and of ways in which this medium structures processes of identity-formation, self-presentation, and social interaction (e.g., Zhao, Grasmuck, and Martin 2008; Bouvier 2012; Van Dijck 2013; Gergalou 2018; Ditchfield 2019).

Moreover, further investigations are needed in order to assess whether our analysis of Facebook in terms of a specific type of ontological precariousness could be extended to address the status of other social media platforms such as Twitter, Instagram, LinkedIn, or TikTok. Whether Noica's conceptual framework could be employed to construct a comprehensive ontology of social media is not yet clear, but it undoubtedly deserves further consideration.

Both authors contributed equally to the paper.

Notes

1. Noica's use of the notion of *spirit* relies upon Hegel's concept of *Geist*, which is generally associated with supra-individual factors such as community and culture. See Noica 1980 for his most sustained engagement with Hegel's philosophy.
2. Originally published in 1981 and translated in English by Alistair Ian Blyth in 2009.
3. These concepts of Hegel are usually translated as *universality, particularity*, and *singularity*, as for example in George Di Giovanni's translation of *The Science of Logic* (Hegel 2010). Hegel defines the terms as follows: "Allgemeinheit, Besonderheit und Einzelheit sind abstrakt genommen dasselbe, was Identität, Unterschied und Grund. Aber das Allgemeine ist das mit sich Identische ausdrücklich in der Bedeutung, daß in ihm zugleich das Besondere und Einzelne enthalten sei. Ferner ist das Besondere das Unterschiedene oder die Bestimmtheit, aber in der Bedeutung, daß es allgemein in sich und als Einzelnes sei. Ebenso hat das Einzelne die Bedeutung, daß es Subjekt, Grundlage sei, welche die Gattung und Art in sich enthalte und selbst substantiell sei" (Hegel 1979: 314). See also Lukács 1954 for an insightful discussion of these concepts in Kant, Schelling, and Hegel.
4. Aristotle's discussions of these categories can be found in various of his works, including *Physics, Metaphysics, De Anima, Categories*, and *Posterior Analytics*. For a useful collection of textual evidence from Aristotle's works addressing particularly the notion of *tode ti*, see Corkum (2019: 41–8).
5. In Blyth's translation, *catholitis, todetitis, horetitis, ahoretia, atodetia*, and *acatholia*.
6. For discussions of the Aristotelian notion of *tode ti* see Smith (1921), Yu (1994), and Corkum (2019).
7. As Noica acknowledges, such a description of religion in terms of todetitis might fail to apply to Christianity: "If it has created a historical situation unusual among other religions, Christianity owes this also to the fact that it has had the strength to maintain the individual incarnation of the Deity to the very end. It might be said that the incarnation represents the Deity's gift not to the world but to itself: divine Being was thus able to emerge from the nothingness and lack of identity that was perfection" (67).
8. For a discussion on how users select their identity categories for their self-presentation on Facebook, see Bouvier (2012).
9. Lavric (2005: 270).

10 Ibid.: 200.
11 Questions regarding the nature of identity on Facebook and the ways in which identity is structured by medium-specific forms of social interaction have been addressed by many scholars from a large variety of disciplinary backgrounds; see, for example, Gergalou's book-length study (2018), and several articles including Zhao, Grasmuck, and Martin (2008); Van Dijck (2013); and Ditchfield (2019).
12 Noica (2009b: 274).

Works Cited

Bouvier, G. (2012), "How Facebook Users Select Identity Categories for Self-Presentation," *Journal of Multicultural Discourses*, 7 (1): 37–57.

Corkum, P. (2019), "This," *Ancient Philosophy Today: DIALOGOI*, 1 (1): 38–63.

Ditchfield, H. (2019), "Behind the Screen of Facebook: Identity Construction in the Rehearsal Stage of Online Interaction," *New Media & Society*, 22 (6): 927–43.

Gergalou, M. (2018), *Discourse and Identity on Facebook*, New York: Bloomsbury.

Hegel, G. W. F. (1979), *Enzyklopädie der philosophischen Wissenschaften Vol. 1*, Frankfurt: Suhrkamp Verlag.

Hegel, G. W. F. (2010), *The Science of Logic*, trans. G. D. Giovanni, Cambridge: Cambridge University Press.

Noica, C. (1980), *Povestiri despre om după o carte a lui Hegel*, București: Cartea Românească.

Noica, C. (2009a [1978]), *Six Maladies of the Contemporary Spirit*, trans. A. I. Blyth, Plymouth: University of Plymouth Press.

Noica, C. (2009b [1981]), *The Becoming within Being*, trans. A. I. Blyth, Milwakee: Marquette University Press.

Lavric, S. (2005), *Ontologia lui Noica: O Exegeză*, București: Humanitas.

Lukács, G. (1954), "Die Frage der Besonderheit in der klassischen deutschen Philosophie: Das Problem von Allgemeinheit, Besonderheit und Einzelheit in der Logik und Kategorienlehre bei Kant, Schelling und Hegel," *Deutsche Zeitschrift fur Philosophie*, 2 (4): 764–807.

Smith, J. A. (1921), "*Tode ti* in Aristotle," *Classical Review*, 35: 19.

Van Dijck, J. (2013), "'You Have One Identity': Performing the Self on Facebook and LinkedIn," *Media, Culture & Society*, 35 (2): 199–215.

Yu, J. (1994), "Tode Ti and Toinde in *Metaphysics 7*," *Philosophical Inquiry*, 16 (3–4): 1–25.

Zhao, S., Grasmuck, S., and Martin, J. (2008), "Identity Construction on Facebook: Digital Empowerment in Anchored Relationships," *Computers in Human Behavior*, 24: 1816–36.

Togliere di scena

(Origin Italian)

Lucia D'Errico

Literally translating as "taking out of the stage" with the implication of "un-staging," the Italian locution *togliere di scena* was employed by theater director and actor Carmelo Bene (1937–2002) to designate his own countertheatrical practice. If traditional prose theater is an action of staging ("mise en scéne," or *messa in scena* in Italian) plays that are conveyed primarily through a textual dimension by means of adding elements to the text (diction, action, costumes, scenography, music, etc.), Bene pursues the opposite aim: to subtract, to amputate, to mutilate the text; finally, to take it out of the stage.

My interest in this concept stems from a concrete situation that I, as practicing musician, have been witnessing directly and palpably: the impasse, that is, generated by the clash between the need to relate to today's enormous accumulation and increasing availability of repertoire from the past on the one hand, and the imperative for innovation and novelty that still haunts current rhetorical assumptions around musical and artistic production on the other hand. Not only each of these conditions seems to problematically exclude and segregate the other, but both are also increasingly exposing their own unsustainability. The first condition gives rise to modes of art making rooted in uncritical replication, conservation, or monumentalization of the past, where the past re-produces itself and novelty is considered as undesirable, or at best (and what is even worse) as a cosmetic actualization directed at fostering the audience's hedonistic "involvement" with cultural heritage; the second condition has gradually and almost unnoticeably transitioned from being associated with now growlingly problematic notions of modernism and avant-garde (Agamben 1999a and 1999b; Badiou 2012) toward an even more problematic neo-capitalist imperative for production, no matter how the immateriality and intangibility of such production in an artistic context would seem to mitigate its consumeristic undertones. The rehearsal of Bene's theatrical methods through the concept of *togliere di scena*, and the opportunity offered by the present volume to revitalize such concept in order to put it to use in today's artistic practice and thought, is for me part of an urgent strategy out of this impasse. Bene's practice is a radical move that turns theater on its head, decidedly departing from reconstructive and monumentalizing approaches; and yet, Bene loathes the notions of innovation and avant-garde. As paradoxical as it might sound, his practice's "innovative" charge is all the more explosive as it relates to pre-existing and rather conventional repertoire of prose theater (e.g., Camus, Shakespeare, Wilde, Marlowe, Laforgue, or Byron). Bene is not after the constitution of a novel way of being on stage, or the construction of a new language; his approach is negative, and precisely through this negativity it becomes all the more positive and constructive. Bene needs a form of "re-writing" of the past because he relies on it to ward off, with one single stroke, both reconstruction and innovation.

Simulacra and Minoration: The Outside of Theater

The first target of Bene's practice is faithfulness to the theatrical text as implied in the *messa in scena*. Bene's operation is not oriented toward producing "good copies" of the primary plays he relates to, where "copies" here is an explicit reference to the Platonic theory of ideas, whose theatrical counterpart would be a meticulous and correct enunciation of an original text through the lens of the interpreter's subjectivity. Instead, Bene's operation is oriented toward the *simulacrum*, in the sense indicated by Gilles Deleuze in his first appendix to *The Logic of Sense* as a means to overturn Platonism (2004: 253–66). The simulacrum is a fundamental diversion from the affirmation of the same, based on the production of an effect rather than on the reproduction of an appearance. Bene implements the simulacrum's power through rewriting pieces of classical repertoire in a radically divergent way: instead of relating to the text as an origin to be reproduced over and over, such rewritings *produce* a new (non-written) text, what Bene calls *scrittura di scena* (writing of the scene). The process of *togliere di scena* subtracts and eliminates precisely the centrality of the text as incarnation of the One and the Same, and its operative effect as generative principle of theatrical performances.

Such subtractive approach leads Bene to define his own theater as a "theater of absence" (see Giacchè 1997: 114); and on an explicit level, he does suppress certain identifiable elements from the plays. For example, his *Richard III* has no male characters save for Richard; his *Romeo and Juliet* has no Romeo. At the same time, his understanding of absence is also far from an explicit (we could say all-too-easy) portrayal of absence by means of the poetics of void, silence, or the physical nonappearance of actors or other theatrical elements onstage. All these operations would remain subtractions *within* the theatrical discourse, and therefore still work under the aegis of representation. By contrast, Bene multiplies: he heaps theatrical props, overloads the scenic space, rants in unceasing monologues that leave no room for silence and are often even doubled by pre-recorded voices. But then, how does he pursue absence, what is actually subtracted?

The fundamental gesture of *togliere di scena* is the starting acknowledgment that first of all we have a *scena*, and that such primary *scena* is always already present even *before* the act of staging begins. The *scena* functions as a framing which determines a locus of territorialization, and which therefore traces a boundary between an inside and an outside. It has therefore a selective function, determining what can enter it and what cannot but be left outside of it: first of all, it is a space of power. Thus, in opposing the theater of power and of representation, Bene cannot be content with rearranging what happens *on stage*. He has to take a step back, pursuing the subtraction *of* the theatrical discourse itself. Bene's stagings indicate the possibility of an outside the scene, which can never be represented because it is unrepresentable. He calls this outside *l'osceno* ("the obscene") which through a productive paraetymology becomes the *o-skené*, the outside-the-scene (Bene 2002); that is, a gesture revealing that which cannot be said, shown, and put on a stage because unsayable, or simply unthinkable as belonging to theater. We could reconceptualize the *scena* in Bene's work as an "image of theater," in an acceptation based upon Deleuze's famous formulation of "image of thought" (2000: 94–102; 1994: 129–67): the frame that already dictates a set of assumptions on how thought (or theater in this case) should be conceived, prompting it to operate in certain directions and preventing it from taking others. Reworking such an image, pointing to a space outside of the scene, implies a multiple stance against the traditional theatrical logic of representation, where plays (and the theatrical past with them) are reproduced, reconstructed, repeated.

If we take for good what Salvoj Žižek in his book *Event* (2014) phrases as the quintessential philosophical act, namely "a change of the very frame through which we perceive the world and engage in it" (n.p.), then Bene's theater is first and foremost philosophical. It is not incidental that in the short text dedicated to Bene's theater, "One Less Manifesto," Deleuze goes so far as to state that Bene's plays are "critical essay[s]" (1997: 239) on the original plays they depart from, therefore making his activity "inseparably creative and critical" (241). Through a process that is eminently artistic and concretely situated, Bene questions and problematizes the traditional function of the actor, of theater, and of the theatrical past, constituting a theoretical reflection through practice. When Deleuze writes, "this critical theater is a constitutive theater. Critique is a constitution" (239), he is proposing a vision of the theatrical and artistic space as the eminent locus for an act of theoretical reflection and active problematization. It is through this creative/critical posture that Bene manages both to break free from pre-given codes (the text) and to suspend pre-given territories (theater as representation and as spectacle). Theatrical performance is then what remains when the primary play is subtracted: the expression of a futural afterlife of the play, the deployment of its otherwise dormant virtualities.

Deleuze defines the ensemble of Bene's practices of subtraction as the "minor treatment" (243) of the primary play. In opposition to the movement ascending to the major (magnification), he proposes an opposite direction toward *minoration*, which consists in individuating elements of power and subtracting them both from what is represented in the theatrical event (in the scene) and from the representational operation of theater itself (outside the scene). "Magnifying" the play consists of extracting a unifying vision or practice out of the motley and incongruous elements that constitute the heterogeneous humus of theatrical practices—and of life practices, we could say. For Deleuze, magnification amounts to the play's (or the author's) "normalization" (243), that is, to their insertion into a stabilized grid of codification, institutionalization, territorialization—all of which are elements that concur with the mechanism of representation. As a means to break away from representation, Deleuze phrases Bene's practice as a "becoming-minor" of the theatrical play, and of theater performance itself. Deleuze uses the concept of "minor" (which appeared for the first time in a collaborative text that he wrote with Félix Guattari, *Kafka: Towards a Minor Literature* [1986]), with extreme specificity. Importantly, minoration has nothing to do with statistic minority, nor with the representation (again) of a conflict between the power of the major and a minority trying to upheave it. It is insoluble from a process of becoming, while "majority designates the power or weakness of a state, of a situation" (Deleuze 1997: 255), and therefore relates to a state of being.

Phoné and Writing

The hypersaturation through which Bene pursues the *togliere di scena* passes through a fundamental and central component: sonic emission. Sound, meant as a substance characterized by infinite variation and utter unknowability, is designated by Bene as the *phoné*. The use of this word should not lead into false assumptions: while the immediate reference for this term appears to be

Jacques Derrida (1997), Bene explicitly rejects interest in the philosophical usage of the word. Actually, the meaning (or rather, non-meaning) he assigns to this term goes in the opposite direction from Derrida's, for whom the primacy assigned to phonic substance (or phonocentrism) epitomizes the voice of the logos, which would lie at the core of the metaphysics of presence. The contrary is rather the case: for Bene sound becomes a subtractive force, entertaining a paradoxical relationship with the text: while sound generates in and through text, it can only relate to text in a friction, as a remainder or excess that manages to jeopardize the textual while being inextricable from it. The *phoné* is the tool through which the "abyss between the written and the oral" (Bene 2013: 79, translation mine) is exacerbated, rather than the bridging that would happen in traditional theatrical practice through the means of diction and correct voice emission. The materiality of performance, the subverting force of the *phoné*, is a rebellion to the "already said" of mediation and interpretation. In this respect, Bene could not be farther away from a metaphysics of presence, pursuing absence—again, the *togliere*, and not the *mettere*.

Bene explores the extreme materiality of the voice, its guttural, demented, involuntary levels (not seldom bordering on the groan, the whisper, the scream, the cackle). But his most powerful vocal strategy is perhaps not so overt, namely what he himself describes as *parlarsi addosso*. The translation of this Italian locution deserves a short detour. Literally meaning "to speak onto oneself," it is often used in the figurative sense of "loving to hear oneself talk," designating vain verbosity or self-indulgent use of jargon. However, such locution also hints to base bodily activities (as would be used in *pisciarsi addosso*, "to piss in one's pants," or *piangersi addosso* "to cry onto oneself," referring also to self-pity). *Parlarsi addosso* indicates both autistic self-referentiality, and at the same time an involuntary, usually unpleasant dribbling of physiological liquids on one's own body. Both these undertones are important to understand Bene's technique and strategy. *Parlarsi addosso* means articulating sound not in order to communicate (which again would be a representational technique), therefore short-circuiting into the actor's autism language's pretense to be actually able to convey any meaning at all. And it also means to spill, to drool the unpleasant and disturbing remainder that oozes through the fissures of language: that which language is not (and which disturbs us). This is why perhaps the most fitting definition of Bene's *phoné* would be "that which is not" (the distance with Derrida's understanding of the term could not be more evident: for Derrida, the *phoné* would be what metaphysically "is").

The *phoné* is therefore a strategy that counters the selective mechanism of the *scena*: while the scena promotes or excludes elements by framing or unframing them, proceeding to align them to each other in the perfect and well-wrought apparatus of representation, the *phoné* emphasizes the caesuras between what is being said and the physical act of saying it, between text and sound, between sound and meaning, between the theatrical characters and their material embodiment. The *phoné* is the strategy for engendering a break, a split, a disturbance, and therefore a destabilization of the text that ultimately leads to its dissolution. The materiality of the voice fights against writing, against the text, against the internal concordance of the relations, even fights against itself—presented, often in the form of playback, as an echo or as a delay. *Parlarsi addosso* is achieved with the use of head resonators, bones, stomach, introjecting the voice's sound in the cavities of the body instead of projecting it in the space between the actor and the audience. And (again paradoxically) this subtraction of diction and of vocal magnification happens also through amplification: in this case, technical and physical amplification with the use of microphones. Shortening the space between the point of sonic emission and its projection surface, the microphone becomes a technology for allowing a microscopic space of non-communication to occupy and saturate the whole theatrical dimension. At the same time, this gesture diminishes (again, subtracts) the declamatory self of the actor, and emphasizes his automatic, involuntary, and uncontrolled multiple selves. Introjected in bones and flesh or pulverized into sheer electricity, the body of the actor is dissociated and prevented from coalescing into a consistent identity (the carefully concocted creation of a character by traditional actors).

The Operator as Macchina Attoriale

We have seen how Bene deploys the *phoné* to short-circuit the separation between text and stage. This strategy is reverberated on a further level through the transformative process that Bene enacts from actor to *macchina attoriale* (actorial machine) or *operatore* (operator). Here Bene addresses yet another classical separation, namely the political division of labor between text (author) and its enactment (actor), which traditionally requires the mirroring of a mutual recognition and communication between the two sides. For Bene, both text and enactment have then to be incorporated within a single role. It is not enough to be a "great actor," even if this remains a fundamental premise; the "great actor" has to take the courage to step beyond himself. What the *macchina attoriale* produces is first of all innumerable selves: Bene is a reader, a translator, an actor, and a *capocomico*, he decides on lighting, music, amplification, regie, and scenography. The crucial aspect of this multiplication of roles is its happening *onstage*, saturating every possible subject position in the theatrical space. The fact that Bene expresses himself through several media (as filmmaker, as writer, as poet, as cinema actor) is only an accidental (and per se almost irrelevant) effect of such transition from actor to *macchina attoriale*. This plethora of roles is far from corroborating each other to constitute a sort of ultimate super-actor, or to engender a *Gesamtkunstwerk* (what would be the paramount act of magnification and therefore of normalization of the work of art). All these roles rather step on each other's toes; as Bene would have it, one has to find strategies to stumble, to create handicaps for oneself (Bene 2002).

The *macchina attoriale* and the *phoné* are linked in the same method of subtraction: the actorial machine is what "remains" of the actor through the passage of dissolution he undergoes in the materiality of the *phoné*. The implementation of an apparatus profoundly nourished by extensive extra-theatrical devices or experiences (electronic amplification, music, cinema, television, etc.) does not point toward a multidisciplinarity that would try to enliven the theater of the past through the *actual* or the *quotidian*, supposedly drawing it closer to the tastes and understanding of today's audiences. Rather, it is again the construction of an absence, and if it does something to modern audiences it is exposing them to the impossibility of relating neutrally, as it were, to the historicity of plays from the past. Audiences live on their skin the sense of a separation, of a dissociation, of a missed communication whose target is again the Same and the One of a supposedly neutral recognizability and capture.

Bene therefore does not reassemble or recompose material from past repertoire in a cynical pastiche strategy, nor does he "add literature to literature" (Deleuze 1997: 239–40), nor again does he pursue the reduction of the caesura of writing by inscribing his own presence into the scene—what would happen through improvisatory practices, or theatrical experiences where the "reality" of the actor is staged. Bene rejects first of all that such a "reality" exists, because that would again imply a sameness between oneself and "a self" (Bene here would agree with Lacan's famous saying: "if a man who thinks he is a king is mad, a king who thinks he is a king is no less so" [Lacan 2006: 139]). Through the operator, the "great actor" is continuously displaced. Displaced toward the work and out of himself, not a *soggetto* (subject) anymore, enacting and acting on the work, but *soggetto* (subjected) to the work's external array of virtual forces, not "playing it" but being played by it (again the *macchina*: the operator is automatic, involuntary). As Giacchè phrases it, the actor now is not free *to do*, but is freed *from doing*: suspended, "exposed to his own thoughts, that will not belong to him but will possess him [...] as visions" (Giacchè 1997: 17, translation mine).

Conclusion: Futures for a Concept

If every de-framing implies the closure of a re-framing, we are constantly faced with the strenuous, joyous task of questioning the images of thought—or images of theater for that matter—arising from the ashes of the ones that have been challenged by our predecessors, however painstakingly. The task for today's artists and thinkers presented with the "toolkit" of Bene's concepts of methods cannot be their replication, but rather the breeding of possible futures out of them. Bene's *togliere di scena* employs specific and situated strategies, strategies that by now have in turn become historical, thus adding up to the reservoir of past "repertoire" at our disposal. But there is more than that to it: this concept invites us to rehearse the necessarily always different interrogation of the space that we reserve for our past in the present time. More than in indicating a possible way for relating to the past, the future of this concept lies in its exposing the very possibility of *a* different relation. It lies in its reminding us that the "outside" of the present time is not necessarily either the utilitarian and futuristic "new" or the archival reservoir of the "old," but that it can be the futural, diagrammatic deployment of the virtual forces that are always already *present* in what we regard as our *past*. To the reader and appropriators of this toolkit, be they artists, thinkers, listeners, scholars, I wish the ever-new discovery of how to become machinic operators of such virtual forces.

Works Cited

Agamben, G. (1999a), *The Man without Content*, Meridian, Crossing Aesthetics, Stanford, CA: Stanford University Press.

Agamben, G. (1999b), *The End of the Poem: Studies in Poetics*, Meridian, Crossing Aesthetics, Stanford, CA: Stanford University Press.

Badiou, A. (2012), "Art and Philosophy," in Joseph T. Tanke and Colin McQuillan (eds), *The Bloomsbury Anthology of Aesthetics*, New York; London: Bloomsbury, 601–12.

Bene, C. (2013), *Sono apparso alla Madonna*, 4th edition, Milan: Bompiani.

"Carmelo Bene." (2002), *Fuoriorario cose (mai) viste*, Raitre, Rome.

Deleuze, G. (1994), *Difference and Repetition*, trans. Paul Patton, New York: Columbia University Press, First published 1968 as *Différence et repetition* (Paris: Presses universitaires de France).

Deleuze, G. (1997), "One Less Manifesto," in Eliane Dal Molin and Timothy Murray (trans.), *Mimesis, Masochism, and Mime: The Politics of Theatricality in Contemporary French Thought*, Timothy Murray (ed.), Ann Arbor: University of Michigan Press, 239–58. First published 1979 as "Un manifeste de moins" in *Superpositions* by Carmelo Bene and Gilles Deleuze (Paris: Minuit), 85–131.

Deleuze, G. ([1972] 2000), *Proust and Signs*, trans. Richard Howard, London: Athlone Press, First published 1964 as *Proust et les signes* (Paris: Presses universitaires de France), Translation first published 1972 (New York: G. Braziller).

Deleuze, G. ([1990] 2004), *The Logic of Sense*, trans. Mark Lester, Charles Stivale, Constantin V. Boundas (eds), London: Continuum, First published 1969 as *Logique du sens* (Paris: Minuit). This translation first published 1990 (New York: Columbia University Press).

Deleuze, G., and F. Guattari (1986), *Kafka: Toward a Minor Literature*, trans. Dana Polan, Minneapolis: University of Minnesota Press, First published 1975 as *Kafka: Pour une littérature mineure* (Paris: Minuit).

Derrida, J. (1997), *Of Grammatology*, trans. Gayatri Chakravorty Spivak, Corrected ed. Baltimore: Johns Hopkins University Press, First published 1967 as *De la grammatologie* (Paris: Minuit).

Giacchè, P. (1997), *Carmelo Bene: Antropologia di una macchina attoriale*, Milan: Bompiani.

Lacan, J. (2006), "The Mirror Stage as Formative of the *I* Function as Revealed in Psychoanalytic Experience," in Bruce Fink (trans.), *Ècrits*, New York: Norton, 75–81. Essay first delivered as a paper in 1949. Book first published 1966 as *Écrits* (Paris: Seuil).

Žižek, S. (2014), *Event: A Philosophical Journey through a Concept*, Brooklyn, NY: Melville House.

29

Ubuntu: Be-ing Becoming (Capable of Being Affected)

(Origin Nguni language group)

Chantelle Gray

Only an affected being can question, which presupposes that it can above all be called into question by its affection.

(Stiegler 2013a: 120)

Two specters are haunting Earth in the twenty-first century: the specters of ecological catastrophe and automation.

(Frase 2016)

Personal and societal need for the biosphere and the cosmos can hardly be overstated in the Ubuntu perspective.

(Chuwa 2014: 18)

In *Uncontrollable Societies of Disaffected Individuals*, Bernard Stiegler laments the ubiquity of disaffected individuals in our contemporary societies of hyper-control, which is to say persons no longer capable of being affected. He attributes this to the reduction of the *totality* of life to consumption so that even individuation and transindividuation processes—the processes by which we become—are "short-circuited by marketing and advertising," effectuating a collective disindividuation in which there "is no longer any '*we*'; there is only the '*they*'" (Stiegler 2013b: 86). For Stiegler this transformation is provoked especially by digital technologies, the progeny of industrialization which placed "*cultural control* at the heart" of its processes, thus rendering culture—and specifically media culture—"a strategic function of industrial activity," starting with radio and television which were effectively allocated to marketing (2011: 4-5). With the advent of the computer, new globally integrated forms of marketing, consumption and governmentality would emerge, aided in particular by the juncture of five major developments in recent history, namely the proliferation of data and data gathering; the development of deep convolutional networks of algorithms deployed for the analyses of data through processes such as pattern recognition; vast improvements in processing power and networks for the instantaneous or near-instantaneous and low-cost transmission and analyses of data; advancements in data storage options; and improvements in hardware (Bratton 2015: 111; Kalpokas 2019: 2–3).

It was Gilles Deleuze who pinpointed the computer as the specific machine associated with what he termed "control societies." Grappling with the convergence of cybernetics and capitalism, Deleuze proposed that Foucault's disciplinary societies, characterized by enclosed spaces that operate according to a logic of molding or form-imposition—the school, the barracks, the university, the factory—had begun to stratify as societies of control, where the predominant logics were no longer that of molds and surfaces but of modulation and self-regulation (1992: 4). It is worth noting here, as Yuk Hui has, that modulation is not used consistently in Deleuze's oeuvre. In *Difference and Repetition*, for instance, modulation is used to "resist the idea of moulding, which has been central to Western ideas of the relationship between form and materiality at least since Aristotle," and which is typical of hylomorphism that "understands being in terms of form and matter, conceived as absolutely distinct categories" (Hui 2015: 76). In other words, modulation is used here to denote an intensive variation or flux in a metastable system. Deleuze, drawing on philosopher Gilbert Simondon, who himself drew on theories of thermodynamics, thus understands both the contingent "structure" and becoming of the individual not in terms of ontological dimensions, but in terms of ontogenetic processes or phase-shifts between at least two disparate states. Modulation, here, is the response to a disparation or tension, where the disparateness forms the primer for individuation, a partial and relative resolution to a prior tension or *problematique*. Modulation, which "operates in terms of *disparation*," thus replaces Aristotle's hylomorphism, which "operates dialectically" as "form+matter=synthesis" (Hui 2015: 77; see also Simondon 2009: 10 and Deleuze 1994: 246). We see, then, that modulation, in the sense that it is used in *Difference and Repetition*, takes on a positive valence because it gives us information about how ontogenetic processes function and how they can give rise to genuinely novel forms of thought and experience.

In his essay on the "Postscript on the Societies of Control," however, Deleuze begins to grapple with the manner in which digitization transforms modulation itself—a process described by Stiegler in terms of the short-circuiting of at least three operations: ontogenetic processes of individuation, sociogenetic processes of transindividuation and epistogenetic processes of knowledge production and transmission across and between generations. The first short-circuit is described by Deleuze as the transfiguration of persons into banks of information for marketing and data mining, which is to say the transformation of individuals into *dividuals* (Deleuze 1992: 5). In effect, ontogenetic individuation processes are disrupted or reticulated through automations, reconfiguring individuation as individua*lization* and *dividuation* in which subjectivity is either contracted narcissistically, actuating a neurotic condition in which the collective is denied, or bypassed entirely so that the individual becomes reduced to a "collection of infra-individual data" that are "recomposed at a supra-individual level under the form of a profile" (Rouvroy and Stiegler 2016: 11, 12). Concomitant to such disruption of psychic or individual individuation by automation is that of society, in the sense that the synthesis of collective or social memory—which aids the production of shared horizons and social practices of collective meaning that carry across the passage of time—is interrupted. In other words, processes by which collective secondary retentions, or inter- and transgenerational knowledges, are interiorized are systematically and systemically replaced by digital and automated systems that themselves become the material for circuits of transindividuation.

As is the case with many of his concepts, Stiegler adopts "transindividuation" from Simondon to philosophically explain the passaging of life as recurrent phase-shifts, but whereas individuation refers to a partial and relative resolution to a prior tension in the individual, *transindividuation*—as the term implies—resides *between* the "I" and the "we" in a procedure of co-individuation, transforming both "through one another" (Stiegler and Rogoff 2010). When, however, the explicit construction of social memories becomes automated vis-à-vis digitization, the metastabilization of our time-consciousness and collective future expectations are disrupted and reticulated because transindividuation is transformed into *cyberindividuation*, marked by concurrent processes of automation and disindividuation. Modulation thus takes on a negative valence in the Postscript.

For Stiegler, it is not automation *per se* that is a problem—all societies, individuals, and even cells deal with sets of automatisms which, in fact, are the basis of life. "A biological cell, for example, is a sequence of instructions and this sequence of instructions is automatic. The reproduction of life is automatic. When you have something that is not automatic, it is a mutation, which produces a monster" (Stiegler in Nony 2015: 16). The problem, then, lies rather with the way in which *digital* automations "short-circuit the deliberative functions of the mind" (Stiegler 2016: 25), thereby instantiating dividualizing or disindividuating processes which, for Stiegler, unlike Simondon, is not a neutral operation that forms part of all individuation processes but implies, on one level, the short-circuiting of individuation (ontogenetic) and transindividuation (sociogenetic) processes and, on another level, the proletarianization of knowledge—the loss of work-knowledge (*savoir-faire*), life-knowledge (*savoir-vivre*), and conceptual knowledge or, to put it differently, the short-circuiting of epistogenetic individuation processes (Stiegler 2016: 164). This loss of knowledge provokes a veritable becoming-unreasonable of the world because as the "real" becomes increasingly replaced by *algorithmic reason*, noetic life is automated and reticulated, inducing a loss of reason, and reasons for living. The shift to digital automation, as we see here, is not merely technical for Stiegler, meaning a transition from analogue to digital, but *organological*, a question of life; that is, of the cosmos and the living subject.

It is here that we find a curious link to *ubuntu*, a Nguni term translating as "personhood" or "humanness," but which denotes African ontology, epistemology, and ethics. Originating in the Zulu language, with the equivalent *batho* in the Sotho language, *ubuntu* "consists of the prefix *ubu-* and the stem *ntu-*," evoking "the idea of be-ing in general" (Ramose 2003: 271).

Ubu- or "enfolded be-ing," which is to say preindividuated being, is always "oriented towards unfoldment" or individuation, the manifestation of "itself in the concrete form or mode of ex-istence of a particular entity" (Ramose 2003: 271). Ontologically speaking, the separation between *ubu-* and *ntu-* is formal rather than literal and denotes the co-constitutive enfoldment of what Deleuze might call the virtual (pre-individual field of multiplicities) and the extensive (the actual and actualized). But the movement from *ubu-* to *ntu-* is also the movement from ontology to epistemology, from "be-ing becoming" to be-ing knowing. This sympoetic emergence is, moreover, not restricted to individual selves because it immediately implicates transindividuation processes with *communalism* and *interdependence* as core values of *ubuntu* (Kamwangamalu 2008: 115–16) but also, I want to suggest following Magobe Ramose and Simondon, as a *metastable condition* of "be-ing becoming" anchored in and oriented by an epistemological coupling to the maxim *umuntu ngumuntu nga bantu* (*motho ke motho ka batho*), meaning "to be a human be-ing is to affirm one's humanity by recognizing the humanity of others and, on that basis, establish humane relations with them" (Ramose 2003: 272).

Generally, *ubuntu* is associated with the individuation of persons and the social being from which emerges a knowledge of how to live an ethical life. Thus, it is often described as a "humanistic ethic which in its articulation" is aimed at countering any conduct that is dehumanizing (Murove 2014: 37). John Mbiti argues accordingly that *ubuntu* is grounded in the maxim "I am because we are" which he opposes to the Cartesian adage "I think, therefore

I am" (Mbiti 1970: 141). Properly speaking, though, *ubuntu* surpasses a concern with human dignity and even the human as such because it is, more substantially, occupied with cosmic harmony and wellbeing. "The interactive and symbiotic interrelationship between living beings and between the biosphere and the cosmos is fundamental" to both understanding and actualizing *ubuntu* (Chuwa 2014: 60). One finds, for example, that *ubuntu* is closely related to *ukama*, a Shona word meaning "relationship or being related," but which is also "based on the totemic system whereby" people see themselves tenanted to a natural species or animal, "thereby instilling a sense of belonging to the wider environment" (Moruve 2014: 44). Humans, therefore, "have duties and obligations to provide good stewardship, treasure and safeguard their environment for the current and for future generations as a matter of ethics" (Chuwa 2014: 88). Correspondingly, *ubuntu* is connected to three dimensions of life: the dimension of the living (*umuntu*), the dimension of those who have passed from this life (the ancestors), and the dimension of those who are yet to enter into it. Since two of these levels pertain to that which is unseen and unknowable, emphasis is placed on the preservation and recognition of *u-nkulu-nkulu*—that which is ineffable, indefinite, and indescribable (Ramose 2003: 278). Together, these cosmological assumptions imply a dimension of *ubuntu* "that surpasses anthropocentricism" and point to an organological account of life involving not only organic but also inorganic matter (Murove 2014: 43).

Although *ubuntu* is associated with the inorganic, it is neither commonly nor theoretically aligned with technology—at least not beyond the Linux open-source operating system.[1] There is, however, some use in alloying the two concepts because there exists, as should be clear by now, a number of overlaps between work on *ubuntu* and Stiegler's media theory, informed by Simondon's work on technology and individuation. To be clear, the process of alloying, as I use it here, draws on Deleuze's understanding thereof according to which two or more heterogeneous series are placed into continuous variation so that there "is a succession of operations, but each operation is as if bounded by determinable thresholds, and in a given order" (Deleuze, Parnet and Pinhas 1979). Alloying *ubuntu* and technology is thus not an attempt to change the meaning/s of *ubuntu*, but to create an encounter between the two concepts in the hope that it prompts the beginnings of a response to what Peter Frase calls the two specters of the present day in his book, *Four Futures: Life After Capitalism* (2016), namely the ecological crisis and automation, which have provoked extensive disindividuation processes that have themselves triggered the disaffection of individuals. Our contemporary crisis is, accordingly, not only about immanent Anthropogenic doom and automation, but also about their effects—perhaps especially about their effects, such as the poverty in the capacity to be affected and the attendant capacity to then think about how and why we have become disaffected.

We have already seen that in Stiegler's work, as in *ubuntu*, the individual is not given in advance but marks, rather, a *passage*, a relation of negotiation between the "I" and the "We," but also between the "I," the "We" and the cosmos which, in the contemporary mode of modernization is co-imbricated with globalization—which is not merely technological, but digital and automated—and the Anthropocene, the ongoing ecological catastrophe. For Stiegler, this is best viewed as a pharmacological situation or transitional period during which we encounter the *pharmakon*—that which is at once a remedy and a poison. What determines which of these immanent conditions becomes amplified depends on our attention to and care of it. Here it becomes obvious why the algorithmic and ecological *pharmaka* have become destructive: because of a lack of attention and care, by which Stiegler means a "rational form of care" that maintains reason through the "formation and training of deep attention" aimed at the production of long circuits or inter- and transgenerational knowledges and practices (2013a: 22). When *pharmaka* are not carefully attended to, individuation process are disrupted, effectuating disindividuation which amounts to "a destruction of the social body itself," in turn engendering "disaffected psychic and social individuals," "ruining their affective capacities" which, essentially, amounts to a question of ethics because it pertains to the disintegration of "knowledge of the abode"— "that which gives me my place within the circuit of affects through which the process of psychic and collective individuation constitutes itself" (Stiegler 2013b: 7–8). Far from simply managing the effects of a pharmacological encounter, a society, for Stiegler, must become capable of adopting the new situation by *inventing* "new ways of life" and "*reopening* the indetermination of a future" (Stiegler 2011: 12). *Ubuntu*, as be-ing becoming—individually, socially, epistemically, and ethically in a cosmological mode—speaks to this experience of equilibrium and non-equilibrium or, to put it differently, to the synthesis and metastabilization of our time-consciousness. Ramose holds, in fact, that the "logic of *ubu-ntu* is distinctly rheomodic in character. It is the logic of and for the preservation of be-ing as a whole-ness" (2003: 275). From this perspective, *ubuntu* connotes the technics—or technology and techniques—of being, where technics is not opposed to culture as both are immediately a question of being and a function of ontogenesis for the preservation and perseverance of be-ing as wholeness. *Ubuntu* is, as such, a cosmopraxis that can teach us to pay *attention* to and *take care of* our contemporary pharmacological situation beyond the "technical fantasies of planetary 'deterritorialization' of the species and colonialization of the solar system" (Viveiros de Castro and Hui 2021: 400). I want to suggest, though, that it is not only a cosmopraxis, but a *cosmotechnics*—a technics of be-ing becoming according to which "all technics are fundamentally cosmological and all cosmologies are fundamentally technical," though not in a universalizing or essentialist manner but, instead, as a question of locality that "implies multiple epistemologies and epistemes which can contribute to reflection on the development" and co-imbrication of technology and the ecological (Lemmens 2020: 5).

Returning here to Ramose's argument that *ubuntu* is a logic of and for the preservation of be-ing as a whole-ness, we find a link with an authentically Spinozist concept, namely the tendency to persevere in being, closely connected with his understanding of affect and which I want to link, in closing, to Stiegler's concern for disaffected individuals. What does it mean to persevere in being? For Deleuze, reading Spinoza, simply for something to "to realize its power of action" (Deleuze 1980)—to become capable of being affected and affecting the world in turn, thus taking care of the pharmacological situation and, in so doing, "creating a passage to the act of a genuine possibility of sublimation through the reconstitution of the life of the spirit, that is, an industrial but ecological economy of cognitive and affective functions forming a new civilizational model on the basis of a reorientation of our contemporary industrial reality" (Stiegler 2013b: 126).

Note

1 See https://ubuntu.com/

Works Cited

Bratton, B. H. (2015), *The Stack: On Software and Sovereignty*, Cambridge and London: MIT Press.

Chuwa, L. T. (2014), *African Indigenous Ethics in Global Bioethics, Interpreting Ubuntu, Volume 1*, London and New York: Springer.

Deleuze, G. (1980), "Seminar on Spinoza: The Velocities of Thought, Lecture 4, 16 December 1980," *The Deleuze Seminars*, https://deleuze.cla.purdue.edu/seminars/spinoza-velocities-thought/lecture-04-0 (accessed July 17, 2021).

Deleuze, G. (1992), "Postscript on the Societies of Control," *October*, 59: 3–7.

Deleuze, G. (1994), *Difference and Repetition*, trans. P. Patton, London: Athlone Press.

Deleuze, G., C. Parnet, and R. Pinhas (1979), "Metal, Metallurgy, Music, Husserl, Simondon," *Web Deleuze*, February 27. https://www.webdeleuze.com/textes/186 (accessed July 5, 2021).

Frase, P. (2016), *Four Futures: Visions of the World after Capitalism*, London and New York: Verso (e-book).

Hui, Y. (2015), "Modulation after Control," *New Formations*, 84 (84–5): 74–91.

Kalpokas, I. (2019), *Algorithmics Governance: Politics in the Post-Human Era*, Switzerland: Palgrave Macmillan.

Kamwangamalu, N. M. (2008), "Ubuntu in South Africa: A Sociolinguistic Perspective to a Pan-African Concept," in M. K. Asante, Y. Miike and J. Yin (eds), *The Global Intercultural Communication Reader*, London and New York: Routledge, 113–22.

Lemmens, P. (2020), "Cosmotechnics and the Ontological Turn in the Age of the Anthropocene (Editorial Introduction)," *Angelaki*, 25 (4): 3–8.

Mbiti, J. (1970), *African Religions and Philosophy*, New York: Doubleday.

Murove, M. F. (2014), "Ubuntu," *Diogenes*, 59 (3–4): 36–47.

Nony, A. (2015), "Bernard Stiegler on Automatic Society as told to Anaïs Nony," *Third Rail Quarterly*, 5: 16–17.

Ramose, M. B. (2003), "*Ubuntu* Philosophy," in P. H. Coetzee and A. P. J. Roux (eds), *The African Philosophy Reader*, London and New York: Routledge, 270–80.

Rouvroy, A. and B. Stiegler (2016), "The Digital Regime of Truth: From the Algorithmic Governmentality to a New Rule of Law," trans. A. Nony and B. Dillet, *La Deleuziana*, 3: 6–29.

Simondon, G. (2009), "The Position of the Problem of Ontogenesis," *Parrhesia*, 7: 4–16.

Stiegler, B. (2011), *The Decadence of Industrial Democracies, Disbelief and Discredit, Volume 1*, trans. Daniel Ross and Suzanne Arnold, Cambridge: Polity Press.

Stiegler, B. (2013a), *What Makes Life Worth Living? On Pharmacology*, trans. D. Ross, Cambridge: Polity Press.

Stiegler, B. (2013b), *Uncontrollable Societies of Disaffected Individuals, Disbelief and Discredit, Volume 2*, trans. D. Ross, Cambridge: Polity Press.

Stiegler, B. (2016), *Automatic Society, Volume 1: The Future of Work*, trans. D. Ross, Cambridge: Polity Press.

Stiegler, B. and I. Rogoff (2010), "Transindividuation," *e-flux*, 14. https://www.e-flux.com/journal/14/61314/transindividuation/ (accessed June 14, 2020).

Viveiros de Castro, E., and Y. Hui (2021), "For a Strategic Primitivism: A Dialogue between Eduardo Viveiros de Castro and Yuk Hui," *Philosophy Today*, 65 (2): 391–400. https://doi.org/10.5840/philtoday2021412394

Uri (우리 [uri]): Sound and the Porous Self
(Origin Korean)

Suk-Jun Kim

Uri (우리 [uri]): *Korean pronoun.*

1) A first-person plural used to refer to both the person who speaks and the other who listens, or several people including the speaker and others who listen.

2) A first-person plural used to refer to many people including the person who speaks and others who are not senior to the speaker and with whom the speaker is engaged.

3) (used in front of some nouns) a word used to show to someone who is not senior to the speaker that the person who speaks is in a close relationship with someone else.

A Small Confusion, or the Problematic of the Collective Aural

I remember many supervisions with my students in composition where we take pain in explaining and understanding what their composition is supposed to do; how they should sound when played to an audience and how the audience would experience it. The strange thing is that this pain of the students explaining about the piece and that of my understanding of what they mean continues even after we listen to the said piece of composition. After all, we heard the same piece, the same aural phenomenon, at the same time and in the same place; still there is so much we do not agree, so much in the piece about which we do not think we understand each other. At least, it seems clear, despite that we can acknowledge our *temporal and spatial togetherness* of the experience, we are not sure if we are listening to the same things in the piece.

The difficulty and confusion in talking about our aural experiences of a sound event, let alone highly structured aural phenomena like a piece of composition, is common and widespread like an innocuous ailment. My interest in this symptom has grown over the years for various reasons, and in this article, I will examine two words (or conceptions that they connote or engender) that confuse our discussion of what we hear, which are important for us to access the key problematics of the collective aural. I will then discuss the problems of language in our attempts to share aural experiences and form the collective aural, and finally I will invite us to consider *uri* to probe, in "we-ness" of *uri*, a tacit inclusiveness or a being-together in a shared experience which I will compare with what Žižek calls "a parallax view" (Žižek 2006).

Audience as a Non-Binding, Futile Construct for the Collective Aural

One of the problems in the discourse of the collective aural has to do with a construct which pre-configures the discourse of the aural and sets it in motion: *the audience*. What is peculiar about the audience in this context is that its configuration (at least when it is initiated) is not separate or distant from those who are engaged in the discourse. Quite to the contrary, this audience includes you and me, or rather, you and I are an integral part that seeds the emergence of the audience; we *are* the audience. A quick survey of literature on sound will demonstrate this inclusiveness of the audience. When Smalley invites us to his "personal listening experience" of a nightly soundscape over a window in his house, focusing on source-bonding sounds and their spatial zones that overlap, nest, and combine with each other, and gestural and sweeping sounds that engender a model for what he terms *space-form*, a spatio-mophological model in acousmatic listening for enacted, spectral, and perspectival spaces (Small 2007), it is clear that we are the audience in this soundscape, beautifully rendered by Smalley's careful and extensive sonic diary. The vantage point he places himself to listen from is mine and yours, and listening, however imaginal, is collective. When Norman writes in *Noise Example ONE* where she discovers that "[t]*here is a noise at the end of the track*," besides her who is caught up with the noise, I am also standing in the audience, listening *together* to the last track of the CD due to the faulty CD writer on her computer (Norman 2004: 144). When I was writing that "I hear the sound of short and long inhaled and exhaled breaths" in Paul Koonce's electroacoustic composition *Out of Breath*, I was of course inviting, and expecting, you, the reader, to join me to this listening (Kim 2010: 47). In aural discourse, we all are the audience.

The question is, why is then that the audience becomes increasingly perceived to be a third party, and that talking about it alienates you and me, us, and threatens to sabotage our discourse of the collective aural? One possible answer is because the audience for (and to) us today is always already a social, political, aesthetic, and, perhaps, imaginary construct that has emerged amid the advancements of information technologies married with consumerism and fetishized individualism at its another height, aptly coined as "I-Culture" by Dyson (2009). As a result, the audience loses its collective aurality. As soon as we enunciate it, it loses you and me, and consequently, it becomes a meaningless, futile object that does not bind us together anymore. We still imagine and perhaps also dream of an audience as a collective, but it really is a mixture of each and every hearing/listening subject who has lost the power of experiencing the aural collectively; caught in this conception of audience now, we all listen individually. It is thus not only convenient, but natural for us not to bring *us the audience* to the core of the discourse of the aural, but to hang it somewhere so that we can all acknowledge its existence without even bothering to mention it necessarily.

Tyrannical Workings of the Hearing|Listening

The other problematic in the discourse of the collective aural that I would like to examine is hearing|listening. Here "|" sits between the two words to denote the inconceivable, but forcefully implemented—the tyranny of language and all that it subjugates (!)—cut to the aural. In western philosophical considerations of sound, the relation between hearing and listening has often been taken rather crudely where, it is thought, hearing involves less attention of the self who is engaged in the act than listening does. It follows that once such an act is taken either aesthetically (as in acousmatic/electroacoustic music, for example) or ethically (as in acoustic ecology, for example), hearing, often placed to be less significant than listening, is an incomplete act that needs to be ushered into the latter.

As a composer and sound artist for whom English is a second language, I have been particularly and increasingly frustrated by this division of hearing and listening. At first, it seemed casual and harmless, and even useful, to have two different words. We can use "hear" when we perceive a sound, and "listen" when we attend to it. But giving priority to listening over hearing normalizes the break and engulfs the gap between the two. In Korean, in comparison, there is only one word for the act of hearing|listening: 듣다 [tɯt͈a]. The same verb is conjugated to indicate when a sound is heard: 들리다 [tɯlʎida]. But the act is linear with no break between the two.

This forceful division of the single, linear act is further performed by Pierre Schaeffer, a prominent example as such, with his four modes of listening—*ouïr, entendre, ecouter,* and *comprendre*—where the self's engagement with the aural is compartmentalized based on the "intentional noetic act" of the self (Kane 2016: 27). While logical in its approach, this formulation, as shown in the case of Schaeffer, assumes that the self in each stage can also be logically compartmentalized. More crucially (as I think it is devastating to the discourse of the collective aural), it isolates the self to the aural from whomever they may be sharing it together with by promoting and aestheticizing or moralizing listening over hearing. Nancy writes of the isolation of the self in listening:

> To be listening will always, then, be to be straining toward or in an approach to the self (one should say, in a pathological manner, *a fit of self*: isn't [sonorous] sense first of all, every time, a *crisis of self*?).
> (Nancy 2007: 9)

But this isolation of the self is not what Shaeffer had initially intended. Rather, his whole project had aimed at "conveying to others how to listen to *musique concrète*" by "articulat[ing] that 'special state of mind' [nurtured by reduced listening] and instill it in others" (Kane 2016: 26). In other words, he wanted to share the experience of his listening with others, which is not only the core of the discourse of the collective aural, but what I think composing really means. But the method he instructed, in effect, was to cut up the act into a schema of four planes—subject|object|abstract|concrete—under the crude division of hearing|listening, and to drive the self into the lonely act of listening—there is this stern, didactical voice that orders us, *LISTEN, not just hear!* It seems that, in reduced listening, there is no *us*, as it promotes each subject's individual listening mode and does not allow for the happenstance of hearing that we all do unconsciously but that cannot be grasped and dissected to parts and planes.

A similar didactical tone of the voice can be heard from R. Murray Schafer's project on acoustic ecology. I often wonder why I feel that, despite the apparent care for one's hearing in the world, Schafer's listening seems aggressive.

> When the soundwalker is instructed to listen to the soundscape, he is audience; when he is asked to participate with it, he becomes composer-performer. In one soundwalk a student asked participants to enter a store and to tap the tops of all tinned goods, thus turning the grocery

store into a Caribbean steel band. In another, participants were asked to compare the pitches of drainpipes on a city street; in another, to sing tunes around the different harmonics of neon lights.

(Schafer 1993: 213)

Here, the split between hearing|listening appears less forceful than Schaeffer's, but still, it is ever-present. More so, when Schafer says of hearing, I think he really means listening, and when he means of listening, what he really means is to seek things out by ear and make them aural. Thus, Schafer's listening is always active, issuing outward from the self. His famous *Ear Cleaning* is an act of seeking out silence: "Stop making sounds for a while and eavesdrop on those made by others" (Schafer 1993: 208). But when he shows how it is done in NFB's *R. Murray Schafer: Listen* where he says, "What happens if my voice stops; what do you hear then?" as he moves closer to an old movie project, turns it off, and holds up a small placard, which reads *Listen* (NFB 2017:00:04:14 - 00:05:03), the awkwardness I am experiencing from this theatrical act is not only (or necessarily) because it is "challenging and even frightening" as Schafer argues his way of listening should be; it is because I feel such a transition is unnatural. I have been listening all along, and now Schafer in the video stops the movie projector (which was making wonderful sounds to listen to by the way), stops talking, and asks me to listen, and I wonder, what else was I doing just then?

Difficulties in Considering the Collective Aural

To return to the difficulty in talking about what we hear, perhaps this may have to do with the language we are destined to use to communicate. Language, or any communicative utterances for that matter, is not well suited for us where our goal is to share our experiences from what we hear. Predominantly visual-oriented and object-based (or thing-based) both in what many words point to or depict (or fail to do so; see Olsen 2010; Olsen 2013) and in how these words are structured to mean anything, language, written or spoken, often fails us in elucidating our aural experiences; *they are perpetually confounded in language*. Hence some (composers and sound artists, for example) choose not to be engaged at all in this unending cycle of the meaning-making operation; others see significance in it, not necessarily because they hope it will shed any light on our experiences, but because they want to let emerge potentialities of this operation that would form an assemblage of other related experiences; in other words, they see language as a tool not for meaning-making operation, but for experience-making one. Many so-called lectures by Cage may be examples of such an operation (see Cage 1961; Kim 2018). For now, let us examine the symptom of the confounding.

This confounding, at first, is understandable because there are no readily available visual signposts which our discussion can refer to when needed. At best, there are representations of sound and of aural experiences, but even when we may be able to say that we can see what we hear, what we are possibly seeing is that of which we hear, not what we hear (see Nancy 2007: 10). It is not only the visual that is absent from and causes the peculiarity of the discourse of aural experiences. The discourse is littered with futile and empty desires, as we attempt to articulate to what we mean, where we mean, how we mean. It never solidifies into something visible, tangible, or tactile, which Cox terms "the ordinary ontology," determined "by the sense of sight and touch." The shadowy existence of the aural experiences leads him to consider "a very different sort of ontology and materialism" of sound that will "provoke us to modify our everyday ontology and our common sense of conception of matter" (Cox 2017: 101). Moreover, sound will have already passed us and so will its effect, though lingering for a while, by the time when we try to speak of it. All this is because our experiences of the aural exist solely in time. Neither to be seen, to be able to be spoken of nor to be stopped even for a while, they, though real, never seem to be able to be shared.

On the other hand, and here I can only project, perhaps this confounding is inescapable, and even desirable because it may be one of the ways (perhaps the only way) in which we are just able to relate to, but not to become one with, those experiences of the aural; that is to say, every effort, including (and *especially*) those which are through language, in accessing and sharing them with others will *need to* lead not to clarity, but to the *thickening of the experiences*. But this is merely a projection for now because, in order for it to be meaningful, I'd need to show you that aural experiences are *resonators (those which return to themselves)* of the unconscious that are always via language. But I am not yet prepared to explore this idea sufficiently in this article. Instead, let us return to the potential of the collective aural and examine how it could be possible despite the difficulties above, which I hope will give us a sideways glance at that idea.

Porous Self in *Uri* and Its Parallax Listening

If our aural experiences cannot be shared (or can be shared but we are suspicious of what we share), why then do we want to share them at all? For Szendy, the act of listening not only carries a sense of responsibility, "a *you must*"; but it also, and because of this *you must*, leads to one's desire for shared listening because without it, there is no listening at all:

> *To listen to oneself listening* (if that were possible) ..., to fold listening onto itself and onto oneself, isn't that also risking not hearing anything anymore of what is available to be heard, isn't that *becoming deaf*? ... The listener I am is nothing, does not exist so long as you are not there. ... The listener I am [*que je suis*] can happen only when I follow you [*je te suis*], when I pursue you. I could not listen without you, without this desire to listen to you listening to me, not being able, since I am unable to listen to me listening.
>
> (Szendy 2008: 142)

Without you, according to Szendy, listening cannot take place; otherwise, the self's listening is folding back to the self, "neither to a proper self (I), nor to the self of an other, but to the form or structure of *self* as such, that is to say, to the form, structure, and movement of an infinite referral [*renvoi*], since it refers to something (itself) that is nothing outside of the referral" (Nancy 2007: 9). Instead, Nancy points out, "to be listening is thus to enter into tension and to be on the lookout for a relation to self," where this relation is not to "'me', (the supposedly given subject), or to the 'self' of the other (the speaker, the musician, also supposedly given, with his subjectivity), but to the *relationship in self*" (Nancy 2007: 12). The question is, then, what is this "you" (for Szendy) or "self" (for Nancy) that is in tension, in relationship in listening? Here I would like to briefly examine a Korean word, *uri* (우리 [ʊri]) for a possible answer.

Those who do not speak Korean may find the use of *uri* strange. Besides its main function as a first-person plural pronoun (i.e., *we* in English), *uri* is often used in verbal conversation as a substitute for "my." Even as a plural pronoun, it may include or exclude those who listen to the speaker, depending on the context and the speaker's intention. In other times, *uri* is used to express intimacy and empathy toward the listener(s). Often called "we-ness" (Choi and Choi 1994), the sense of a being-togetherness or a *tacit* inclusiveness among people (both the speaker and those who listen to the speaker, and even those who are there or not there, those named or unnamed) is deep in Korean psyche. On the other hand, while the notion of the self is common in Western society, there is no equivalent concept of the self in Korean. Although it is often translated as "Jagee (自己 in Chinese characters, *Na* in Korean vernacular), which literally means 'one's own body'" (Park and Han 2018), the translation does not carry the same concept of the self in the west.

This absence of the western concept of the self and the deeply rooted collective "we-ness," of which the usage of *uri* is a telling example, open up the possibility of another self who has no clear boundary against others, a porous self that is us, you and me, the audience, in listening to the collective aural. With its tacit inclusiveness, *uri* as a porous self prepares us for what Žižek calls the *as if* or the *leap of faith* in the collective aural, which, Žižek argues, is required for the emergence of shared meaning in language. The subjects can only break the deadlock of the chain of the endless referral in language "by simply taking for granted, presupposing, acting *as if* we *do* mean the same thing" because "[t]here is no language without this 'leap of faith'" (Žižek 2006: 241). We can also posit that the porous *uri,* with its being-togetherness in a shared aural experience, may allow us to stand on neither of the presupposed hearing|listening planes or of the individual|collective aural planes, putting into practice a *parallax listening*, a term taken from the "parallax view," which is an "in between stance" termed by Kojin Karatani (Žižek 2006: 231). Just as the parallax view is exercised to "assert the antinomy [in the precious Kantian sense of the term] as irreducible ... conceive the point of radical critique not as a certain determinate position as opposed to another position, but as the irreducible gap between the positions themselves, the purely structural interstice between them" (Žižek 2006: 232), the parallax listening rejects the short-circuiting or the synthesis of the hearing|listening or of the individual|collective aural planes, and opens a "new dimension that emerges in the gap" (Žižek 2006: 234) between the aural (the phenomenal)|sound (the noumenal) where we *uri* can listen together.

Works Cited

Cage, J. (1961), *Silence Lectures and Writings*, Middletown, CT: Wesleyan University Press.

Choi, S. C., and Choi, S. H. (1994), "We-ness: A Korean Discourse of Collectivism," in *Psychology of the Korean People: Collectivism and Individualism*, Seoul, Korea: Dong-A Publishing & Printing.

Cox, C. (2017), "Sonic Thought," in B. Herzogenrath (ed.), *Sonic Thinking: A Mediaphilosophical Approach*, New York, NY: Bloomsbury Publishing USA, 99–110.

Dyson, F. (2009), *Sounding New Media: Immersion and Embodiment in the Arts and Culture*, Berkeley, Los Angeles and London: University of California Press.

Kane, B. (2016), *Sound Unseen: Acousmatic Sound in Theory and Practice*, New York, NY: Oxford University Press.

Kim, S. J. (2010), "Imaginal Listening: A Quaternary Framework for Listening to Electroacoustic Music and Phenomena of Sound-images," *Organised Sound*, 15 (01): 43–53.

Kim, S. J. (2018), *Humming (The Study of Sound)*, New York: Bloomsbury Academic.

Nancy, J. L. (2007), *Listening*, trans. C. Mandell, New York: Fordham University Press.

NFB. (2017), *R. Murry Schafer: Listen*, April 4, https://www.youtube.com/watch?v=rOlxuXHWfHw (accessed July 1, 2021).

Norman, K. (2004), *Sounding Art: Eight Literary Excursions through Electronic Music*, Aldershot, UK: Ashgate Publishing.

Olsen, B. (2010), *In Defense of Things: Archaeology and the Ontology of Objects*, Lanham, MD: Rowman Altamira.

Olsen, B. (2013), "Reclaiming Things: An Archaeology of Matter," in Carlile, P. R., Nicolini, D., Langley, A. and Tsoukas, H. (eds), *How Matter Matters: Objects, Artifacts and Materiality in Organization Studies*, Oxford: Oxford University Press, 171–96.

Park, J., and Han, G. (2018), "Collectivism and the Development of Indigenous Psychology in South Korea," in W. W. Li, D. Hodgetts and K. H. Foo (eds), *Asia-Pacific Perspectives on Intercultural Psychology*, New York, NY: Routledge, 53–74.

Schafer, R. M. (1993), *The Soundscape: Our Sonic Environment and the Tuning of the World*, Rochester: Destiny Books.

Smalley, D. (2007), "Space-form and the Acousmatic Image," *Organised Sound*, 12 (1): 35–58.

Szendy, P. (2008), *Listen: A History of Our Ears*, trans. C. Mandell, New York: Fordham University Press.

Žižek, S. (2006), *Interrogating the Real*, ed. R. Butler and S. Stephens, London and New York: Continuum.

"Utbrytningsdröm": Swedish Audio-Visual Expressions of a Desire for Leaving Far

(Origin Swedish)

Andreas Jacobsson

French film critic, film historian, and film maker Jean Béranger (1924–2000) devoted a major part of his scholarly career to documenting Nordic and Swedish cinema, and particularly the famous Swedish film maker Ingmar Bergman. In both his auteur study *Ingmar Bergman et ses films* (1959), and his exposé over Swedish film history *La grande aventure du cinéma suédois* (1960), Béranger describes one of Ingmar Bergman's early career films, *A Ship Bound for India* (*Skepp till Indialand*, 1947), as fully absorbed by "l'Utbrytningsdrömmen" (218).[1] *Utbrytningsdröm* is a concept he found untranslatable into French with sufficient precision. The concept, according to Béranger, captures "a desire to escape your destiny and leaving far" ("désir d'échapper à son sort, en partant au loin") (218). The suffix "-dröm" in Swedish is generally translated into "dream" or "wish" in English, but is here translated to désir into French (that will say "desire" in English). By not performing a literal translation into French, Béranger signals that something culturally specific is at stake in this form of dream.

The story in the film *A Ship bound for India*, is telling about Johannes, a young man (Birger Malmsten) that lives in the shadow of his abusive and alcoholic father, Captain Blom (Holger Löwenadler). Supported by his submissive mother Alice (Anna Lindahl) he endures his everyday life up to a certain point. All three family members are dreaming of a radical life change: Captain Blom is gradually going blind—he dreams of living a different "fuller" life with another, younger woman in the form of the cabaret artist Sally (Gertrud Fridh), that he also brings to live together with him and his family. Blom has, without his family's knowledge, rented an apartment as his own personal refuge where he from time to time can completely disappear and dream about breaking away far. Alice's dream is focused on the life she thought she would have had together with a loving husband, but was ultimately denied. Her dream of breaking free is quite different from that of her husband, but still an utbrytningsdröm from her everyday life, that has imprisoned her existence. Johannes is dreaming of breaking free from his father's firm and destructive grip, and strives for living an independent life far away, but also in finding meaning in romantic love. The social pressure has taken the physical form of a lump in the back of his neck, and Johannes is regarded as a hunchback.

By bringing Sally into the family circle Captain Blom introduces a catalyst that activates the utbrytningsdröm for all involved parties. For Blom, Sally is the one he imagines will help him to break free from his current life and family. For Johannes, Sally becomes an object of romantic and sexual attraction, driving a final wedge between him and his father when Sally accompanies him to a deserted island and they make love in an abandoned light house. For Alice, the young rival motivates her to speak frankly about her own personal utbrytningsdröm with her husband—regardless if his mind is impervious. For Sally, being brought into the conflict-ridden and emotionally charged family circle is for her a potential way out at the same time as it is a dead end. Blom has to fulfill his dream before he loses his sight and it becomes too late to for him to break away. His desire for change drives him to try to murder his son, and when his utbrytningsdröm crumbles—try to commit suicide. Ultimately Blom, Alice, and Sally fail to realize their dream, only Johannes actually breaks away (and go far away) by going to sea on a commercial ship.

In the only substantial published study that focuses on *Ship bound for India*, Hugo Wortzelius (1947), characterizes the central motif in the film as striving for belonging and finding a way in life to move past loneliness and anguish. A motif he stated was on the rise both in Sweden and in other film cultures in Europe. He regards Bergman as the central Swedish artistic interpreter of this motif (229). Wortzelius never mentioned the concept "utbrytningsdröm" in his article, but he captures a similar sentiment as Béranger by quoting the following line from the dialogue in the film: "It is better to leave and never find your way back, than not move at all" (author's translation of the Swedish original, "Det är bättre att ge sig iväg och aldrig hitta tillbaka än att inte röra sig ur fläcken"). Wortzelius interpretation of the motif is that there is a dissonance between a stifling reality and the characters' individual dreams of another and different life, a dissonance he connects to the somber sentiments permeating the post-war context in the Swedish society and in Europe in general.

Béranger (1959) approaches the concept from a different film historical angle than Wortzelius. He discovered Bergman while he was in Sweden, but he watched several of the films in Paris after coming back from Stockholm. As a French film critic Béranger had developed a sensibility for detecting a clear affinity between Bergman and the pre-war French noir films by auteurs such as Jean Renoir and Marcel Carné. Béranger highlights that Bergman found his inspiration in films with mainly Jean Gabin in leading roles—as *The port of Shadows* (*Le quai des brumes* 1938), and *Daybreak* (*Le jour se leve* 1939). An aspect that clarifies the connection between Bergman and the French noir genre is that the films take place in the vicinity of harbors and open water. The water ways are opening for far away travel and establishes a sense of fluidity and constant movement in the depictions. The desire in Bergman's utbrytningsdrömmar can thus be described as mirrored in a nautical metaphor of constant motion, this is to be found in a variety of early Bergman films, as *Summer Interlude* (*Sommarlek* 1951) and *Summer with Monika* (*Sommaren med Monika* 1953). There is a "becoming" depicted in these films representing the life of youthful breaking away juxtaposed with an established idea of the Swedish society as on the one hand a secure "People's home" and a bourgeoning welfare state, and on the other hand as a stifling social structure restricting youthful expressions. Enmeshed in the Nordic darkness the brief summer months provide an opening for experiencing freedom for the young protagonists.

Comparing the utbrytningsdröm in *A Ship Bound for India* with the French Noir films it is possible to argue that there is a connection by the focus on the fine line between the destructive vis-à-vis the productive power of romantic liaisons. For example, Bergman scholar Birgitta Steene has discussed the motif and Bergman's inspiration from French film noir. She highlights that young couples are "sometimes predestined/.../to remain outsiders in society, sometimes finding strength in their relationship to face members of established society, and always yearning for freedom of their own ..." (Steene 1995: 150). However, it is a predominantly male perspective promoted by these films.

Toward a Definition of Utbrytningsdröm

A number of international critics and researchers from different linguistic backgrounds—French, English, German, Italian, and Spanish—have picked up on the relevance for applying the concept of utbrytningsdröm in relation to specifically Bergman's films (e.g., Cowie 1992; del Río Kuroiwa 2004; Steene 1995; 2005; Chiesi 2018), but also as a common motif to be found in the Swedish cinema of the 1940s. For example, according to the British film historian Peter Cowie (1992) the concept captures, "the quintessential Nordic desire to escape—what Swedes calls the *utbrytningsdröm*" (134). But besides framing a filmic motif in a specific time of film history, the concept is tacit and vaguely presented, mentioned by the film critics and researchers as a taken for granted concept that Swedes use to describe a desire to break away. However, utbrytningsdröm is not a concept that is frequently used in contemporary colloquial Swedish. Rather it is connected to a specific era and can thereby initially be considered as a predominantly film historical concept describing a certain motif in Swedish cinema. Often referring to, but not exclusively to, films by Ingmar Bergman.

The pertinent question that arises then is if, how and for what purpose the concept still is meaningful to use in a contemporary film and media philosophical context. By taking a closer look at the specific utbrytningsdröm in *A Ship Bound for India* it is more radical and multifaceted than the depiction of the youthful summer outings in the other two Bergman films mentioned above. A key to defining the concept is found in the film's original Swedish title, which captures both the idea of an unspecified location somewhere far away and different, and an old-fashioned exoticist way to talk about India as an oriental place with the term "Indialand"—rather than the regular term for the actual geographical location of India, that the slightly misleading English translation implies. In relation to this, utbrytningsdröm can be defined as a strong desire to leave everything behind, to break free from all social structures and relations, and travel (by sea) to a location somewhere unspecified and radically different. It is not then the same thing as escapism in the sense of fleeing from reality, but rather a desire of drastically and completely replacing one's own social reality.

In light of this discussion, utbrytningsdröm can be defined as a "relational" concept that operates on three different levels simultaneously: 1) as a film historic Swedish motif describing a relational tension between the individual and the social environment, 2) as a cultural-historical aspect in relation to the common-sense idea of Swedish national culture, or so-called Swedishness, 3) as intercultural and intertextual audio-visual encounters from a Swedish perspective.

A factor that connects the three different levels of the definition is how the perceived "untranslatability" of the concept points in the direction of relations and movement, rather than to a culture-specific static aspect of national culture. As French philosopher Barbara Cassin has presented and problematized the idea of untranslatable concepts in the *Dictionary of Untranslatables: A philosophical Lexicon* (2014), they are capturing an ongoing process of constant translation and negotiation between languages (and cultures): "An untranslatable is not what one doesn't translate but what one doesn't stop (not) translating" (2016: 243). This entails that the Swedishness depicted by the concept is in constant motion and therefore changes over time and context and requires repeated negotiation. Utbrytningsdröm is then relevant to activate as an audio-visual heuristic of Swedishness, rather than a factual description of a cultural trait.

The reproduction of discourses of national cultures has for a long time constituted the common sense of how film history has been written (although this tradition has been thoroughly criticized the last decades, it is still prevalent). The intercultural aspect of utbrytningsdröm open for a retrospective problematization of this tradition in relation to Swedish cinema—already Ingmar Bergman was negotiating his filmmaking with inspiration from the French noir films, but he was reminded by his producer Lorens Marmstedt that inspiration and negotiation are quite different from imitation: "You have to remember that Birger Malmsten is no Jean Gabin and you are *most definitely* no Marcel Carné" (author's translation of the Swedish original) (1990: 132). The Swedishness depicted in *A ship Bound for India* and the other early Bergman films, that the characters desire to break away from consist of an idealization of individualism. This idealization includes striving for political and social consensus and a love for nature and leisure time.

In reality this was an idealization of what could best be described as a middle-class life (Frykman and Löfgren 1987). The stifling social structures that the utbrytningsdröm is a reaction toward are hence connected to a class hierarchy that presumably had been eradicated in the rational social democratic consensus society—a tangible absence producing emotions of alienation and anxiety that transcends the immediate post-war sentiments for individuals that were feeling out of place. This second cultural historical aspect of the utbrytningsdröm uncovers a political layer of meaning, clarifying that the concept is permeated with contextually situated ideological tensions. Not the least in relation to collective societal structures and individual aspirations for breaking away and fulfilling "myths of personal success stories" (Sjögren 1976: 73).

The ideological tension is a connecting bridge between the second and third aspects in the definition of the concept. These two aspects depend to a high degree on each other and are often very hard to separate. Interculturality in the sense of describing interactional processes of diversity is rarely neutral. It is rather more relevant to regard interculturality as an inherently ideological concept (Dervin and Jacobsson 2021). With this updated definition of utbrytningsdröm, the concept's relevance is expanded from describing a film historical motif to a concept for thinking about Sweden as a contemporary intercultural society. Film scholar Olle Sjögren has introduced the idea that it is possible to understand the "maturity" of the utbrytningsdrömmar of a generation by analyzing their relations with other audio-visual cultures (1992: 50). Following Sjögren, in addition to discussing utbrytningsdrömmar as relations between film cultures in the terms of interculturality and intertextuality, it is possible to argue that the concept also is applicable to analyze intergenerational differences (in the Swedish society), and how tensions between ideas of Swedishness, class, and interculturality are depicted in contemporary films. Approaching audio-visual depictions as documents to think with utbrytningsdrömmar, in different times and contexts, can be treated as cultural symptoms opening for new ideas of how to analyze a process of constantly moving fluid Swedishness.

Two Contemporary Examples of Audio-Visual Utbrytningsdrömmar

Approaching utbrytningsdrömmar from the perspective of contemporary audio-visual culture is to direct one's attention to a very different society in comparison with 1940s post-war Sweden. The reasons for breaking away and the focus of the dreams have shifted drastically. The most interesting utbrytningsdrömmar are now primarily found in films depicting the demographically altered, multicultural society that Sweden has developed into since the era of work migration in the 1960s–1980s, and a continuing migration with among others a large number of refugees coming to Sweden during the last decades. The Swedish society is now unquestionably multicultural, with approximately a quarter of the population of so-called foreign decent.[2]

Two examples that are particularly illuminating regarding depictions of updated versions of utbrytningsdrömmar are the film, *Eat Sleep Die* (*Äta sova dö*, Gabriela Pichler 2012) and the television series, *Snabba Cash* (2021). Both these examples display a clear connection between the desire to break away and a renewed understanding of class as partly an issue of intercultural relations in a multicultural society. In *Eat Sleep Die* the main protagonist Raša (Nermina Lukac), a young working-class woman of Bosnian decent take pride in being the fastest packer of salad in the factory. When the company is downsizing its workforce Raša is laid off. Her whole sense of self-worth and her identity is connected to being a skilled and conscientious worker. She is living with her father who has health issues and therefore only able to work intermittently. The film is depicting everyday life in the south of Sweden from a working class as well as a migrant perspective in a "documentary" rhapsodic style of filming. The societal restraints she is trying to break away from are an alienating rigid social welfare system out of touch with time that fails to provide any help in her search for work. The working-class environment portrayed in the film is filled with people from a variety of cultural and linguistic backgrounds, the common denominator is their strive for employment—either keeping the job they already have, or trying to find a new one. The utbrytningsdröm is here articulated as a tension between the individual and the collective, being an outsider equals being unemployed. In series av sequences Raša try out creative strategies for finding her own way out of her social predicament.

The tv-series *Snabba Cash* (a spin-off of a trilogy of popular fiction films) depicts the effects of a hyper-segregated metropolitan area in Stockholm, where breaking away for the people living in the outskirts of the city consists of either turning to criminality and dealing drugs or crossing the huge gap to the established society mainly reserved for the majority Swedes. A young woman, Leya (Evin Ahamd) on the verge of realizing her business venture and transcending the border to the established hyper-individualized business world, is constantly dragged back by old friends and family. She has to perform a very intricate social balancing act constantly orienting between gang murders, her criminal boyfriend and the highflying entrepreneur supporting her business ideas.

These two utbrytningsdrömmar of the contemporary generation of audio-visual expressions focuses on the desire of strong independent young women aiming to break free from their subordinate position in a society where class and cultural backgrounds are gradually becoming more and more important, at the same time as it is also gradually becoming harder to distinguish. Raša and Leya are expressing two very different utrbytningsdrömmar, but they have both in common that breaking away far is no longer represented by some unknown "exotic" location you reach by transoceanic ships. For many young people categorized as outsiders in multicultural societies the distance they have to traverse cannot be measured in kilometers. The only way to realize their utbrytningsdröm, which here just as well could be rephrased as "breaking into," is to completely replace their social reality.

Both these audio-visual expressions are also clear examples of the impurity and fluidity of film history by entering in audio-visual dialogue with in the case of *Eat Sleep Die* different "neorealist" filmic traditions and in the case of *Snabba Cash* Nordic and Global Noir genre expressions, in a similar manner as *A Ship Bound for India* (and for that matter countless other films) the intercultural aesthetical aspect of the concept utbrytningsdröm undermines static assumptions of cultural specificity. Even though there is a counterforce of cultural essentialization in *Snabba Cash* with the portrayal of the outskirts of Stockholm as inherently destructive environments.

From this perspective utbrytningsdröm is still a relevant concept to use to think with films for understanding the Swedish society—connecting and clarifying distinctions between different generations of Swedes, demographic and ideological shifts, and intercultural relations.

Notes

1 The Swedish term utbrytningsdröm is the indefinite form singular. In the text the indefinite form plural utbrytningsdröm*mar* and the definite form singular utbrytningsdröm*men* are also used.
2 The definition of foreign descent in Sweden is: an individual that is either born abroad or born in Sweden with both parents born abroad.

Works Cited

Béranger, J. (1959), *Ingmar Bergman et ses films*, Paris: Le Terrain Vague.
Béranger, J. (1960), *La grande aventure du cinéma suédois*, Paris: Le Terrain Vague.
Béranger, J. (1968), *Le nouveau cinema Scandinave*, Paris: Le Terrain Vague.
Bergman, I. (1990), *Bilder*, Stockholm: Nordstedts.
Cassin, B., Apter, E., Lezra, J., and Wood, M. (eds) (2014), *Dictionary of Untranslatables: A Philosophical Lexicon*, Princeton: Princeton University Press.
Cassin, B. (2016), "Translation as Paradigm for Human Sciences," *Journal of Speculative Philosophy*, 30 (3) (2016): 242–66.
Chiesi, R. (2018), *Il cinema di Ingmar Bergman*, Rome: Gremese editore.
Cowie, P. (1992), *Le cinéma de pays Nordiques*, Paris: Editions du Centre Pompidou.
del Río Kuroiwa, S. E. (2004), *Fresas salvajes y Persona: El encuentro con uno mismo y las relaciones humanas en el cine de Ingmar Bergman*, Lima: Pontifica universidad cató.
Dervin, F., and Jacobsson, A. (2021), *Teacher Education for Critical and Reflexive Interculturality*, London: Palgrave Macmillan.
Frykman. J., and Löfgren, O. (1987), *Culture Builders: A Historical Anthropology of Middle-Class Life*, New Brunswick, NJ: Rutgers University Press.
Sjögren, O. (1976), *Filmens Ledbilder: Marxistiska Filmanalyser*, Stockholm: Nordstedts.
Sjögren, O. (1992), "Det blågula stjärnbaneret: Om amerikanska smältbilder i svensk film," in R. Lundén and E. Åsard (eds), *Networks of Americanization: Aspects of the American Influence in Sweden*, Stockholm: Almqvist & Wiksell international.
Steene, B. (1995), "'Manhattan Surrounded by Ingmar Bergman': The American Reception of a Swedish Filmmaker," in R. W. Oliver (ed.), *Ingmar Bergman: An Artist's Journey, On Stage, On Screen, In Print*, New York: Arcade Publishing, 174–97.
Steene, B. (2005), *Ingmar Bergman: A Reference Guide*, Amsterdam: Amsterdam University Press.
Wortzelius, H. (1947), "Ensamhet och gemenskap: Reflexioner kring Ingmar Bergmans 'Skepp till Indialand,'" *Biografbladet*, 28 (4) (Winter 1947): 229–35.

Wellevenskunst

(Origin Dutch)

Rick Dolphijn

To do well and to rejoice are the best assets of all human beings
(Weldoen ende vrolijck wezen is het alderbeste ghoed alder menschen)
Dirk Volkertsz. Coornhert

Wellevenskunst is a term coined by the Dutch philosopher, artist, politician, musician, writer, and theologian Dirk Volkertsz. Coornhert (1522–90). Coornhert lived in an era known for the intellectual rise of Humanism (he was fifteen years old when Erasmus died), a time in which the spirit of the Italian Renaissance had reached the north of Europe, meaning that the rethinking of its artistic and intellectual traditions, in light of a renewed attention for Antiquity (pre-Christian Europe), led to fundamental changes in society at large. Coornhert, especially at the beginning of his career, explored the freedom this brought to the arts. He excelled in playing flute and was well known for his engravings (Hendrick Goltzius, who would rise to great fame, was one of his students).

It seems that he changed directions in life after being properly introduced to Stoicism. He was already in his thirties when he started learning Latin, initially as he wanted to read Augustine and to analyze how he discussed the original sin (which was an idea Coornhert would fiercely disagree with throughout his life). Yet when he mastered it, he began translating the works of Boëthius, Cicero, and Seneca, major works in the history of Stoic thought, for the Dutch market. He never cared to learn Greek (though he played with it in his aliases, later in life). Though a relatively well-known school in thought, the dominant (Christian!) intellectuals in those days considered Stoicism (and Epicureanism) rather sinful (with its emphasis on happiness), and especially the kind of spiritualism that Coornhert would in the end adhere to (a *Stoic* spiritualism which for instance allowed him to write an ethics without citing the Bible) would make him a "dangerous" thinker.

Although he was considered dangerous, or better "a heretic" (rather than someone who questioned the existence of God, a heretic—not surprisingly-was someone who somehow questioned the authority of the church), Coornhert did not in any way stop him from speaking truth to power, it seems. Known for his fierce critiques (mainly on those loyal to the church) and his unapologetic and ruthless debating style (which he also often practiced with intellectuals/friends such as the Leiden-based professor Justus Lipsius), Coornhert became a key figure in Dutch artistic and academic life since the middle of the sixteenth century. Simon Schama (1987), in his *Embarrassment of Richess* referred to Coornhert as the patriarch of culture in sixteenth-century Netherlands. In the public debate, priests and influential theologians, all too often put his claims aside simply referring to him arriving so late at the game, as they considered him the artist who learned Latin only in his thirties and, and because he didn't seem to have a proper education (though coming from a fairly wealthy Amsterdam family), they called him "an outsider," or a "self-made man" (for instance in a debate he had with the rector of Leiden University, prof. Saravia). Despite their disapproval (or arrogance) though, or perhaps because of, Coornhert was highly esteemed throughout the Netherlands, selling a lot of books and pamphlets throughout the Republic for several decades and becoming the point of reference in the open minded, creative and liberal debate. Coornhert not just paved the way for his students but also set the tone for the arts and for philosophy in the times to come, the seventeenth century, also referred to as the Golden Age of the Netherlands, contributing to the artistic and intellectual climate in which also free spirits like artists, scientists, writers like Hendrik Spieghel came to fruition.

*

The intellectual debates in his days, besides their early explorations in humanism and rationalism (a term also much more radical than we read this today as it at could already implicitly question the all-might of God), were heavily signed by the consequences of the Reformation and the Contra reformation. Of course, there was no "outside" of Christian belief in sixteenth-century Europe, especially not when the discussions were open to the general audience (which means also in the correspondences). Yet although Christ was everywhere, the ideas central to Christianity, and to the rule of Roman Catholicism, were openly discussed in the Netherlands, especially in comparison to the neighboring countries. The Netherlands in the sixteenth century had already become quite a "free haven" for the critical and liberal theologians and philosophers of Europe, though it was only in the seventeenth century, when Sephardic Jews and Huguenots started to play an increasingly important role—especially with the rise of Amsterdam—that it was obvious throughout the continent, that one had to go to the Netherlands (and often Amsterdam), to find artistic and intellectual freedom. (This for instance led to the fact that so many books were published in the Netherlands. Amsterdam was even referred to as Bibliopolis.)

It is impossible to come up with one explanation of why this free atmosphere came about, but the particular geophysical circumstances of the Netherlands must have played an important role: surrounded by stronger empires (France, England, and later Germany), the Netherlands always focused on trading between these empires, and thus, especially in its urban centers, its communities were never organized in a very hierarchical way. Next to that, the Netherlands—as the name (in plural) already tells us- always consisted of a series of countries (it was a republic of seven lands when the "unification" was effectuated in 1581, starting from a confederation that was defined by a defense alliance and a customs union). Though small in size, these different countries, especially until the end of the eighteenth century, valued their independence strongly. They had different legal systems (in which different religious groups also had their own legal systems again) and there was never an authority able to tighten the rules for everyone (nota bene; the Republic officially also did not have a capital).

In a way this lack of a central authority in which a highly diverse community, or better, a multiplicity of communities, was able to prosper and to live together in peace, reminds us of the coming of the Renaissance itself, when the many different city states that are now part of Italy, gave rise to an unprecedented revival of the arts and sciences. Much earlier, it seems to resemble the geography of ancient Greece, as Gilles Deleuze and Félix Guattari note, with its fractal structure, where each island and each city is at once "near enough and far enough away" (1991, 87) from the other, from the neighboring empire, and from the deserted sea, so it would always welcome the stranger. Kojin Karatani, in his book *Isonomia and the Origins of Philosophy*, agrees with this geological analysis of Greece as the philosophers earth, and focuses in particular on Ionia, a small series of settlements on the coast of Asia Minor, at the heart of the Greek world: a new colony, free from the traditions of the clans, where a new type of covenant gave rise to a new type of community (based on *isonomia*, the equality of law) that was never centralized (which is why people also speak of the Ionian tribe). Ionia was the homeland of the first philosophers (Thales, of Anaximander and of Heraclitus) but also of a distinct school of art (with for instance Theodorus of Samos) famous for (for instance) the Archaic female figures at the Acropolis in Athens.

*

Coornherts *wellevenskunst* found its *philosophical earth* in the situation as I briefly described it above, which was the liberal intellectual and artistic climate in the Netherlands in the sixteenth century. It was a situation in which free spirits such as Coornhert (and the many creative minds and free thinkers to follow), were able to reach out to an audience, and play a role in the public debate. It was also a situation in which the Protestantism of John Calvin (1509-64), the theologian who, can be considered much more conservative than Martin Luther, became very popular. Looking at this from our twenty-first-century perspective, it is not easy to understand how the rise of liberals such as Coornhert was accompanied by the rise of the gained popularity, of course, much to the dislike, of course, of especially Coornhert.

It is important to stress immediately that the ideas of Calvin were not so much appreciated because of their conservatism, which would be a contemporary analysis of his thinking. Rather, even more so than with Luther and the other reformers gaining influence in his time, we should understand that the reforms that Calvin proposed were much more rigid and far-reaching and were strongly opposed to how Catholicism had practiced Christianity up until then. Calvinism was simply *more* revolutionary. Let's also not forget that John Calvin was a humanist by training and received a doctorate in (humanist) law. His first publication was a commentary on Seneca *De clementia* (1532), much in line with how Coornhert started his intellectual career. In this book he actually proved himself a loyal follower of Erasmus who had published on Seneca a few years earlier (1529). On top of that, Calvin, in his early work, did not seem greatly interested in the Bible and issues of religion at all.

Obviously, that changed, and it should not be very surprising that Coornhert, who, as said, shared with Calvin a love for Seneca and the Stoa, fiercely disagreed with how the later Calvin became so devoted to the Bible and (especially at a later age) so intolerant toward other interpretations of Christianity (and other interpretations of the Bible). Their shared interest in Stoicism, in searching for ways to live one's life not subjected to worldly passions, was succeeded by a major conflict concerning the role of the church in this this life. Coornhert wrote a text (very much directed at Calvin) in which he questioned the rituals of the Catholic Church (and actually also the protestant churches that were being formed), Calvin wrote a response to "a rude Dutchman."

Of course, their differences were in the end unbridgeable. And both were unapologetic. Calvin, over the years, turned into a merciless ruler of his own reformation, went back to Geneva after living in exile in Germany, which he turned into a model reformed city. He even set up a university there and saw his influence grow significantly during the last decade of his life, especially in Northern Europe. Though it should be mentioned that his followers, in the Netherlands, represented a very small fraction of the Dutch population, as it was only in the late eighteenth and in the nineteenth century especially that Calvinism became the dominant protestant community (which is one of the reasons that Schama questions the famous claim by Max Weber that the rise of capitalism was due to the rise of Protestantism). Coornhert's writings, on the other hand, not only in philosophy, but also his plays, his letters, etcetera, would never stop fiercely arguing against the religious and the worldly institutes of his age and its key principles (on predestination, on freedom of religion, against the capital punishment of heretics). It led to several imprisonments and bannings. At the end of an eventful life, he was forced to spend his final years in Gouda, after he was given asylum there, thanks to its liberal burgomaster and probably because of the lobbying of the numerous publishers located in the city (like Jasper Tournay).

*

The book *Zedekunst is Wellevenskunst*, in which the concept of our interest plays a key role, was written in 1585 in Embden (today in Germany), where he was banned to at the time. It was published in 1587 anonymously, in Gouda probably, without even mentioning the publisher and the city in which it was pressed. Like his other works, this book was written in Dutch (and not in Latin) which was highly unusual in his days. In fact, *Wellevenskunst* was the first book on Ethics in a vernacular language in Europe. Of course, this was consequential to the situation in the Netherlands, as described above, and in particular to Coornhert's position in the Dutch debate: the way he, contrary to the religious establishment, was interested in the everyday, embodied, search for the good. Coornhert was different from contemporaries such as Thomas More or Erasmus whose works served an international (European) community of freethinkers (the so-called Republic of Letters). *Wellevenskunst* was a bestseller in the Netherlands, and, like Coornhert's other writings, was aimed at the intelligent and critical community that could be found *throughout* the Netherlands (for the first time). He wrote it, as he put it himself; "niet voor den scherpzinnighen gheleerden, maar voor den leergierighn ongheleerden" (*Wellevenskunst* II 5.2.) (trans.; not for the astute scholars but for the studious uneducated).

Of course, it was not simply a political choice to write this book on Ethics in the local language; writing it in Dutch was in many ways reflected in its content. For whereas the intellectual books written in Latin in those days were addressing themes important to the European intellectual community, Coornhert searched for ways to *situate* his ethics, meaning that more than his humanist peers he was interested in the Dutch tradition in thought, the Dutch discussions on the freedom of religion and morality, and the ways these discussions allowed him to actually write a book on Ethics in sixteenth-century Europe without quoting the Bible once. At this time, there was a war going on in the Netherlands and Coornhert decided it was time to search for ways to unite the different perspectives searching for a practical ethics, one that did not start from one particular religious belief but that adopted a naturalist idea of God that allowed him to respect the classic virtues, wisdom, justice, strength, and temperament (after Cicero's *de Officiis*), by stressing the everyday importance of charity and good citizenship (*burgerschap*).

But writing a book in one's own language also allowed Coornhert to practice ethics as a practical philosophy. Though seemingly concerned with a spiritualism that would count for all, the book is in fact rooted in Stoicism (see also Kalff 1889). Coornhert's *Wellevenskunst* continuously stresses the search for the empirical, the embodied good, and a control over the passions, an affirmative approach to life (a love for life as it were) and a firm rejection of any idea of goodness that promoted the values of the church (or of the churches that, at the time, were being set up). He may seem to take a more "moderate stance" in this book, if we compare it to his earlier work, but that is by all means—again—a contemporary interpretation of what how this happened in the sixteenth century. Coornhert started with this project after an exchange with Spieghel (as the preface (entitled "toe-eyghen brief") explains), and elaborated on his earlier ideas of the *oikeiosis*, the Stoic doctrine which says that any ethics starts from "the dearest thing," which is, one's own body and being, one's essence. Yet as he wanted to write a book not so much in critique of the church but as a book which offered an art of life for all, Coornhert refuses to take position. Because of his conciliatory efforts and his practical ideas on free speech (emphasizing forbearance and tolerance), Coornhert became a key advisor of William of Orange, the stadtholder who would unite the Netherlands and liberate them from the Spanish crown. Rejecting the drive "to search for oneself" (for which he, as so often, invented a neologism (*eigenzoekelijkheid*)) was key to the art of living well.

*

The Dutch Golden Age is an epoch, roughly coinciding with the seventeenth century, in which Dutch scientists, artists, philosophers, fueled by a sharp rise in economic and (maritime) military power, lead the world. In terms of philosophy, without a doubt, Spinoza has made the biggest impression, with a system of thought that was in many ways so radical, so strongly opposed to how Christian powers had organized society, subjectivity and the everyday life, that even today, 350 years later, his writings can easily be used to question the dogmas implicitly and explicitly at work in the intellectual debates today. Spinoza himself seemed to have lived the life of a hermit, spending most of his days as a lens grinder, moving around the country as he was well aware that his writings (of which very few were published during his lifetime) were highly disputed. Much has been written already about his intellectual friends (Jarig Jelles, Pieter Balling, Jan Rieuwertsz) and the circles of freethinkers (Remonstrants, Collegiants) that were of crucial importance to Spinoza's philosophical life. The collected works of Coornhert were published in 1632, forty-two years after Coornherts death, the year Spinoza was born, and these three massive books sold well throughout the Netherlands. Coornhert, together with for instance the brothers Sozzini, was surely a key inspiration for many within Spinoza's circles. The fact that Coornherts work was not a documented part of Spinoza's library when he passed away (see Sluis & Musschenga), can be because he lent his copies to others, but more likely, also given Spinoza's careful nature, would be that this was kept a secret (which would also explain why Spinoza does not make direct reference to Coornhert in his work).

Spinoza was born more than a century after Coornhert was born and the Netherlands, at that time, had certainly changed for the good. Although Calvinism was still on the rise, especially the city of Amsterdam had turned into a truly global city, with people from so many nationalities walking the docs; the most prosperous and inclusive city of Europe where creatives and free spirits found their refuge. Spinoza's Ethics, written in Latin, was not, like Coornhert's *Wellevenskunst*, situated in the Netherlands. Much more like the work of Erasmus, it aimed at the European intellectuals, which could also have been a good reason not to mention Coornhert. And although this needs further study, obviously, it is all too clear that Coornhert's ideas in many ways resonate with Spinoza's Ethics. The Stoicism, the emphasis on living well (on "joy" as Spinoza would say), but also the analysis of the *"herts tochten"* (the "passions"). Too often, Coornherts practical *wellevenskunst* and how he rethinks spirituality (as a search for the good for everyone) is considered more abstract than Spinoza's emphasis on the immanent, but an affirmative reading of Coornhert, keeping in mind the situation from which he wrote, will reveal a philosophy, that, perhaps even more so than Spinoza's, gives us neologisms (in Dutch) that practice a very earthly, embodied, and creative search for *wellevenskunst* (the art of living well). Too often, Coornhert is seen as just another Erasmian, whereas especially his *wellevenskunst* shows us a philosopher much more responsible for his residence, more entangled with the world around him, sensitive to the passions and affects that make up his world, sympathetic to the differences that matter to being.

Works Cited

Bonger, H. (1989), *Spinoza en Coornhert*, Leiden: Brill.
Coen, M. (2019), "'Non erubescat Hollandia': Classical Embarrassment of Riches and the Construction of Local History in Hadrianus Junius' Batavia," in Karl A.E. Enenkel and Konrad Adriaan Ottenheym (eds), *The Quest for an Appropriate Past in Literature, Art and Architecture*, Leiden: Brill, 361–82.
Coornhert, D. V. (1982), *Zedekunst Is Wellevenskunste*, Utrecht: HES Publishers.
Deleuze, G. and Guattari, F. (1991), *What Is Philosophy?*, trans. Hugh Tomlinson and Graham Burchell, New York: Verso.
Kalff, G. (1889), *Geschiedenis der Nederlandse Letterkunde in de 16de eeuw*, vol. II, Leiden: Brill, 317, 319.
Karatani, K. (2017), *Isonomia and the Origins of Philosophy*, Durham: Duke University Press.
Land, J. P. N. (2010), *De wijsbegeerte in de Nederlanden (1889)*, Ann Arbor: University of Michigan Library.
Simon, S. (1987), *The Embarrassment of Riches: An Interpretation of Dutch Culture in the Golden Age*, New York: Random House.
Sluis, J. V. and Musschenga, T. E. (2009), *De boeken van Spinoza*, Groningen: Rijksuniversiteit Groningen, Universiteitsbibliotheek.
Veen, M. (2001), *"Verschooninghe van de roomsche afgoderye": de polemiek van Calvijn met nicodemieten, in het bijzonder met Coornhert*, Leiden: Brill.

Line and Bump

(Origin Transcultural)

Cora Bender

Concepts and the Other

What benefit can a transcultural media theory gain from reflecting, integrating, and experimenting with non-Western media concepts? What can be pitfalls and problems of this process? An especially interesting example for a piece of transcultural theorizing is the confluence of South American indigenous thinking and the philosophical work of Gilles Deleuze and Felix Guattari in the concept of *perspectivism*, coined by the noted Brazilian anthropologist and public intellectual Eduardo Viveiros de Castro (1998, 2013). His touchstone is the concept of "the Other as an a priori structure" proposed by Gilles Deleuze in a number of publications (Deleuze 2015 [1969]; Deleuze and Guattari 1994 [1991]) as "a condition of the field of perception": "the existential possibility of those parts of the world that lie beyond actual perception is guaranteed by the virtual presence of an Other that perceives them; what is invisible to me subsists as real by being visible to an other." Viveiro de Castro's urgent plea: "Without an Other the category of possibility disappears; the world collapses reduced to the pure surface of the immediate" (Viveiros de Castro 2013: 478).

This Other, so essential to perception and, really, conception, has been an issue in anthropology as the problem of the "native's point of view" since the discipline's pioneering methodological serve issued by Bronislaw Malinowski in his well-known introduction to his study *Argonauts of the Western Pacific* (1922): "[…] the final goal, of which an Ethnographer should never lose sight […] is, briefly, to grasp the native's point of view, his relation to life, to realize his vision of his world" (Malinowski 2005 [1922]: 19).

This seemingly simple methodological requirement, since, has arguably served as the discipline's single most important common denominator as much as its favorite object of contention.

One of Viveiros de Castro's main epistemological propositions in these debates is to refer to Deleuze's concept of "concepts" in order to review and re-center anthropology's most peculiar and "Victorian" notions such as hau, mana, totem, kula, potlatch, and tabu, some of which had fallen out of use for a number of decades and recently made a surprising comeback, most notably "new animism" (Harvey 2013). In Viveiros de Castro's view, they bear witness to the fact that anthropology is a space where "theories emerge through the imaginative efforts of societies on which the discipline hopes to shed light" (Viveiros de Castro 2013: 486), "unsettling what we think we know in favor of what we may not even have imagined" (Holbraad and Pedersen 2017: 2). This programmatically renewed brand of anthropology quickly gained traction. In 2011, a new journal appeared on the international stage, which took its attention-provoking title, *HAU—Journal of Ethnographic Theory*, from "Marcel Mauss' reading of the Māori term hau as 'Spirit of the Gift,'" as the editors explained with reference to Marcel Mauss' famous *Essai sur le Don* (Mauss 1954 [1925]). HAU became the flagship of a new scene of fresh scholarship answering the "call to revive the theoretical potential of all ethnographic insight, wherever it is brought to bear, to bring it back to its leading role in generating new knowledge. Above all, we see ethnography as a pragmatic inquiry into conceptual disjunctures" (daCol and Graeber 2011: vii), HAU's editors urged, "[w]e would rather our Mongolianists show that 'nomadic machines' are not actually what Deleuze and Guattari thought they were, and instead return to the moment in which philosophers like Deleuze and Guattari themselves turned to ethnography for its conceptual riches (drawing on everything from Bateson's plateau to Clastrean theories of the State)" (daCol and Graeber 2011: xiv).

The journal team made the project of translating concepts their main raison d'être:

> As for the choice of name, HAU stems from what Eduardo Viveiros de Castro in his generous endorsement of the journal calls 'the felicitous equivocation.' Since what is Marcel Mauss' reading of the Māori term hau as 'Spirit of the Gift' if not the quintessence of everything that is equivocal, everything that is inadequate, but also, everything that is nonetheless endlessly productive and enlightening in the project of translating alien concepts?
>
> (daCol and Graeber 2011: vii)

In the present article, I would like to sidestep HAU's—and really, Viveiros de Castro's—elaborate concept of productive equivocation and instead emphasize a different aspect of Deleuze's and Guattari's concept of concepts, which addresses concepts in terms of *signature, regeneration*, and *geography*:

"[...] concepts are and remain signed: Aristotle's substance, Descartes's cogito, Leibniz's monad" (7), and "they have their own way of not dying while remaining subject to constraints of renewal, replacement, and mutation that give philosophy a history as well as a turbulent geography" (Deleuze and Guattari 1994 [1991]: 8).

In my view, two main questions emerge with the endeavor to bring indigenous concepts into the constraints of circulation in Western philosophy. The first concerns the role of the mediators of this process, namely the anthropologists involved; the second question concerns an indigenous concept's signature and to whom it belongs. What I aim to come up with, in the end, is an argument to first and foremost treat indigenous concepts as *indigenous media*. Indigenous media, generally, come with a complex signature of both translation *and* sovereignty (Bender 2015). This peculiar nature of indigenous concepts distinguishes them from other philosophical concepts such as "Leibniz's monad," and often represents a productive irritation in otherwise "transparent" (Bowker and Star 2000) academic practices of translation and circulation.

In order to arrive at this point, I will take a historical detour from Viveiros de Castro's Deleuze and HAU's hau: Before I return to HAU and the question of anthropological concepts' signature in the last paragraph, I will introduce a key transcontextual encounter of indigenous thought and Western media theory which took place in the mid-1950s in a journal edited in Toronto by Edmund Carpenter and Marshall McLuhan with the title *Explorations* and with ambitions not entirely unlike those of HAU, namely to recast the basic conditions of knowledge at a crucial historical moment in time.

In the view of Marshall McLuhan, the launching of the Soviet satellite Sputnik was not only a turning point in the history of media, a media revolution, but also an act of creation: "For the first time the natural world was completely enclosed in a manmade container. (...) 'Ecological' thinking became inevitable as soon as the planet moved up into the status of a work of art" (McLuhan 1974: 49). At the core of this new ecological understanding of media lies a distinction between different kinds of media: on the one hand, the media of classical European modernity, first and foremost alphabetic writing and print; on the other hand, new electronic media such as TV and radio. This distinction between "lineal" and "non-lineal" media can be shown to originate from McLuhan's close collaboration and spirited exchange with two anthropologists associated with what became later known as the Toronto School: Edmund Carpenter (1922–2011) and Dorothy Demetracopoulou Lee (1905–75).

Lineal and Nonlineal Codifications of Reality

In 1953, Edmund Carpenter, a specialist in the cultures of Canadian Inuit, and Marshall McLuhan, who both worked at the University of Toronto, received a grant by the Ford Foundation for an interdisciplinary media research project which led to the institution of the Seminar on Culture and Communication, and to the establishment of the co-edited avant-garde periodical *Explorations* (Prins 2011). *Explorations* eventually brought together an interdisciplinary research team of more than eighty contributors, among them A. Irving Hallowell, Harold Innis, Ashley Montagu, Rhoda Métraux, Melford Spiro, and Northrop Frye, "striving to understand the implications of postwar new media of communication: photography, film, radio, television, even early computing" (Darroch and Marchessault 2016: v), and eventually arriving, in McLuhan's words, at *Understanding Media* as a "basic art situation which is more significant than the information or idea 'transmitted'" (McLuhan 1954: 1; McLuhan 1994 [1964]). The team of Explorations was also joined in 1954 by anthropologist Dorothy Lee who soon became what Edmund Carpenter later called "Exploration's most influential force" (Carpenter 2001: 240).

Dorothy Demetracopoulou was born in 1905 as the youngest of nine children of a Greek evangelical pastor who was the ambassador of Greece in Istanbul (at the time Constantinople). A childhood spent in this multiple liminality probably predisposed her for her later interests in anthropology and philosophy (Bender 2014). She received a sound education at Vassar College and, in 1927, embarked on her first field work trip among the Wintu at Mount Shasta in California in the context of her PhD studies under Alfred Kroeber. She wrote her dissertation on *The Loon Woman Myth: A Study in Synthesis* (Lee 1933) and in the following years went on to expand her research into an exacting and sophisticated philosophical linguistics of Wintu. An important source of inspiration for her was her husband Otis Lee, a student of Dewey's who became Director of the department of Philosophy at Vassar in 1938.

> "[Her husband] asked Dorothy how various tribesmen might answer certain philosophical questions. After she'd finished dinner and helped four children with schoolwork, she wiped the kitchen table clean and sat down to answer those questions. The result was a series of remarkable essays on languages that lacked or minimized temporal tenses, adjectives, metaphors, first-person singular, as well as all equivalents to our verbs 'to be' & 'to become'; languages that blurred the distinction between nouns & verbs, that conjugated and declined from plural to singular, but also possessed forms alien to Standard Indo-European languages."
>
> (Carpenter 2001: 239)

In 1959, Dorothy Lee published a volume of her essays under the title *Freedom and Culture* which quickly became popular among students of anthropology and neighboring disciplines. Shortly after, she went to Harvard to work with the sociologist and education researcher David Riesman; however, she never felt comfortable amidst the hustle and bustle of the elite institution, and eventually left for California, where she joined Edmund Carpenter at the San Fernando State College in 1961.

One of her main strengths was the close reading she gave the texts that anthropologists recorded from the people they worked with, a technique she had been trained in by her teacher and colleague Ruth Benedict (1887–1948):

> [Ruth Benedict] taught us to read an ethnography as we would visit a tribe: to accord equal dignity to every datum, to read slowly and repeatedly, delving beyond the interpretative words of the writer, till we could savor the culture. [...] At a time when we were trying to be scientific in the old Pearsonian sense, deleting the observer from the observed, she was not only scientific in the Einsteinian sense, including the observer, but went beyond this, defining the observer as a total person, apperceiving with immediacy as well as cognitively.
> (Lee 1949: 346)

This concept of research, "apperceiving with immediacy as well as cognitively," is, in my view, a striking example of "perspectival anthropology" (Viveiros de Castro) avant la lettre. This is most apparent in her essay *Lineal and non-lineal codifications of reality* which was published in 1957 in the seventh volume of *Explorations*, flanked by Carpenter's article *The New Languages* and another one by Lee with the title *Symbolization and Value*. Lee's concern is with "the codification of reality, and more particularly, with the nonlineal apprehension of reality [...] in contrast to our own lineal phrasing" which she illustrates with Malinowski's famous ethnographic paradigm of the South Pacific Trobriand Islands already mentioned in the introduction (Lee 1957: 27; Malinowski 1922). Lee's assumption is that "a careful study and analysis of a different code and of the culture to which it belongs [...] may even, eventually, lead us to aspects of reality of which our own code excludes us" (Lee 1957: 27). In order to illustrate this, she ventures a comparison between two entirely different ways of comprising experience into patterns of perception, which for brevity's purpose we may address as the codes of the line and that of the bump, respectively:

> In our own culture, the line is so basic, that we take it for granted, as given in reality. We see it in visible nature, between material points, and

we see it between metaphorical points such as days or acts. It underlies not only our thinking, but also our aesthetic apprehension of the given; it is basic to the emotional climax which has so much value to us, and, in fact to the meaning of life itself. [...]. But is the line present in reality?

(Lee 1957: 32-3)

In a close reading of Bronislaw Malinowski's Trobriand ethnography she points out that what for Malinowski and his Euro-American audience looked like a Trobriand village arranged in concentric circles, that is, lines, was referred to by the Trobrianders by words "prefixed by the substantival element *kway* which means bump or aggregate of bumps, [...] the element which they use when they refer to a pimple or a bulky rash; or to canoes loaded with yams. [...] Are they blind to the circles? Or did Malinowksi create the circles himself, out of his cultural axiom?" (Lee 1957: 33).

In light of Trobriand concepts, she shows that the Western convention of drawing lines is, ultimately, a pervasive moral discourse:

Our conception of personality formation, our stress on the significance of success and failure and of frustration in general, is based on the axiomatically postulated line. [...] But failure is devastating in our culture, because it is not failure of the undertaking alone; it is the moving, becoming, lineally conceived self which has failed.

(Lee 1957: 41)

By contrast, Trobriand thinking actually more abhors than ignores the intentionality underlying lineality:

[When Trobriand activity] assumes lineality, [it is considered] utterly despicable. [For instance] some men are accused of giving gifts as an inducement to their kula[1] partner to give them a specially good kula gift. Such men are labeled with the vile phrase: he barters. But this means that, unvalued and despised, lineal behavior does exist.

(Lee 1957: 35)

I have seen lineal pictures of nervous impulses and heartbeats, and with them I have seen pictured lineally a second of time. These were photographs, you will say, of existing fact, of reality; a proof that the line is present in reality. But I am not convinced, perhaps due to my ignorance of mechanics, that we have not created our recording instruments in such a way that they have to picture time and motion, light and sound, heartbeats and nerve impulses lineally, *on the unquestioned assumption of the line as axiomatic.* The line is omnipresent and inescapable, and so we are incapable of questioning the reality of its presence.

(Lee 1957: 33; italics by author, C.B.)

This is the central elaboration of her anthropological comparison between lineal and non-lineal modes of codifying reality which inspired Carpenter's and McLuhan's reflections on media bias and lineal print culture. It was the catalyst for a seminal shift from studying communication as manipulation (Schüttpelz 2002) toward media theory proper, from studying the utility of media as tools of mass communication, to "Understanding Media" as an ecology—not in the then-conventional epistemology as an adaptive system based on the survival of the fittest, but as an ecology which simultaneously contains and reflects humans and their worlds, and as a multi-perspectival work of art which comprises humans, technology, and the planet as a whole.

In 1953, Harry Hoijer, an anthropologist from Chicago studying Athapaskan languages, organized a big conference under the title "Language in Culture" which was dedicated to a programmatic discussion inspired by the work of Edward Sapir's student Benjamin Lee Whorf, who had passed on in 1941. It was Harry Hoijer, now largely forgotten, who coined the term *Sapir—Whorf Hypothesis* as a catchword for different approaches to linguistic relativity. In absentia, Dorothy Lee was attacked by a proponent of anthropological Acculturation Studies, Robert Redfield from Chicago. He marked her position as deterministic, allegedly promoting a simplistic congruence between grammar and worldview. The background to this has to be seen, in my view, in a post-Second World War turn of the discipline toward policy- and problem-oriented approaches using social science to screen and patrol social order in the American multi-cultural conglomerate as well as in its overseas sphere of influence and domination. This utilitarian turn, in Lee's terms: "lineality" at its worst, directed large sums of research money into the discipline and boosted its numbers while it turned anthropology's ethnographic methods from media of translation into tools of objectification and intervention. Redfield's misrepresentation of Lee's research marked the beginning of her marginalization in her own academic community while at the same time, she integrated anthropology into the multidisciplinary, open debates of *Explorations*, and thus changed both profoundly. "I see anthropology as far more than the study and presentation of man," Carpenter wrote in 1965, eight years after *Exploration*'s last issue. "It's experiencing man: sensing, apperception, recognition. It's art" (Carpenter 1965: 55–6).

Re-Cycling Concepts

Nowadays, the work of translating indigenous concepts takes place in a new academic ecology of non-lineal "social" media, which, on the one hand, accelerate its circulations, and on the other hand, facilitate the intervention of indigenous actors and the public reception of indigenous voices. In 2018, while *HAU—Journal of Ethnographic Theory* underwent a thorough restructuring of its editorial work and publishing model after a prolonged crisis,[2] the Mahi Tahi, a collective of New Zealand and Māori scholars, published an open letter in which they shared their reasons for taking issue with HAU's signature of hau:

> We note that on the front page of your journal's website it does not mention the Māori origins of the word, hau, simply describing it thus: "HAU takes its name from Mauss's Spirit of the Gift, an anthropological concept that derives its theoretical potential precisely from the translational inadequations and equivocations involved in comparing the incomparable."
>
> [...] How well have the journal's recent practices, decisions and approaches lived up to the Māori concept of hau, a concept that the journal has continually stated is its central ethos? In other words, has the word become a misappropriated marketing tool [...]? [W]hat types of mutually beneficial relationships do you hope to foster with Māori scholars and communities?
>
> (Mahi Tahi 2018)

The open letter also refers to an article on *The "Hau" of Research: Mauss Meets Kaupapa Māori* (Stewart 2017)[3] which provides further insight on the issue of hau's signature from a Māori point of view. The data underlying Mauss' notion of the hau as the "spirit of the gift," Stewart shows, originate from letters written by a Māori named Tanati Ranapiri to the anthropologist Elsdon Best on whose rendition Mauss relied in his *Essai sur le Don*. Stewart retraces how in these collaborations, "Ranapiri's written words became verbatim scientific data in the archives of anthropology, which have been debated and theorized about ever since by many non-Māori scholars." Even though the letters were distorted by non-Māori purposes and in many cases sent into general circulation attached with the wrong signature, they founded "a great conversation about the gift" (Stewart 2017: 8). In Stewarts view, this case provides us with the question of "the hau of research" and an important argument for a Māori re-vision, a regeneration, and a translation, really, of Western educational philosophy that "offers its gifts to humanity and to the future" (Stewart 2017: 9).

The letter and the article highlight the issues of obligation and cultural copyright that indigenous voices raise against what they necessarily perceive as the recklessness of conceptual mavericks who misunderstand the translation and circulation of indigenous concepts as a playground for outside purposes and self-interested transgressions. By contrast, the anthropological business of "taking people serious" is not as radically new as Viveiros de Castro and his partisans make it seem. As becomes obvious in the work of Dorothy Lee and Edmund Carpenter, translation is a precarious knowledge practice situated never entirely *within* but always *in between* the worlds it explores, and for better or for worse, in the context of participant observation, it is more than any other academic practice susceptible to feedback from its research fields and interlocutors.

I would like to conclude with a plea for a critical historical media anthropology as a key condition of transcultural theorizing, and for an understanding of the translation of concepts as a precarious activity involving not one, not two, but at least three positions—anthropologist, interlocutor, and audience—which, under the conditions of the internet and social media, are never absolutely fixed but can be seen as temporarily inhabited by different proponents who observe and comment on each other. However, these fluid conditions of circulation are, and in fact, have always been productively disturbed by the interferences of indigenous sovereignty. Addressing indigenous concepts as indigenous media—media that translate *and* set boundaries, at the same time—renders visible many otherwise blurred issues of shared historicity and mutual obligations established through the fieldwork and translation process. In my view, transcultural media heuristics need to assume not so much a certain political morality in the hope of getting impregnated, once and for all, against criticism but rather "*Haltung*, a particular stance in the pursuit of knowledge" (Rabinow 2019: 484). This entails an obligation to not run away with other peoples' cultural media to sell them on some opaque academic market. It also entails a constant readiness to return to the incisive moment of ethnographic encounter when an indigenous interlocutor finds it worthwhile to open a window onto her world, and we do our best to *listen*. Then, we strive to embed the concepts that were shared with us in the complex cultural re-creation of thick description which only fieldwork can provide.

Notes

1 Kula, or Kula Ring, is a ceremonial exchange system made famous by Malinowski's path-breaking ethnographic monography Argonauts oft he Western Pacific (1922).
2 https://www.haujournal.org/index.php/hau/announcement/view/22, 08.01.2022.

3   Georgina Stewart is an associate professor in Te Kura Mātauranga School of Education, at Auckland University of Technology (AUT) in Auckland, Aotearoa New Zealand.

Works Cited

Bender, C. (2014), "Dorothy Lee: Lineare und nicht-lineare Kodifizierungen der Realität. Auf Spurensuche nach einer Vordenkerin der Medientheorie," *Zeitschrift für Medienwissenschaft*, 6 (11): 166–76.

Bender, C. (2015), "Indigenous Knowledge in the Production of Post-Frontier American Culture," *Journal of Transcultural Studies*, 6 (2). doi: https://doi.org/10.17885/heiup.ts.20202, 18.01.2022.

Bowker, G., and Leigh Star, S. (2000), *Sorting Things Out: Classification and Its Consequences*, Cambridge, MA: MIT Press.

Carpenter, E. (1965), "Reply to Charles Campbell Hughes," *Current Anthropology*, 6 (1): 55–6.

Carpenter, E. (2001), "That Not-So-Silent Sea," in D. Theall (ed.), *The Virtual Marshall McLuhan*, Montreal: McGill Queens University Press, 236–61.

Collins, Samuel G. (2019), "Social Media," in H. Callan (ed.) *The International Encyclopedia of Anthropology*, Oxford: Wiley, 1–11.

DaCol, G. and Graeber, D. (2011), "Foreword. The Return of Ethnographic Theory," *HAU: Journal of Ethnographic Theory*,1 (1): vi–xxxv.

Darroch, M., and Marchessault, J. (2016), "Explorations, 1953–57. Introduction to the Eight-Volume Series of the 2016 Edition," in *Explorations*, 1. Studies in Culture and Communication, Eugene, OR: Wipf & Stopck, v–xxv.

Deleuze, G. (2015 [1969]), *The Logic of Sense*, trans. M. Lester and C. Stivale, London: Bloomsbury Academic.

Deleuze, G., and Guattari, F. (1994 [1991]), *What Is Philosophy?*, trans. H. Tomlinson and G. Burchell, New York: Columbia University Press.

Harvey, G. (2013), *Handbook of Contemporary Animism*, Durham, UK: Acumen.

Holbraad, M., and Pedersen, M.A. (2017), *The Ontological Turn. An Anthropological Exposition*, Cambridge: Cambridge University Press.

Lee, D. (1933), "The Loon Woman Myth. A Study in Synthesis," *Journal of American Folk–Lore*, 46: 101–28.

Lee, D. (1949), "Ruth Fulton Benedict (1887–1948)," *Journal of American Folk-Lore*, 62: 345–7.

Lee, D. (1957), "Lineal and Non-Lineal Codifications of Reality," *Explorations*, 7: 27–42.

Mahi, T. (2018), "An Open Letter to the HAU Journal's Board of Trustees," https://www.asaanz.org/blog/2018/6/18/an-open-letter-to-the-hau-journals-board-of-trustees, 07.01.2022.

Malinowski, B. (2005 [1922]), *Argonauts of the Western Pacific. An Account of Native Enterprise and Adventure in the Archipelagoes of Melanesian New Guinea*, London: Routledge.

Mauss, M. (1954 [1925]), *The Gift. Forms and Function of Exchange in Archaic Societies*, trans. I. Cunnison, intr. E. E. Evans-Pritchard, Glencoe: Free Press.

McLuhan, M. (1954), "Notes on Media as Art Forms," *Explorations*, 2: 1–8.

McLuhan, M. (1974), "At the Moment of Sputnik the Planet Became a Global Theater in Which There Are No Spectators but Only Actors," *Journal of Communication*, 24 (1): 48–58.

McLuhan, M. (1994 [1964]), *Understanding Media. The Extensions of Man*, Cambridge: MIT Press.

Prins, H. (2011), "In Memoriam: Edmund Snow Carpenter," *Anthropology News*, 52 (9): 24.

Rabinow, P. (2019), "Contemporary Counterconduct," *HAU: Journal of Ethnographic Theory*, 9 (2): 483–91.

Schüttpelz, E. (2002), "'Get the message through'. Von der Kanaltheorie der Kommunikation zur Botschaft des Mediums: Ein Telegramm aus der nordatlantischen Nachkriegszeit," in I. Schneider and P. Spangenberg, (eds), *Medienkultur der Fünfziger Jahre*, Opladen: Westdeutscher Verlag, 51–76.

Stewart, G. (2017) "The 'Hau' of Research: Mauss Meets Kaupapa Maori," *Journal of World Philosophies*, 2: 111.

Viveiros de Castro, E. (1998), "Cosmological Deixis and Amerindian Perspectivism," *Journal of the Royal Anthropological Institute*, 4 (3): 469–88.

Viveiros de Castro, E. (2013), "The relative native," *HAU: Journal of Ethnographic Theory*, 3 (3): 473–502.

Viveiros de Castro, E. (2015), "Perspectival Anthropology and the Method of Controlled Equivocation," in *The Relative Native. Essays on Indigenous Conceptual Worlds*, Chicago: HAU Books, 55–74.

Contributors

Babson Ajibade is Professor of African Arts and Visual Culture in the Department of Visual Arts and Technology, Cross River University of Technology. He holds a PhD (Social Anthropology) from the University of Basel, and a PhD (Scene Design) from the University of Calabar. His research has covered popular culture, youth culture, and African visual culture. A visual artist scene designer, Babson has consulted for a variety of organizations such as Future Histories, Talawa Theatre Company, and the V&A Theatre Collections, London; Family Health International (FHI) and USAID-funded Malaria Action for States (MAPS) in Nigeria, among others.

Cora Bender is a cultural/social anthropologist and media scholar. She has held deputy and guest professorships at the University of Texas at Austin, the University of Vienna, the LMU Munich, and at the Cluster of Excellence "Asia and Europe in a Global Context" at the University of Heidelberg. At present, she is employed at the University of Cologne Center for Media and Modernity Studies. Her research focuses on knowledge culture and media in indigenous North America, and on indigenous modernity and globalization. Her research interests also include media and visual anthropology, medical anthropology, research methods, and histories of anthropology and media studies.

Sebastian Kawanami-Breu is a PhD candidate and visiting researcher at the department for Media Studies, Humboldt-Universität zu Berlin. He also works as an adjunct lecturer at Tama Art University, Tokyo. His current research investigates the epistemology of visual pattern recognition and algorithmic modeling from the viewpoint of a 'History of Epistemic Things'. Besides working in the field of performing arts as an advisor/dramaturge for artists such as Okada Toshiki, Rimini Protokoll, Saeborg or faifai, he is also known as the Japanese translator of "Capitalist Realism" by the late Mark Fisher. After living in Tokyo for most of the last decade, he is currently based in Berlin.

Budhaditya Chattopadhyay is an artist, media practitioner, researcher, and writer. Incorporating diverse media, creative technologies, and research, Chattopadhyay produces works for large-scale installation and live performance addressing contemporary issues of environment and ecology, migration, race, and decoloniality. Chattopadhyay has received numerous residencies, fellowships, and international awards. His sound works have been widely exhibited, performed, or presented across the globe, and released by Gruenrekorder (DE) and Touch (UK). Chattopadhyay has an expansive body of scholarly publications in the areas of media art history, theory and aesthetics, cinema and sound studies in leading peer-reviewed journals. He is the author of three books, *The Nomadic Listener* (2020), *The Auditory Setting* (2021), and *Between the Headphones* (2021). Chattopadhyay holds a PhD in Artistic Research and Sound Studies from the Academy of Creative and Performing Arts, Leiden University, and an MA in New Media from the Faculty of Arts, Aarhus University. https://budhaditya.org/.

Didi Cheeka is an off-Nollywood filmmaker and critic. He is the editor of Lagos Film Review and co-founder/curator of Lagos Film Society—an alternative cinema center dedicated to the founding of Nigeria's first arthouse cinema. Didi is artistic director of Decasia—1st Berlin-Lagos Archival Film Festival.

Lucia D'Errico is an artist-researcher in the field of music with a specific focus on performance, experimental practices, and transdisciplinarity. Her research interests include contemporary philosophy, psychoanalytic theory, semiotics, and epistemology. After completing her PhD in the framework of the ERC-funded project *MusicExperiment21* (2013–18), she is currently a postdoc fellow at the Orpheus Institute, the co-editor of the recently launched book series *Artistic Research* at Rowman & Littlefield Int., and the coordinator of the doctoral program docARTES (Ghent, Belgium). She is the author of *Powers of Divergence. An Experimental Approach to Music Performance* (2018), and the co-editor of *Artistic Research: Charting a Field in Expansion* (2019). She is active as a composer, sound artist, guitarist, video performer, and graphic designer.

Bogdan Deznan is a PhD candidate at the University of Bucharest. He is also a research associate of the Cambridge Centre for the Study of Platonism (University of Cambridge). The topic of his doctoral dissertation is the concept of deification in the thought of the Cambridge Platonists (primarily Benjamin Whichcote, John Smith, Henry More, and Ralph Cudworth) and how this issue relates to the larger early modern theological and philosophical contexts. His primary research interests concern the history of theological and philosophical ideas in the early modern period, the appropriation of

Patristic and Platonic/Neoplatonic sources in the seventeenth century, the theological underpinnings of natural philosophy, and the interplay between metaphysical and theological discourses.

Rick Dolphijn is an associate professor based at Humanities, with an interest in transdisciplinary research at large. He wrote *Foodscapes, Towards a Deleuzian Ethics of Consumption* (2004) and (with Iris van der Tuin) *New Materialism: Interviews and Cartographies* (2012) and is finishing his new monograph entitled *The Cracks of the Contemporary; A Meditation on Art, Wounds and a Damaged Earth*. He has published widely on new materialism, ecology/ecosophy, feminist/postcolonial theory, and contemporary art and is interested in the developments in continental philosophy and speculative thought. His academic work has appeared in journals like *Angelaki*, *Rhizomes*, *Collapse*, and *Deleuze Studies*. He edited (with Rosi Braidotti) *This Deleuzian Century: Art, Activism, Life* (2014/15) and *Philosophy after Nature* (2017). Most recently he published an edited volume entitled *Michel Serres and the Crises of the Contemporary* with Bloomsbury Academic.

Agnieszka Dytman-Stasienko is an associate professor in the Department of Media and Communication, University of Lower Silesia. Her field of research includes computer mediated communications, webstudies, infoactivism, digital activism, culture jamming, analog and digital liberation technologies, communication of protest, propaganda, and persuasion studies. She is an author of a book: *The Celebration of Grabbed Signifiers. The May Day in Communist Poland – Ideology, Ritual, Language* (Wroclaw 2006) [In Polish]. She has been an organizer (with Jan Stasienko) of cyclic Language and Multimedia Conferences (2004, 2006, 2008). She has served as visiting scholar in the Department of Communication, SUNY College at Brockport, USA (2010/11), and the Centre for Digital Media, and Simon Fraser University in Vancouver, Canada (2013/14). Her current project is an analysis of the origins of digital activism within the field of media technologies in communist Poland.

Lorenz Engell is professor of Media Philosophy at Bauhaus-Universität Weimar, Germany, where he was the founding Dean of the Faculty of Media from 1996 to 2000 and was co-director of the IKKM (Internationals Kolleg für Kulturtechnikforschung und Medienphilosophie) from 2012 to 2020, a research institute funded by the German Federal Government. His research interests comprehend philosophy of film and of television, media anthropology, philosophy of the comedy and studies on seriality and causality. Recent publications are *"Thinking Through Television"* (2019),

"*Medienanthropologische Szenen*" (co-editor, 2019), "*Mediale Anthropologie*" (co.-ed, 2015), "*Film Denken. Essays zur Philosophie des Films*" (co-author, 2015). "*Fernsehtheorie zur Einführung*" (2012), "*Playtime*" (2010) and "*Körper des Denkens*" (co-editor, 2013), and *The Switch Image. Television Philosophy* (Bloomsbury 2021). He is also co-editor of the "*Kursbuch Medienkultur*" (1998), of the "*Zeitschrift für Medien- und Kulturforschung (ZMK)*", and the "*Film Denken*" book series.

Victor Fan is Reader in Film and Media Philosophy, King's College London and Film Consultant of the Chinese Visual Festival. He is the author of *Cinema Approaching Reality: Locating Chinese Film Theory* (2015) and *Extraterritoriality: Locating Hong Kong Cinema and Media* (2019). His forthcoming book, *Cinema Illuminating Reality: Media Philosophy through Buddhism*, will be published in 2022. His articles appeared in journals including *Camera Obscura, Journal of Chinese Cinemas, Screen*, and *Film History*.

Chantelle Gray (PhD) is an associate professor in the School of Philosophy at North-West University, South Africa. Her research interests span Continental Philosophy, queer theory, media studies, film studies, and critical algorithmic studies, although she specializes in Deleuzoguattarian philosophy. She is the co-convener of the biennial South African Deleuze & Guattari Studies Conference (www.deleuzeguattari.co.za) and serves on the editorial board of *Somatechnics*. Her books include *Deleuze and Anarchism*, co-edited with Aragorn Eloff (2019) and *Anarchism after Deleuze and Guattari* (2022, Bloomsbury).

Mohammad Hadi is an Iranian freelancer living in Berlin. Having done a master's degree in Linguistics from Tehran University, he did another Master in European Humanities between Perpignan and Tübingen. In 2012 he was awarded an EMJD Scholarship to fulfill his PhD between Tübingen, Bergamo, and Barcelona. He defended his PhD dissertation in Tübingen on Derisive Realism. He is the founder of *rhizastance*, an independent critical and clinical platform of interviewing thinkers around the globe.

Bernd Herzogenrath is Professor of American literature and culture at Goethe University of Frankfurt am Main, Germany. He is the author of *An Art of Desire: Reading Paul Auster*, *An American Body|Politic: A Deleuzian Approach* and editor of a.o. *The Farthest Place: The Music of John Luther Adams* and *Deleuze|Guattari & Ecology*. At the moment, he is planning a project, *cinapses: thinking|film* that brings together scholars from film studies, philosophy, and the neurosciences (members include António Damasio and Alva Noë). His latest publications include the collections *The Films of Bill Morrison. Aesthetics of the Archive* (2017), *Film as Philosophy* (2017), and *Practical Aesthetics* (Bloomsbury, 2020). He is also (together with Patricia Pisters) the main editor of the media-philosophical book series *thinking|media* with Bloomsbury.

Andrei Ionescu is a postdoctoral researcher at the University of Bucharest, exploring the ways in which literature, philosophy, and cognitive science deal with mental health/illness. He was a research associate with Ghent University and Princess Nourah bint Abdulrahman University, and completed his doctoral studies at the University of Padua with a dissertation exploring failures of understanding in human interaction. He is the author of a book, *Disrupted Intersubjectivity: Paralysis and Invasion in Ian McEwan's works* (Bloomsbury, 2020), and of several articles on topics including social interaction, the relationship between science and literature, and the interaction of human and nonhuman realities in modern and contemporary fiction.

Andreas Jacobsson, PhD film studies, is senior lecturer in child and youth studies at University of Gothenburg, Sweden. Jacobsson's research focuses on world cinema (African and Latin American Cinemas), intercultural film, intercultural encounters in science fiction, intercultural epistemology and education, and audio-visual depictions of death.

Kajri Jain is Professor of Indian Visual Culture and Contemporary Art at the University of Toronto. Her research focuses on images at the intersections between religion, politics, art, and vernacular business cultures in India; she also writes on contemporary art and photography. Jain is the author of *Gods in the Time of Democracy* (2021), on monumental sculptures in post-liberalization India, and *Gods in the Bazaar: The Economies of Indian Calendar Art* (2007), on printed icons. Her work has appeared in *Art History*, *Third Text*, *Current Anthropology*, *The Immanent Frame*, *Capitalism and the Camera*, the *Cambridge Companion to Modern Indian Culture*, and *New Cultural Histories of India*.

Gretchen Jude is a performing artist and scholar of sound practices, with degrees in Electronic Music (MFA, Mills College) and Performance Studies (PhD, University of California Davis) as well as certificates in Sawai Koto and Deep Listening. Jude's work aims to harmonize personal, embodied experience with rapid cultural and technological changes. Jude's writing has been published in *Performance Philosophy*, *Critical Stages*, *Capacious: Journal for Emerging Affect Theory*, and *Sounding Out!*, while their music has been released on Full Spectrum, Susuultrarock, and Edgetone Records. Jude collaborates extensively with musicians, choreographers, filmmakers, and academics and practices diverse performance traditions, including Japanese *nagauta* 長唄 and *hauta* 端. Gretchen Jude is Assistant Professor of Film and Media Arts at the University of Utah.

Woosung Kang is a professor in the Department of English, Comparative Literature, and American Studies at Seoul National University, Korea. He was a visiting scholar at University of Pennsylvania (2012–13) and a visiting professor at National Taiwan University (2019–20). His research area includes American literature, politics of aesthetics, critical theories, psychoanalysis, film theory, and Asian cinemas. He is the author of *Emerson and the Writing of the Moment in the American Renaissance* (2003), *A History of American Literature* (2007), *Freud Seminar* (2019), and co-authored *Painting as the Gaze of Philosophy* (2014) and *Poe Translated* (2014). He translated books on Deconstruction into Korean, and is now working on two books, *The Geography of East Asian Cinema* and *Political Derrida*.

Jukka-Pekka Puro (PhD) works as a senior lecturer in University of Turku. His research focus is mainly in the fields of media history, theory, and phenomenology. Puro has edited and written several scientific books and published dozens of articles in the leading Finnish as well as international media studies journals since the early 1990s.

Veli-Matti Karhulahti (PhD) works as a Senior Researcher in University of Jyväskylä (Academy of Finland, 312397). His primary research focus is the psychology and philosophy of play and games. Karhulahti has worked around the world in multiple institutions such as the MIT (Boston), ITU (Copenhagen), and Yonsei (Seoul), and his monograph *Esport Play* (2020) is now out by Bloomsbury.

Suk-Jun Kim is Senior Lecturer in Electroacoustic Music and Sound Art at the University of Aberdeen, UK. A composer and sound artist, Kim has received first prizes at Bourges Electroacoustic Music Competition, Metamorphoses in Belgium, and CIMESP (Concurso Internacional de Música Eletroacústica de São Paulo). He was a resident composer at the DAAD Artists-in-Berlin Programme in 2009. He is the author of *Humming (A Study of Sound)* by Bloomsbury and *Hasla* by Kehrer Verlag Heidelberg and recently published his solo CD *Humming* by Vox Regis.

Behrooz Mahmoodi-Bakhtiari holds a PhD in Linguistics, and is Professor of Linguistics and Persian at the Department of Performing Arts, University of Tehran. Doing a second PhD in Film Studies at Goethe University Frankfurt, he is interested in Iranian Cinema, Poetics and Aesthetics of Film, and Semiotics of Film and theater.

Shintaro Miyazaki is a (Junior)-Professor in Digital Media and Computation (with tenure track) at the Department of Musicology and Media Studies, Humboldt-Universität zu Berlin. In the early 2000s he has studied German Media Studies under Georg Christoph Tholen and later Media Archaeology with Wolfgang Ernst (PhD defended in 2012). From 2014-21 he has been a Senior Researcher at Critical Media Lab of the Academy of Art and Design, University of Applied Sciences and Arts Northwestern Switzerland working with Claudia Mareis. He inquires how we can generate moments of (non-modernistic) criticality which would emancipate us from our self-imposed ignorance of the algorithmic infrastructures we are captured by and at the same time keep this knowledge alive, open, schizo-rhizomatic and ideally free from oedipal and capitalistic drives.

Ana Peraica is the author *The Age of total Images, Fotografija kao Dokaz* (2018), and *Culture of the Selfie* (2017). She is also the editor of Smuggling Anthologies (2015), *Victims Symptom* (2009), and *Žena na raskrižju ideologija* (2007). She teaches at Media Art Histories of Department for Image Science, Danube University Krems as well as on the Media Art Cultures (ERASMUS MUNDUS) by a consortium of universities, Danube University and Aalborg, Lodz and Singapore. Since 2019 she also teaches at History Department, Central European University (CEU), Budapest.

Vít Pokorný teaches philosophy, anthropology, and media studies at the University of J. E. Purkyně in Ústí nad Labem and he is a researcher at the department of Contemporary continental philosophy of the Institute of Philosophy of the Czech Academy of Sciences and assistant professor at the Department of Political Sciences and Philosophy of the Purkyně University in Ústí nad Labem. He publishes in philosophy and cognitive anthropology. His theoretical interests include theory of perception and imagination, enactivism, philosophy of media or rhizomatics. He was a co-applicant in the research grant *Methodological precedence of Intertwinng: theory and application,* and currently (2020-2) in another grant project called *Phenomenological investigations of sonic environments.* He is an author of a philosophical texbook *Postmoderní filosofie,* then two monographies *Myslet z psychedelických zkušeností: transdisciplinární interpretace* and

Psychonauticon: Transdisciplinary Interpretation of Psychedelic Experiences, and also an editor and co-author of the collective monograph *Antropologie smyslů*. In his work, he attempts on finding connections between various disciplines—philosophy, anthropology, aesthetics, or ecological thinking in order to formulate a complex transdisciplinary perspective.

Liana Psarologaki is an artist, architect engineer, and academic, originally from Greece and based in East Anglia. She holds a PhD from the University of Brighton (2015), an MA in Fine Art at UCA Canterbury (2010), and a combined Master's in Architecture from the National Technical University of Athens (2007). Awarded many times for academic excellence, her work is internationally presented and published contributing in the current debate on empirical ontologies of architectural space, with a focus on post-theory. Dr Psarologaki is a Deleuze scholar, senior lecturer, and the Head of Architecture at University of Suffolk, UK.

Bhaskar Sarkar, Department Chair and Associate Professor of Film and Media, UC Santa Barbara, is the author of *Mourning the Nation: Indian Cinema in the Wake of Partition* (2009) and a wide range of articles. He is the co-editor of *Documentary Testimonies: Global Archives of Suffering* (2009), *Asian Video Cultures: In the Penumbra of the Global* (2017), and *Routledge Companion to Media and Risk* (2020). He is currently completing a monograph, *Cosmoplastics: Bollywood's Global Gesture,* and working on two others: *Pirate Humanites,* and *Tripping the Light Fantastic: LA Queer Underground Clubs of the Long Nineties.*

Holger Schulze is full professor in musicology at the University of Copenhagen and principal investigator at the Sound Studies Lab. His research focus is the cultural history of the senses, sound in popular culture, and the anthropology of media. He was invited visiting professor at the Musashino Art University in Tokyo, at the University of New South Wales in Sydney, at the Berlin University of the Arts, and the Humboldt-Universität zu Berlin. He was associated investigator at the cluster of excellence Image Knowledge Gestaltung at the Humboldt-Universität zu Berlin and vice chair of the European Sound Studies Association. He served as curator for the Haus der Kulturen der Welt Berlin, is founding editor of the book series Sound Studies, and produced radio features for Deutschlandfunk Kultur. He writes for Merkur, Seismograf, Neue Zeitschrift für Musik, Positionen. Recent book publications include: *Sonic Fiction* (2020), *The Bloomsbury Handbook of Sound Art* (co-editor, 2020), *The Sonic Persona* (2018), *Sound as Popular Culture* (co-editor, 2016).

Jukka Sihvonen, professor emeritus of film studies at the University of Turku, has published several books (mostly in Finnish) on different film genres (children's films, war movies) and film theory. His most recent book (*Mieluummin en* ['I would prefer not to'] Turku: Eetos 2020) is about the aesthetics and ethics of resistance.

Soudhamini has a Masters in English Literature from the Stella Maris College, Madras, and a Post Graduate Diploma in Film Direction from the FTII, Pune. She began her career assisting *avant garde* filmmaker Mani Kaul, and has since then been working across platforms and genres making short fiction, feature length nonfiction and installation works, receiving commissions from India as well as International institutions like the ZDF, Germany, and the Prince Claus Fund, Netherlands. Her work has been shown at many International venues including the Oberhausen, the Fid Marseille, Cinema du Reel, Festival dei Popoli and Leningrad International Film Festivals, and she has officiated on International Selection Committees and Competition Juries. Following many years as Visiting Professor at leading film and art schools in India, Soudhamini taught full time at the film program at Srishti, Bengaluru, from 2013. In 2017–18, she was Artist-Scholar in Residence at Chapman University, California, as a Fulbright Nehru Research Fellow for Academic and Professional Excellence. In July 2018 she began her Practice-based PhD in Narrative VR at the School of Communication and Creative Arts, Deakin University, Melbourne, where she is currently based. Her academic writing, both published and unpublished, can be found at https://deakin.academia.edu/Soudhamini.

Jan Stasieńko serves as a full professor and the Director of Research in the Department of Media and Communication, University of Lower Silesia. He also holds a position of the Head of the Centre for Games and Animation, ULS. In 2010–11 and 2013–14 he has served as a visiting fellow in SUNY Brockport Department of Communication (USA) and the Centre for Digital Media and Simon Fraser University, Vancouver (Canada). He is a member of Beyond Humanism Net. In his research he focuses on digital media and culture, cultural history of (new)media, posthumanism and media technologies, webstudies, narrative structure of video games, educational contexts of gaming, animation history and anthropology, video games and CGI in the context of disabilities. He published several books: *Media Technologies and Posthuman Intimacy* (2021), *Posthuman Studies Reader: Core readings on Transhumanism, Posthumanism and Metahumanism* (with Evi Sampanikou 2021), *Capturing Motor Competencies. People with*

Disabilities as Actors in Motion Capture Sessions (2015), *Alien vs. Predator?, Computer Games and Literary Studies* (2005) [In Polish].

Erik Steinskog is Associate Professor of musicology at the Department of Arts and Cultural Studies, University of Copenhagen. He earned a PhD in musicology from the Norwegian University of Science and Technology (NTNU), with the dissertation "Arnold Schoenberg's *Moses und Aron*: Music, Language, and Representation." His current research includes Afrofuturism, African American music, and questions about music, race, gender, and sexuality. He is the author of *Afrofuturism and Black Sound Studies: Culture, Technology, and Things to Come* (2018).

Julia Vassilieva is an Australian Research Council Research Fellow and a lecturer at Monash University. Her research interests include narrative theory, cinema and the brain, cinema and philosophy, and specifically work of Sergei Eisenstein. She is an author of *Narrative Psychology: Identity, Transformation and Ethics* (2016) and a co-editor of three volumes: *The Eisenstein Universe* (with Ian Christie, Bloomsbury, forthcoming), *Beyond the Essay Film* (with Deane Williams, 2020), and *After Taste: Cultural Value and the Moving Image* (2013). Her publications also appeared in *Camera Obscura, Film-Philosophy, Continuum: Journal of Media & Cultural Studies, Screening the Past, Critical Arts, Kinovedcheskie Zapiski, Rouge, Lola, Senses of Cinema, History of Psychology*, and a number of edited collections.

Susana Viegas is an appointed research fellow in Philosophy of Film and a full member of IFILNOVA, FCSH—Universidade Nova de Lisboa. She received her PhD in Philosophy (Aesthetics) from the Universidade Nova de Lisboa in 2013 with a doctoral thesis on Gilles Deleuze's philosophy of film, and an FCT PhD Studentship during the years 2007 through 2011. She was a postdoctoral research fellow at the University of Dundee and Deakin University with the project "Rethinking the Moving Image and Time in Gilles Deleuze's Philosophy" (2014–19).

Sebastian Wiedemann is a Filmmaker-researcher and Professor at UPB – Universidad Pontificia Bolivariana (Colombia). He holds a PhD in Philosophy, Art Practice & Learning from the University of Campinas (Brazil). His field of interest includes Deleuzian Studies, Research-Creation, Embryology of Creative Processes, Audiovisual composition and Cinematic Modes of Experience. He investigates at the intersection of experimental cinema and philosophy the possibility of a cinematic thinking as poetic ethology and radical kino-madology that expresses itself as more than human learning between writing, curating and filmmaking. He is the author of "Deep Blue: Future Memories of A Livings Cinematic In-Between" (2019) and the editor of the book *Conexões: Deleuze e Cosmopolíticas e Ecologias Radicais e Nova Terra e…* (2019).

Helena Wu is Assistant Professor of Hong Kong Studies at the Department of Asian Studies of the University of British Columbia. She has published on the topics of Hong Kong cinema, literature, culture, and media in *Interventions: International Journal of Postcolonial Studies* (2018), *Chinese Martial Arts and Media Culture* (2018), *Hong Kong Keywords* (2019), *Global Media and China* (2020), and *Journal of Chinese Cinemas* (2020). Her book *The Hangover After the Handover: Places, Things and Cultural Icons in Hong Kong* (2020) explores the fabrication and the intermediation of local icons, relations, and identities.

Index of Subjects

sixteenth century 31, 218, 272, 358, 360, 362
seventeenth century 31, 358–9, 380

affordance 7, 35, 148, 189
algorithms 215, 332, 382
ambiguity 198, 254
antropofagia 8, 45–6, 54
apparatus 18–19, 90–1, 93, 98, 123, 187, 205, 211–16, 236, 239, 281–3, 326–7
audience 30, 63, 79–80, 118, 145, 178, 183, 189–91, 217, 219–21, 248, 258, 266, 306, 321, 326–7, 339–42, 346, 358, 360, 370, 373
audio technology 234, 238

bazaar 9–10, 63–74, 110, 380
Buddhism 26, 120, 133–7, 139, 141, 291, 296, 299–301, 303, 305–12, 379

Cahiers 16, 33, 165–7, 174
Caste 13, 99, 103–6, 108, 110
caste sensorium 13, 99
ćmiatło/shlight 11–12, 87–93, 95–7
collective aural 30, 339–44, 346
collective disindividuation 331
colonial missionary 15, 153
colonialism 71, 100, 107–8, 120, 153, 159–60, 162, 265, 274, 386
community 59, 65–7, 72, 77–8, 82, 118, 163, 275, 291, 296, 319, 359, 361–2, 371
Confucianism and neo-Confucianism 14, 134–7, 139–40, 300, 305, 308, 312
Contract 10, 37, 66, 69, 71, 165, 333
cosmotechnics 337–8

cultural history 118, 143, 149–50, 240, 383, 385
cyborg 7, 14, 35, 39, 41, 121, 129–30, 236

Dhvāni 13, 113–20
Dutch Golden Age 362

echo 5–6, 17, 56, 83, 102, 117, 145–6, 175–9, 181, 236–7
education 19, 153–5, 157–63, 195–6, 201, 203, 294, 356, 358, 368–9, 372–3, 380, 385
efficiency 10, 38, 65, 67
embodiment 11, 21–2, 41–2, 75–9, 81–3, 102, 107–8, 110, 156, 234–5, 251, 254, 326, 346
ethic 29, 31
ethnography 68, 102, 366, 369, 370
Eurocentrism 100, 119
Explorations 32, 358, 367–9, 374
expressed, the 71, 185, 189, 197, 201–2, 207, 209, 233, 246, 262, 271, 292–3

fabulation 8, 53
flow 39, 77–8, 83–4, 93, 97, 102, 128, 284–5
Facebook 27, 189, 314–20
fluid politics 11, 77–8, 80
French film *noir* 351

Gemeinschaft and *Gesellschaft* 66–7
Gestell 14, 121, 123–4, 126, 128, 130–1
Global South 10, 73, 113, 115, 118–20
Góng 14–15, 133–8, 140
gonggong 15, 136–40

hau 366, 372
HAU – Journal of Ethnographic Theory 366–7, 374–5
hearing|listening 341–3, 346
Hong Kong 10–11, 75–6, 81–6, 308–11, 379, 386
hyper-identity 272
hypocrisy 23, 47, 253, 255–8

ice 12, 88, 90–7
iconosphere 279, 286, 287
illusion 18, 173, 189–92, 196, 199, 257, 301
imagology 271, 273–4
immanence 52, 188, 192, 292–3
immersion 7, 18, 35–42, 189–90, 192, 346
information 7, 67–9, 74, 91, 94–5, 119, 123, 130, 209, 211–2, 214, 218, 232, 235, 316, 332–3, 341, 368
intercultural 108, 110, 115, 118, 187, 338, 347, 352–6, 380
interface 19, 126, 199, 205–6, 209–16
intermediality 197, 200
Iran 218, 220, 222, 229, 257

kinosophy 8, 45–6, 49–53

languaging 10, 82
light xi, 12, 36, 47, 49–51, 88–91, 184, 187, 193, 282, 286, 343, 350, 370, 383
lineality 370–71
liquid embodiment 11, 76–7, 79, 81
literacy 19, 195, 201–3
loud/loudness 179–81

machine 9, 14, 35, 40, 48, 55–6, 58–62, 118, 121–31, 146, 162, 171, 174, 190, 198, 200, 202–3, 213, 215, 232, 234, 247, 270, 280, 282–3, 326–7, 366
machine selfie 55–62

manifesto 8, 28, 37, 43, 45–6, 53–4, 130, 162, 203, 323, 328
Māori 366, 372
market 10, 18, 63–74, 77, 189
measure 22, 25, 65, 188, 251, 280, 284
media 4–6, 8, 10–12, 15, 19–21, 25–7, 31–2, 45–6, 56, 73, 77–8, 83, 85, 87–90, 94–7, 100–1, 109, 113, 118, 120, 143, 146–50, 190, 195–7, 199–203, 206, 211, 214–16, 220, 233, 238, 240–1, 270, 273, 275–7, 279, 282–5, 293, 295–7, 309–10, 311, 314–15, 317–20, 327, 331, 335, 346, 352, 365, 367–8, 371, 373–9, 382–6
media environments 293
mediators 32, 275–6, 367
modern 7, 10, 38–40, 58, 64–7, 70, 72–4, 79, 111, 120, 122, 146, 158, 193, 230, 265, 267, 276, 294–6, 308, 311, 314, 327, 380
modulation 36, 205, 217, 332–3, 338
moral 51, 64–6, 69, 134, 140, 149, 154, 160, 253, 255–7, 370
myth 125, 145, 187, 213, 249, 269–70, 272, 274–5

naqqāli 20, 217–21, 226, 229–30
networks 5, 26, 36, 64, 70–1, 76, 94, 215, 291, 293–4, 332, 356
noise 15, 17, 65, 95, 146, 148, 177–9, 181, 240, 283, 286, 340
nonduality 183, 185, 187
non-lineal 367, 369–71, 374
Nordic 151, 161, 164, 349, 351, 355

OTKAZ 243–51
one-man show xi, 217, 219
ontological malady 27, 313
ontology 24, 28, 41, 141, 190, 203, 272, 279–82, 308, 334, 344, 347
oral tradition 153, 156, 218
Orient, the 64, 210
o/Other, the 5, 12, 13, 20, 32, 76, 83, 189, 263, 365–7

Index of Subjects

parallax listening 344, 346
"People's home" 351
phenomenology 105, 110, 147, 149–50, 173, 186, 381
phone 55, 57, 146, 325–7
photography 8–9, 12, 56–7, 60–1, 89, 91–3, 95, 98, 125, 214, 238, 368, 380
piratical 73–4
plasmatic voice 232, 239
popular imagination 16, 65, 136, 159–60
post-human 7, 9, 40–1, 129, 338

Rasa Theory 114
rationality 66, 68, 70
religion 27, 31, 47, 49, 72, 101, 103–4, 108–10, 141, 144, 153, 156–7, 162, 164, 183, 255–6, 306, 311, 314–5, 319, 338, 360–2, 380
rend 22, 253
resonance 4–6, 13–14, 67, 83, 100, 103, 113, 115–17, 119–20, 181, 187
risk 45, 64, 69, 161, 239, 315, 383

Saek 14–15, 133, 136–40
Sankofa 23–4, 261–7
Saudade 24, 47, 269–78
Schalten und Walten 25, 279–81, 283, 285–6
selfie 8–9, 55–62, 382
self-image 56–61, 143, 145
self-picture 56, 60–1
senses 13, 35, 43, 50, 103–6, 110, 147, 176, 184, 189, 210, 234, 383, 385
sensibility 166–9, 173, 237, 350
sensing 19, 35, 105, 115–16, 167–9, 172, 195–6, 371
šahr-e farang 221–2
situation 16–17, 55, 165–71
social media 27, 295, 314–15, 318–19, 373–4
Stimmung 23, 257–8

storytelling 20, 200, 217–18, 222, 229–30
South Asia 13, 105, 108, 114–15
South Asian religion 103, 110
Stoicism 357, 360, 362–3
subtraction 323–4, 326–7
śūnya 14, 133–5, 137, 141
switch 279–80, 283–4, 286–8

Taoism 14, 26, 134–5, 299–300, 303, 305, 308
Tathāgatagarbha 26, 299–300, 302, 304–5, 308
telegraph 89–90, 93–5, 97–8
theater 21–2, 27–8, 90, 217–18, 230, 243–4, 246, 321–4, 327–8, 376
thinking with 19, 205, 270
todetita 27, 313–14
traditional 3, 20, 27, 42, 67, 71, 82, 88, 90, 93, 118, 153, 156–8, 160–1, 201, 210, 217, 221–2, 229, 261, 269–70, 279–80, 282, 286, 293–5, 310, 318, 321, 323, 325–6
transcreation 8, 46
transindividuation 29, 331–4, 338
translation 8, 17, 21, 23, 26, 27, 32, 45, 46, 55, 56, 88, 99, 101, 103, 105, 107, 108, 134, 146, 156, 177, 179, 198, 206, 207, 208, 236, 237, 238, 253, 256, 257, 262, 279, 291, 294, 299, 300, 303, 304, 305, 308, 325, 345, 349, 352, 367, 371, 372, 373
Trobriand Island 369–70

ubuntu 29, 331, 334–7
utbrytningsdröm 30, 349–56
untouchability 99, 105–7, 109
untranslatability 99, 107, 253–4, 257, 272, 305, 308, 352

veoma 7, 35, 37, 40–1
vernacular 71–2, 269, 345, 361, 380
virtual 11, 18, 78, 82, 167, 173, 183, 187–93, 327–8, 334, 365, 374

virtuality 173, 188, 191
vocalic body 235–6
voice 6, 20–1, 28, 83, 113, 116–17, 119, 231–40, 325–6, 342–3
vulnerability 256

wellbeing 335
we-ness 345–6
worldmaking 295

Yogācāra 301–4, 311

Index of Names

Abe, Kinya 291–2, 294, 297
Acerbi, Giuseppe 143–5, 150
Amane, Nishi 294
Arendt, Hannah 292, 297
Aristotle 122, 209, 313–14, 319–20
Auster, Paul 19, 195, 199–200, 202–3, 379
Awolowo, Obafemi 158, 160–1

Bābā šhamal xi, 20, 226, 227, 229
Babb, Lawrence 101–2, 107, 109
Bauman, Zygmunt 11, 32, 77–81, 85
Beck, Johann Tobias 144–5
Bene, Carmelo 27–8, 321–7, 329
Benjamin, Walter 24, 102, 259, 272
Béranger, Jean 30, 349–51, 356
Bergman, Ingmar 30, 349–53, 356
Bhāviveka 302, 309
Birla, Ritu 65, 71, 74
Braidotti, Rosi 7, 35, 42, 378
Buddha 133, 301, 306, 311–12

Cage, John 14, 114–15, 119–20, 181, 344, 346
Calvin, John 31, 360
Carpenter, Edmund 32, 367–72
Carroll, Lewis 196–9, 202–3
Cassin, Barbara 352, 356
Cavarero, Adriana 233, 240
Chion, Michel 234, 240
Chow, Rey 82, 85
Confucius 14, 134–7, 139–40, 305, 308, 312
Coomaraswamy, Ananda K.114
Coornhert, Dirk Volkertsz 31, 357–8, 360–4

Dath, Dietmar 17, 32, 170–3
de Andrade, Oswald 8, 45–6, 53–4

de Campos, Haroldo 8, 46, 54
de Oliveira, Manoel 274
Deleuze, Gilles 1–8, 11, 14, 18–19, 28, 31–3, 35, 37, 42–3, 45, 51, 53–4, 76–7, 94, 98, 127–9, 131, 167, 173, 187–8, 191–2, 195–203, 206, 209, 216, 254, 258–9, 261, 267, 270, 273–5, 277, 286, 288, 322–4, 327–9, 332–5, 337, 359, 364–7, 374, 378–9, 383, 385, 386
Derrida, Jacques 28, 88–9, 98, 175, 182, 283, 288, 325, 329, 381
Dharmapāla 302, 304, 310
Dukaj, Jacek 11–12, 87–98
Cavarero, Adriana 233, 240
Chion, Michel 234, 240

Eck, Diana 99–101, 107
Eisenstein, Sergej 243–51

Fales, Cornelia 235, 240
Finland 15, 144–6, 150–1
Fisher, Mark 41, 43, 376
Flusser, Vilem 93, 98, 213–14, 216

Geertz, Clifford 68–70, 74
Gomes, Miguel 274, 277
Gonda, Jan 100, 185, 192
Guattari, Félix 3, 5–6, 8, 11, 14, 31–3, 43, 45, 54, 77, 94, 98, 127–9, 131, 254, 270, 273, 277, 286, 288, 324, 359, 364–7, 374, 379
Guru, Gopal 105–6, 108, 110

Han, Byung-Chul 37–8, 42, 302, 345
Hasan Kačal 20, 222, 224–6, 229
Haraway, Donna 37, 43, 169, 173
Hatami, Ali 217, 221–2, 226, 229–30
Hafez 254, 258–9

Hegel, G.W.F. 261–3, 267, 313, 319–20
Heidegger, Martin 14, 38, 42–3, 98, 121–4, 127, 130–2, 147, 150, 280, 283, 288, 307
Herzogenrath, Bernd 132, 197, 203, 205, 216, 346

Ife 155

Jain, Kajri 12–13, 65, 72, 74, 103–4, 108, 110, 380

Kaurismäki, Aki 145, 150–1
Kirchner, Barbara 17, 32, 170–3
Kittler, Friedrich 95–6, 98, 214, 283–4, 288
Kumārajīva 303, 305, 311

Lacan, Jacques 14, 123–8, 132, 293, 297, 327, 329
Laozi 10, 75–6, 78, 85, 300, 310
Lavric, Sorin 319–20
Lee, Bruce 10, 75–6, 79–81, 84
Lee, Dorothy Demetracopoulou 32, 367, 368–73
Levy, Pierre 18, 187–8, 191–2
Lourenço, Eduardo 271–3, 275–7

Mahony, William 185–6, 192
Martin, Alice 198, 203
Mauss, Marcel 366, 372
McHugh, James 103–5, 108, 110
McLuhan, Marshall 32, 176, 182, 192, 206, 209, 214, 216, 282, 288, 367–8, 371, 374–5
Monty Python's Life of Brian 65
Mou Zongsan 134–6, 141

Nāgārjuna 133–5, 141, 301–2
Nakahira, Takuma 238, 240
Nancy, Jean-Luc 58, 61–2, 176–7, 181–2, 342, 344–5, 347
Nietzsche, Friedrich 4, 196–7, 201, 258

Noica, Constantin 27, 313–16, 318–20
Nokia 146

Òdùdúwà, 155–6, 163
Olajubu, Bunmi 155
Òlódùmàrè 156–7, 163
Òrìsànlá 153

Pauline, Mark 14, 123–5, 129, 132
Peirce, Charles Sanders 280, 288, 305, 311

Ramose, Magobe 334–8
Ray, Rajat K. 65–6, 70, 74
Rumi 228

Sarukkai, Sundar 105–6, 108, 110
Survival Research Laboratories (SRL) 123–4, 131–2
Rocha, Glauber 46, 54
Sankara 186–9, 191
Sauvagnargues, Anne 36–7, 40, 43
Schafer, R. Murray 176, 182, 342–3, 347
Schulze, Holger 16–17, 33, 169, 171, 173, 383
Serres, Michel 178–9, 182, 378
Shirazi, Hafez 254, 258, 259
Simondon, Gilbert 29, 43, 332–5, 337–8
Sjögren, Olle 353, 356
Spector, Regina 72, 74
Spieghel, Hendrik 358, 362
Spinoza, Baruch 7, 52, 76, 128–9, 131, 258–9, 306, 311, 337, 363–4
Stauff, Markus 287, 289
Stelarc 14, 125, 129–32
Stiegler, Bernard 29, 125, 132, 309, 311, 331–8

Tetsuo 14, 125–8
Tesla, Nikola 91–2
Tomokawa, Kazuki 20, 237, 240

Valéry, Paul 16–17, 33, 165–71, 173–4
Viveiros de Castro, Eduardo 32, 46, 54, 336, 338, 365–6, 369, 373, 375

Wonhyo 15, 136–41
Wortzelius, Hugo 350, 356

Xuanzang 303–4, 308, 310, 312

Young, La Monte 114–15
Yoruba 15–16, 153–64

Zielinski, Siegfried 95–6, 98

www.ingramcontent.com/pod-product-compliance
Lightning Source LLC
Chambersburg PA
CBHW052139300426
44115CB00011B/1440